The Historic Rama

Indian civilization at the end of Pleistocene

CW01497542

Nilesh Nilkanth Oak

TO,

Dr. Padmakar Vishnu Vartak

Praise for: The Historic Rama

It was a fascinating ride. The pictures helped enormously. It is funny, logical, unapologetic, interesting, thought-provoking and most importantly, it requires a higher amount of reader participation. This is not a book for reading before bed or in a leisurely mood. This book is best read with a pen and a paper nearby.

The book is excellent. I also enjoyed the last appendix on the 'origins of weekday names and division'. It seemed like a relief when I reached the appendix, but ended up re-reading it in order to fully comprehend the gist of it.

Thank you so much for the work you have done to unearth the timelines of Ramayana. Reading the book gives me Goosebumps. I never had such an experience before. Hindus were blamed for not keeping track of time. Your research disproves it totally, clearly showing how the use of motion of celestial bodies serves as the ultimate timekeeper.

I love the quotations you give at the beginning of every chapter which sets the tone of that chapter. The Vanara search party and the problem following it run like a detective novel.

Congratulations for an amazing, meticulous and painstaking work. I salute your devotion and hard work. I have no knowledge or appreciation of arguments connected with astronomy. I had read Pushkar Bhatnagar's book and also heard his lecture. Your book has prompted me to read books by Vartak, Yardi and others. I had found Bhatnagar's dates very attractive because they tally with the anthropological history of India. A date of 12000 BCE will need pushing back the history of agriculture in India to almost 5000 years earlier than its documented evidence. However, who knows, some new discoveries are waiting to be made as has happened in case of the use of iron.

As I was reading, I got transported to Rama's time and went through the journey. I liked your set of questions that the dating of Ramayana does to the world history. Overall I am impressed and this will do a lot to revive interest in Ramayana and lend credence to the epic just as the discovery of Troy did to Homer's Iliad.

The book is gripping, fascinating and it is hard to put it down.

I had a wonderful evening today explaining to my family how the 24 hour day, the 7 day week, the names of the weekdays, the sequence of weekday names, are all based on a system founded on logic of astronomy observations. And the week had an Out-of-India migration just like the Zero! So next time some AIT-Nazi talks you down, ask him what weekday it is! Nilesh ji, a big thanks to you, Sudarshan Bharadwaj and Shri Suhas Gurjar.

BHARAT is REBORN, as its most famous son, Lord Rama, has finally found a throne on world's time-line! And it is an open challenge from Nilesh Nilkanth Oak to the world to try and dethrone Lord Rama from that throne if they think they are intellectually up to the task.

It was an incredible experience to read your wonderful book. I cannot say that I understood lot of the astronomical stuff. However, I understood most of it because your presentation was very logical. In few places I thought some of the points were repetitious. But I think I understand why you chose to reassert your points. I did not realize that our tradition and history went so far back! Thanks again for this wonderful book. I am looking forward to reading your next book.

Praise for
'When did the Mahabharata War happen? The Mystery of Arundhati'

You have done a great job. I requested astronomers to consider if Arundhati had gone ahead of Vasisth in 1971, when I published 'Swayambhu'. But nobody cared. You are the first to do the great job!
- Dr. P V Vartak (Author of 'Swayambhu' & 'Wastav Ramayana')

Grueling and unfaltering logic

I have to thank you for being the cause for a quantum leap in my own knowledge of general astronomy as well as Hindu astronomy / calendrical systems over a very short span of time. In some ways the effect of your book has some parallels with Rajiv Malhotra's 'Being Different', though in a very different context. RM never intended his book as a primer on Dharma / Hinduism - but nevertheless it introduced many aspects of Dharma in a light which would be new even to a practitioner. Similarly, even though I am sure you never intended your book to act as an exploration of key astronomical principles and Vedic astronomy - that has definitely been a key side benefit, at least from my perspective.

I have verified Nilesh Oak's elimination of "errors". A bow! Excellent!

It is interesting how all Indologists the world over talk about linguistics and horse, but never mentions archaeoastronomy! Perhaps the focus of the national and international debate on Aryan Invasion/Migration Theory needs to change.

Your rigorous methodology was simply a pleasure to read and that got me started off on my efforts to dabble in archeoastronomy. Please accept my best compliments on such a wonderful book.

"Indology" has been populated by linguists and my respect for their work has gone down by several notches when I look at the shoddy assumptions many are prone to make. Science and rigor the way Nilesh Oak has used seems to be unknown to these Indologists. I bet that not one of those horse bone chewers can understand what Archeo-astronomy means. Their awareness extends to looking at Archeo-asses and saying it was not Equus caballus.

I do not want to sound obsequious, but the work you have done is nothing less than tremendous. Thank you, and keep it up.

I am simply '*natmastak*' to Shri Oak for the amazing piece of deductive reasoning applied by him in interpreting the 'Arundhati is leading Vasistha' remark. I think Shri Oak is not only on sound footing but also has clearly exhibited every '*lakshan*' of a true seeker of knowledge in the finest Indian traditions. I cannot recall if he mentioned whether anybody else (other than him) thought of the EOA approach. If he is the first one, he deserves billions of thanks from all the Bharatiyas in the last 7000+ years. *Oak saheb, aamcha maanacha mujra sweekar karava hee vinanti.*

It is absolutely fantastic! I loved the way Nilesh presents the cases - as experiments and problems! He did his work a lot of justice by opting for this format. The Mahabharata War did not take place anytime after 4380 BC" is really one of the biggest achievements of his work! That is the roadblock that needs to be placed before all those writing anything on history, especially Westerners and their lackeys doing so in India. Anybody from now on opening his mouth to refute Indian Antiquity needs to be asked, "So how do you explain Arundhati walking in front of Vashishta?" I presume they too would be scratching their heads at least as long as Nilesh did, 15 years, before the solution to the mystery hit him!

CONTENTS

FOR MY FANS

By definition, you would have already read 'When did the Mahabharata War happen? The Mystery of Arundhati (2011)', 'Ancient Indian History' blog, watched few of my YouTube videos or attended my talks.

If not, at a minimum, you need to get hold of my first book and read it, along with this book, just to qualify. ☺

Many Will Enter, Few Will Swim

Writers are like baby turtles (or like tadpoles). Hundreds of them hatch, but only a handful of them survive the trip from the sand dunes into the sea. I have worked hard to get this far, but I am also keenly aware that my fans buying books, then reading them and discussing them with the curious and the likeminded, and then telling their friends to buy them too that is what keeps me in this business.

Without your support and encouragement, there would be no 'The Historic Rama'. Thank you all.

Special Thanks

I would also like to extend special thanks to everyone who has bought my previous book in large quantities; to give out as gifts during social gatherings, religious functions, birthdays, weddings, and to their younger relatives for no specific reasons. Thank you all.

If you would like to gift more than 10 copies of my books, it may be possible to obtain better cost per book. Write to me at NileshOak@gmail.com.

I would also like to extend special thanks to those who have acted as mentors to me in varied capacity, and have gone out of way to assist me in ways unimaginable. In spite of such support, they prefer that I not mention their names. Thank you all.

ACKNOWLEDGMENTS

Many readers of my book on the timing of the Mahabharata War suggested that I also research on the timing of Ramayana. Rajesh Arya suggested the title of this book. Appendix-A (Origin of Weekday Names) was based on information made available by Suhas Gurjar (Jyotirvidya Parisanstha – Pune). Sudarshan Bharadwaj conducted background research and compiled first draft of Appendix-A. Ashwini Manjul created the front cover design(s). Haresh Gala brought to my attention numerous Ramayana blogs, research articles and books. Ramesh Rahalkar brought to my attention few curious references from Ramayana and I will analyze them in my future books.

There are many who assisted and encouraged me through trying times, cheered me up through my writer's block, read and re-read drafts of this book or suggested modifications. In no particular order, they are,

S. M. Sullivan, Denavi Patil, Uschi Ringleb, Mangesh & Maya Murdeshwar, Bimal Trivedi, Pradipta Banerjee, Chandraish Sinha, Sujata Shukla, Pravin Datar, Madhavi Nath Sinha, Wim Borsboom, Mukta & Gyanesh Khare, Kaushal Vepa, Arya Tara Oak, Sucheta Godbole, Jagy Pattur, Mariana Baca, Suguna Vepa, Sanjay & Nayana Ponkshe, Suhas Gurjar, Anil Oak, Ashish & Dipika Hairat, Sasha Under Midnattssol, Aniruddha Ainapure, Sudarshan Bharadwaj, Pankaj & Pradnya Oak, Casey Kang, Atul & Ashwini Manjul, Rajesh Arya, Benn Konsynski, Anand & Rupali Dalvi, Neeta Kajale, Vivek Ramakrishnan, Anish Patani, Horacio Francisco Arganis Juarez, Anantha Narayanan, Sameer Kurundkar, Prabhakar Phadnis, Ravi Patil, Vijay Iyengar, Virendra Rathore, Preeti Shah, Ali Raza Zaidi, Aashay Gune, Haresh Gala, Amey Modak, Linda Jauneau, Sunil Ganu, Pragati Bhasin, Abhitosh Tripathi, Alka Godbole, Sandeep & Seema Mulay.

The views represented in this book are my own and not necessarily of those who have been kind to me, directly and indirectly in this endeavor. Paramatma inspired me and sustained my faith in the words of Valmiki. Popper's specific approach to falsification and corroboration of a theory allowed me to interpret words of Valmiki. This was a wonderful journey. Many exciting projects are also in the pipeline.

INTRODUCTION

Those who dance are considered insane by those who can't hear the music.

- Friedrich Nietzsche

After I published 'When did the Mahabharata War Happen?' one of my friends asked her husband, who also happens to be my friend:

"What might have motivated Nilesh to write a book on subject such as 'Mahabharata'?"

"Unbearable Itch," my friend responded.

My friend answered it in the sense of 'Just because', i.e. there is truly no good answer. However his original answer, in Marathi, loosely translated into English as 'Unbearable Itch' meant much more than 'just because'. I thought of answering my friend's question.

If I have to answer, not unlike her husband, in one word, here it is: Curiosity. I met many who discussed the subject of Mahabharata and Ramayana. Unfortunately, majority of them discussed it with many blind assumptions, where careless opinions of others were mixed with unguarded speculations of their own.

One of the many astronomy references from the Mahabharata text made me curious. Outcome of that curiosity was my previous book. In that book, I successfully interpreted all (200+) astronomy observations from the Mahabharata text and conclusively validated 5561 BCE as the year of Mahabharata War. Even more critical, my work falsified all previous claims, and will falsify any future claim for the year of Mahabharata War anytime after 4500 BCE. I decided to do the same with astronomy observations of Valmiki Ramayana.

One other acquaintance of mine asked a similar question: "Why bother?" which I interpreted it to mean, 'Why be curious about anything, and in this specific case – curious about the timing of Ramayana. Of course one cannot force 'curiosity' on others. Still the question 'why be curious?' can be answered.

Curiosity encourages one to clarify one's doubts and uncover the truth, or at least get much closer to the truth. A curious person does not just take someone's word for it. He discovers the truth for himself. A curious person will dig deeper into the details, and while he may or may not solve the problem at hand, he will certainly uncover many more clues to previously unanswered questions. A curious search, besides answering the question at hand, leads to growth of knowledge. For example, in the context of Mahabharata and Ramayana, while my curiosity was about 'when', I uncovered tremendous insights about 'how' and 'why'.

Notice that children are curious. Children are like an empty canvas, waiting to be filled with knowledge and experiences. They don't have predetermined expectations fogging their judgment. Curiosity opens up one's mind and takes one beyond existing and tired biases within the field of knowledge. It expands the borders of existing knowledge. Curiosity releases your inner child.

For example, I began my work on the dating of Mahabharata War with no predetermined timeline in mind. In fact I would have been perfectly happy to run into the conclusion that Mahabharata is nothing but a fiction. I was ready for that outcome. It is just that each single piece of evidence led me to a viewpoint away from the notion that Mahabharata could be a fiction.

Curiosity reduces stress. It does a lot more than reducing stress. It allows one to experience something fresh. New discoveries and experiences are one of the most exciting acts of living. They stimulate one's mind and free one's creative emotion. There is daring in discovering something fresh.

A curious mind dives beneath the surface of common acceptance and this curiosity, especially one that results in new discoveries, will extend to all daily pursuits where one will comprehend the details better which in turn results in better understanding the process. A solution to the problem leads to many new problems, of higher dimension and of more complexity. This is why when one's curiosity leads to new discoveries, many novel questions emerge which in turn stretch the boundaries of one's mind. Every new problem and new awareness, leads one to another stimulating challenge.

Curious people look at a challenge from multiple angles. Over time this becomes a habit. They discover alternative ways of accomplishing the same task. The greater the pool of possible solutions, the more likely it is that they will find a better way to get things done.

If variety is the spice of life, then there is nothing more boring than repetition. When one allows one's curiosity to send one in new directions, one adds variety into one's life. To understand a problem is to try solving it and fail at it. Human beings tend to be more positive toward the things they understand. While there are no guarantees for success in solving a given problem, curiosity is the motivating force that encourages us to tackle challenging questions and even if we fail, it naturally broadens our horizon and improves our understanding. Curiosity brought me in touch with optimistic and intelligent people around the world.

I will end this preamble on 'curiosity' with words engraved on Sanskrit Prize Medal:

तत्सुखं सात्त्विकं प्रोक्तमात्मबुद्धी प्रसादजं

(Knowledge obtained through one's own intellect and reason brings forth a most contented happiness.)

Mahabharata is richer in astronomy observations and, by luck I could employ three distinct sets of astronomy observations: (1) Arundhati, (2) Planetary positions and (3) Bhishma Nirvana. My work led to well defined interval for the plausible year of Mahabharata War and also the specific year of Mahabharata War.

Researcher of history has to employ whatever evidence he can gather and also has to be content with whatever evidence is available. I began my work on Ramayana by defining 5561 BCE as the lower bound of this time interval. This assumption is rather trivial since no ardent student of Indian literature disputes antiquity of Ramayana over Mahabharata. I found such sharp limit, on the lower bound for the search of Ramayana timing, extremely useful.

Skeleton key to 'The Historic Rama'

The book can be informally divided into three parts: Part I (Chapters 1-5), Part II (Chapters 6-16) and Part III (Chapters 17-23). Part I presents the background necessary for comprehending exciting discoveries that follow in Part II. Part II constitutes not only the efforts to determine the broader time interval of Ramayana but also the timing of specific instances of Rama's life over a period of more than 40 years. Part III begins with the analysis of conflicting observations from Valmiki Ramayana and also offers their resolution. Part III analyzes four specific efforts of past researchers in determining the timing of Ramayana. Part III concludes with author's original contributions, descriptions of problems (from Ramayana) not addressed and the implications of author's research for the timeline of ancient Indian history and world civilizations.

Chapter one & two define the problem, propose hypothesis to solve it and outline the method of testing. Chapter three emphasizes, otherwise obvious point of, Ramayana occurring before Mahabharata, with the assistance of internal references from these two epics. Chapter four & five equip the reader with astronomy background, necessary to comprehend and enjoy rest of the book.

While chapter six establishes broader time interval of 7000 years-Epoch of Ramayana, chapter seven establishes specific millennium of Ramayana. Chapters 8 through 16 develop, and corroborate, detailed timeline for specific instances of Rama's life for more than 40 years of his life.

Chapter 17 enumerates conflicting and contradictory observations of Valmiki Ramayana, discusses potential solutions and also resolutions. Critical analysis of the work of other researchers is presented in chapters 18, 19 & 20. Chapter 21 provides excellent chronological narrative of Valmiki Ramayana along with Ramayana timeline. Chapter 22 makes a case for author's proposal as the best proposal among the available proposals of Ramayana and chapter 23 concludes with implications of this revolutionary work for, but not limited to, world civilizations, Sindhu-Sarasvati civilization, ancient Indian history and age of Veda.

Two appendices at the end of the book are stand alone short notes. Valmiki Ramayana references employed in determining the timing of Ramayana are at the end.

1

THE PROBLEM

Our whole problem is to make the mistakes as fast as possible

- *John Archibald Wheeler*

Our whole and sole problem in this book is to determine the timing of Ramayana. All past attempts, and there are not many, to determine the timing of Ramayana are based on inductive methodology where efforts were made to fit astronomy data from Valmiki Ramayana for a proposed date(s).

For example, Late Shri Pushkar Bhatnagar began with the present, and searched for a year that *supposedly* matched astronomy observations and positions of grahas as described for the timing of Rama-Janma (birth of Rama). Dr. P V Vartak began with the timing of Mahabharata War (5561 BCE) and going backwards (since Ramayana is before Mahabharata) settled somewhere near 7300 BCE as his proposed timeline for Ramayana. Two other efforts simply state their proposed timeline without explaining their methodology.

I want to begin with the timing of Mahabharata War - 5561 BCE as the lower bound for the timing of Ramayana. This milestone is useful however all it tells us is that Ramayana happened sometime before 5561 BCE. Thus I defined my problem as to find out:

1. At a minimum, upper bound for the timing of Ramayana

2. Preferably, a time interval, not unlike provided by Epoch of

Arundhati during my work on timing of Mahabharata War, that defined both upper and lower bounds for the plausible timing of Ramayana.

3. If lucky, specific days/months/years for the events of Ramayana

What is Ramayana?

The Ramayana is the oldest epic of humanity, written in Sanskrit. Literally translated, it would mean 'Rama's Journey'. The epic consists of 24000 verses in seven Kanda (books) and 500 Sarga (chapters). The Ramayana is the story of royal prince Rama, whose wife (Sita) was abducted by Ravana, king of Lanka (modern Sri Lanka)

Valmiki composed Ramayana. Valmiki is regarded as India's *Adi-Kavi* - first poet, and Ramayana as India's *Adi-Kavya* - first poetry. Not that there were no poets and poetry before Valmiki or Ramayana, however when it came to epic poetry, Ramayana is the oldest epic poem, at least one that has survived. This original epic poem is known as Valmiki Ramayana, to distinguish it from many of its variations that occurred over time.

The Ramayana is *Itihasa*, similar to the Mahabharata, and thus includes a narrative of past events. The incidents described in the Ramayana took place during *Treta* Yuga. The key incidents described in Ramayana took place at what is today called Northern India, Central India, Southern India and Sri Lanka.

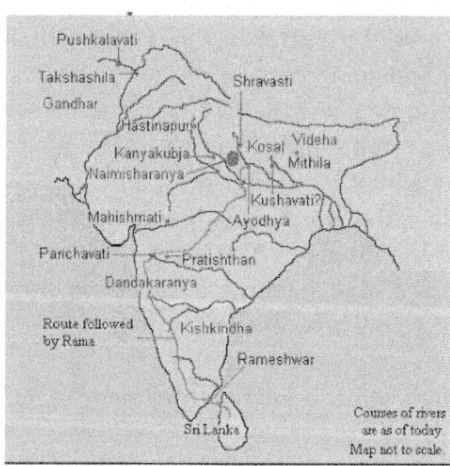

Bharat during Ramayan times.

The Problem: When did Ramayana happen?

The problem this book tries to solve is to determine the timing of Ramayana. The problem of when exactly the instances described in Ramayana occurred, and also when exactly the Ramayana was composed.

Our approach in determining the timing of Ramayana would be identical to the one employed in determining the timing of Mahabharata War, namely – interpretation of astronomical and chronological observations. I had employed references to seasons in discounting specific proposals of other researchers for the timing of Mahabharata War. This experience taught me the importance of 'seasonal' observations. This specific insight, i.e. descriptions of seasons and their use to determine timing of specific events, is due to Dr. P V Vartak. Observations of seasons played important role in determining the chronology of Ramayana events.

Ramayana has fewer astronomy observations than Mahabharata. Unlike Mahabharata text, where most of the astronomy observations are related to the timing of Mahabharata War (+/- 2 years); astronomy observations of Ramayana are spread over ~30 years of Rama's life.

I asked few researchers, who had attempted 'timing of Mahabharata War', if they have also attempted 'timing of Ramayana'. All of them admitted their inability and commented that astronomy evidence from Valmiki Ramayana was not sufficient in determining the timing of Ramayana. Of course same things were being said about the quality of astronomy observations of Mahabharata. Many researchers of Mahabharata used this argument of 'quality' (i.e. lack of quality) of astronomy data to even justify their arbitrary methods. Many of them tried to fit few observations from a list of 200+ astronomy observations for their favorite proposal(s) of Mahabharata. Some of these attempts were so naïve that their proposed dates (for Mahabharata War) can be shown to be incorrect – and mind you, with the help of very observations they claimed to have employed in determining their proposal!

Dogma & Dogmatically driven timing of Ramayana

Majority of Indians who accept Rama as Avatar or great king believe that Ramayana occurred a long time ago. This arrow of time, to the past, is good enough for them. While a student of history may find such an approach frustrating, this is not a dogmatic approach. Hinduism is not based on shaky foundations of History-centrism seen in other religions of the world and may be due to this very reason, followers of Hinduism are not troubled by lack of specificity of their ancient history.

Let's look at the relevant, relevant for our purpose, meanings of 'Dogma' and 'Dogmatic':

Dogma (noun): A doctrine that is proclaimed as true without proof

Dogmatic (adjective):

1. *tending to force one's own opinions on other people*

2. *characterized by assertion of unproved or improvable principles*

3. *lacking tolerance or flexibility or breadth of view*

4. *characterized by an authoritative, arrogant assertion of unproved or improvable principles*

5. *forcibly asserted as if authoritative and unchallengeable*

6. *based on assumption rather than empirical observation*

Recognize that while the word is often used in the context of religious doctrine, the principle itself is not a prerogative of religious views. We can categorize the dogmatic viewpoint, as it relates to the timing of Ramayana into two camps. Keep in mind that it is indeed illusive to pinpoint members of this group, but they do exist and you would have already come across them during educational, social, religious and family gatherings. We have two dogmatic viewpoints regarding the timing of Ramayana:

1. *Ramayana is a fiction. Thus question of determining the actual timing of Ramayana is redundant.*

2. *Ramayana happened about a million years ago.*

Since Ramayana as a 'written text' exists in our times, the group holding first dogma may, and only may, spend time simply researching and determining the timing of when Ramayana was 'written'. Their efforts have led to a time period of anywhere from 1300 BCE to 1800 CE, for the timing of the writing of Ramayana, since they base their efforts on the age of handwritten manuscripts.

The group holding second dogma arrive at their million year timeline (in antiquity) based on the statement of Valmiki Ramayana that the timing of Rama was that of *Treta*-yuga. They combine this information with one of the many definitions of 'Yuga' (or more specifically – length of Yuga) and arrive at their timing of Ramayana.

Of course either of these dogmatic views could be right. However, anyone holding such views is required to address this issue in an empirical and/or scientific manner. In short, they need to move this beyond opinion. This will enable their proposals to change from mere dogma into something that can be tested, corroborated and critically discussed. It may enable others to provide criticism of their logic.

While we have nothing to offer in way of jump start to the group that holds first dogma (Ramayana as fiction), Dr. P V Vartak has provided a jump start, for those willing, from the second group (Ramayana occurred about one million years ago), to take their proposal to the next stage, in the form of one Ramayana observation and its plausible corroboration with geological evidence.

Here comes the jump cable:

The logic of the second group for their timeline of Ramayana is derived, loosely, based on one of the many definitions for the duration of Kali, Dwapara and Treta yugas.

e.g., Duration of Kali Yuga = 432,000
Duration of Dwapara Yuga = 864,000

Assuming Kali-Yuga to have begun only ~5000 years ago (3102 BCE) and considering that Ramayana occurred in Treta-Yuga, one may estimate timing of Ramayana,
= 5000 (Kali-Yuga) + 864,000 = 869,000 years when Treta-Yuga ended.

And thus approximately speaking, one may propose that Ramayana must have occurred more than 800K (~one million) years ago.

Dr. P V Vartak presents one observation[1] in support of above conjecture.

Himalaya and Vindhya, these mountains were comparable (in their height?) and appeared as if they are looking at each other.

Vartak refers to geological view of Himalaya being one of the youngest mountains and that its height is increasing continuously, even in our times. Thus assuming,

Height of Vindhya = Height of Himalaya, during Ramayana times,

And employing general consensus of geologists related to rate of increase of height of Himalaya, namely ~3 feet per every 100 years,

Vartak calculates,

Average height of Himalaya = 29029 Feet
Average height of Vindhya = 5000 Feet
Number of year required for difference in their height,
= (29029 – 5000) / (3/100) = 800967 years.

Please note that Vartak has proposed 7300 BCE, and not one million years in antiquity, as the time period of Ramayana. However, Vartak has provided this wonderful jump-start to those who believe Ramayana occurred some million years ago <u>and</u> who are <u>courageous to research further </u>with the aim of bringing their cherished timeline out of 'dogma'.

We must realize that the evidence provided above is capable of corroborating 'one million year' proposal of Ramayana however such proposal must be corroborated by other independent evidence, which is lacking at the present. On the other hand, there is ample evidence that goes against the 'one million year' proposal.

We should also mention another piece of geological evidence (Clift, et.al) that alludes to river Yamuna flowing as a separate and eastward river, as it flows today and as it flowed in Ramayana times[346, 347], only after 47000 BCE. This evidence may place upper limit on the timing of Ramayana to 47000 BCE and is thus capable of falsifying any proposal that claims Ramayana to have occurred more than 50,000 years ago.

Deracination & Deracinated Timing of Ramayana

If you belong to this group, you know who you are. We will not go into the causes of this deracination, but will simply state the litmus test for deracination.

If someone asks you, during a social or religious gathering, or you ask yourself during your alone or lonely moment:

"Is Ramayana real? Did it really happen?"

You are in the presence of a deracinated individual, crowd or your own self!

Very Brief review of Ramayana Research

While more than 125+ different dates were proposed for the timing of Mahabharata War, only handful of dates have been proposed for the timing of Ramayana.

Ramayana occurred long time before the Mahabharata. This assertion along with my proposed date for the Mahabharata War (5561 BCE) allows us to eliminate much that is worth discarding.

We already looked at a viewpoint that holds a belief that Ramayana occurred some one million years ago. This group bases their view/opinion on the specific notion for the duration of years for Kali, Dwapara and Treta yugas. They could be correct in their assumption of Ramayana occurring more than 800K years ago, however, we have no way of testing their timeline. Essentially, their theory and their proposed timeline are irrefutable. These researchers did not profess any evidence other than blind leap of faith in descriptions of Yugas (from Puranas) and their interpretations for the length of various Yugas. We have presented two geological evidences, one capable of corroborating and another capable of falsifying 'one million year' proposal.

It is equally relevant to mention outcome of the belief held by the group of the first dogmatic kind (Ramayana is fiction). Some of them claim that Valmiki Ramayana was composed anywhere from 1500 BCE to 100 CE. There is no dearth of opinions for dates within this range (1500 BCE- 100 CE) however there exists complete lack of evidence for any of these proposals. We should also realize that some of them, claiming such late dates for the composition of Ramayana also claim that Ramayana was composed after Mahabharata. I assert that claims for composition of Ramayana after that of Mahabharata are careless opinions and are falsified rather easily.

I came across four distinct attempts to determine the timing of Ramayana:

(1)   In their book 'Ancient History of India through Vedic Astronomy', Dr.

S P Sabrathnam, N P Ramadurai & V Sundaram proposed 17 January 10205 BCE as the day of Rama- Janma. I will call this proposal – SRS – after the combined initials of three authors.

(2) Dr. P V Vartak proposed 4 December 7324 BCE as the day of Rama-Janma. His references to dating are per Gregorian calendar (and not Julian calendar).

(3) Late Shri Pushkar Bhatnagar proposed 10 January 5114 BCE as the day of Rama-Janma.

(4) Shri M. R Yardi proposed a broader and approximate time period of 1500 BCE for the timing of Ramayana.

Later on we will show how these four proposals for the timing of Ramayana are wrong. We will also show how evidence from Valmiki Ramayana (astronomy and seasons) falsifies these four proposals.

Those who have read my work on Mahabharata (When did the Mahabharata War Happen? The Mystery of Arundhati) will immediately realize that entire evidence presented in that book (and the proposed year-5561 BCE, for Mahabharata war) would instantaneously falsify proposals of both M R Yardi (1500 BCE) and Pushkar Bhatnagar (5114 BCE). Of course we will also demonstrate how proposals of Dr. P V Vartak (7324 BCE), SRS (10205 BCE) or Shri Pushkar Bhatnagar (5114 BCE) are falsified either based on key astronomy observations of Valmiki Ramayana or based on the very observations (astronomy and chronology) employed by these researchers. Mr. Yardi's work on dating of Ramayana is too naïve and too superficial to enable criticism. Mr. Yardi proposed 1500 BCE as the approximate timing for Ramayana, without any critical thought and his proposal is falsified rather easily.

SRS proposed only 3 dates: Rama-Janma, *Ravana-Vadha* and Rama's coronation. SRS do not tell us how they arrived at their proposal. We are unable to analyze this proposal as it is devoid of theory and/or Ramayana references in support of proposed dates.

Dr. P V Vartak is meticulous and detailed in his explanations. My proposed date for the timing of Ramayana is far removed in antiquity from that proposed by Dr. P V Vartak. My work, presented in this book, became possible due to detailed analysis of Vartak. Dr. P V Vartak and his work on Ramayana were my inspiration for this book and for my previous book. I have dedicated this book to him.

I deal with evaluation and falsification of proposed timings of Ramayana by P V Vartak, SRS, Pushkar Bhatnagar and MR Yardi in Chapters 18, 19 & 20.

Method of Investigation

We will employ hypothetico-deductive method. This is the method of Science. Richard Feynman, Noble Laureate in Physics, describes the process of science as follows:

(1) Make *a guess (Propose a theory)*

(2) *Compute consequences (Predictions derived from this theory)*

(3) *Compare these consequences against evidence, observations or experimental tests. (Testing of Theory: Predictions of a theory are tested against evidence)*

One begins by guessing a potential solution to solve the problem. Theory is a sophisticated name for a guess; Guess = Theory. Next step is to compute the logical consequences of a theory. The consequences could be both quantitative and qualitative, however quantitative consequences are preferred. The goal of this exercise is to develop specific statements (consequences emerging out of a theory) that place restrictions on what is permissible by the theory and also what is not permissible by that theory. Next step is to compare the consequences against experience, observations, outcome of specially designed experiment, simulations, nature, etc.

Experiments are designed in such a way so as to test the consequences. The outcome of experiments may provide support for predicted consequences of a theory. In this case, the experiment <u>failed to disprove the theory</u>. On the other hand, outcome of an experiment may produce troubles for the theory by generating unexpected results, results that conflict with expected consequences of a theory, in which case one must begin by guessing again, i.e. another theory!

By this method, one can disprove any theory but one cannot prove new theory. It is not important where the guess comes from but it is very important that the guess, i.e. its consequences should agree with the experiments and observations. It is never correct to criticize the guess itself. Scientific way to falsify a guess (theory) is to show how the implied consequences of a theory do not stand the scrutiny of nature, observations, experience or outcome of experiments. That is why it is important to know what the consequence of a given theory are and anyone proposing a theory must strive for definite consequences – as definite, as quantitative and as clear as possible. This is because one cannot disprove a '<u>vague</u>' theory!

It is not unusual that many researchers (and laypeople) erroneously think of a theory as a good theory because it cannot be disproved. Any theory that cannot be disproved is inferior and probably not scientific. A falsifiable theory is a scientific theory and our goal is to prove our theories wrong and do it as fast as we can. That is the only way to make progress. This also means one should make bold guesses and then ardently attempt to prove them wrong.

Many well meaning researchers are willing to make bold guesses (which is great) but do not realize the importance of aggressively searching for errors in their own theories and admitting them when found. While argumentative discussion is to be avoided (since it does not lead to the growth of knowledge), it is a characterstic of a mediocre mind to either not participate in critical rational discussions or simply walk away, without admitting one's errors or without changing position, even when critical discussion and evidence has led one to such an outcome.

The Ramayana Text

Many researchers create unnecessary confusion and big deal about the existence of many versions of Ramayana. Some of them insist on cleansing these versions, of course due to misunderstood notions about method and process of science, before undertaking research to determine the timing of Ramayana. This is indeed an incorrect proposition.

All versions of Ramayana, as far as I know, recognize Valmiki as its original composer. Ramayana story has seen multiple variations among these latter editions – mainly due to prevailing beliefs of their composers, predominantly guided by their religious orientation (Buddhism, Jainism, Islam), intent (devotional literature) or cultural influences (Ramayana versions from Thailand, Indonesia, Malaysia, Japan, China, etc.). Multiple versions of Ramayana provide us with good illustration of how an historical tale may add flavors depending on who is re-telling it.

While these versions may provide a confusing mass to a student of Ramayana, for a researcher working on determination of the timing of Ramayana, choice of Ramayana version should not be confusing at all.

A researcher interested in determining the timing of historical instances in Ramayana has only one choice for his research – Valmiki Ramayana. Of course Valmiki Ramayana, as it comes to us, comes in multiple versions, and I have used all available, available to me, versions of Valmiki Ramayana in determining the timing of historical instances described in Ramayana.

2

THEORY, CONJECTURES
&
BACKGROUND ASSUMPTIONS

Your work is not to drag the world kicking and screaming into a new awareness. Your job is to simply do your work – sacredly, secretly and silently, and those with 'eyes to see and ears to hear' will respond.

- The Arcturians

Theory

My theory has two theses:

1. *All astronomy observations are visual observations of the sky*
2. *Ramayana author employed analogies of corresponding seasons, descriptions of nature (flowers, trees, rain, clouds, tides, stormy sea, etc.,), sky views and planetary configurations while describing the incidents of Ramayana.*

Background Assumptions

1. *Ramayana happened before Mahabharata, and thus before 5561 BCE.*
2. *Valmiki wrote Ramayana long before the occurrence (the events of Mahabharta) and composition of Mahabharata.*
3. *At a minimum, Rig-Veda, Sama-Veda and Yajur-Veda existed before Ramayana*

4. *The state of astronomy is as described in Ramayana*

5. *It is not unreasonable to assume that Ramayana has gone through numerous recensions however no objective criteria exist to decide what is original and what is interpolated. I have used the Ramayana text as is (specific editions are mentioned elsewhere in the book). I have documented all astronomy observations <u>corroborating</u> and <u>contradicting</u> my timeline*

6. *Valmiki Ramayana is the only reference text used in determining the timing of Ramayana. It is well understood that Valmiki Ramayana, as available, has transliteration and transcription errors.*

I received tremendous response to my book 'When did the Mahabharata War Happen - The Mystery of Arundhati'. This was personally gratifying. In spite of this appreciation, I realized that while readers were impressed by the findings of that book, many of them failed to understand the critical distinction between inductive and deductive reasoning. Many also confused between portions of an observation that are testable and portions of observations that are not testable. For examples, many readers spent enormous time (on forums but also via email communications with the author) on discussing questions such as:

1. *Why Arundhati-Vasistha (AV) observation was stated among the list of evil omens?*

2. *Why would Vyasa state something as 'evil omen' that existed as such for thousands of years (since 11091 BCE) before the first day of Mahabharata War (16 October 5561 BCE)?*

3. *Was the separation between Arundhati and Vasistha discernible at the time of Mahabharata War, to a naked eye?*

4. *Did Vyasa choose this observation due to its significance for declining morals at the time of War?*

5. *Why did Vyasa choose AV observation and not other star-pair observations?*

While question five is nonsensical, even previous four questions, while interesting by themselves, are completely irrelevant in the context of the theory I proposed (visual observations of the sky) and for testing subsequent consequences of that theory. And while question three is realistic, even that question ignores the basics of a theory I proposed that has telescopic vision in its postulates. Many of these issues arise due to the confusion between inductive and deductive reasoning.

Differences between inductive vs. deductive method is not a trivial matter and a reader must understand it to appreciate the beauty of deductive logic and why this approach leads to growth of knowledge.

Deductive Method

Sir Karl Popper summarizes deductive approach as follows:

1. *All scientific knowledge is hypothetical or conjectural*
2. *The growth of knowledge, and especially of scientific knowledge, consists in learning from our mistakes.*
3. *Learning from our mistakes is achieved by boldly proposing new theories and then searching systematically for the mistakes we have made, i.e. by the critical discussion and the critical examination of our theories.*
4. *Among the most important arguments used in this critical discussions are arguments from experimental tests. Other important arguments include consistency, testability and falsifiability of a theory.*
5. *Experiments are constantly guided by theory, by theoretical hunches of which the experimenter is often not conscious, by hypotheses concerning possible sources of experimental errors, and by hopes or conjectures about what will be a fruitful experiment.*
6. *I had firsthand experience of this point throughout my testing of astronomy observations of the Mahabharata text. The experience was similar while testing astronomy observations of Valmiki Ramayana.*
7. *What is called scientific objectivity consists solely in the critical approach. One proposing the theory is expected to be biased*

*towards it. This is natural. What is important for anyone pro-
posing a theory is to realize that others will be eager to criticize
existing theories and proposals, i.e. they will be eager to refute
your pet theories if they can. This is the critical approach.*

8. *This fact should encourage those proposing theories to try to refute their own theories themselves. This would, if practiced, im-
pose some discipline on researchers. I came across many theories (and proposals) on the dating of Mahabharata War (and
few proposals on the dating of Ramayana). To propose a theory
is to make one self vulnerable and thus I appreciate work of all
these researchers. At the same time, I was disappointed by their
style of research. Their flaws were not limited to inductive logic,
which unfortunately is accepted, erroneously, as valid method of
doing science. These researchers cared little about consistency
of a theory, and rather than making their theories falsifiable,
they were falsely, may be unknowingly, proud of their irrefutable theories.*

9. *Scientists/researchers are not any more objective than other
people. It is not the objectivity or detachment of individual scientist that makes for objectivity. Rather it is the detachment
and objectivity (as Marathi saying goes, "बाप दाखव नाहीतर श्राद्ध कर")
of science itself – the friendly-hostile cooperation of scientists,
i.e. their readiness for mutual criticism which makes for objectivity.*

10. *There is even something like a methodical justification for individual scientists to be dogmatic and biased. Since the method of
science is that of critical discussion, it is of great importance that
the theories criticized should be tenaciously defended. For only
in this way can we learn their real power. And only if criticism
meets resistance can we learn the full force of a critical argument.*

11. *The fundamental role played in science by theories or hypotheses or conjectures makes it important to distinguish between
testable (or falsifiable) and non-testable (or non-falsifiable) the-*

ories.

12. *Only a theory which asserts or implies that certain conceivable events will not, in fact, happen is testable. The test consists in trying to bring about, with all the means we can muster, precisely these events which the theory tells us cannot occur.*

13. *Thus every testable theory may be said to forbid the occurrence of certain events. A theory speaks about empirical reality only in so far as it sets limits to it.*

14. *Every testable theory can thus be put into the form 'such and such cannot happen'.*

Deduction vs. Induction

Books have been written on this subject and I encourage readers to read 'The logic of Scientific Discovery' and 'Conjectures & Refutations' by Sir Karl Popper for additional insights. However I want to explain the difference between deductive and inductive reasoning, in brief.

Deductive reasoning is a basic form of valid reasoning. Deductive reasoning, or deduction, starts out with a general statement, or hypothesis, and examines the possibilities to reach a specific, logical conclusion. The scientific method uses deduction to test hypotheses and theories.

In deductive reasoning, if something is true of a class of things in general, it is also true for all members of that class. For example, "All men are mortal. Harold is a man. Therefore, Harold is mortal." For deductive reasoning to be sound, the hypothesis must be correct. It is assumed that the premises, "All men are mortal" and "Harold is a man" are true. Therefore, the conclusion is logical and true.

It's possible to come to a logical conclusion even if the generalization is not true. If the generalization is wrong, the conclusion may be logical, but it may also be untrue. For example, the argument, "All bald men are grandfathers. Harold is bald. Therefore, Harold is a grandfather," is valid logically but it is untrue because the original statement is false.

A common form of deductive reasoning is the syllogism, in which two statements — a major premise and a minor premise — reach a logical conclusion. For example, the premise "Every A is B" could be followed by another premise, "This C is A." Those statements would lead to the conclusion "This C is B." Syllogisms are considered a good way to test deductive reasoning to make sure the argument is valid.

Inductive reasoning is the opposite of deductive reasoning. Inductive reasoning makes broad generalizations from specific observations. Even if all of the premises are true in a statement, inductive reasoning allows for the conclusion to be false. Here's an example: "Harold is a grandfather. Harold is bald. Therefore, all grandfathers are bald." The conclusion does not follow logically from the statements.

Ramayana Observations

We can classify observations from the text of Valmiki Ramayana as follows. This classification is for the sake of clarity:

1. *Astronomy observations*
2. *Observations of seasons, trees, flowers, weather, animals, vegetation, etc.*
3. *Chronological – related to age of Ramayana personalities, duration of specific journeys and also observations that conflict with linear sequence of time, e.g., need to conjecture multiple Ravanas, ages of Rama and Sita at the time of scheduled coronation, length of time searching for Sita.*
4. *Descriptions of Technology (Pushpak Vimana, Nala-Setu, Flying ability of Vanara and Riksha, Many heads of Ravana, Conjuring abilities of Rakshasas, fighting abilities of Indrajit, etc.,)*

Observations from categories one, two and three would assist us in determination of Ramayana timeline. Observations from category four are interesting by themselves and need further research. However, we must understand that in _no way_ these observations affect our theory of visual astronomy observations in determining the timing of Ramayana. We should emphasize this point as it is misunderstood most often. For example, a question such as why 'Arundhati-Vasistha' observation of Mahabharata text was part of the list of bad omens may be interesting, but has no implication for my theory of visual astronomy observations in determining the timing of Mahabharata War.

I also listed and analyzed any and all observations from each of the above categories that I could not corroborate or explain. These would provide seed observations for improving upon or falsifying my theory.

Simulations, Tests & Observations

Voyager 4.5™ from Carina Soft was used throughout this book in testing astronomy observations of Valmiki Ramayana. Locations of Ayodhya, Nashik (Panchavati), Hampi/Bellary in Karnataka (Kishkindha) and Candy (Sri Lanka) were used for corresponding places in Ramayana, for simulation of appropriate astronomy observations.

Four distinct astronomy observations were responsible for allowing me to establish a lower bound (~10000 BCE) and a plausible upper bound (17500 BCE) for the timing of Ramayana.

The timing of Mahabharata War (5561 BCE) itself provides the lower boundary on the timing of Ramayana, without even looking at the observations of Ramayana. Four distinct Ramayana observations did provide us with latest time interval of 10000 BCE-17500 BCE, for the timing of Ramayana. This time interval of few millenniums does not eliminate possibility of Ramayana occurring in further antiquity, however it does place a distinct limit on the latest time interval when it could have occurred, i.e. Ramayana did not occur any time after 10,000 BCE.

Let's begin by emphasizing lower bound on the timing of Ramayana. The year of Mahabharata War (5561 BCE) provides us with an excellent lower limit. Let's explore connections between Ramayana and Mahabharata. The importance of 5561 BCE will also become clear when we test specific observations, especially conflicting observations, of Valmiki Ramayana.

3

Ramayana before Mahabharata

Setting the Lower Boundary

पवनः पवतामस्मि रामः शस्त्रभृतामहम
झषाणां मकरच्श्रास्मि स्रोतसामस्मि जान्हवी

Of purifiers I am the wind, of the wielders of weapons I am Rama, of
fishes I am the shark and of flowing rivers I am the Ganga.
(Bhagavad Gita 10:31, Mahabharata – Bhishma Parva)

Ramayana & Mahabharata

I have made a case in my book on the Mahabharata war, for 5561 BCE
as the year of the Mahabharata War. It is then natural that Ramayana
happened in further antiquity, i.e. before 5561 BCE.

P V Vartak addressed this issue in his book 'Wastav Ramayana' and I
reproduce number of his points below:

1. If Ramayana was written after Mahabharata, it is not unreason-
    able to expect Valmiki to mention contemporary king(s) of
    Hastinapur. Ramayana does not have even cursory mention of
    the king(s) of Hastinapur. In fact the descendants of the
    Pandavas, beginning with Parikshita, are well known and are

documented elsewhere however none of them are mentioned in Ramayana. On the other hand, Mahabharata does mention contemporary king(s) of Ayodhya (Deergha*Yajna*) [Mahabharata Sabha CE 27] and Kosala (Brihadbal) [Sabha 30 & Drona CE 46]. Both of them fought on the side of the Kauravas.

2. No portion of Mahabharata is to be found in Ramayana; on the other hand 'Ramopakhyana' is part of Mahabharata.

3. No mention of any of the kings of Ayodhya, subsequent to Rama, in Ramayana. This would have been the case if Ramayana was written long after Ramayana and after Mahabharata.

4. Ramayana is called Adi-Kavya. Mahabharata author and those who prepared latter versions of Mahabharata (recensions) have not questioned status of Ramayana as Adi-Kayva or of Valmiki as Adi-Kavi.

5. Ramayana was popular during the time of the Pandavas and Mahabharata. Mahabharata has numerous instances where personalities of Mahabharata refer to instances of Ramayana or employ analogies from Ramayana. Bhurishrava began his fast when Arujna cut the hand of Bhurishrava. Satyaki killed Bhurishrava while the latter was fasting. The Kauravas criticized Satyaki (Drona 143:85-86). Satyaki responded by saying that, "In ancient past, Valmiki has written of Indrajit telling Hanuman that while it is true that women are not to be killed, doing things that cause suffering to a enemy is one's duty nevertheless'. This verse appears in Ramayana (Yuddha 81:29-30). Author of Mahabharata is clearly attributing this reference to Ramayana (and thus Valmiki). This also shows that Ramayana was popular and familiar to the extent Satyaki could quote a verse out of it in an appropriate context. Satyaki quoting this verse reinforces the idea (1) The verse was composed/sung by Valmiki (2) it was composed prior to Mahabharata (3) and that Ramayana was a kavya even during the time of Mahabharata. It is true that Satyaki did not use the word Ramayana but rather 'verse sung by ancient sage Valmiki'.

6. Bhima asserts connection between him and Hanuman by specifically referring to 'Ramayana' (Vana CE 147:11)

7. During Bhima-Hanuman dialogue, Bhima tells Hanuman, that similar to Hanuman's crossing the ocean, Bhima could have crossed the ocean and carried the mountain'. Thus Bhima shows awareness of Hanuman crossing the ocean. Bhima was also aware of Hanuman's inflated appearance at the time of ocean crossing and requests Hanuman to exhibit that inflated form to Bhima. When Hanuman exhibited his gigantic form, Bhima expressed his surprise at the need for Rama to go and defeat Ravana, when Hanuman could have done it singlehandedly. This conversation makes it clear that Bhima was thoroughly familiar with instances from Ramayana.

8. Yudhishthir was equally familiar with Ramayana. When he thought of playing 'Dyuta' for the second time, even after being defeated and excused once, he justified his decision by quoting 'Rama falling prey to illusion of Golden deer, in spite of knowing the impossibility of its existence and states that when time of destruction arrives, even an intelligent person may not act properly. (Sabha 76)

9. Yudhishthir requested Markandeya to tell about Rama in detail (Vana 274)

10. Hanuman asked for a boon from Rama (Uttara 40). Vyasa quote identical details (Vana 148) in Mahabharata.

11. Mahabharata author has quoted instances from Ramayana (Ayodhya 10:33) in Mahabharata (Vana 277:22-23), and from dialogue between Tara and Vali (Ramayana) in Mahabharata (Vana 280).

12. Mahabharata refers to Rama as the best among the holders of Weapons (Bhishma 34, Vibhuti Yoga – chapter 10 of Bhagvad Gita)

13. While comforting Yudhishthir after the War, Krishna told Yudhishthir instances of 16 Kings and that all of them died and thus not to remain in sadness for the killing of his (Yudhishthir) own sons. Krishna tells the story of Rama as one of the 16 kings

and also clearly mentions Rama going to forest for 14 years(Shanti 29)

14. Vyasa recalls story of Rama in brief to Yudhishthir (previously told by Narada to King Srinjaya). This brief mention of Rama refers to Rama spending 14 years in forest due to order of his father, defeating 14000 rakshasas in Janasthana, Ravana abducting Sita, Rama-Ravana yuddha and killing of Ravana (Drona 59)

15. Bhima defeated Brihadbal of Kosala and Deergha*Yajna* of Ayodhya (Sabha CE 27) and also conquered Uttara Kosala (Sabha CE 30). Ramayana clearly states that the area mentioned as Ayodhya, Kosala and Uttara Kosala were under one King (King of Ayodhya) during the time of Ramayana and Rama consciously split it into two. Rama established Lava in Uttara Kosala with Shravasti as its capital and Kusha in Kosala with Kushavati as its capital. Ayodhya lost its importance as center of power after that and thus it appears that Ayodhya was reinstated after Ramayana times but before Mahabharata, for Deerga*Yajna* to be its King.

16. Abhimanyu killed Brihadbal of Kosala (Drona 47)

17. Bhima conquered Janaka of Videha (Sabha 30). It appears that Videha was mentioned because of its ancient connection with Ramayana.

18. When Rama was contemplating 'Rajasuya' (Uttara 83), only two names (of Kings) were mentioned – Mitra and Soma, who had done Rajasuya in the past, and Bharata commented that royal families disappear if someone does Rajasuya. No one refers to Yudhishthir and his Rajasuya *Yajna*. This would have been the case if Mahabharata happened before Ramayana.

19. Vyasa has quoted, casually, an analogy of Hanuman lifting the mountain, in describing the scene of Bhima lifting an elephant during the fight between Karna and Bhima (Drona 139). Same Vyasa has not mentioned this incident of Hanuman during Ramopakhyana of Mahabharata. This point is suggestive of the fact of how popular Ramayana was during Mahabharata times.

20. Mahabharata refers to 'Gopratar' as renowned Holy place near Sharayu (Vana 283) and mentions that from this spot Rama left for heaven along with his servants, army and horses/elephants etc. The places associated with Ramayana were thus familiar during Mahabharata times.

21. Harivamsha (VishnuParva, Adhyaya 31:44-45 refers to a verse uttered by Ravana and then states the verse itself

22. After mentioning the descriptions of the construction of 'Setu' of Ramayana, Vyasa mentions (Vana 283) that this Setu is famous by the name 'Nala-Setu' (in Mahabharata times).

23. Descendants of Rama are described in Harivamsha (Adhyaya 15). There are 21-22 descendants between Rama (Ramayana) and Brihadbala (Mahabharata). In addition Harivamsha 15:36 says that "I have recounted the legends of some (only) important personalities of this dynasty.

1. Sagara	18. (Animitra & Raghu)
2. Panchajana aka Asamaj	19. Duliduha (from Animitra)
3. Amshuman	20. Dilipa
4. Dilip	21. Dirghabahu aka Raghu
5. Bhagiratha	22. Aja
6. Shruta	23. Dasharatha
7. Nabhaga	24. Rama
8. Amabarish	25. Kusha
9. SindhuDwip	26. Atithi
10. Ayut Ajit	27. Nishada
11. Ritaparna (expert in game of Dice + Friend of Emperor Nala)	28. Nala
	29. Nabha or Nagha
	30. Pundarik
12. Artaparni	31. Kshema-Dhanva
13. Sudasa	32. Devanika
14. Saudasa aka Kalmashpada alias MitraSaha	33. Ahignau
	34. Sudhanva
15. SarvaKarma	35. Anal
16. Ananaranya	36. Uktha
17. Nighna	37. Vajranabha

38. Shankha aka Vyushitashva
39. Pushpa
40. Artha
41. Siddhi
42. Sudarshan

43. AgniVarna
44. Shighra
45. Maru
46. Brihadbala

24. Bhagavata Purana also presents the list of descendants of Rama. (Canto 9, chapter 12) That list is as follows:

1. Rama
2. Kusha
3. Atithi
4. Nishada
5. Nabha
6. Pundarika
7. Kshemadhanva
8. Davanika
9. Aniha
10. Pariyatra
11. Balasthala
12. VajraNabha (Sagana)
13. Vidhriti
14. Hiranyanabha
15. Pushpa
16. Dhruvasandhi
17. Sudarshana
18. Agnivarna
19. Shighra
20. Maru
21. Prashruta
22. Sandhi
23. Amarshan
24. Mahaswan
25. Vishwabahu
26. Prasnajit
27. Takshaka

28. Brihadbala (killed by Abhimanyu)
29. Brihadrana
30. Urukriya
31. Vatsavriddha
32. Prativyoma
33. Bhanu
34. Divaka
35. Sahadeva
36. Brihadasva
37. Bhanuman
38. Supratika
39. Pratik
40. Marudeva
41. Sunakshtra
42. Pushkar
43. Antariksha
44. Sutapa
45. Amitrajit
46. Brihadraj
47. Barhi
48. Kritanjaya
49. Rananjaya
50. Sanjay
51. Sakya
52. Shuddodh
53. Langala
54. Prasnajit

55. Kshudraka	56. (Ranaka and Suratha and Sumitra)

Sumitra is listed as last descendant of this dynasty in Bhagavad Purana. This is probably the time when Bhagavata was composed and thus dynasty ended here or only dynasty of Brihadbala ended here which means, Bhagavat might have been composed after this. If this was still told to a Parikshita, this must be another Parikshit, but later recension makers of Bhagavat tried to improve on the gap in narration and thus identified (mis-identified) this Parikshit with previous Parikshit (Son of Abhimanyu).

25. Ramayana Balakanda 66:8, Devarata is described as son of Nimi, on the other hand Ramayana Balakanda 71:3-6 the descendants are described as Nimi-Mithi-Janak-Udavasu-Nandivardhan-Suketu,-Devarata.

Bala 66:8-

1. Nimi
2. Devarata

Bala 70:19-

1. Brahma
2. Marichi
3. Kasyapa
4. Vivaswana
5. Manu
6. Ikshvaku (first ruler of Ayodhya)
7. Kukshi
8. Vikukshi
9. Bana
10. Ananaranya
11. Prithu
12. Trishanku
13. Dhudhumara
14. Yuvanshwa
15. Mandhata
16. Susandhi
17. Dhruvasandhi & Prasnajit
18. Bharata-Dhruvasandhi's son
19. Asita
20. Sagara
21. Asamaj
22. Amshuman

23. Dilipa
24. Bhagiratha
25. Kakustha
26. Raghu
27. Pravrudha-aka-Kalmashpada
28. Sankhana
29. Sudarshan
30. Agnivarna
31. Shighra
32. Maru
33. Prasrusruka
34. Ambarisha
35. Nahusha
36. Yayati (not to be confused with other lineage of Mahabharata or should we?)
37. Nabhaga
38. Aja
39. Dasharatha
40. Rama

26. Vyasa has specifically mentioned Valmiki, the author of Ramayana numerous times. On the other hand no direct or indirect mention of Vyasa is to be found in Valmiki Ramayana.

When above specific points are combined with my established timing of the Mahabharata War, we can assert that Ramayana occurred sometime before 5561 BCE.

.

4

INDIAN CALENDAR

India is, the cradle of the human race, the birthplace of human speech, the mother of history, the grandmother of legend and the great grandmother of tradition. Our most valuable and most constructive materials in the history of man are treasured up in India only.

- Mark Twain

Before we begin analyzing specific observations from Ramayana text, we should set the necessary background in order to understand and appreciate the interpretation of Ramayana observations and their corresponding consequences for determining the timing of Ramayana.

Celestial Time Clock

Reader will find analogy of 'mechanical clock and its mechanism' with that of 'celestial clock' useful. Various celestial motions are not unlike the motions of various gears of wheel train of a mechanical clock. While a power spring is the source of power that moves the wheel train in a mechanical clock, the gravitational forces and the interplay between them are responsible for motions of the moon around the earth, motions of the earth and the precession of equinoxes.

While we carefully control the settings of wheel train and escapement mechanism in order to generate precise and accurate time on the display of a mechanical clock; in case of 'Archeo-astronomy', the task is to interpret 'astronomy observations' in the context of the celestial clock in order to predict precise and accurate timing of either an ancient document containing those astronomy observations or ancient structure that was supposedly aligned according to astronomy coordinates of that time.

The Celestial clock appears complex and it is, but so does mechanical clock to a novice. On the other hand little patience and some willingness to go into the details is all that is required to understand both.

Let's understand this celestial clock. We will begin with solar year.

Solar Year

Solar year is the period of time required for the earth to make one complete revolution around the sun, measured from one vernal equinox to the next. This time interval is equal to 365 days, 5 hours, 48 minutes and 45.51 seconds. It is represented by a Gregorian calendar with 12 months and length of 365 days, unless it is a leap year when the length is 366 days. While the first day of the year in Gregorian calendar is arbitrary, in the sense that it does not coincide with any specific cardinal point, the Gregorian calendar has rules so that it closely approximates the solar year and will continue to do so for next 8000 years without introducing much inaccuracy.

Solar months are 12 in number in the Gregorian calendar system and length of each month is arbitrarily set so that all days of the year together add up to 365.

Solar Day

It is defined as 'the length of time' that elapses for sun to reach its highest point in the sky two consecutive times. This duration is approximately of 24 hours. This is our most familiar 24 hour day. Inventions of mechanical and now digital clocks allow us to measure it from any arbitrary reference point, such as midnight, as is done in our times.

Solar Month

True solar month would/should refer to the time interval when the sun stays in the region of a specific zodiac. However this method is not followed by any existing solar calendars. In that sense, duration and names of solar months (January through December) of Gregorian calendar are arbitrary.

Lunar Year

The moon takes 27.3 days to make a complete round around the earth. However the earth itself moves by significant distance during this time and thus it takes the moon around 29.5 days to reach the same phase with respect to the earth. This is the lunar month.

The length of time for the moon to make one revolution in its orbit is difficult to predict and varies from its average value. Because observations are subject to uncertainty and weather conditions, and astronomical methods are highly complex, there have been attempts to create fixed arithmetical rules. The average length of the synodic month is 29.530589 days.

Lunar year is made up of 12 such lunar months and thus length of the lunar year is equal to 354 (29.5 x 12 = 354) days.

Islamic calendar follows lunar year. Since the lunar year is shorter by 10/11 days from the solar year, Islamic holidays occur 10/11 days earlier each subsequent year. For example the month of Ramadan occurs earlier by a month (with respect to solar calendar) every three years. This also means if month of Ramadan occurs during peak of winter in any given year (Gregorian calendar), it will occur at the peak of summer 18 years in the future.

Tithi (Lunar day)

In Indian calendar system (luni-solar year) a *Tithi* is a lunar day or the time it takes for the longitudinal angle between the moon and the sun to increase by 12^0. *Tithi* begins at varying time of day and vary in duration from 19 to 26 hours.

There are 30 *Tithis* in each lunar month. *Amawasya* is new moon (no moon day). It is followed by Pratipada (1) , Dwitiya(2) , Tritiya (3), Chaturthi (4), Panchami (5), Shashthi (6), Saptami (7), Ashtami (8), Navami (9), Dashami (10), Ekadashi (11), Dwadashi (12), Trayodashi (13), Chaturdashi (14) and Pornima (Full moon day). These *Thithis* are repeated for the second half of the lunar month, beginning with Pratipada, Dwitiya, etc. and ends with *Amawasya* when a new lunar month begins.

Nakshatra (Wives of the Moon)

Predictable rising of the sun provided the ancients a unit of time. However, in order to track the progress of time, one aspires to monitor the motion of a moving object with respect to non-moving (non- moving only in a relative sense since all astral bodies are in motion) object. Observations of the moon's position (moving) with respect to those of nakshatras (not moving) at night provided such an opportunity. Astronomers of Ramayana time used the system of 'nakshatra Ganana', developed by their predecessors, to keep track of time. Nakshatra, which is loosely translated as 'asterism' could be either a specific star (e.g. Chitra) or group of stars (e.g. Krittika) along the ecliptic and is employed as reference in stating the positions of astral bodies (sun, moon, planets, comets, etc.).

It appears that the desired number of nakshatras were determined based on how long it took the moon to complete one orbital cycle. Since the moon completes one cycle through its orbit in 27.3 days, 27 nakshatras were selected. This nakshatra system was also used to track positions of other astral bodies. Since the moon visited each nakshatra once every month, poetically, it was perceived as moon visiting each of his 27 wives each day of the month, until the moon visited all of them, only to repeat the cycle during the next month. These wives of the moon were given specific names, were assigned a devata (deity) and are frequently referred to by the name of their assigned deity. The nakshatras along with their *YogaTara*, Deity, Right Ascension and Declination measurements for the timing of Ramayana are listed below:

Nakshatra Positions on 29 November 12240 BCE
(Dynamic epoch)

Nakshatra	Yoga-Tara	Nakshatra-Devata	RA	Dec
			(Hrs & Min)	(Deg & arc-min)
Chitra	Spica	Twastra (Indra)	0 hr 36 min	$+1^0 47'$
Swati	Zeta Bootis	Vayu	23 hr 16 min	$+38^0 56'$
Vishakha	Zubeneschamali	Indragni	1 hr 54 min	$+22^0 2'$
Anuradha	Dschubba	Mitra	3 hr 1 min	$+16^0 45'$
Jyeshtha	Antares	Indra (Varuna)	3 hr 33 min	$+16^0 18'$
Moola	Nunki	Visve Devah	4 hr 40 min	$+10^0 28'$
P. Ashadha	Shaula	Pitarah (Nirriti)	5 hr 21 min	$+14^0 50'$
U. Ashadha	Kaus Australis	Apah	5 hr 49 min	$+22^0 33'$
Shravana	Altair	Vishnu	7 hr 23 min	$+53^0 9'$
(Abhijit)	Vega	Brahma	(4 hr 45 min)	$(+86^0 22')$
Dhanistha	Sualocin	Vasavah	9 hr 11 min	$+53^0 27'$
Shatabhishaj	Sadalmelik	Indra (Varuna)	9 hr 42 min	$+27^0 14'$
P. Bhadrapada	Markab	Aja Ekapad	11 hr 17 min	$+27^0 26'$
U. Bhadrapada	Algenib	Ahir-Budhyna	12 hr 2 min	$+14^0 19'$
Revati	Kullat Nunu	Pusan	12 hr 52 min	$+0^0 13'$
Ashwini	Hamal	Asvinau	13 hr 39 min	$+0^0 45'$
Bharani	41 Arietis	Yama	14 hr 19 min	$-3^0 14'$
Krittika	Pleiades	Agni	14 hr 54 min	$-13^0 37'$
Rohini	Aldebaran	Prajapati	15 hr 21 min	$-25^0 2'$
Mriga-shirsha	Bellatrix	Soma	15 hr 57 min	$-39^0 38'$
Ardra	Betelgeuse	Rudra	16 hr 36 min	$-40^0 28'$
Punarvasu	Pollux	Aditi	18 hr 45 min	$-18^0 10'$
Pushya	Altarf	Brihaspati	19 hr 33 min	$-34^0 21'$
Ashlesha	zeta Hydrae	Nagas/Sarpah	20 hr 23 min	$-33^0 0'$
Magha	Regulus	Pitarah	21 hr 14 min	$-17^0 16'$
P. Phalguni	Zosma	Aryaman (Bhaga)	21 hr 33 min	$-1^0 1'$
U. Phalguni	Denebola	Bhaga (Aryaman)	22 hr 20 min	$+2^0 39'$
Hasta	Algorab	Savitar (Sun?)	0 hr 17 min	$-11^0 3'$

Some nakshatras have synonyms and were recognized by those synonyms, in addition to being referred to by their presiding deity. For example, 'Bhadrapada' is also called 'Proshtha-pada', 'Dhanishtha' is
called 'Shravishtha' and 'Shatabhisaj' is called 'Shata-taraka'. Some variations can also be seen while assigning presiding deity to a given
nakshatra. These variations, fortunately, do not lead to any confusion.
Existence of other evidence and cross-references within Indian literature (prior to and after Ramayana) are sufficient to understand the

nakshatra referred to. The nakshatra closest to the moon on a given day is 'nakshatra of the day' in Indian calendar system. Determination of the nakshatra of any given day based on visual observation can lead to an error of +/- 1 day.

Lunar Month

There are two definitions of Lunar months – *Purnamanta* and *Amanta*. A lunar month that begins with full moon day and ends on the next full moon day is called *Purnamanta*. A lunar month that begins on *Amawasya* (new moon day) and ends on the next *Amawasya* is called *Amanta*.

I will follow definition of *Amanta* lunar month throughout the book. In the *Amanta* system, lunar months are named after the nakshatra in the vicinity of full moon during that month. Lunar months are named - Chaitra, Vaishakha, Jyeshtha, Ashadha, Shravana, Bhadrapada, Ashwin, Kartika, Margashirsha, Pausha, Magha and Phalgun.

Luni-solar year

Gregorian calendar and Islamic calendar are examples of purely solar and purely lunar calendars, respectively. Indian calendar is decidedly luni-solar from ancient times. Indian Calendar does have regional variations however the core of it can be described without getting into regional nuances.

Basic unit of Indian calendar is lunar day (*Tithi*). For the purposes of defining a year, the next unit of the Indian luni-solar calendar is the lunar month. Lunar month is the time interval either from one new moon to the next or one full moon to the next. The luni-solar calendar based on two successive new moons is called the *'Amanta'* calendar. The luni-solar calendar based on two successive full moons is called the *Purnamanta*. I have followed terminology and assumptions of *'Amanta'* calendar throughout this book.

Indian luni-solar calendar is *'Nirayana'* in nature. The *Nirayana* year is the time taken for the sun to return to the same fixed point on the ecliptic. The *Nirayana* year comprises 12 solar months. The lunar year consisting of 12 lunar month is shorter than the solar *Nirayana* year and hence *Adhika masa* (leap months) have to be added periodically so that the calendar approximates the *Nirayana* solar year. The occurrence of *Adhika masa* is not (cannot be) determined by arithmetical rules of Gregorian calendar. Additionally, some lunar months in the 'Amanta' luni-solar calendar can have skipped days (*Tithi*) or repeated days (*Tithi*) which makes the numbering of days in the month slightly more complicated than usual.

Length of a lunar month = 29.5 days

Length of a lunar Year = 12 x 29.5 = 354 days

Length of solar year = 365.2422 ~ 365 days

Difference between Solar and Lunar year =
365-354 = 11 days.

Adhika masa

Indian calendar makers came up with the ingenious idea of 'Adhika masa (extra lunar month) to enable synchronization between the solar and the lunar year. While the method(s) to determine 'Adhika masa' might have changed over the millenniums, the invention of 'Adhika masa' is very old. Rig-Veda, but also Mahabharata, refers to 'Adhika masa' and thus we have reason to believe in existence of 'Adhika masa' during Ramayana times, since Ramayana is post Rig-Veda, but before Mahabharata. I do not require assumption of 'Adhika masa' in my Ramayana research. Rather the point I want to emphasize is that existence of 'Adhika masa' in calendar calculations during Ramayana time should not surprise us.

While references to 'Adhika masa' exist in Rig-Veda and Mahabharata, no specific method to determine 'Adhika masa' is mentioned. However to clarify the concept of selection and naming of *Adhika masa*, I will illustrate the method employed in India, in our times.

Recall that Lunar month begins with *Amawasya* (*Amanta* reckoning) and that the moon and the sun are together, as seen from the earth, on *Amawasya* day. The ecliptic, path of the sun, is divided into 12 zodiacs (27 Nakshatras) and thus each zodiac is approximately 30^0 ($30^0/360^0$ or 1/12) of the ecliptic. This also means that on an average the sun will travel though area of each zodiac in approximately 30 days. The sun transiting from one zodiac into the next is called 'Sankrantee' (San–Krantee: meaningful movement/transition).

Generally, *Amawasya* (new moon day) falls only once between two

Sangrantees. However occasionally, *Amawasya* may fall twice while the sun is still transiting through the area of a single zodiac. The lunar month defined by this second *Amawasya* is termed as *Adhika masa*.

Let us analyze the basis of *Adhika masa* calculations. The earth is revolving around the sun. The earth completes one circle around the sun in 365.2564 days (365 days 6 hours 9 minutes & 12.96 seconds) whereas the moon takes 29.5306 (29 days 12 hours 44 minutes & 3.84 seconds) days from new moon (*Amawasya*) to the next new moon (next *Amawasya*). Therefore the duration of lunar month is 29.5306 days and number of days in 12 lunar months = 29.5306x12=354.3672 days. The difference between a solar year and a lunar year is 10.8992 days ~ 11 days.

Therefore every year, lunar months (and thus *Tithis*) occur 11 days earlier. In three years this difference reaches up to 33 days, which is more than one month. This difference necessitates insertion of *Adhika masa* every ~three years.

The timing of Adhika masa varies. It may come after an interval of 2 years and 4 months, 2 years and 9 months, 2 years and 10 months or 2 years and 11 months. On an average *Adhika masa* comes in 2 years and 8.5 months. This value can be verified by dividing the duration of lunar month i.e. 29.5 days by 10.9. A lunar year is 10.9 days shorter than solar year therefore after dividing 29.53/10.9 = 2 years and 8.5 months there arises a difference of one month.

Kshaya Masa

Recall that usually *Amawasya* (new moon) falls once between two *Sankrantees, Sankrantee* being sun's transit into the area of next zodiac. On a rare occasion, no *Amawasya* would occur between two *Sankrantees* and when that happens subsequent lunar month is considered as *Kshaya* (elapsed). Let's us understand why this may happen.

Minimum value between two *Sankrantees* is 29 days 10 hours and 48 minutes and maximum value is 31 days 10 hours and 48 minutes; whereas the minimum value between two *Amawasyas* (new moons) is 29 days 5 hours 54 minutes and 14 seconds and the maximum value between two new moons is 29 days 19 hours 36 minutes and 29 seconds. Therefore, it so happens, although rarely, that no *Amawasya* (new moon) falls between two *Sankrantees*. This generally happens after 19 years, or after 141 years, and sometimes after 65, 76 or 122 years. This type of situation is termed as *Kshaya masa*. This is possible during sun's transit through zodiacs with smaller areas such as Scorpio, Sagittarius and Capricorn. This implies *Kshaya masa* most likely happens during the lunar months of Margashirsha, Pausha or Magha.

Why Synchronize?

While *Tithi* (lunar day) is a unit for daily measurement of time, and while lunar month is a unit for monthly measure of time, it is the solar year that determines the seasons. In agrarian culture, the importance of synchronizing lunar and solar years is obvious. Synchronizing lunar days/months with solar year is critical for planting and harvesting of crops. Celebration of festivals, initiation and completion of *Yajnas* and strict adherence to rituals on specific days of the year were all meant to informally educate the society and to aid in maintenance of calendar.

Delta T and Dynamic Time

This is the difference between Universal Time (UTC) and Terrestrial Dynamic Time (TDT). TDT is based on atomic clocks, and it is the standard for precise time keeping in astronomy. It differs from UTC because the earth's rotation is slowing in an irregular manner. This is due to the earth's gravitational interaction with the moon. We must periodically add or subtract "leap seconds" to or from UTC, in order to keep it in sync with where the earth is actually pointing. The accumulated difference between UTC and TDT is called *'Delta T'*.

The current value of *'Delta T'* is about 67 seconds. But in 4000 BCE, the accumulated time correction was about two days, and in much earlier periods, it was only an educated guess. Note that *'Delta T'* affects the time when an astronomical event is observed on earth, and hence the altitude and azimuth where it is seen in the sky.

5

PATH OF THE POLE

The end of our exploring will be to arrive at where we started, and to know the place for the first time.

- T.S. Eliot

Path of the Pole: Precession of Equinoxes

The earth orbits the sun in an almost invariable plane – what we call path of the sun – known as the ecliptic. The earth's axis of rotation in space is inclined to the perpendicular of this plane (the ecliptic) by an angle of about 23.5^0.

Per current theory in vogue, the sun and the moon exert gravitational influence on the earth's equatorial bulge that leads to the change in direction of the earth's axis describing a circle with a radius of almost 23.5^0, about the north pole of the ecliptic, once every 26000 years.

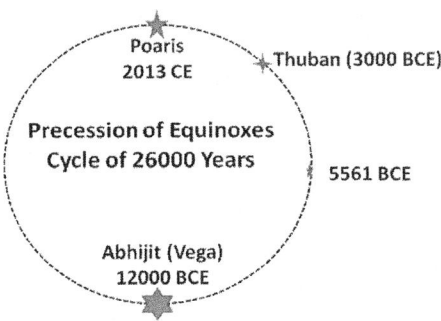

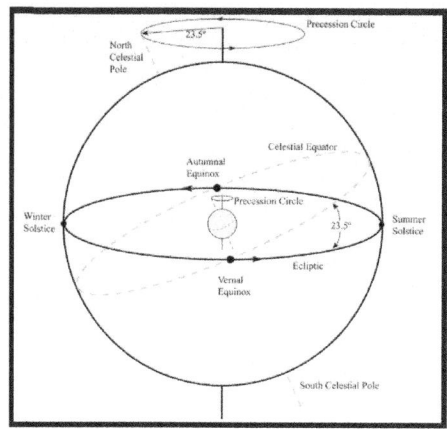

It is good to understand why precession occurs, however what is critical is to understand the consequences of the precession of equinoxes. The point of spring or autumn equinoxes, and summer and winter solstices move slowly –westward – along the ecliptic by about 50 arc-sec per year, or 1^0 every 72 years.

This means that the spring equinox – where the sun crosses the celestial equator from the south to the north every spring – moves backwards through the nakshatra space (the band of sky on both sides (north and south) of the ecliptic) at the rate of one nakshatra every 950 years or so.

Effect of 'precession of equinoxes' on Solar year

Position of the sun, referenced by background nakshatra, for the timing of winter and summer solstices or spring and fall equinoxes would change due to the precession of equinoxes.

Gregorian calendar – our modern calendar, which was a modification of Julian calendar, while adjusted to take into account effect of precession of equinoxes, is incapable (in the sense of Archeo-astronomy) of documenting astronomy changes (references of background nakshatras for specific cardinal points, at any given time).

Solar Year – Gregorian style

Gregorian calendar that began in 1582 CE (AD) is designed in such a way that spring equinox coincides with 20 March, summer solstice with 21 June, autumn (fall) equinox with 23 September and winter solstice with 21 December. The advantage of this calendar is that all one has to remember is these key dates in order to know the cycle of seasons.

The disadvantage of this calendar, at least archeo-astronomically speaking, is that it is disconnected from nakshatra (or zodiac) system. The disadvantage is not obvious, since these calendars (Gregorian but also Julian) were designed recently. The months do slide against the background zodiac, due to the precession of equinoxes, however the calendar itself has no provision to capture this slippage of zodiac against the Gregorian calendar month.

Effect of 'precession of equinoxes' on Lunar year

Lunar month is defined by the position (with respect to the background nakshatra field) of the full moon. If full moon occurs closer to nakshatra Ashwini, it is the lunar month of Ashwin. If full moon occurs close to nakshatra Chitra, it is the lunar month of Chaitra, and so on. We will consider few epochs separated by thousands of years to illustrate the effect of 'precession of equinoxes' on lunar months/year.

Polaris: North Pole Star (2000 CE)

In our times (1800 CE – 2100 CE), the point of summer solstice coincides with nakshatra Ardra (*Yogatara*- Betelgeuse). This means the sun is near nakshatra Ardra during summer solstice. The full moon occurring around this time would be opposite of nakshatra Ardra (point of winter solstice) and that point is in the region of nakshatras Moola and Purva Ashadha, which also means summer solstice coincides with lunar month(s) of Jyeshtha/Ashadha. Nakshatra Ardra is next to that of nakshatra Mrigashirsha which also means winter solstice coincides with the lunar month of Margashirsha. Using same methodology, we can identify lunar months that would coincide with spring equinox and fall equinox. The point of spring equinox is between nakshatras Purva and Uttara Bhadrapada and the point of fall equinox is between nakshatras Uttara Phalguni and Hasta. This means lunar month of Bhadrapada coincides with fall equinox and lunar month of Phalgun coincides with spring equinox.

Cardinal Points & Seasons (Today: 2013 CE)
Spring Equinox – U. Bhadrapada
(Middle of spring – Lunar month of Phalgun)

Summer Solstice – near Ardra
(Beginning of Varsha/Rainy season – Lunar month of Ashadha)
Fall Equinox – near Hasta
(Middle of fall – Lunar month of Bhadrapada)
Winter Solstice – near P. Ashadha
(Beginning of winter – Lunar month of Margashirsha)

The point of spring equinox coincided with nakshatra Uttara Bhadrapada in year 1742 CE. The point of autumn equinox was near nakshatra Hasta in 1742 CE while the point of summer solstice was near nakshatra Ardra and the point of winter solstice was near nakshatra Purva Ashadha. Since nakshatras are used as signposts to indicate location of the sun as it journeys through its path – the ecliptic, we can also say that the sun was in nakshatra Uttara Bhadrapada during *Vasant Sampat* (spring equinox), in nakshatra Hasta during *Sharad Sampat* (autumn/fall equinox), in nakshatra Ardra during summer solstice (Dakshinayan Bindu) and in nakshatra Purva Ashadha during winter solstice (Uttarayan Bindu).

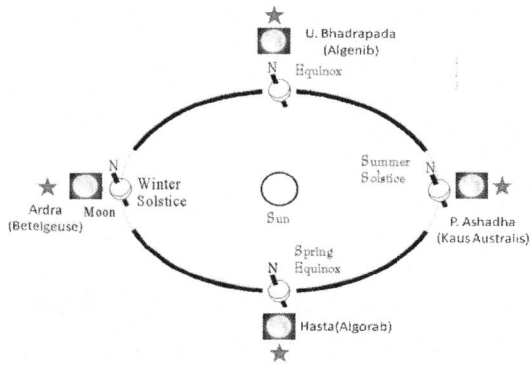

No significant change has taken place since 1742 CE. This is because the movement of the precession of equinoxes is extremely slow and it would take ~1000+ years before a change in location of these cardinal points (equinoxes and solstices), with respect to nakshatras, would become obvious.

Abhijit (Vega): North Pole Star (12000 BCE)

Let's turn the clock backwards by ~14000 years to 12048 BCE, when the earth's axis was pointing towards, and closest to the area of the star

Abhijit (Vega). This point is almost opposite to that of Polaris, our current North Pole star. The point of summer solstice, then, coincided with nakshatra Uttara Ashadha, point of winter solstice was between nakshatras Ardra and Punarvasu, point of spring equinox was near nakshatra Hasta and finally point of fall equinox was near nakshatra Uttara Bhadrapada. The situation is exactly reversed! The point of winter solstice has been replaced by the point of summer solstice (2100 CE vs. 12048 BCE) and point of fall equinox has been replaced by spring equinox. This means the correspondance between these cardinal points (solstices and equinoxes) and lunar months is also reversed!

Thus, 14000 years ago, summer solstice occurred during lunar month(s) of Margashirsha/Pausha, winter solstice occurred during lunar months of Jyeshtha/Ashadha, spring equinox occurred during the lunar month of Bhadrapada and fall equinox occurred during the lunar month of Chaitra.

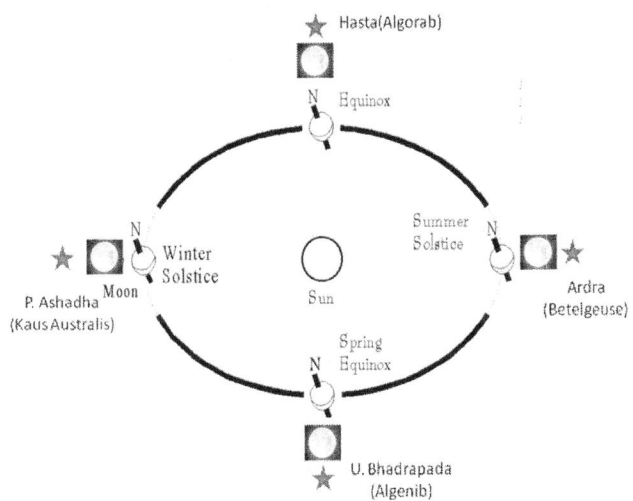

Cardinal Points and Seasons: (12000 BCE or 13500 CE)

Spring Equinox – near Hasta (Lunar months of Bhadrapada/Ashwin/Kartika)

Summer Solstice – near U. Ashadha (Lunar months of Margashirsha/Pausha)

Fall Equinox – near U. Bhadrapada (Lunar months of Phalgun/Chaitra/Vaishakha)

Winter Solstice – near Punarvasu (Lunar months of

Jyeshtha/Ashadha/Shravan)

North Pole: Mahabharata War (5561 BCE)

The Mahabharata War took place in 5561 BCE when fall equinox co-incided, roughly, with the lunar month of Margashirsha/Pausha and winter solstice coincided, roughly, with lunar months of Chaitra or Phalgun. The Mahabharata War occurred during the season of *Sharad* and during the lunar month of *Margashirsha*. Bhishma was lying on the bed of arrows for 98 days (25 October 5561 BCE – 30/31 January 5560 BCE) until the day of winter solstice.

No visible star (visible to naked eye) was available close to the point of North Celestial pole during Mahabharata times (5561 BCE).

Cardinal Points and Seasons: Mahabharata Time (5561 BC)
Spring Equinox – near Punarvasu (Lunar months of Phalgun/Chaitra)
Summer Solstice – near Hasta (Lunar months of
Bhadrapada/Ashwin)
Fall Equinox – U. Phalguni (Lunar months of Margashirsha/Pausha)
Winter Solstice –U. Bhadrapada (Lunar months of Phalgun/Chaitra)

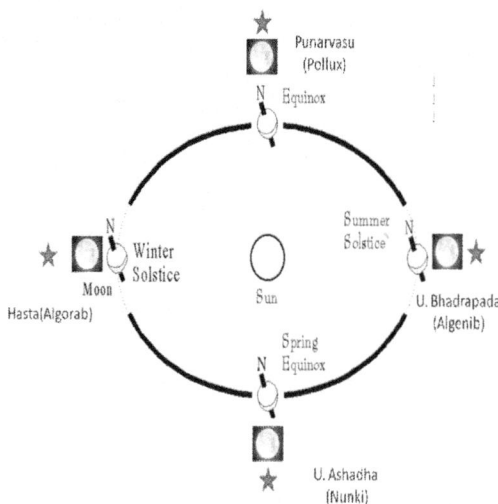

Effect of 'precession of equinoxes' on Seasons

The Indian calendar has 6 seasons – Vasanta (spring), Grishma (summer), Varsha (rain), Sharad (pre-autumn), Hemant (autumn) and Shishir (winter), each season, roughly, made up of two lunar months. Shishir begins with the day of winter solstice and Varsha begins with the day of summer solstice. Two months surrounding spring equinox constitute the season of spring and two months surrounding fall equinox constitute the season of Sharad. Two months leading to the day of summer solstice constitute season of Grishma and two months leading to the day of winter solstice constitute season of Hemant.

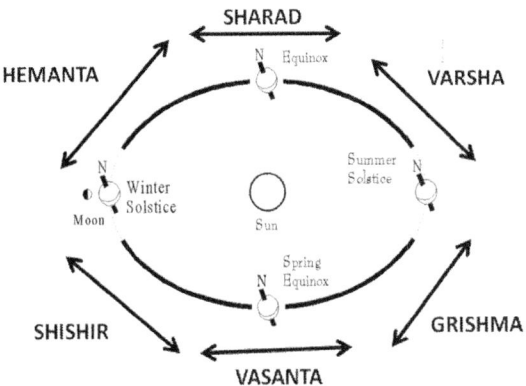

In summary,

Season	Months (2100 CE)	Months (12000 BCE)
Varsha	Jyeshtha-Ashadha	Margashirsha-Pausha
Sharad	Shravan- Bhadrapada	Magha - Phalgun
Hemant	Ashwin-Kartika	Chaitra - Vaishakha
Shishir	Margashirsha-Pausha	Jyeshtha- Ashadha
Vasanta	Magha- Phalgun	Shravan-Bhadrpada
Grishma	Chaitra –Vaishakha	Ashwin –Kartika

It is important to keep in mind that the changes due to the precession of equinoxes are gradual and thus its effect on Indian lunar months, corresponding to specific seasons, is also gradual. For example, if we go back by 2000 years, in further antiquity, to the timing of Mahabharata observation of 'Fall of Vega' (14602 BCE), the seasons would shift only slightly with respect to the lunar months (in comparison to those of 12000 BC).

In 14000 BCE,

Season	Lunar Months
Varsha	Pausha and Magha
Sharad	Phalgun and Chaitra
Hemant	Vaishakha & Jyeshtha
Shishir	Ashadha and Shravan
Vasant	Bhadrapada & Ashwin
Grishma	Kartika & Margashirsha

It is also critical to keep in mind that lunar day recedes by 10-11 days every year against the Gregorian calendar (or against a specific cardinal point), until correction of *Adhika masa* is made every 2.5 years or so. Thus, change of season for a given Indian lunar month is further slowed down by the periodic correction of *Adhika masa*.

Thus, the correspondence between a season and lunar months is approximate and shift of up to one month from the list above is to be expected.

Comprehension of the 'precession of equinoxes' and deep understanding of its effect on the seasons and corresponding lunar months is critical for defining (and comprehending) the broader time interval for Ramayana- Epoch of Ramayana.

6

Epoch of Ramayana

One of the things a philosopher may do, and one of those that may rank among his highest achievements, is to see a riddle, a problem, or a paradox, not previously seen by anyone else. This is an even greater achievement than resolving the riddle. The philosopher who first sees and understands a new problem disturbs our laziness and complacency. He does to us what Hume did for Kant: he rouses us from our 'dogmatic slumber'. He opens out a new horizon before us.

- Karl Popper.

Let's begin with Ramayana observation of the lunar month of Chaitra. When Rama was 17 years old, king Dasharatha decided to coronate Rama. The Ramayana text describes the lunar month of Chaitra as glorious and auspicious and that of 'पुष्पितकाननं (pushpitakanan)', i.e. a month of flowers or a month in which forests bloom with flowers.

Error Elimination – Experiment 1

Chaitra – Month in which forests bloom with flowers[2]

Almost all researchers, writing on Ramayana, assume the timing of the lunar month of Chaitra, during Ramayana times, to coincide with the Vasanta (spring) season. These researchers have casually assumed the timing of the lunar month of Chaitra to be that of spring (Vasanta) season. It is obvious that these researchers have given little thought to this observation of Ramayana.

Ayodhya 3:4

चैत्र: श्रीमानयं मास: पुण्य: पुष्पितकानन:
यौवराज्याय रामस्य सर्वमेवोपकल्प्यताम

In our times (2012 CE) spring equinox is between nakshatras Purva and Uttara Bhadrapada while fall equinox is between nakshatras Hasta and Uttara Phalugni. This means in our times the lunar month of Phalgun can be considered the first month and Chaitra as the second month of spring season. Certainly Ramayana did not happen in our times.

Voyager 4.5 simulation shows us that point of fall equinox coincided with nakshatra Chitra (Spica) around 345 CE and this means full moon of Chaitra coincided with the spring equinox during this time, i.e., in year 341 CE (e.g. 20 March 341 CE). I also tested the extreme limit of Chaitra for Ramayana descriptions, i.e. the first month of Vasanta (spring) season coinciding with the lunar month of Chaitra. The First month of Vasanta (spring) season coincided with the lunar month of Chaitra around 2000 BCE.

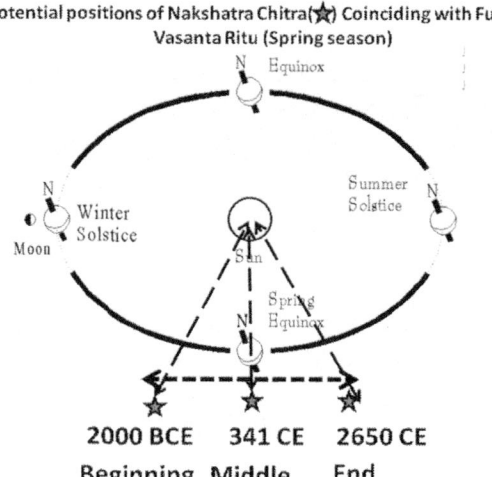

Potential positions of Nakshatra Chitra(☆) Coinciding with Full Moon
Vasanta Ritu (Spring season)

If one accepts that the lunar month of Chaitra coincided with the seasons of spring in Ramayana times, then, such an acceptance falsifies proposals of Vartak, Bhatnagar and SRS; purely based on this one reference.

Thus, unless we are willing to assume that Ramayana occurred during the last 4000 years, we have to go back through a complete cycle of the precession of equinoxes to a time period of ~24000 BCE, i.e., if one still insists on the assumption of season of Vasanta coinciding with that of the lunar month of Chaitra. Alternately, we have to look for other explanations.

Since the lunar month of Chaitra is described as month of flowers, we can safely eliminate seasons of Hemant (cold) and Shishir (very cold). That leaves us with seasons of Vasanta, Grishma, Varsha and Sharad to choose from. I have already eliminated season of Vasanta.

Let's look at 5561 BCE, the year of Mahabharata War, when the point of summer solstice was near nakshatra Chitra. This means the lunar month of Chaitra coincided with (opposite of summer solstice) the first month of winter. Since Ramayana occurred before Mahabharata, we have to go back from 5561 BCe, in further antiquity.

The next available season of flowers (i.e. going back in antiquity) that would coincide with the lunar month of Chaitra would be that of Sharad. We find that the point of spring equinox coincided with nakshatra Chitra (i.e. position of the sun near nakshatra Chitra) around 13000 BCE. This corresponds to lunar month of Chaitra coinciding with (opposite of spring) the middle of Sharad season, another season of flowers. Considering a time interval of +/- 30 degrees from this point, I could estimate time interval of Ramayana, based on this observation, to be from 10500 BCE until 15000 BCE. The rationale for estimating time interval for position of nakshatra Chitra, separated from the position of the sun by $+/- 30^0$, is due to the fact that any given season (in this case – season of Sharad) roughly extends over two months. Reader should recall that the sun travels through $~30^0$ in one month.

This Ramayana observation then allows us to define the timing of Ramayana to be sometime during 10500 BCE – 15000 BCE.

"Unbelievable! Impossible! " says the Reader.

I hear you. I said the exact same words and no one was around to hear them. Fortunately, we have learnt from our previous research that what may appear impossible is possible and no matter how unbelievable the conclusion is, one has to accept it at the face value. If it is impossible and/or wrong, other evidence will falsify it anyway.

Potential positions of Nakshatra Chitra(★) Coinciding with Full Moon
Sharad Ritu (Pre-autumn))

End	Middle	Beginning
10500 BCE	13000 BCE	15000 BCE

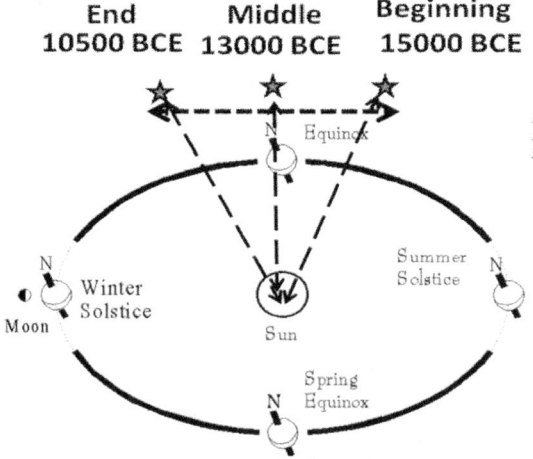

Are there any other observations in Ramayana text that would lead us to the same time interval? That is the question I asked myself. The answer did not take long.

Error Elimination – Experiment 2

Setting Sun near Pushya, during the season of Hemanta[3]

Ramayana text refers to the setting of the sun near nakshatra Pushya during the season of Hemant (autumn).

Aranya 16:12

निवृत्ताकाशशयना: पुष्यनिता हिमारुणा:

शीता वृद्धतरायामास्त्रियामा यान्ति साम्प्रतम

For the purpose of simulation, let's assume the timing of this observation to be at the middle of Hemant season. This amounts to 30^0 (or 2 hrs of Right ascension before the point of winter solstice) away from the point of winter solstice and towards the point of fall equinox.

The point of winter solstice coincided with nakshatra Pushya around 13500 BC, with that of middle of Hemant season, around 15500 BCE and with that of the beginning of Hemant season, around 17500 BCE.

Potential positions of Nakshatra Pushya(☆) with respect to Sun's position
Season of Hemanta (Autumn)

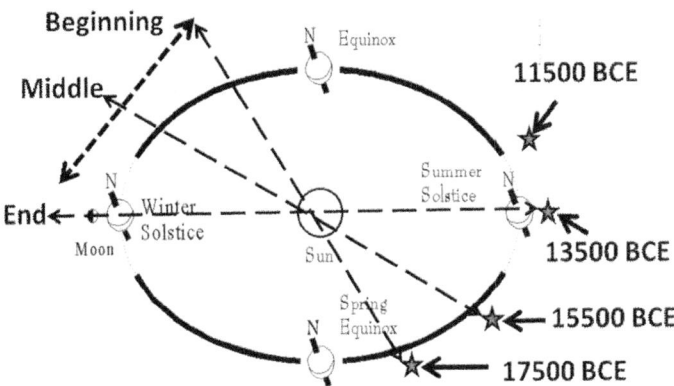

Since the observation of the sun setting near nakshatra Pushya, during the season of Hemant (autumn), is a visual observation, one may make a case for extending this period further. One may assert that nakshatra Pushya would have been visible at the western horizon, immediately after the setting of the sun. While determining specific amount of separation between the sun and nakshatra Pushya could be anyone's guess, what we can comfortably state is that the separation of nakshatra Pushya from the position of the setting sun (during season of Hemant) does not need to be more than 30 degrees, i.e. nakshatra Pushya east of the setting sun by 30 degrees. This assumption would place lower limit on the timing of Ramayana as late as 11500 BCE.

This observation is capable of pinpointing a broad time interval of 11500 BCE – 17500 BCE, which interestingly enough, coincides with the conclusion drawn from Ramayana observation for month of Chaitra and it coinciding with the season of flowers.

These two observations (Error Elimination – Experiments 1 and 2) lead us to a broad interval of 10500 BCE – 17500 BCE.

Error Elimination – Experiment 3

Brightly Shining North Pole Star[4]

Ramayana observation (Yuddha Kanda) describes the North Pole star as very bright pole star. When I read and re-read this portion of Ramayana text, I could not understand the reference to the North Pole star. I still don't. However, many translators have translated this Ramayana text as referring to North Pole star and all researchers, as far as I am aware, also accepted this translation. I went through multiple translations, looking for word to word translation, and to my delight, found that the word 'BrahmaRashi' appears to have been translated by these Ramayana researchers as referring to North Pole star.

Yuddha 4:48

ब्रह्मराशिर्विशुद्धश्च शुद्धाश्च परमर्षयः
अर्चिष्मन्तः प्रकाशन्ते ध्रुवं सर्वे प्रदक्षिणम

ब्रह्मराशि = Dhruva; the very bright pole-star, विशुद्धश्च = is becoming clear; सर्वे = all; शुद्धा= the pure; परमर्षयः= great sages; अर्चिष्मन्तः= having bright light; प्रकाशन्ते= are shining; प्रदक्षिणम= going round from left to right; ध्रुवं= of Dhruva star.

Dhruva, the very bright pole-star is becoming clear. All the pure great sages having bright light are shining around Dhruva star.

Those of you who have read my first book (*When did the Mahabharata War Happen?*) may remember my interpretation of 'BrahmaRashi' as referring to nakshatra Abhijit (Vega). I decided to take a leap of faith and test this hypothesis.

Wait a minute! I did not have to test it.

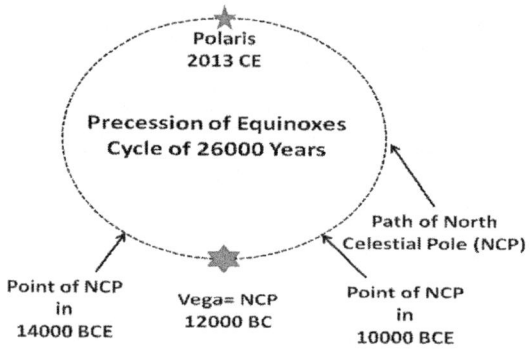

We had done it when we tested observation of Abhijit from the Mahabharata text (in the book- *When did the Mahabharata War Happen?*

The Mystery of Arundhati) and we already know that nakshatra Abhijit was discontinued as nakshatra sometime around 14500 BCE (when nakshatra Dhanishtha coincided with the point of summer solstice and was given the status of first Nakshatra, by Indian astronomers). Star Abhijit (Vega) was closest to the point of North celestial pole around 12000 BCE. Taking a time interval of 2000 years on each side, we can then estimate the time interval for this Ramayana observation, when star Abhijit (BrahmaRashi) was North Pole star (10000 BCE – 14000 BCE) as the plausible time interval for Ramayana.

Star Abhijit (Vega) is indeed bright, brightest of all North Pole stars along the path of Celestial North Pole. We all should be aware by this time that the Celestial North Pole charts a circle by its movement over a period of 26000 years, due to the precession of equinoxes.

Identification of Abhijit (Vega) as Pole star for our proposed timing of Ramayana is straightforward. However I do want to bring very interesting fact/coincidence to reader's attention. This straightforward corroboration of Vega/Abhijit as Pole Star was further buttressed by identification of *Abhijit* with 'BrahmaRashi' since we have seen a convincing case for identification of 'BrahmaRashi' with Vega (*Abhijit*) in my book on the timing of Mahabharata War.

This Ramayana observation thus corroborates timeline predicted by previous two Ramayana observations.

Where to search for the timing of Ramayana

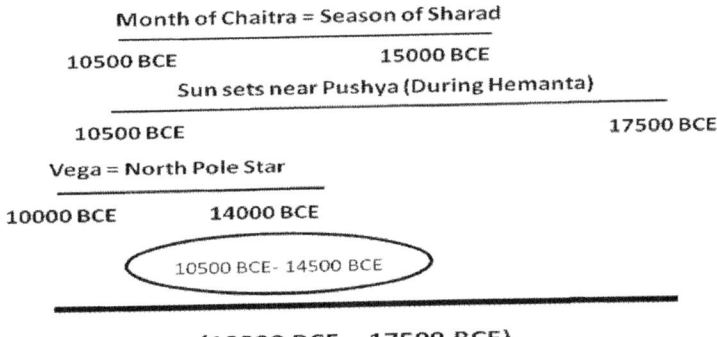

(10000 BCE – 17500 BCE)
Time Interval: Searching for the timing of The Ramayana

7

Ramayana Millennium

Needle in a Haystack

Now the world in general doesn't know what to make of originality; it is startled out of its comfortable habits of thought, and its first reaction is one of anger.

- Somerset Maughm

Three observations of previous chapter lead us to a broad time interval of seven millenniums (10000 BCE – 17500 BCE) and a plausible time interval of four millenniums (10500 BCE – 14500 BCE).

This is progress indeed since 'Arundhati' observation had also given us a broad interval of six millenniums (11091 BCE – 4508 BCE) for the plausible timing of Mahabharata. In case of Mahabharata, we were provided with two specific years to test, proposed by previous researchers, which fell within the Epoch of Arundhati.

Haystack

Ramayana text has many astronomy observations. Key astronomy observations, with potential to corroborate a specific timing of Ramayana incidents, are as follows:

1. The sun setting on nakshatra Pushya during the season of

Hemant (autumn) [3].

2. North Pole star (BrahmaRashi) shining brightly[4].

3. Nakshatra Moola, nakshatra of Nairuktas, afflicted by a comet, at the time of Rama's march along with Vanara army, from Kishkindha to Lanka[5].

4. Nakshatras of Rama and Dasharatha being afflicted by Sun, Mars and Rahu[15].

5. Five grahas in an exalted state at the time of Rama-Janma[18].

6. Conjunction of the sun & the moon with Venus & Jupiter, as Sumantra and Guha met Rama & Laxman, at Chitrakuta[88].

7. Solar eclipse at the time of Khara-Rama Yuddha[94].

8. Analogy of group of grahas rushing towards the sun and the moon, during the Khara-Rama Yuddha[98].

9. Khara looked like Mars rising in the midst of stars, during the Khara-Rama Yuddha[99].

10. Vali & Sugriva fight that began at the time of sunset appeared like a fight between Mercury and Mars in the sky[107].

11. Plausible solar eclipse at the time of second dual between Vali and Sugriva[108].

12. Vali compared with lost brilliance of the sun during an eclipse[109].

13. Two fighting brothers resembled similar to the sun and the moon in the sky[110].

14. Sugriva lost his brilliance, like the moon during an eclipse[111].

15. Southern Vanara party began their search in the south, for Sita, with star Abhijit as reference[130].

16. Timing of the full moon (and plausible lunar eclipse) when Hanuman visited Lanka [163-167].

17. View of the sky from nakshatra *Punarvasu* through nakshatra *Shravana*, when Hanuman returned from Lanka[175].

18. Rama and Vanara army march from Kishkindha on nakshatra Hasta[176].

19. As Vanara army marched towards Lanka, Laxman and Rama were carried by Angada and Hanuman, and they appeared bright like the moon and the sun, conjoined with two major grahas (Jupiter and Venus) [177].

20. As Vanara army marched towards Lanka, star Trishanku (Acrux) along with his Purohit, could be seen shining brightly before them (south) and Venus behind them. Bright Vishakha could be seen free from the evil influence and the bright pole star (BrahmaRashi) and seven sages shining brightly [178].

21. The war began around the time of full moon [225, 226] and during the season of Sharad [218, 227-228].
22. Rama-Ravana Yuddha (last day of the War): Analogy of an eclipse and Mercury attacking nakshatra Rohini[282].
23. Rama-Ravana Yuddha (last day of the War): Mars attacking nakshatra Vishakha, nakshatra of Kosalas[283].
24. Rama to Shatrughna: When summer is over and rainy season arrives, you should kill Lavana[302].
25. Shatrughna sent ahead the army (along with elephants and horses) and he himself stayed with Rama for a month and then he too departed[303].
26. After spending only one month in Ayodhya, Shatrughna left and reached *ashram* of Valmiki after traveling for two nights[304].
27. Sita gave birth to twin boys, the very night Shatrughna arrived at the *ashram* of Valmiki[305].
28. Twin boys (Lava & Kush) of Sita were born on nakshatra Shravana, during the rainy season[306].
29. Analogies of Mars afflicting nakshatra Rohini, when Hanuman was searching for Sita in Lanka[349] and also when Vanara army marched towards Lanka, after crossing the ocean[350].
30. Analogies of nakshatra Rohini tortured/afflicted by some evil graha [351-356].

Ramayana text refers to time of *Ravana-vadha* as that of *Amawasya* and when Mercury was near Rohini. Ramayana text might have referred to plausible solar eclipses at the time of Khara-Rama fight, killing of Vali, killing of Ravana and plausible lunar eclipse when Hanuman met Sita in Lanka.

It is very important to understand that unless an eclipse is clearly mentioned, analogies of eclipses may form only corroborative evidence for an eclipse at the time of a specific instance, however, they cannot be taken as evidence that eclipse indeed occurred. Numerous analogies of Mars or evil grahas afflicting nakshatra Rohini are dispersed throughout the Ramayana text. Many other instances describe a view of the sky, nakshatra of the day or season of the year.

All above descriptions qualify as observations that would be crucial in determining and corroborating the timing of Ramayana, however, their value is only 'corroborative'. After all, seasons occur once every year, specific nakshatra occurs once every lunar month and specific position of the sun, with respect to any given nakshatra, occurs once every year.

Many researchers place so much emphasis, erroneously, on occurrence of eclipses. Such an emphasis is indeed misplaced. Eclipses are not as rare as these researchers make us believe, especially when we are scanning through thousands of years of antiquity. Therefore, while these observations can be used (and should be used) to corroborate or falsify a given proposal for the timing of Ramayana, they are incapable, by themselves, to propose a year for the specific instance of Ramayana.

I was looking for a year (needle) in a haystack of some 6000 years that would allow me to nail down a specific instance of Ramayana (Rama-Janma, scheduled coronation of Rama, Ravana-Vadha, Rama-Sita wedding, Rama returning to Ayodhya, etc.).

I was looking for a needle and celestial needle is what I found. Before we analyze the specific Ramayana observation, here is quick and essential primer on Comets.

Comets

A comet far from the sun is only the nucleus. The nucleus is the so called dirty ice ball, a stuck-together mixture of water ice, other frozen gases and solid particles – the dust or 'dirt'. The ice ball may be dozens of miles in diameter, or just a mile or two. A distant comet is very faint and hard to find.

As comet gets closer to the sun, solar heat vaporizes more and more of the frozen gas and it spews out into space, blowing some dust out, too. The gas and dust form hazy, shining cloud around the nucleus. This cloud is the coma.

The glow from a comet's coma is partly the light of the sun, reflected from millions of tiny dust particles, and partly emissions of faint light from atoms and molecules in the coma. The dust and gas in a comet's coma are subject to disturbing forces that can give rise to a comet's tail or two.

The pressure of sunlight pushes the dust particles in a direction opposite the sun, producing the comet's dust tail. The dust tail shines by the reflected light of the sun and has these characteristics: a smooth, sometimes gently curved appearance and a pale yellow color. The tails of a comet can be millions to hundreds of millions of miles long.

Comet's tail steams behind it when comet is headed towards the sun. When the comet has rounded the sun and heads back toward the outer solar system, the tail still points away from the sun, so the comet now follows its tail! The comet behaves to the sun as an old-time courtier did to his emperor: neither turns nor turned his back on his master.

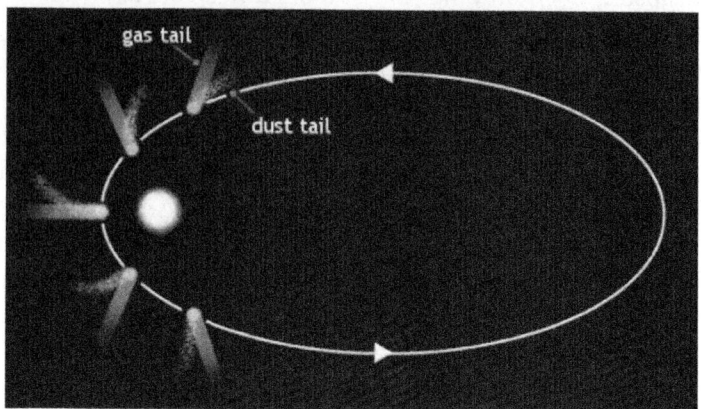

Comets are visible from the earth, in all their glory, just before sunrise and just after sunset. This time interval can last for few hours depending on relative position of the sun, the comet and the earth.

Celestial Needle of Ramayana Text

I went through my list of Ramayana observations. There were indeed few promising observations however their ability to provide information was not any more precise than provided by three observations [2-4] of Error ellimination experiments one, two and three.

Next I looked at planetary observations such as positions of slow moving grahas – Jupiter and Saturn, and found nothing meaningful on that front. The closest I came across were positions of Mars, however problem with Mars is that it completes one cycle in less than 2 years. This means one has to test positions of Mars some 3500 times (7000 years being total duration of exploration, i.e. from 10000 BCE through 17000 BCE).

At this point, I was looking for some specific Ramayana observation that would have allowed me to narrow down this time interval further. The Ramayana text has good number of planetary observations however they are too generic in nature (unlike those of the Mahabharata text). I made a daring decision, partly driven by my experience, of similar observation, during my Mahabharata research.

What could be the rare and infrequent event that we could use which also was described in Ramayana? An observation came to mind and I decided to try it out. Testing this observation was challenging, weird in its logical selection, but with one great benefit. If we could test it, and if by luck, we succeeded in validating this observation, it held the key to validation of six millennia long time interval for the plausible timing of Ramayana and would have allowed us to test rest of Ramayana observations. Of course lack of validation for this observation would have brought my efforts to a dead end. On the other hand, a validation of this observation was no guarantee for corroboration of numerous other planetary observations.

The observation occurs in *Yuddha Kanda* of Ramayana text. In retrospect, I could not have selected a better observation.

The testing was cumbersome.

Error Elimination - Experiment 4

Comet afflicting Moola - Nakshatra of Nairuktas[5]

Laxman refers to a comet afflicting nakshatra Moola, as Rama and his Vanara army walked towards Lanka[5].

नैरृतं नैरृतानां च नक्षत्रमभिपिड्यते
मूलं मूलवता स्पृष्टं धूप्यते धूमकेतुना
सरं चैतद्विनाशाय राक्षसानाम उपस्थितम
काले कालगृहीतानां नक्षत्रं ग्रहपीडितम

I had employed Dynamic Visual Astronomy (DVA™), during my Mahabharata research. I decided to employ identical methodology. Identification of a comet near nakshatra Moola was no guarantee for correct identification of Ramayana War year however reader must understand that it is a <u>necessary condition</u> for any proposed timing of Ramayana.

A comet, when visible, will usually span through more than one nakshatra space. The Ramayana text referred to a comet afflicting nakshatra Moola. Initially I tried to spot a comet that is not visible but one that stays in the vicinity of nakshatra Moola (similar to Haley's comet in the vicinity of nakshatra Pushya, an astronomy observation from the Mahabharata text) when not visible. I had no luck identifying any such comet. This meant I had to look for a comet that would have been visible in the vicinity of nakshatra Moola, and <u>only</u> in the vicinity of nakshatra Moola.

I locked the position of nakshatra Moola (Shaula) and with a step change of one day, simulated the sky, beginning with 16000 BCE. This simulation indeed tested my perseverance. I continued to visualize other observations that I could test while performing this simulation. Unfortunately (or fortunately) I could not come up with another distinct Ramayana observation that would have been as decisive as this observation of a comet near nakshatra Moola.

Laxman's Comet

Numerous days and simulations later, I noticed a small comet flutter by nakshatra Moola. The comet in Voyager simulation is identified as 2P/Encke. Interestingly, the comet only appeared (became visible) near nakshatra Moola and disappeared in the same region, as desired (anticipated) for the specific condition that would have corroborated Ramayana description. The timing of this observation was that of September 12209 BCE.

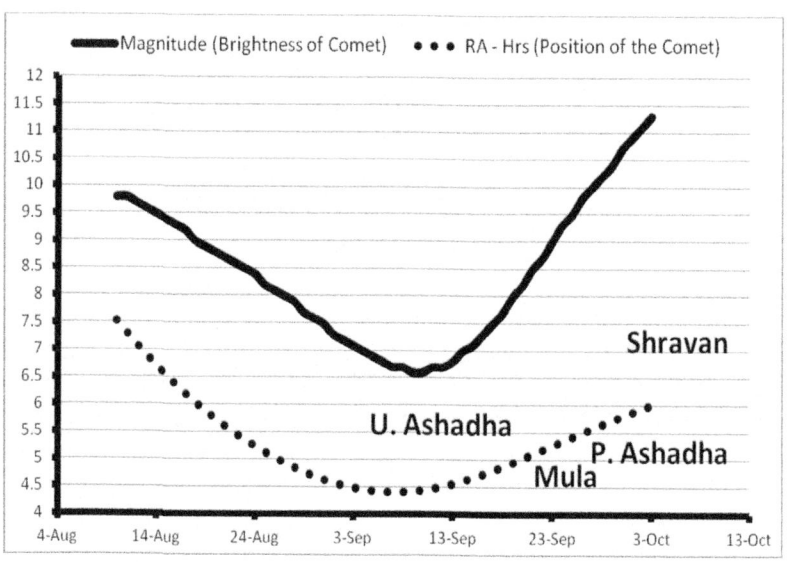

The comet was at its brightest when in the region of naskhatra Moola. <u>Recognize that lower the magnitude, brighter the object seen in the sky</u>. For examle, we may say that the sun has the lowest magnitude and the moon has the second lowest magnitude among astral objects.

Over the next many months I re-ran simulations, screening through entire time interval of the 'Epoch of Ramayana' (10000 BCE -17500 BCE) to identify another instance of a comet becoming visible in the region of nakshatra Moola, from list of all known comets – in Voyager simulation. I did not come across any other such instance, however, I encourage researchers to run their own simulations and report if they come across such a scenario.

We should recognize that identifcation of a visible comet near naskhatra Moola in September of 12209 BCE provides us with a plausible year of Rama-Ravana Yuddha. However the truthfulness of such a prediction depends on the corroboration and resistance to the falsification shown by other Ramayana observations.

Laxman, virtuous brother of Rama, was the first human being, in documented history of humanity, to observe/notice this comet and thus I consider it most appropriate to name the comet after Laxaman – Comet Laxman.

My next task was to make predictions for the timing of key instances of Ramayana, based on September 12209 BCE as the timing of Rama's march from Kishkindha to Lanka.

Predictions for key instances of Ramayana

We can predict years for key instances of Ramayana, based on the timing for the observation of the comet 'Laxman' afflicting nakshatra Moola.

Rama was 16 years old when sage Vishwamitra came to king Dasharatha and to request Rama's assistance in protecting the *Yajna*. Rama, Laxman, Bharata & Shatrughna were married to daughters of king Janaka and king Kushadwaja, few days after.

Rama & Sita lived in Ayodhya for a year when king Dasharatha decided to coronate Rama. Thus, Rama was 17 years old at the time of his scheduled coronation and this is when he left for the forest.

Rama, Laxman and Sita spent 14 years in the forest, at the end of which Rama went to Lanka, along with Vanara army and defeated Ravana. Rama returned to Ayodhya immediately, after killing Ravana.

Year of Rama-Ravana Yuddha

Comet Laxman was seen near nakshatra Moola as Rama and his Vanara army traveled towards Lanka. This year was 12209 BCE. The comet was in apparition during the month of September and was brightest around 9-10 September 12209 BCE. The corresponding lunar month was that of Margashirsha/Pausha and the time of summer solstice.

Since Ramayana text stated that Rama did return to Ayodhya at the end of the 14th year[6] of his 'forest stay' and since he had left for the forest on his birthday – Chaitra Shuddha Navami, we can calculate the timing for the month of Chaitra occurring after 9-10 September 12209 BCE. Chaitra Shuddha Navami occurred on 17 December 12209 BCE and we can mark it as the approximate (and tentative) time of Rama's return to Ayodhya from Lanka. Thus Rama-Ravana Yuddha took place in the year 12209 BCE.

Day of Rama's return to Ayodhya from Lanka

I am indebted to Dr. P V Vartak for identification of Ramayana observations related to the return of Rama from Lanka to Ayodhya. I am confident that I would have found these observations eventually; however, this wonderful gift of Dr. Vartak reduced my work and also provided additional corroboration for the timing of *Ravana-vadha*.

Many researchers continue to assume that Rama returned to Ayodhya in the lunar month of Chaitra. This is not the case, if one looks carefully at the evidence of Valmiki Ramayana.

Dr. Vartak did not adjust his corresponding timeline either for the *Ravana-Vadha* or for the arrival of Rama in Ayodhya, even though he acknowledged the required correction of one lunar month related to the timing of *Ravana-Vadha* and also of Rama's return to Ayodhya.

Rama reached *ashram* of sage Bharadwaj on fifth (panchami) lunar day of the month[6, 7]. Specific lunar month is not specified however Ramayana text also refers to Hanuman telling Bharata, that Bharata would meet Rama, on nakshatra Pushya[8], the next day, i.e. day after Panchami[7]. This means Rama returned to Ayodhya on the 6th day of the lunar month of Vaishakha. We can determine this day to be 13 January 12208 BCE.

Day of Rama's departure for the forest

Rama was away from Ayodhya for 14 years[6]. He left Ayodhya on his birthday (Chaitra Shuddha 9), which was also the scheduled day of his coronation as set by king Dasharatha, when Rama became 17 years old.

Rama spent 14 years away from Ayodhya and then after defeating Ravana, returned to Ayodhya. Thus, we can calculate the timing of Rama's scheduled coronation day to be that of 20/21 December 12223 BCE. We did this by going backwards 14 years (from year of Rama-Ravana Yuddha) to the day of Chaitra Shuddha 9.

Day of Rama Janma

Going backwards by 17 more years, we can estimate the day of Rama Janma to be 29 November 12240 BCE.

King Dasharatha was approximately 60 years old at the time of Rama Janma and thus we can estimate Dasharatha's birth year to be around 12300 BCE.

Vishwamitra Arrives in Ayodhya

Vishwamitra arrived at the court of king Dasharatha when Rama turned 16. Rama turned 16, per lunar month/year calculations, on 3 December 12224 BCE. Day of Vishwamitra's arrival could be estimated to be around this day (+/-1 day).

Vishwamitra asked king Dasharatha for Rama's assistance for 10 days. King Dasharatha granted this request. Rama and Laxman left with sage Vishwamitra on 5 December 12224 BCE and arrived at *Siddhashrama* on 8 December 12224 BCE. Rama and Laxman protected six day long *Yajna* of sage Vishwamitra, i.e. until 14 December 12224 BCE. Next day, after *Yajna* was completed, Rama and Laxman accompanied sage Vishwamitra on his journey to Mithila. They reached Mithila on 18 December 12224 BCE. King Janaka was performing *Yajna* and 12 days were remaining for its completion. Rama lifted Shiva-Dhanushya (bow of Shiva) on 19 December 12224 BCE. King Janaka completed his *Yajna* on 30 December 12224 BCE.

Rama-Sita Wedding

King Dasharatha arrived in Mithila, along with his entourage, on 29 December 12224 BCE. King Janaka sent messengers to invite his brother Kushadhwaja on 30 December and Kushadhwaja arrived in Mithila before 2 Jan 12223 BCE.

Three kings – Janaka, Dasharatha and Kushadhwaja held discussions and finalized the day of wedding on 2 Jan 12223 BCE. Rama-Sita wedding took place on 4-5 Jan 12223 BCE.

Composition of Valmiki Ramayana

Rama was 17 years old at the time of his departure to the forest and since he lived away from Ayodhya for 14 years, he was 31 years old when he returned to Ayodhya. Lava and Kusha were born within a year's time after Rama and Sita returned to Ayodhya and thus we can estimate the year of their birth to be that of 12208 BCE. Lava and Kush were approximately 12 years old when they arrived at the court of Rama to recite Valmiki's Ramayana and thus Valmiki composed Ramayana sometime between 12208 BCE and 12196 BCE.

We can define, albeit tentatively, 13th Millennium BCE as the Ramayana Millennium.

Our next task is to test if these predictions, for events in Rama's life, corroborate with evidence of Valmiki Ramayana. We will test our predictions against astronomy, chronology and seasonal evidence of Valmiki Ramayana.

8

THE DAY RAMA LEFT FOR THE FOREST

लक्ष्मीश्चन्द्रादपेयाद्वा हिमवान्वा हिमं त्यजेत
अतीयात्सागरो वेलां न प्रतिज्ञामहं पितुः

*Beauty may leave the moon, Himavaan may become bereft of snow,
the ocean may transgress its shores but I will never violate the promise
given by my father (Valmiki Ramayana - Ayodhya 112:18)*

To build an internally consistent chronology for Ramayana instances, for
a given theory and proposal, is rather straightforward. But what evidence do we have to accept the dates for the specific events of Ramayana as reliable, for any given proposal? Is there anything in Valmiki
Ramayana text that would offer independent corroboration for these
predictions?

What is corroboration?

Corroboration is confirmation or support of a claim/evidence
through independent, authoritative and credible evidence. In a scientific investigation, we don't question the theory itself, but rather consequences of the theory and corroborative evidence presented in the context of these consequences of the theory. Corroborative evidence is
evidence that tends to support a proposition (theory and/or consequences of a theory) that is already supported by some initial evidence
and thus confirming the proposition.

Corroboration does not prove anything. Good corroboration simply asserts that specific evidence that was tested in the context of a theory (and consequences resulting from that theory) <u>failed to disprove</u> that theory.

Rama Janma & Scheduled coronation of Rama

Ramayana text mentions that the astronomical/planetary situation prevailing at the time of the scheduled coronation of Rama, when he was 17 years old, was also similar to that of the time of his birth. Specific astronomy observations mentioned at the time of his birth are distinctly different from those described at the time of his scheduled coronation, making comparison between two events challenging. Having said that, astronomy observations at the time of Rama's scheduled coronation are more specific than that of his birth and thus we will first analyze astronomy descriptions at the time of Rama's scheduled coronation.

Let's begin with the day of scheduled Rajyabhishek (coronation) of Rama when he turned 17.

Error Elimination – Experiment 5

Scheduled Coronation of Rama & Sharad season

King Dasharatha decided to coronate Rama one year after Rama-Sita wedding and when Rama turned 17. King Dasharatha set the date during the lunar month of Chaitra and on nakshatra Pushya, i.e. one day after Rama would have turned 17. This day was 20/ 21 December 12223 BCE, which also occurred during the season of Sharad (pre-autumn).

King Dasharatha describes the lunar month of Chaitra as that of forests blooming with flowers[2], which corroborate well with the season of Sharad. Additional descriptions of rain and peacocks[9] also corroborate the lunar month of Chaitra with that of Sharad season and therefore with 13th Millennium BCE.

इति ब्रुवन्तं मुदिताः प्रत्यनन्दन्नृपा नृपम
वृष्टिमन्तं महामेघं नर्दन्तमिव बर्हिणः

Numerous analogies to 'Sharad season' also corroborate the timing of scheduled coronation of Rama. King Dasharatha's assembly is described as similar to the autumnal sky, spangled with bright grahas and stars that would shine brightly when illuminated by the moon[10]. Queen Kaikayi rising from her bed is compared with rising orb of the autumnal moon[11]. Rama's palace is compared with an autumnal cloud[12]. When Rama heard that Kaikayi had imposed the condition on Rama to go to the forest for 14 years, he did not shed his characteristic and native joy any more than autumnal moon, with its intensely bright rays, loses its natural splendor[13]; and hearing Sumitra, Kausalya's grief disappeared like an autumnal cloud[14].

Error Elimination – Experiment 6-A

Sun, Mars & Rahu encroaching Birth Nakshatra(s) [15]

Interpretation of all past Ramayana Researchers

Ayodhya Kanda of the Ramayana text states:

अवष्टब्धं च मे राम नक्षत्रं दारूणग्रहैः
आवेदयन्ति दैवज्ञाः सूर्यानअंगारकराहु भि

Almost all translators interpret above observation as follows:

King Dasharatha says,

Astrologers inform me that fearful grahas (Sun, Mars and Rahu) have taken possession of my Nakshatra.

If we accept translation of past Ramayana researchers/translators, it would mean, the sun and Mars were close to each other and the node (Rahu) was also close to the sun and Mars.

Fortunately location of the sun can be determined with reasonable accuracy since the lunar day, when this conversation took place, was somewhere around the day of Chaitra Shuddha 7/8. This information fixes the position of the sun somewhere between nakshatra Purva Bhadrapada and nakshatra Bharani, with median position around nakshatra Revati.

My proposed date corroborates well for positions of the sun and Mars.

None of the proposed dates, <u>including mine</u>, corroborate the position of Rahu, if we interpret the position of Rahu to be same as that of the sun and Mars. I request readers and future researchers to search the time interval of 10500 BCE through 17500 BCE to identify year(s) when the sun, Mars and Rahu would be in the region of nakshatra Revati (+/- 2 nakshatra) and then to test if such year(s) would also corroborate remaining Ramayana observations. Readers or other researchers should also test positions of five grahas for such a date to see if the Ramayana observation of their exalted states can also be corroborated.

Error Elimination – Experiment 6-B

Sun, Mars & Rahu encroaching Birth Nakshatra(s) [15]

My Interpretation

Let's look at the same text again. This time we will look at word to word translation and possible alternate meanings it may generate.

अवष्टब्धं च मे राम नक्षत्रं दारूणग्रहैः
आवेदयन्ति दैवज्ञाः सूर्यानंगारकराहु भि

दैवज्ञा - Astrologers, आवेदयन्ति - are informing, दारूणग्रहै - fearful grahas, अवष्टब्धं – have encroached, are encroaching. मे - I, राम - Rama, च - and/also, सूर्यानंगारकराहु भि - the sun, Mars and Rahu (node of the moon)

My translation is as follows:

King Dasharatha says,

Astrologers are informing that fearful grahas - (Sun, Mars and Rahu) have taken possession of Nakshatras of King Dasharatha and Rama.

Ramayana text does not explicitly state nakshatra of King Dasharatha. However it can be estimated with reasonable confidence. When Dasharatha utters this statement, the timing is that of the lunar month of Chaitra and lunar *Tithi* of 1-2 days before Chaitra Shuddha 9.

This means position of the sun is somewhere between nakshatra Purva Bhadrapada and nakshatra Bharani, with Revati as the median. Thus we can conjecture 'Revati' (or Uttara Bhadrapada or Ashiwni) as Nakshatra of Dasharatha.

Rama was born on Punarvasu and thus Punarvasu is his (birth) nakshatra. Let's look at the positions of the sun, Mars and Rahu on 20-21 December 12223 BCE.

The sun and Mars were together, between nashatras Uttara Bhadrpada and Revati. The location of Rahu was near nakshatra Pushya. Thus Rahu was near nakshatra Pushya (next to Punarvasu - Janma Nakshatra of Rama) on the day of scheduled coronation of Rama.

Reader may keep in mind that the point of node (Rahu), i.e. intersection of the path of orbit of the moon and the sun (as perceived from the earth) is not a point, but rather a line and thus position of Rahu is to be seen as region of the sky rather than a specific point in the sky.

Rama's Coronation (scheduled)	20/21 December 12223 BCE
Astral Body	**Right Ascension**
Punarvasu (Pollux)	18 hr 46 min
Moon	18 hr 41 min
Rahu	19 hr 12 min
Ashwini (Hamal)	13 hr 40 min
Revati (Kullat Nunu)	12 hr 53 min
Mars	12 hr 32 min
Sun	12 hr 25 min
Uttara Bhadrapada (Algenib)	12 hr 3 min
Purva Bhadrapada (Markab)	11 hr 18 min

All three references to the sun, Mars and Rahu corroborate well for 20/ 21 December 12223 BCE, the day of scheduled coronation of Rama, per this interpretation of mine.

Error Elimination – Experiment 7

Rahu near Punarvasu

There is one additional Ramayana observation in support of our conjecture of position of Rahu near Pushya/Punarvasu, rather than near Revati. The Ramayana text states that the King (Dasharatha) entered the residence of Kaikayi as the moon would enter the sky overcast with white clouds and marked with the presence of Rahu[16].

This observation corroborates position of Rahu and the moon (Rahu and moon were near Pushya/Punarvasu) on the day of scheduled coronation.

Error Elimination – Experiment 8

Rama Janma and positions of Sun, Mars & Rahu

Ramayana text states[17] (Ayodhya 15:3)

उदिते विमले सूर्ये पुष्ये चाभ्यागतेऽहनि
अभिषेकाय रामस्य द्विजेन्द्रैरुपकल्पितम

GP version also adds another line to the above that states,

"Lagne Karkatake Prapte, Janma Ramasya cha stithe"

The translation would be,

Best of Brahmanas were prepared to do Rama's coronation after sunrise, when nakshatra was Pushya (moon in Pushya) and situation <u>similar to the time of Rama's birth</u>.

'Situation similar to the time of Rama's birth' could mean simply the timing of Chaitra Shuddha 9. On the other hand, if this reference also means positions of grahas, we will have to explore planetary situations separated by 17 years and evaluate their positions and compare for similarities between two instances, i.e. Rama Janma and scheduled coronation of Rama, 17 years after his birth.

Going back by 17 years, i.e. at the time of Rama-Janma (29 November 12240 BCE), Rahu was near Ardra (i.e. still in the vicinity Punarvasu) and thus positions of Rahu at the time of Rama Janma and at the time of scheduled coronation of Rama corroborate Ramayana observation of similar astronomy conditions during Rama Janma-and his scheduled coronation[17]. The sun and Mars were also together and near Uttara Bhadrapada. These positions of the sun, Mars and Rahu are similar (if not identical) to their positions at the time of scheduled coronation of Rama.

Rama Janma	29 November 12240 BCE
Astral Body	**Right Ascension**
Punarvasu (Pollux)	18 hr 45 min
Moon	17 hr 57 min
Rahu	17 hr 35 min
Ashwini (Hamal)	13 hr 39 min
Revati (Kullat Nunu)	12 hr 52 min
Mars	11 hr 5 min
Sun	11 hr 9 min
Uttara Bhadrapada (Algenib)	12 hr 2 min
Purva Bhadrapada (Markab)	11 hr 17 min

Ramayana text refers to additional astronomy descriptions at the time of Rama Janma.

Error Elimination – Experiment 8

Exalted Grahas @ the time of Ram Janma[18]

The astronomy observations at the time of Rama Janma are certainly confusing with the exception of the nakshatra of the day – Punarvasu.
The exact text of Ramayana, at the time of Rama Janma states[18],

ततो यज्ञे समाप्ते तु ऋतू नाम षट समत्ययुः
ततः च द्वादशे मासे चैत्रे नावमिके तिथौ
नक्षत्रे अदिती दैवत्ये स्व उच्छ संस्थेषु पंचसु
ग्रहेषु कर्कटे लग्ने वाक्पता इंदुना सह
प्रोद्यमाने जगन्नाथम सर्व लोक नमस्कृतम
कौसल्या अजनयत रामं सर्व लक्षण संयुतम
विष्णो अर्धं महाभागम पुत्रं ऐक्ष्वाकु नन्दनम
लोहिताक्षम महाबाहुं रक्त ओष्ठम दुंदुभी स्वनम

When six seasons (one year) had passed, during the 12th month, on the 9th day of Chaitra, when the Nakshatra was presided by its Deity Aditi (Punarvasu) and when five grahas were exalted.

The nakshatra was Punarvasu (Devata= Aditi) and 5 grahas were exalted. Jupiter (Vak-pati) was along with the moon (or they were in similar positions, i.e. ascendant, descendant, etc.).

While commentators/researchers have added specific interpretations of what exalted grahas mean, Valmiki Ramayana does not provide definitions of what it means to have a graha (or planets) in exalted state.

GP edition refers to the sun, Mars, Saturn, Jupiter and Venus as five grahas and their appearance in zodiacal signs of Aries, Capricorn, Libra, Cancer and Pisces, respectively, qualifies them as being exalted. Vartak and Bhatnagar refer to similar interpretation.

While Vartak and Bhatnagar claim to have grahas in exalted positions for their proposed timeline, this is not the case. Grahas are not in exalted state (as per definition) for my proposed day either. In short, notwithstanding the claims to contrary, no researcher has shown five grahas in exalted positions (per astrology rules and/or their own interpretation) for their proposals.

Table lists positions of five astral bodies (Sun, Mars, Saturn, Jupiter and Venus) for 4 different proposed dates for Rama Janma. Second column shows desired positions of these astral bodies to qualify as being in 'EXHALTED' state. Epoch of 2000 CE was used for 'Right Ascension values' in defining areas of Zodiac and also positions of astral bodies. Time: 12:00 PM

Astral Body	Exhalted State	29 November 12240 BCE	4 December 7323 BCE (Gregorian)	10 January 5114 BCE	17 January 10205 BCE
	(Required positions)	(Actual positions)	(Actual positions)	(Actual positions)	(Actual positions)
	(per Indian Astrology)	OAK	VARTAK	BHATNAGAR	SRS
Sun	Aries (1 hr 46 min - 3 hr 24 min)	0 hr 5 min	1 hr 36 min	23 hr 28 min	**2 hr 3 min**
Mars	Capricorn (20 hr 7 min - 21 hr 58 min)	0 hr 5 min	5 hr 24 min	3 hr 19 min	8 hr 23 min
Saturn	Libra (14 hr 21 min - 15 hr 54 min)	18 hr 25 min	17 hr 22 min	16 hr 21 min	20 hr 26 min
Jupiter	Cancer (8 hr 0 min - 9 hr 21 min)	19 hr 38 min	7 hr 7 min	11 hr 0 min	5 hr 55 min
Venus	Pisces (23 hr 30 min - 1 hr 46 min)	21 hr 14 min	4 hr 30 min	**23 hr 32 min**	2 hr 21 min

I conjecture that exalted state of grahas, assuming my proposal is a valid proposal, may refer to their being present in the sky along with the sun at the same time, i.e. all five grahas (excluding the sun) in the sky along with the sun. In addition, Jupiter was setting (western horizon) when the moon was rising (on eastern horizon) at ~ 3 PM on this day.

My proposed timing corroborates the description of 'exalted status of grahas', if my conjecture (grahas being present in the sky along with the sun) is accepted. Proposals of Vartak and Bhatnagar do not corroborate, per this explanation.

Error Elimination – Experiment 9

Exalted Grahas @ the time of Scheduled Coronation

I have already shown the similarity in positions of the sun, Mars and Rahu between the timing of Rama Janma and the timing of his scheduled coronation 17 years after his birth.

I decided to test, purely out of curiosity, the positions of grahas at the time of scheduled coronation of Rama, in the light of observation of so called exalted grahas (and descriptions of Jupiter/moon) of Rama Janma.

Astral Body	Exhalted State	20/21 December 12223 BCE	29 November 7306 BCE (Gregorian)	5 January 5089 BCE
	(Required positions)	(Actual positions)	(Actual positions)	(Actual positions)
	(per Indian Astrology)	OAK	VARTAK	BHATNAGAR
Sun	ies (1 hr 46 min - 3 hr 24 m	1 hr 21 min	1 hr 16 min	23 hr 28 min
Mars	corn (20 hr 7 min - 21 hr 58	1 hr 32 min	5 hr 48 min	3 hr 19 min
Saturn	a (14 hr 21 min - 15 hr 54 m	8 hr 38 min	7 hr 38 min	16 hr 21 min
Jupiter	ncer (8 hr 0 min - 9 hr 21 m	5 hr 6 min	18 hr 22 min	11 hr 0 min
Venus	ces (23 hr 30 min - 1 hr 46 m	4 hr 12 min	1 hr 30 min	23 hr 32 min

All 5 grahas were in the sky along with the sun on 20/21 December 12223 BCE. Position of the moon was identical (not a surprise as same time of the lunar day and lunar month). Position of Jupiter was not on the western horizon when the moon was rising.

Error Elimination – Experiment 10

Rama leaves for the forest[339]

स तमन्तः पूरे घोरमार्तशब्दं महीपतिः

पुत्र शोकाभिसंतप्तः श्रुत्वा चासीत्सुदुःखित

नाग्निहोत्राण्यहूयन्त सूर्यश्चान्तरधीयत

व्यसृजन्कवलान्नागा गावो वत्सान्न पाययं

त्रिशंकुर्लोहिताङ्गश्च बृहस्पतिबुधावपि

दारुणाः सोममभ्येत्य ग्रहाः सर्वे व्यवस्थिताः

नक्षत्राणि गतार्चींषि ग्रहाश्च गततेजसः

विशाखाश्च सधूमाश्च नभसि प्रचकाशिरे

अकस्मान्नागर: सर्वो जनो दैन्यमुपागमत

आहारे वा विहारे वा न कश्चिदकरोत्मन:

Astronomy content of above Ramayana references is limited to verses 10 & 11 and is extrmely generic. It states that Mars, Jupiter, Mercury and other grahas assumed a menacing aspect and that was also the case with star Trishanku (Acrux). Other than star Trishanku, rest of the obesvations (Mars, Jupiter, Mercury and nakshatra Vishakha) are too generic. Trishanku could be seen at night during this time.

All we can say is that this observation certainly does not contradict our timeline.

Error Elimination – Experiment 11

Return of Rama to Ayodhya on Pushya [6-8]

Most of the Ramayana researchers simply assumed that Rama returned to Ayodhya on Chaitra Shuddha 9, after 14 years away from the kingdom. This casual assumption, in part, is driven by the fact that Rama left Ayodhya on Chaitra Shuddha 9 when he was 17 years old.

Credit goes to Dr. P V Vartak, for recognizing implications of Ramayana references related to Rama's arrival at the *ashram* of sage Bharadwaj on fifth (panchami) lunar day of the month and Rama's scheduled meeting with Bharata the next day on nakshatra Pushya.

Rama killed Ravana in the battle and installed Vibhishan on the throne of Lanka. Vibhishan offered *Pushpak Vimana* for Rama's speedy return to Ayodhya. Rama arrived at the *ashram* of sage Bharadwaj on the 5th lunar day [6, 7]. Sage Bharadwaj asked Rama to meet Bharata the next day, the day being lunar day of Pushya[8].

Two possibilities exist for 6th lunar day of the month coinciding with nakshatra Pushya: either 6th day of the Krishna Paksha of Ashwin/Kartika or 6th day of the Shuddha Paksha of Vaishakha/Jyeshtha. Since Margashirsha was already over when Rama left for Lanka, it is clear that Rama arrived in Ayodhya on Vaishakha Shudda 6, on Pushya nakshatra. The day was 13 January 12208 BCE. The timing of his arrival is also consistent with his pledge not to return to Ayodhya until 14 years were completed. In addition, this day occurred only six days after *Amawasya* day, when Ravana was killed by Rama on the battlefield.

9

Rama-Sita Wedding

नातन्त्री वाद्यते वीणा नाचक्रो वर्तते रथः
नापतिः सुखमेधते या स्यादपि शतात्मजा

A Veena cannot exist without its strings. A chariot cannot exist without its wheels. Without her husband a woman can never live happily even though she has a hundred sons.

(Valmiki Ramayana - Ayodhya 39:29)

King Dasharatha was getting old. When winter was over[19] (i.e. spring had begun), and at the suggestion of Brahmans and his royal priest, king Dasharatha ordered his minister to organize *yajna* recommended by Brahmanas. King Dasharatha asked ministers to invite sage Rishyashringa to Ayodhya.

When considerable time had elapsed and when sage Rishyashringa was in Ayodhya and when the season of Vasanta (spring) set in, king Dasharatha felt the urge to begin the *yajna*. *Yajna* ground was set on the northern bank of river Sharayu and *yajna* horse was let loose. The Yajna horse returned after a year and the *yajna* commenced.

Upon completion of 'Ashwamedha *yajna*' and thus free from past sins, king Dasharatha asked sage Rishyashringa to perform appropriate *yajna* in order to obtain sons, and sage Rishyashringa commenced 'Putra-Kameshthi" *yajna*. King Dasharatha distributed '*payas*' of this *yajna* to his queens. Soon queens were pregnant and after six seasons had elapsed, from the end of Putra-Kameshthi *yajna*, they gave birth to Rama, Bharata, Laxman and Shatrughna.

Error Elimination – Experiment 12

End of Putra-Kameshthi *Yajna* in Sharad season

Rama was born during the lunar month of Chaitra and we have shown that this was the season of Sharad. Ramayana text states that the princes were born after passing of six seasons i.e. one complete year after the end of *yajna* [18].

तततो यज्ञे समाप्ते तु ऋतू नम षट समत्ययु:

तत: च द्वादशे मासे चैत्रे नावमिके तिथौ

नक्षत्रे अदिती दैवत्ये स्व उच्च्छ संस्थेषु पंचसु

ग्रहेषु कर्कटे लग्ने वाक्पता इंदुना सह

प्रोद्यमाने जगन्नाथम सर्व लोक नमस्कृतम

कौसल्या अजनयत रामं सर्व लक्षण संयुतम

This also means the timing of the end of Putra-kameshthi *yajna* was same as that of the lunar month of Chaitra and thus, that of Sharad season. Ramayana text has one analogy in support of Sharad season as the season when *yajna* ended [20].

हर्षरश्मिभीरुदयोतम तस्यान्त: पुरमाबभौ

शारदस्याभिरामस्य चन्द्रस्येव नभोऽशुभि:

This Ramayana observation corroborates our assertion of lunar month of Chaitra coinciding with the Sharad Season.

Rama's childhood

Princes turned from infants to toddlers and soon into young adults. All of them were trained in horse riding, archery and subtleties of warfare, administration and Dharma.

Vishwamitra arrives in Ayodhya

Rama was barely 16 years old [22] when sage Vishwamitra arrived in Ayodhya to request Rama's assistance.

ऊनषोडशवर्षो मे रामो राजीवलोचन:

न युद्धयोग्यतामस्य पश्यामि सह राक्षसै:

Sage Vishwamitra had almost completed his *yajna*[23] however Rakshasas were not allowing it to be completed[24] and sage Vishwamitra wanted Rama's assistance for 10 nights[25].

अभिप्रेतमसंसक्तमात्मजं दातुमर्हसि

दशरात्रं हि यज्ञस्य रामं राजीवलोचनं

The Ramayana text is not explicit as to when exactly sage Vishwamitra arrived at the court of king Dasharatha. What we do know is that king Dasharatha was discussing the subject of Rama's marriage with his ministers at that time. In addition, king Dasharatha refers to Rama, in his conversation with sage Vishwamitra, as merely 16 years old.

I conjectured that the timing of Vishwamitra's arrival in Ayodhya coincided with Rama completing 16 years. Rama completed 16 years, per lunar *nakshatra/tithi*/month, on 3 December 12224 BCE. I have assumed that sage Vishwamitra arrived at the court of king Dasharatha on 3 or 4 December 12224 BCE.

Rama & Laxman with Vishwamitra: First 10 days

Day 1:

Rama and Laxman left Ayodhya, along with sage Vishwamitra, the next day, 5 December 12224 BCE. This is the day when they walked for around 12 miles along the bank of river Sharayu[26]. Sage Vishwamitra awarded 'Bala' and 'Atibala' *vidya* to Rama[27] and they slept/stayed on the bank of river Sharayu for the night[28]. This is the end of 5 December 12224 BCE.

Day 2:

Next morning[29] they continued their journey and arrived at the confluence of rivers Sharayu and Ganga[30]. They reached a hermitage by the evening and spent their night most comfortably[31]. This day was 6 December 12224 BCE.

Day 3:

Next day (7 December 12224 BCE), they crossed Ganga[32] in the morning and entered *Tataka-van*. They encountered Tataka; sage Vishwamitra ordered Rama to kill her and Rama killed Tataka. They spent the night at *Tataka-van*[33].

Day 4:

Next morning sage Vishwamitra congratulated Rama on his accomplishment and that day (8 December 12224 BCE) imparted Rama with the knowledge of various missiles[34]. At the end of the day they arrived at *Siddhashrama*, their final destination where they had to guard the *yajna* for next six days and nights. They slept at *Siddhashrama*. This was the end of 8 December 12224 BCE.

Day 5 through 10 (Six days of *yajna*):

Rama and Laxman took rest overnight[35] and in the early morning (9 December 12224 BCE), after ablutions, stood in front of sage Vishwamitra. The sages of Siddh*ashrama* explained Rama and Laxman their duties of guarding the *yajna*, day and night, for six days[36]. Rama and Laxman guarded the *yajna* for six days and nights (9-14 December 12224 BCE). Rakshasas - Marich and Subahu attacked on 14 December 12224 BCE i.e. on the last day of *Yajna*. While Marich was thrown away by an arrow of Rama, Laxman killed Subahu. *Yajna* was completed and sage Vishwamitra felicitated both brothers as he offered his evening prayers. This was the end of 14 December 12224 BCE.

Siddhashrama to Mithila

Day 11:

Next day (15 December 12224 BCE) both brothers, after a good-night's rest, were ready[37]. Sage Vishwamitra told two princes about the upcoming *yajna* planned by king of Mithila and suggested that they should accompany Vishwamitra and his companions to Mithila[38]. They left for Mithila with many (100s) carts[39] and after traveling a long distance, spent their night on the bank of river Shona[40]. Sage Vishwamitra and two princes continued to converse into the late night and when half of the night was over, the moon slowly rose in the sky[41]. The timing of moonrise on this day, per Voyager simulation, was at 11:40 PM.

Error Elimination – Experiment 13

Late Moonrise[41]

Late moonrise during the travel of Vishwamitra and Rama/Laxman corroborates well with my proposed timeline.

गतोऽर्धरात्रः काकुत्स्थ कथाः कथयतो मम

निद्रामभ्येहि भद्रं ते मा भूद्विघ्नोऽध्वनीह नः

निष्पन्दास्तरवः सर्वे निलीना मृगपक्षिणः

नैशेन तमसा व्याप्ता दिशश च रघुनन्दन

शनैर्वियुज्यते संध्या नभो नेत्रैरिवावृतं

नक्षत्रतारागहनं ज्योतिर्भिरवभासते

उत्तिष्ठति च शीतांशुः शशी लोकतमोनुदः

हलादयन्प्राणिनां लोके मनांसि प्रभया विभो

Day 12:

Next day (16 December 12224 BCE), they woke up early and proceeded on their journey[42] and reached river Ganga by noon[43]. Sage Vishwamitra told two brothers many stories related to river Ganga. They decided to stay on the bank of Ganga as evening approached[44].

Day 13:

Next day, having passed through a beautiful night[45] they decided to cross river Ganga[46]. This day was 17 December 12224 BCE. They saw city of Vishala and Vishwamitra educated them on its history. They spent the night at Vishala and traveled to Mithila the next day[47].

At the *Ashram* of Ahilya and Gautama

Day 14:

They reached the *ashram* of Gautama. Vishwamitra told them history of Ahalya[48]. This day was 18 December 12224 BCE.

Arrival in Mithila

They reached Mithila the same day[49]. King Janaka, hearing the news of arrival of sage Vishwamitra, came in a hurry to welcome him. King Janaka told them that the total duration of *yajna* would be 12 days[50]. (It is not clear if *yajna* was going to continue for 12 more days or the total duration of *yajna* was 12 days). In either scenario, the *yajna* would have continued for next 12 days, i.e. 19-30 December 12224 BCE.

Rama lifts Shiva-Dhanushya (Bow of Shiva)

Next morning (19 December 12224 BCE), king Janaka invited sage Vishwamitra and two princes to his court. Rama broke the Shiva-dhanushya on this day[51]. King Janaka expressed his wish to offer Sita to Rama, in marriage, and asked permission of sage Vishwamitra to send messengers to Ayodhya, to convey the news to king Dasharatha and request Dasharatha to arrive at Mithila[52].

Dasharatha arrives in Mithila

Messengers of Janaka took three days to reach Ayodhya[53]. Thus estimated time interval of messengers travel is 20/21 through 23/24 December 12224 BCE. Dasharatha's advisors suggested that they leave for Mithila the next day[54].

King Dasharatha left for Mithila with his army the next day[55] (24/25 December 12224 BCE) and reached Mithila after four days[56] (29 December 12224 BCE). The moment king Janaka heard of Dasharatha's arrival, he set about preparing for latter's reception. King Janaka told Dasharatha (29 December 1224 BCE) that they would decide the *muhurta* of Rama-Sita wedding, next day (30 December 12224 BCE) as soon as his *yajna* was concluded[57], the day (30 December) being the last day of *yajna*. Both parties spent the night happily[58].

Kushadhwaja arrives in Mithila

Next morning (30 December 12224 BCE), after completing the final rites of his *yajna*, king Janaka asked his family priest, Shatananda, to invite king's brother, Kushadhwaja of Samkasha[59]. Messengers were dispatched on horses[60] and king Kushadhwaja arrived in Mithila in no time[61]. While exact date of the arrival of Kushadhwaja cannot be inferred from the Ramayana text, we can safely say that he was in Mithila on or before 1-2 Jan 12223 BCE.

Rama-Sita Wedding

Janaka sat down with Dasharatha and Kushadhwaja to decide the muhurta for the wedding, on 1-2 Jan 12223 BCE, when nakshatra was Magha and decided to perform the wedding, three days after, on nakshatra Uttara Phalguni[62] (i.e. on 4 or 5 Jan 12223 BCE).

Rama-Sita wedding as well as weddings of Rama's three brothers took place on 4 or 5 Jan 12223 BCE. Next day (5 or 6 Jan 12223 BCE) sage Vishwamitra left for his own hermitage and king Dasharatha also proceeded towards Ayodhya[63].

Mithila to Ayodhya

King Dasharatha, his entourage, his four sons and their wives returned to Ayodhya.

The day of Rama-Sita wedding appears to be that of Vaishakha Shuddha 11 or 12. In addition, Dasharatha and his party would have taken longer than 4-5 days to reach Ayodhya (since they reached Mithila in 4 days). Thus, Dasharatha and party, along with his sons and their newly wedded wives, reached Ayodhya sometime during lunar month of Vaishakha.

Let's look at corroborative instances for my proposed timeline of Rama-Sita wedding and observations from the Ramayana text. Entire timeline from the arrival of sage Vishwamitra to court of Ayodhya and leading to the wedding day of Rama-Sita is corroborated for my proposed timeline.

Error Elimination – Experiment 13

Rama was 17-18 year old when he left for the Forest

King Dasharatha refers to the age of Rama as of 16 years when sage Vishwamitra arrived in his court[22]. Queen Kausalya refers to the age of Rama as of 17 years old when he leaves for the forest[64]. Thus a period of one year had gone by between Rama's wedding and his leaving for the forest.

दश सप्त च वर्षाणि तव जातस्य राघव

अतीतानि प्रकाङ्क्षन्त्या मया दुःखपरीक्षयं

In Gorresio's text of Ramayana, Kausalya refers to Rama being 18 years old[311].

अद्यैव मरणं मेऽस्तु को वार्थो जीवितेन मे

अद्य जातस्य वर्षाणि दश चाष्टौ च तेऽनघ

Reader should understand that difference between Kausalya's two statements is that of 'figure of speech'. I have seen people in India, in my times referring to their age as sometimes number of years completed and at other times as number of years completed + 1.

Error Elimination – Experiment 14

Sita in Ayodhya for a year, before leaving for the Forest

Statement of king Dasharatha tells us that Rama was ~16 years old just before Rama-Sita wedding and statement of Kausalya tells us that Rama was ~17 year old when he was scheduled to be coronated and when he left for the forest.

Gorresio's Text of Ramayana (G Ramayana Aranya 53:3-4) corroborates Sita living in Ayodhya for a year before leaving for the forest[313].

संवत्सरं चाध्युपिता राघवस्य निवेशने

भुज्जाना मानुषान भोगान सर्वकामसमृद्धिनी

ततः संवत्सराद्वर्ध सममन्यत मे पतिं

अभिषेचयिन्तु राजा संमत्र्य सचिवैः सह

Error Elimination – Experiment 15

Sita was almost of same age as Rama[312]

Sita's age was not that different from that of Rama. Valmiki Ramayana[312] states:

पतिसंयोगसुलभं वयो द्रष्ट्वा च मे पिता
चिन्तामभ्यागमद्दीनो वित्तनाशदिवाधनः

Perceiving my age to be such when union with a husband can be easily had, my father felt anxiety, feeling distressed as a desititute would through loss of fortune.

This means Sita was at least 14-16 years old at the time of her wedding. Menstruation among girls may begin as early as 9 years however the range for the beginning of menstruation is from 9 to 16.

Error Elimination – Experiment 16

When did *Yajna* begin and end?

One of the many purposes behind *yajna* was to keep track of time. It appears that *yajna*s of varying durations were performed. For example, king Dasharatha performed 'Ashwamedha' *yajna* first and then sat down for 'Putra-kameshthi' *yajna*. The timing for the completion of *yajna* appears to be during the season of Sharad[20].

Sage Vishwamitra did *yajna* for six days when he was accompanied by Rama and Laxman. It is possible that Vishwamitra might have begun this *yajna* long time ago but had to complete last six days of this *yajna* and needed protection of Rama and Laxman. In this case, the *yajna* ended during the month of Chaitra and thus during Sharad season.

King Janaka had planned either *yajna* of 12 days or 12 days of *yajna* were remaining when sage Vishwamitra, along with Rama and Laxman, arrived in Mithila. Again, this *yajna* ended during the month of Chaitra and thus during the Sharad season.

While when *yajna*s begun is difficult to say, it appears that they ended during the Sharad season[20].

Let's look at Ashwamedha and Putra-kameshthi *yajna*s of King Dasharatha. This sacrifice was over by the Sharad[20] and king Dasharatha gave *'payas'* to his queens. Soon the queens became pregnant[65]. After one year, from the conclusion of Ashwamedha and Putra-Kameshthi, the queens gave birth to Rama, Laxman, Bharata and Shatrughna. The language used for passing of one year between the end of *yajna* and birth of Rama is very specific – six seasons – twelve months rolled away until the 9th lunar day of Chaitra[18]. Since the *yajna* (Ishti) was concluded during the Sharad season[20] and the fact the boys were born one year after[18], the season of their birth is also that of Sharad (month being Chaitra) and this fact corroborates well with 13th Millennium BCE.

Chaitra Pornima (full moon of Chaitra) and Sharad Sampat (fall equinox) coincided in 13th Millennium BCE, e.g. 12963 BCE, 12955 BCE, 12944 BCE, 12936 BCE, 12925 BCE, 12914 BCE,------, 12390 BCE, 12371 BCE, 12363 BCE, 12344 BCE, -----, 12238 BCE, 12230 BCE, 12219 BCE, 12208 BCE.

Thus timing for the completion of *yajna* and descriptions related to birth of Rama also allude to 13th Millennium BCE.

Error Elimination – Experiment 17

Sharad Season

Rama is described, after receiving mystic spells of Bala and Atibala, as shone like the glorious sun, casting innumerable rays, of the Sharad season (pre-autumn) [66].

10

Ayodhya to Chitrakuta

आत्मानं नियमैस्तैस्तैः कर्षयित्वा प्रयत्नतः
प्राप्यते निपुणैर्धर्मो न सुखालभ्यतेसुखं

Dharma, which is the source of all happiness, can be attained, even by a skilled person, only after observing various disciplines for his own purification and after great effort subjecting him to great strain and stress. One cannot attain such dharma by leading a life given to the pleasures of the senses.

(Valmiki Ramayana – Aryanya 9:31)

Rama was just short of completing his 16 years when sage Vishwamitra arrived at the court of king Dasharatha to request assistance of Rama[22]. Rama (and Laxman) went along with sage Vishwamitra to assist the latter in his *yajna* and subsequently visited Mithila, where Rama wedded Sita.

Rama was 17 years old at the time of his scheduled coronation[64]. King Dasharatha scheduled coronation of Rama on nakshatra Pushya[17, 67-73] and during the lunar month of Chaitra[2]. Thus, Rama and Sita had spent approximately one lunar year (12 months), together, by the time of his scheduled coronation. The day of scheduled coronation was 20/21 December 12223 BCE.

Death of King Dasharatha

Rama, Sita and Laxman left for the forest and king Dasharatha sunk in despair[74]. Dasharatha could not control his grief and remained delirious. He noted that five nights had passed since Rama left Ayodhya[75]. King Dasharatha recalled his misdeeds during that night, on the 6th night since Rama left[76] and died around the midnight of that very night[77].

Calculating from 21 December 12223 BCE - the day of Rama's departure for the forest, it would mean king Dasharatha died during the night of 26-27 December 12223 BCE. Residents of Ayodhya came to know of their King's death on 27 December 12223 BCE[78].

Messengers Leave for Kekaya capital

Sage Markandeya and other sages urged sage Vasistha, the next day (27 December 12223 BCE), to install any of the princes on the throne immediately (GP Ayodhya Chapter 67). Royal sage Vasistha dispatched the messengers to Kekaya capital in order to fetch Bharata and Shatrughna right away, and messengers left immediately and reached Kekaya capital by the fastest route (GP Ayodhya Chapter 68).

Bharata arrives in Ayodhya, from Kekaya

Bharata and Shatrughna left for Ayodhya immediately and reached Ayodhya in seven days[79].

While I could not determine when exactly Bharata/Shatrughna arrived in Ayodhya, what we do know from the Ramayana text is that they were present to perform 10-11th day rituals (10-11 days after the death of king Dasharatha) for deceased Dasharatha[80]. Thus we know that Bharata was present in Ayodhya on 5 Jan 12222 BCE, 10 days after Dasharatha died.

Error Elimination – Experiment 18

Days of Moonless nights

Bharata also performed some of these rites, the timing of which is described as moonless nights, i.e. on a day close to Amawasya[81]. Bharata performed 11th and 12th day rituals on 6th and 7th January 12222 BCE, respectively[80]. The lunar Tithis (days) for 6 & 7 January 12222 BCE corresponds to Chaitra Krishna Navami and Dashami and thus corroborate well with Ramayana observation of moonless nights. The moonrise on these days was at ~3 AM and 4 AM, respectively.

Sage Vasistha asked Bharata to accept the throne on the 14th day (9 Jan 12222 BCE) after Dasharatha died[82]. Bharata rejected the request and rather offered to spend 14 years in place of Rama, in the forest[83].

Bharata orders construction of roads and camps

Bharata ordered construction of roads and camps suitable for army and members of royalty, to travel from Ayodhya to bank of Ganga and construction began in earnest (GP Ayodhya Chapter 80).

It is difficult to determine how much time was spent in these construction projects however it can be estimated to be substantial, based on the scope of the construction work described in the Ramayana text.

Error Elimination – Experiment 19

Bharata leaves for Chitrakuta during the Lunar month of Vaishakha[84]

Bharata arrived in Ayodhya, from Kekaya, within 10 days after the death of king Dasharatha. After the cremation rites were performed, sage Vasistha urged Bharata to accept the throne of Ayodhya. Bharata ordered construction of roads from Ayodhya to bank of Ganga.

I could not find information that would have allowed me to estimate the duration of this construction interval.

The incident below appears to be after the construction was over. We can conjecture this time to be sometime around the full moon of Sharad season.

Ramayana text describes the assembly of Bharata (in Ayodhya) similar to the full moon night of Sharad season, enriched with well known grahas[84].

तामार्यगणसम्पूर्णां भरतः प्रग्रहां सभां
ददर्श बुद्धिसम्पन्नः पूर्णचन्द्रां निषां इव
आसनानि यथान्यायमार्याणां विशतां तदा
अदृश्यत घनापाये पूर्णचन्द्रेव शर्वरी

Of course this is an anology. Full moon of autumn is all we can deduce and that key grahas were also in the sky.

I conjecture this day to be that of 26 January 12222 BCE. Evening sky, just after sunset, would have shown Saturn, Jupiter, Venus and

Mercury along with the full moon.

Bharata left Ayodhya for Chitrakuta to be around full moon of Vaishakha, i.e. around 26 January 12222 BCE. This was indeed the full moon of Sharad season.

Bharata leaves for Chitrakuta

Bharata and his army camped at the town of Shrigaverapura (ruled by Guha) and then proceeded to the hermitage of sage Bharadwaja[85]. Bharata met sage Bharadwaj and then proceeded to search for Rama around Chitrakuta. The timing seems to be that of the autumn (late Sharad – Hemant) as trees shed flowers and are compared with dark rain bearing clouds pouring water[86].

Bharata meets Rama at Chitrakuta

Bharata reached Rama's hut at Chitrakuta and met with Rama, Laxman & Sita on 10 April 12222 BCE (*Amawasya* of Ashadha). On Pratipada (first day) of Shuddha Paksha during the lunar month of Shravana (11 April 12222 BCE), Bharata asked for sandals of Rama[87]. This was the peak of winter, i.e. one month into the Shishir season.

Error Elimination – Experiment 20

Bharata meets Rama at Chitrakuta

I proposed 10 April 12222 BCE as the day when Bharata met Rama at Chitrakuta. I made this proposal based on Ramayana text where meeting of Bharata and Rama is described as[88]

तत: सुमन्त्रेण गुहेन चैव
समीयतू राजसुतावरण्ये
दिवाकरश्चैव निशाकरश च
यथाम्बरे शुक्रबृहस्पतिभ्यां

The two princes (Rama & Laxman) then embraced Sumantra and Guha, in the forest, similar to the sun and the moon conjoining with Venus and Jupiter in the heaven.

11 January 12222 BCE and 10 April 12222 BCE are two instances when conjunction of sun/moon (*Amawasya*) along with conjunction of Venus/Jupiter occurred. Conjunction of Venus/Jupiter occurred twice within a span of 3 months due to the fact that Venus went retrograde during this time.

I rejected 11 January in favor of 10 April for the following reasons. If Rama had left Ayodhya on 21 December 12223 BCE, he had hardly reached Chitrakuta by 11 January 12222 BCE and still, Bharata was definitely in Ayodhya. In addition, the construction of roads and camps had not begun at this time.

Bharata meets Rama at Chitrakuta	10 April 12222 BCE
Astral Body	**Right Ascension**
Sun	19 hr 35 min
Moon	19 hr 35 min
Venus	17 hr 52 min
Jupiter	17 hr 43 min

Bharata met Rama on or around 10 April 12222 BCE. If correct, this meant Rama was living on Chitrakuta, per my proposed timeline, for some three months, since he left Ayodhya on 21 December 12223 BCE (and assuming he reached Chitrakuta in ~20 days).

It is then interesting to note that GP manuscript translator refers to the long time spent by Rama at Chitrakuta[89] as covering a period of about three months. I do not know the rationale or information used by this translator (GP) to arrive at his estimate of three months. I am pointing it out for its coincidental corroboration with my proposed timeline.

Error Elimination – Experiment 21

Bharata meets Rama during Shishir Season[90]

The day of 10 April 12222 BCE was 23 days after the day of winter solstice (Day of winter solstice ~17 March 12222 BCE) and thus during the peak of winter (Shishir) season. Do we have corroborative evidence for the timing of Bharata-Rama meeting at Chitrakuta during the winter season? We definitely do have additional evidence.

As Bharata began search for the residence of Rama on Chitrakuta, he saw in the vicinity, great heaps of dried dung of deer and buffaloes, kept ready for protection against cold[90].

ददर्श च वने तस्मिन्महत: संचयान्कृतां

मृगाणां महिषाणां च करीषै: शीतकारणात

Now, heaps of dried dung of deer and buffaloes could be stored for the purposes of cooking in general. However, Ramayana text specifically refers to its purpose, i.e. to protect against cold.

This is additional corroboration for the specific timing of Bharata-Rama meeting but also for the 13th Millennium BCE (and lunar month of Chaitra as month of Sharad season during Ramayana times) as Ramayana Millennium.

Error Elimination – Experiment 22

Bharata returns to Ayodhya

Ramayana text is not explicit on when Bharata returned to Ayodhya from Chitrakuta. It appears that Bharata left Chitrakuta and arrived at Ayodhya by the end of spring, i.e. during Grishma season[91].

पुष्पनद्धां वसन्तान्ते मत्तभ्रमरशालिनीं

द्रुतदावाग्निविप्लुष्टां क्लान्तां वनलतां इव

Ayodhya appeared like a flowering creeper laden with blossom in the spring-tide, frequented by a swarm of intoxicated bees, that is suddenly consumed by a forest fire and withering.

This timing appears to be corroborated by comparison of otherwise joyful times that accompanied this season of Grishma (end of spring) [92].

11

PANCHAVATI TO KISHKINDHA

अनागत विधानं तु कर्तव्यं शुभमिच्छता
आपदं शङ्कमानेन पुरुषेण विपश्चिता

A wise man should foresee tragedy or misfortune and take action to prevent or overcome such tragedy or misfortune, well before it strikes. Thus, only he can enjoy a safe and good life.

(Valmiki Ramayana – Aryanya 24:11)

Dandakaranya

Rama, Laxman and Sita spent more than 10 years[343] at Dandakaranya. At the end of this 10 year period, they moved to Panchavati, near modern day Nashik, Maharashtra, India.

Rama, Laxman and Sita settled in Panchavati for about two years and another season of Hemant arrived[93].

वसतस्तस्य तु मुखं राघवस्य महात्मनः
शरद्व्यपाये हेमन्त ऋतुरिष्टः प्रवर्तते

Ramayana text provides descriptions of Hemant season at Panchavati and describes the incident of Shurpanakha. I conjectured, based on this sequence, that Shurpanakha arrived at the residence of Rama either during the season of Hemant (autumn) or sometime afterwards. This is the time of January-March 12210 BCE.

Laxman loped the nose and ears of Shurpanakha. Angry Shurpanakha approached her brothers – Khara and Dushana. In response, Khara sent 14 of his chosen men to attack Rama and Laxman. Rama destroyed all the 14 men of Khara.

Shurpanakha witnessed destruction of Khara's men by Rama and she returned to Khara. At this point, Khara and his brother Dushana, along with a big army, marched towards Rama. I propose this day to be that of 28 March 12210 BCE. As Khara, Dushana and their army marched towards Rama, terrible clouds showered inauspicious blood-red water. A solar eclipse also occurred on this day.

Error Elimination – Experiment 23

The Solar Eclipse[94]

Foreboding danger, buzzards, jackals and vultures uttered shrill notes; and female jackals invariably bringing disaster in war and presenting a terrible aspect shirked with their mouths vomiting flames. A headless human figure resembling an iron club appeared near the sun.

The great graha Rahu (node) obscured the sun, the wind blew violently and the sun became lusterless. Stars flashing like fireflies appeared when there was no night.

Error Elimination – Experiment 24

Solar eclipse in the evening[95]

A fearful and thick darkness that caused the hair to stand prevailed. Neither the quarters nor the intermediate points were clearly discernible. Evening shades resembling canopy, drenched with blood, fell before expected time (sunset) while frightful beasts and birds cried[95].

बभूव तिमिरं घोरमुद्धतं रोमहर्षणं

दिशो वा विदिशो वापि सुव्यक्तं न चकाशिरे

क्षतजार्द्रसवर्णाभा सन्ध्याकालं विना बभौ

खरस्याभिमुखं नेदुस्तदा घोरा मृगा: खगा:

Voyager simulation shows the beginning of solar eclipse around 4:30

PM, and 2 hours before the sunset (6:30 PM) at Panchavati/Nashik.

While exchange of hot words began between Khara and Rama, Khara resumed the fight by stating that <u>while he wanted to say much more, he would not as the sun was setting and that may cause interruption in the fight, which he wanted to avoid</u>[96]

कामं बह्यपि वक्तव्यं त्वयि वक्ष्यामि न त्वहं

अस्तं गच्छेद्धि सविता युद्धविघ्नस्ततो भवेत

Error Elimination – Experiment 25

The season of Khara-Rama fight[97]

The time of this fight, as proposed by me – 28 March 12210 BCE, falls during the peak of winter (10 days after the winter solstice). The description of nature at the time of this solar eclipse corroborates this season.

संलीनमीनविहगा नलिन्य: पुष्पपङकजा:

तस्मिन्क्षणे बभुवुश्च विना पुष्पफलैर्द्रुमाः

Lotus ponds found their lotuses withered and their fishes and aquatic beings hidden in its depths. The trees were bereft of their blossom and fruits[97].

Error Elimination – Experiment 26

Grahas attacking Sun & Moon[98]

Valmiki compares Khara, Dushana and their companions attacking Rama and Laxman with that of grahas attacking the sun and the moon[98].

सा   भीमवेगा समराभिकामा

सुदारुणा राक्षसवीर सेना

तौ राजपुत्रौ सहसाभ्युपेता

मालाग्रहाणामीव चन्द्रसूर्यौ

Position of the sun and the moon together refers to *Amawasya* and possible time of solar eclipse. Voyager simulation shows all five visible grahas in the sky – Mercury, Venus, Mars, Jupiter and Saturn at the time of solar eclipse.

And while I am not making a case for Valmiki being aware of Uranus, Neptune and Pluto, I want to simply bring it to the attention of readers that these three grahas, not visible to the naked eye, were also in the sky at the time of solar eclipse.

Error Elimination – Experiment 27

Khara in the middle of his army

Similar to

Mars risen in the middle of Stars[99]

Khara reached Rama's hermitage and Valmiki describes Khara standing in the middle of his army, similar to Mars in the middle of stars[99].

स तेषां यातुधानानां मध्ये रतो गत: खर:
बभूव मध्ये ताराणां लोहिताङ्ग इवोदित:

Voyager simulation shows beginning of solar eclipse at around 4:40 PM, with Mars close to the zenith, i.e. at the center of the visible sky over Panchavati.

Error Elimination – Experiment 28

Sun became invisible[100]

Ramayana text mentions 'sun becoming invisible' few times in the context of Rama's fight with Khara. Granted the reason for the covering of sun is said to be due to unlimited arrows in the sky covering the sun[100].

शरजालावृत: सूर्यो न तडा स्म प्रकाशते
अन्योन्यवधसंरम्भादुभयो: सम्प्रयुध्यतो:

Ravana comes to Panchavati

Rama defeated Khara, Trishira and Dushana.   Akampana left

Dandakaranya and reached Lanka. He narrated the whole story to Ravana. Akampana suggested Ravana to kidnap Sita, instead of fighting with Rama.

Ravana boarded his chariot and reached the *ashram* of Marich, son of Tataka; described his plan and requested assistance of Marich. Marich convincingly described dangers of Ravana's plan. Ravana obliged and returned to Lanka.

Realizing that no response from Ravana was forthcoming, Shurpanakha reached Lanka and entered Ravana's court. Shurpanakha scolded Ravana for his ignoring the destruction of Khara, Dushana and their army and instigated Ravana to abduct Sita.

Ravana weighed merits and demerits of his decisions, ascertained strengths and weaknesses of his plan, made up his mind and asked his charioteer to get his chariot ready and headed towards the ocean (coast) from Lanka. Ravana crossed the ocean and arrived at the *ashram* of Marich. Ravana reiterated his plan and Marich tried to dissuade Ravana from latter's plan and encouraged Ravana not to provoke Rama. Ravana reproached Marich and commanded the latter to help him in his mission. They mounted the chariot of Ravana and after crossing through towns and forests, mountains and rivers, states and cities; reached Dandakaranya and arrived at *ashram* of Rama in Panchavati.

Error Elimination – Experiment 29

Ravana & Marich in Panchavati

Time of Vasanta/Grishma[101]

सशैलं सागरानूपं वीर्यवानवलोकयं
नानापुष्पफलैर्वृक्षैरनुकीर्ण सहस्रशः
कदल्याढकिसम्बाधं नालिकेरोपशोभितं
सालैस्तालैस्तमालैश्च तरुभिश्च सुपुष्पितैः

Ravana left Lanka and traveled through mountains and forests filled with trees bearing varieties of flowers and fruits. He traveled along coastline that looked most charming with its plantain groves and was embellished with coconut, sal, Palymrya, Tamala and other trees in full blossom[101].

Assuming a remarkable and attractive form of a deer, Marich began moving about near Rama's *ashram*. Sita noticed the golden deer and asked Rama to capture it.

Error Elimination – Experiment 30

Ravana & Marich in Panchavati

Time of Vasanta/Grishma[102]

प्रलोभनार्थं वैदेह्या नानाधातुविचित्रितं
विचरन्गच्छंते सम्यक्षाद्वलानि समन्ततः
रुप्यबिन्दुशतैश्चित्रो भूत्वा च प्रियदर्शनः
विटपीनां किसलयान्भङ्क्त्वादन्विचचार ह

Marich, in the form of a golden deer, began moving around on the
green pastures. Putting on an enchanting appearance with hundreds
of silvery spots and lovely to look at, the golden deer (Marich) nibbled
tender shoots (new grass blades) of trees[102].

Laxman rightly judged the golden deer to be the trick of Marich. Rama did not quite disagree with it and still decided to go after the golden deer.

Error Elimination – Experiment 31

Ravana & Marich in Panchavati

Time of Vasanta/Grishma[103]

अथावतस्थे सुश्रांतश छायामाश्रित्य शाद्वले
मृगैः परिवृतो वन्यैरदूरात्पत्यदृश्यत

Beguiled by him (Marich) and feeling helpless, Rama felt enraged, and
seeking the shade of a tree, thoroughly exhausted as he was, stood at
ease on a spot covered with velvety grass.

After chasing the golden deer for a long time, finally Rama killed the golden deer (Marich). Marich uttered a cry precisely resembling the voice of Rama… "Alas Sita, Ah Laxman" and passed away. Rama was worried at the potential consequences of Marcia's trickery, and still, he spent time collecting meat and other edible stuff on his way and hastily returned to his *ashram*.

Hearing the voice of Rama (in reality, imitation by Marich) Sita asked Laxman to run and help Rama. Laxman, however, did not move as he was confident of Rama's prowess but also due to his wish to obey strict commands of Rama of guarding Sita. Sita became upset and said many undeserving words to Laxman and showed no willingness to listen to logical assertions of Laxman, upon which Laxman left in search of Rama.

Error Elimination – Experiment 32

Ravana & Marich in Panchavati

Time of Vasanta/Grishma[104]

तत: सुवेषं मृगया गतं पतिं
प्रतीक्षमाणा सहलक्ष्मणं तदा
निरीक्षमाणा हरितं ददर्श तं
महद्वनं नैव तु रामलक्ष्मणौ

Looking out for her husband (Rama), who had gone hunting with Laxman, Sita only saw <u>the vast green forest</u> but not Rama & Laxman.

Ravana approached Sita and tried to entice her to accompany him to Lanka. When Sita refused, he lifted her forcefully, on the way fought with Jatayu, severely injured Jatayu, and finally reached Lanka.

Error Elimination – Experiment 33

Ravana & Marich in Panchavati

Time of Vasanta/Grishma[105]

आमन्त्रये जनस्थानं कर्णिकारांश्च पुष्पितां
क्षिप्रं रामाय शंसध्वं सीतां हरति रावण:

"I pray to <u>Karnikara trees in blossom in Janasthana</u> – Kindly tell Rama promptly that Ravana is taking away Sita"

I have conjectured that Ravana abducted Sita, from Panchavati, sometime during May-July 12210 BCE. This was the time of Vasanta (spring) season. Six observations of Valmiki Ramayana corroborate timing of Sita's abduction as that of Vasanta (spring) season.

Sita in Lanka

Ravana lodged Sita in a royal palace with attendants and ordered attendants to be most pleasing in their behavior to Sita and also offer her various pearls, gems, gold and precious clothes.

Ravana sent eight of his chosen men for espionage to Janasthana to monitor activities of Rama and Laxman.

Ravana entered his delightful palace where Sita was stationed and showed her his royal opulence and tried his best to coax her into marrying him.

When Sita scolded him in harsh words, he ordered the ladies guarding Sita to move her to *Ashoka-van* and assigned a time limit of 12 months to accept his proposal and threatened her with death, if his proposal was not accepted[106]. Ravana assigned this time limit sometime during October-November 12210 BCE.

Panchavati to Kishkindha

Back in Janasthana/Panchavati, Rama met Laxman and arrived at their *ashram* to realize that Sita had disappeared. They began their search for Sita and met Jatayu who updated them that Ravana had taken away Sita. Jatayu died soon thereafter and Rama cremated Jatayu and continued with their search for Sita. They ran into Kabandha and he advised them to make an alliance with Sugriva and informed them of the way to Rishyamukha Hill and Lake Pampa. Rama and Laxman visited Shabari at the *ashram* of sage Matanga and then proceeded to Lake Pampa.

Seeing Rama and Laxman and not knowing who they were, Sugriva, who was residing on Rishyamukha Hill, went into hiding. Sugriva sent Hanuman to ascertain purpose of Rama and Laxman to arrive near Rishyamukha Hill. Rama met with Sugriva and Sugriva requested Rama to get rid of Vali.

12

IN KISHKINDHA

हत्वा बाणेन काकुत्स्थ मामिहानपराधिनं
किं वक्ष्यसि सतां मध्ये कर्म कृत्वा जुगुप्सितं

What will you say to holy men for your abominable act, having killed me with an arrow even though I had not committed any offense?

(Valmiki Ramayana – Kishkindha 17:35)

Rama promised to kill Vali. Sugriva ascertained actual strength of Rama, shrewdly, by first asking him to kick away skeleton of Dundubhi, and then to pierce with his arrow, one of the seven Sal trees. Sugriva was convinced of Rama's strength and implored Rama to kill Vali.

Sugriva & Vali Dual – First Round

Rama sent Sugriva to challenge Vali to a combat. Rama sat hiding behind a tree. Rama did not hit Vali with an arrow, since two brothers (Sugriva and Vali) resembled so closely with each other that Rama could not distinguish Vali from Sugriva. As a result, Sugriva lost heart and ultimately ran away from the combat to Rishyamukha Hill.

The timing of this first fight appears to be that of the late afternoon and just before the sunset. The day was 21 September 12210 BCE. Mercury and Mars were next to each other on the western horizon.

Error Elimination – Experiment 34

Clash between Mercury & Mars at Sunset[107]

Valmiki describes this fight between two brothers, as they rushed towards each other, as if to finish the fight before impending sunset, and compares them to a clash between Mercury and Mars in the heavens[107].

तं श्रुत्वा निनदं भ्रातुः क्रुद्धो वाली महाबलः
निष्पपात सुसंरब्धो भास्करोऽस्तटादिव
ततः सुतुमुलं युद्धं वालिसुग्रीवयोरभूत
गगने ग्रहयोर्घोरं बुधाङ्गारकयोरिव

Vali who possessed extraordinary strength rushed forth as the <u>sun would slide from the edge of the western mountain</u>. Tumultuous and terrible dual ensued between Vali and Sugriva, <u>resembling a clash between Mercury and Mars in the heavens.</u>

Voyager simulation shows Mercury and Mars next to each other, immediately after the sunset, on 21 September 12210 BCE.

Sugriva & Vali Dual – Second Round

Rama explained his dilemma to discouraged Sugriva and encouraged Sugriva to seek another encounter with Vali. This time Laxman uprooted a blossomed Gajapushpi creeper and tied it around the neck of Sugriva for identification.

Tara, wife of Vali, discouraged Vali, with cogent reasons, from going to the battle. Vali went to meet Sugriva anyway and there ensured a fierce encounter between two brothers. During the fight, Rama struck Vali with an arrow. Vali fell to the ground. The timing of this second fight appears to be on the very next day, and possibly in the morning. The day was 22 September 12210 BCE. There appears to be a solar eclipse on this day.

Error Elimination – Experiment 35

Sun along with galaxy of stars in the sky[108]

कृताभिज्ञान चिन्हस्त्वमनया गजसान्हया
विपरीत इवाकाशे सूर्यो नक्षत्र मालया

Sugriva with creeper around his neck is compared with the sun adorned with galaxy of stars in the sky.

Voyager simulation shows solar eclipse on the morning of 22 September 12210 BCE. This possibility is further corroborated by additional four observations.

Error Elimination – Experiment 36

Sun lost its splendor[109]

स तु रोषपरीताङ्गो वाली सन्ध्यातपप्रभ:
उपरक्त इवादित्य: सद्यो निष्प्रभतां गत:

On hearing the challenge of Sugriva, embitterment overspreading on all his limbs, Vali, golden-hue in color, was immediately rendered non-luminous like the eclipsed sun.

The solar eclipse began in the morning, so Vali who looked bright like morning light (*usha*), immediately became dark like the eclipsed Sun.

Error Elimination – Experiment 37

Resembled Sun-Moon in the sky[110]

तौ भीमबलविक्रान्तौ सुपर्णसमवेगिनौ
प्रवृद्धौ घोरवपुषौ चन्द्रसूर्याविवाम्बरे

The two brothers – who were endowed with terrible might and prowess, were intent on finding out vulnerable points of each other – resembled like the moon and the sun in the sky.

As described earlier, this day was the day of *Amawasya* and thus the moon and the sun were together. In addition, the moon and the sun might have been visible together as it was the day of solar eclipse. This timing of *Amawasya* appears to be further corroborated by one additional observation.

Error Elimination – Experiment 38

Moonless sky = Amavasya[111]

तस्मिन्निपतिते भूमौ हर्यृषाणां गणेश्चरे
नष्टचन्द्रमिव व्योम न व्यराजत भूतलं

Vali fell to the ground, and the earth appeared as dark as the sky with the moon disappeared from it (*Amawasya*).

Error Elimination – Experiment 39

Moon devoured by Rahu- Eclipse in general[112]

इत्येवमुक्तः सुग्रीवो वालिना भ्रातृसौहृदात
हर्ष त्यक्त्वा पुनर्दीनो ग्रहग्रस्त इवोडुराट

Listening to the advice of Vali, Sugriva felt wretched and looked like the moon seized by Rahu. The reference is definitely to an eclipse. As I have shown, the day was that of *Amawasya* and also that there was a solar eclipse. Reader should not forget that the sun and the moon are together at the node (intersection of the paths of the sun and the moon) at the time of solar eclipse.

Death of Vali and Coronation of Sugriva

Dying Vali requested Rama to take care of Angada. Tara rushed to the place where Vali had fallen. Rama consoled all and requested to carry out cremation and final rites for Vali in a suitable manner.

Rama declined request of Hanuman to visit city of Kishkindha and directed that Sugriva may be installed on the throne of Kishkindha and that Angada may become *Yuvaraj*. Rama took a vow to live in a cave till the end of four months of Varsha (rainy) season. Rama also requested Vanara to initiate search for Sita as soon as Varsha season was over.

Sugriva and Vanara party entered city of Kishkindha. Sugriva became the king of Kishkindha and Angada the *Yuvaraj*. Rama retired to Mount Prasravana along with Laxman and began dwelling in a mountain cave.

Arrival of autumn season and Search for Sita

Season of Sharad arrived and the sky became clear. Perceiving this, Hanuman approached Sugriva and advised Sugriva, in friendly manner and with truthful words, to issue orders to the Vanara to do the needful for search of Sita. Sugriva commanded Nila to collect all the troops from all quarters. After this, Sugriva retired to his palace.

Rama waited patiently for Sugriva to make a move and take expedient measures to begin search for Sita. Sugriva remained busy in material pleasures. Rama sent Laxman to Kishkindha and Sugriva asked Hanuman to summon Vanara stationed at various mountain ranges – Mahendra, Himalaya, Vindhya, Kailasa and Mandara, but also from other mountains: Padma, Anjana, Mahasaila, Meru, Dhumra and Maharuna.

Over a period of next several days and weeks, hordes of Vanara arrived in Kishkindha. Sugriva visited Rama and updated him on the arrival of Vanara army into Kishkindha.

Search for Sita

Sugriva sent a search party in each direction. All parties began their search towards the end of Sharad season. Vinata led the search in the east, Hanuman, Nila & Angada led the search party in the most crucial (towards Lanka) direction, i.e. to the south. Sushena led the search in the west and Shatabali to the north. Sugriva did not forget to assign each party a strict time limit of one month to return, and warned them of severe punishment if the strict time limit was not followed.

All parties began their search. They searched a given area multiple times however returned to Kishkindha within a month, dispirited, with the exception of south party which did not return by the time limit imposed by Sugriva.

13

SEARCHING FOR SITA IN THE SOUTH

न निषादेन नः कार्यं विषादो दोषवत्तरः
विषादो हन्ति पुरुषं बालं क्रुद्ध इवोरगः

One should not let one's mind be swayed by despondency (melan-choly). Despondency is very harmful. It kills (destroys) a man just as an angered serpent kills an infant.

(Valmiki Ramayana – Kishkindha 64:9)

Hanuman, Nila, Angada and party left Kishkindha as early as one month after the Sharad season. They began with exploration of the caves and dense forests of Vindhya. They scoured difficult places: mountain peaks, rivers, lakes, forests, groves and mountain ranges however met with no luck in finding Sita. In these early days of search, they subsisted on roots and fruits of various kinds.

Error Elimination – Experiment 40

Season of Sharad/Hemanta[113]

ते भक्षयन्तो मूलानि फलानि विविधानि च
अन्वेषमाणा दुर्धर्षा न्यवसंस्त्रत्र तत्र ह
स तु देशो दुरन्वेषो गुहागहनवान्महां

The search party subsisted on roots and fruits of various kinds. This then appears to be the season of Sharad or early Hemant.

By the time they left this region and moved on to the next, they were already severely tormented with hunger and thirst. They entered the next region and by that time, it appears that the season of winter had arrived.

Error Elimination – Experiment 41

Season of Shishir (winter) [114]

यत्र वन्ध्यफला वृक्षा विपुष्पा: पर्णवर्जिता:
निस्तोया: सरितो यत्र मूलं यत्र सुदुर्लभं
न सन्ति महिषा यत्र न मृगा न च हस्तिन:
शार्दूला: पक्षिणो वापि ये चान्ये वनगोचरा:
स्निग्धपत्रा: स्थले यत्र पद्मिन्य: फुल्लपङ्कजा:
प्रेक्षणीया: सुगन्धाश्च भ्रमरैश्चापि वर्जिता:

They found the trees had no flowers, fruits or even leaves. The streams were devoid of water and they had hard times finding roots. The area was devoid of buffaloes, deer, elephants, tigers, birds and other animals. The area was also devoid of trees, annual plants, climbers or creepers, lotus plants or lotuses.

Significant time elapsed and exhausted Vanara party was encouraged by Angada and Gandhamadan to resume their search.

Error Elimination – Experiment 42

A considerable time elaspsed[115]

कालश्च नो महान्यात:सुग्रीवश्चोग्रशासन:
तस्माद्भवन्त: सहिता विचिन्वन्तु समन्तत:

Hanuman, along with Tara and Angada, began to explore caves and dense forests in the southwestern (Kerala?) ranges of the mountain. They reached the south-western summit of that mountain and while they searched, the time appointed by Sugriva clearly slipped away.

Error Elimination – Experiment 43

A considerable time elapsed[116]

आसेदुः तस्य शैलस्य कोटीं दक्षिण पश्चिमां
तेषां तत्र एव वसतां स कालो व्यत्यवर्तत

The party reached a valley – Rikshabila – difficult to access. However, overcome by hunger, thirst and exhaustion, and thus to seek water, the party decided to enter the valley which was filled with climbers and creepers. The birds – herons, swans, cranes, chakrawaka, their limbs laden with pollen, emerged from the valley. This then appears to be the time of early spring.

Error Elimination – Experiment 43

Time of Early Spring[117]

गिरिजालावृतान्देषान्मार्गित्वा दक्षिणां दिशं
क्षुत्पिपासा परीताश्च श्रान्ताश्च सलिलार्थिनः
अवकीर्ण लतावृक्षैर्देदृशुस्ते महाबिलं
ततः क्रौञ्चाश्च हंसाश्च सारसाश्चापि निष्क्रमं
जलार्द्राश्चक्रवाकाश्च रक्ताङ्गाः पद्मरेणुभिः
अस्माच्चापि बिलाद्धंसाः क्रौञ्चाश्च सह सारसैः
जलार्द्राश्चक्रवाकाश्च निष्पतन्ति स्म सर्वशः
नूनं सलिलवानत्र कूपो वा यदि वा ह्रदः
तथा चेमे बिलद्वारे स्निग्धास्तिष्ठन्ति पादपाः

The search party entered the valley and after walking for some distance arrived at a beautiful spot that was filled with atmosphere of the spring season: Sal, Palmyra, Tamala, Punnaga, Vanjula, Dhava Champaka, Naga and Karnikara trees in blossom with wonderful golden clusters of flowers and tender crimson leaves.

Error Elimination – Experiment 44

Season of Spring[118]

ततस्तं देशमागम्य सौम्यं वितिमिरं वनं
दद्दशुः कांचनान्वृक्षान्दीप्तवैश्वानरप्रभां
सालांस्तालांश्च पुंनागान्ककुभान्वनजुलान्धवां
चंपकान्नागवृक्षांश्च कर्णिकारांश्च पुष्पितां
तरुणादित्यसङ्काशान्वैदूर्यमयवेदिकां
नीलवैदूर्यवर्णांश्च पद्मिनीः पतगावृताः
महद्द्रिः कान्चनैर्वृक्षैर्वृतं बालार्क संनिभैः
जातरूपमयैर्मत्स्यैर्महद्द्रिश्च सकच्छपैः

Valley of Swayamprabha had creepers surrounding the trees, lotus plants surrounded by birds, trees laden with blossom and fruits and with honeys of various kinds available on them. The palaces were filled with collection of aloe wood and sandal-wood, pure foods as well as roots and fruits and delicious honey.

Error Elimination – Experiment 45

Season of Spring[119]

दद्दशुस्तत्र हरयो गृहमुख्यानि सर्वशः
पुष्पितान्फलिनो वृक्षान्प्रवालमणिसंनिभां
कांचनभ्रमरांश्चैव मधूनि च समन्ततः
मणिकांचनचित्राणि शयनान्यासनानि च
महार्हाणि च यानानि दद्दशुस्ते समन्ततः
हैमराजतकांस्यानां भाजनानां च संचयां
अगरूणां च दिव्यानां चन्दनानां च संचयां
शुचीन्यभ्य वहार्याणि मुलानि च फलानि च
महार्हाणि च पानानि मधूनि रसवन्ति च
दिव्यानामम्बराणां च महार्हाणां च संचयां
कम्बलानां च चित्राणामजिनानां च संचयां

Vanara dined on fruits and roots and Hanuman narrated the story of their search to Swayamprabha – manager in charge, of that place.

Error Elimination – Experiment 46

Time limit has elaspsed[357]

एवमुक्त: शुभं वाक्यं तापस्या धर्मसंहितं
उवाच हनुमान्वाक्यं तामनिन्दितचेष्टितां
शरणं त्वां प्रपन्ना: स्म: सर्वे वै धर्मचारिणि
य: कृत: समयोऽस्माकं सुग्रीवेण महात्मना
स तु कालो व्यतिक्रान्तो बिले च परिवर्ततां

While narrating the story of their search for Sita, Hanuman told Swayamprabha that the time limit fixed by Sugriva for search expired, even while Vanara party was roaming in the caves, before approaching Swayamprabha.

Swayamprabha provided Vanara party with directions to get out of the valley and Vanara party resumed their search. The Vanara party now beheld the shoreless ocean. They began searching for Sita in this mountainous region, next to the ocean, established by *Danava* Maya, and while they were busy, another month elapsed[120].

Error Elimination – Experiment 47

Time limit has elapsed[120]

मयस्य माया विहितं गिरिदुर्गं विचिन्वतां
तेषां मासो व्यतिक्रान्तो यो राजा समय: कृत:

They sat exhausted on the hill, in that area and felt alarmed to see treetops of spring season, weighted by flowers and enshrouded by numerous vines (this meant long time had elapsed since the expiration of time limit set by Sugriva for all Vanara search parties to return to Kishkindha).

Error Elimination – Experiment 48

Time of Spring[121]

विन्ध्यस्य तु गिरे: पादे सम्प्रपुष्पितपादपे
उपविश्य महाभागाश्चिन्तामापेदिरे तदा

तत: पुष्पातिभाराग्रांल्लताशतसमावृतां
द्रुमान्वासन्तिकांदृष्ट्वा बभूवुर्भयशंकिता:

And of course one does not have to rely, for predicting the season of this time of Vanara search, on descriptions of nature (trees, leaves, flowers and vines).

Valmiki Ramayana clearly states this to be the timing of Vasanta season (spring). This Ramayana observation also reiterates that time limit set by Sugriva had long expired.

Error Elimination – Experiment 49

Time of Spring & Expiration of time[122]

ते वसन्तमनुप्राप्तं प्रतिवेदय परस्परं
नष्टसन्देशकालार्था निपेतुर्धरणीतले

Angada uttered words that are very critical in determining the timing of Ramayana. This observation also provides exciting corroborative evidence for my timeline.

He begins with reiterating the fact that his search party spent one month while simply searching for Sita, in the valley of Swayamprabha.

Error Elimination – Experiment 50

Full month elapsed within the Valley itself[123]

शासनात्कपिराजस्य वयं सर्वे विनिर्गता:
मास: पूर्णो बिलस्थानां हरय: किं न बुध्यते

And then states (possibly from observations of phases and positions of the moon) to the Vanara party that, based on his calculations – from the time of their departure from Kishkindha, the current time was that of lunar month of Ashwin and that month had also elapsed!

Error Elimination – Experiment 51

Season of Vasanta coinciding with Lunar Month of Ashwin[124]

वयम अश्वायुजे मासि काल संख्या व्यवस्थिताः
प्रस्थिताः सो~पि चातीतः किमतः कार्यमुत्तरम

Vayam –us, we; ashwayuje masi –Lunar month of Ashwin, kalasamkhya vyavasthitha – based on calculations of time, prasthitta – departed, departure, sopichatit – that, kimat – what, karaymuttarmam – next to do

By proper calculations from the time of our departure, now is the lunar month of Ashwin and even that month seems to have passed. What should we do now?

Full Moon of Ashwin & Flag of Indra

I want readers to analyze outcome of Error Elimination Experiment # 51 with the Ramayana text analogy of 'falling down of Vali' with that of 'falling down of the flag of Indra' that was raised, in honor of Indra, during the lunar month of Ashwin on a full moon day, but thrown onto the ground along with its flagstaff after the festival[125].

These references (121-125) assert that in Ramayana times, the flag of Indra was raised and then thrown onto the ground during the lunar month of Ashwin and also that lunar month of Ashwin coincided with that of spring season.

If we run a simulation where full moon of Ashwin coincides with the spring Equinox (i.e. the middle of spring season), we can estimate this time to be around 14200 BCE. We can also simulate the beginning (and the end) of spring season coinciding with the full moon of Ashwin. These simulations provide us with the time interval from 16500 BCE through 11800 BCE.

I want readers to recognize that this estimate falls within the broader time interval defined by me in chapter six, i.e. from 10000 BCE through 17500 BCE. In fact we can update our figure from chapter six as follows:

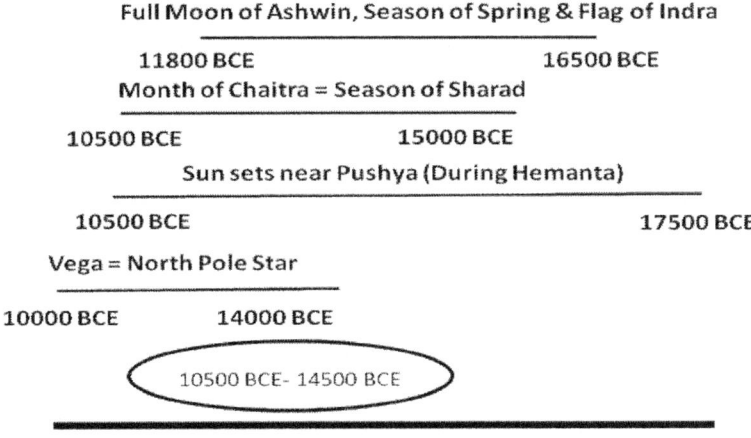

(10000 BCE – 17500 BCE)
Time Interval: Searching for the timing of The Ramayana

Flag of Indra & *Gudhi-Padava*

I conjecture that this Ramayana tradition of raising flag of Indra might have turned into what is celebrated as *'Gudhi Padava'* in Maharashtra when Gudhi (flag) is raised on the first lunar day of spring season. In our times, it falls on first day of Chaitra (Chaitra Shuddha Pratipada). If my suggestion is correct, then we can say that this tradition of *Gudhi Padava* goes back to at least 14000 years! In order for the tradition to stick, one may assert that the significance was associated more with the time of the year (i.e. spring) and not with a specific lunar month. That would explain the preservation of the tradition even when coincidence between lunar months and season of spring changed through some 14000 years. I encourage researchers of Indian history to research this subject further.

The Voyager simulation for year 12209 BCE shows that the lunar month of Ashwin coincided with second half of spring season. Vanara party left Kishkindha, at the earliest, during the second month of Sharad season (pre-autumn), and more likely during the first month of Hemant season (autumn). Thus Vanara party, heading south, searched through the seasons of Hemant, Shishir and Vasanta and still had not found Sita. I assert that numerous and frequent references alluding to 'expired time limit set by Sugriva' is due to this extended search that went way beyond the limit of one month set by Sugriva.

After much search and exhaustion, many of them, headed by Angada, decided to give up their search for the second time. This is due to the fact that they were aware of missing the time limit set by Sugriva, by a huge margin [127-129].

Sampati, elder brother of Jatayu, arrived at the scene. Vanara party came to know of Sita being stationed at Lanka through Sampati.

With renewed vigor, Vanara party marched towards the south (Lanka) and keeping reference of nakshatra Abhijit (It had become the North Pole star during ~12000 BCE) as their guiding light, they marched towards Lanka (south).

Error Elimination – Experiment 52

Vanara party headed South, with reference to Abhijit[130]

अथ पवनसमानविक्रमा:

प्लवगवरा: प्रतिलब्ध पौरुषा:

अभिजिदभिमुखां दिशं ययुर

जनकसुता परिमार्गणोन्मुखा:

Some translators have interpreted 'Abhijit' as referring to the auspicious muhurta – Abhijit. Certainly that meaning is also plausible. And while either interpretation does not affect the proposed timeline, I assert that interpretation of 'Abhijit' as reference star due to it being 'North pole star' (~12000 BCE) is more meaningful.

Soon they arrived at the seashore. Vanara party discussed individual strengths of party members in crossing the ocean, and finally Jambavan encouraged Hanuman to take up the task. Hanuman climbed up the mountain Mahendra, and prepared to take a leap across the sea.

14

HANUMAN IN LANKA

वाच्यावाच्यं प्रकुपितो न विजानाति कर्हिचित
नाकार्यमस्ति क्रुद्धस्य नावाच्यं विद्यते क्वचित

One who is enraged can not discern between what is worth uttering and what not to be uttered. For an enraged person, there is neither an improper act nor ever an improper word to be spoken.
(Valmiki Ramayana – Sundar 55:5)

Hanuman jumped into the sea and began swimming towards Lanka. He eventually landed on the shore of Lanka. Numerous Ramayana references corroborate this time to be that of the spring season [131-133]. Hanuman came across an island on his way to Lanka, and descriptions of the island also corroborate the timing of spring[134].

Hanuman began searching for Sita and the timing was that of close to the full moon day[137]. He heard music of various instruments. He observed Ravana's forces armed with various weapons. Hanuman reached and searched through Ravana's gynaeceum but could not locate Sita. He continued his search, visited palaces of Ravana's key warriors and ministers, saw aerial car – Pushpak, and also noticed Ravana sleeping in his mansion.

Finally he ended up at *Ashoka-vana* and caught sight of Sita. He waited there until moonrise (evening) [137]. This was day two of Hanuman in Lanka.

Hanuman saw Ravana, surrounded by many women, approaching *Ashoka-vana*. Ravana tried to coax Sita and tried to win her. Placing a blade of grass between herself and Ravana, Sita praised Rama and tried to impress upon Ravana consequences between befriending and antagonizing Rama. She advised Ravana to make friendship with Rama and to surrender.

Ravana allowed her a time limit of (additional?) two months to revise her decision and also made it clear that she must share his bed; otherwise he would have her for his morning breakfast[138]! Some of the accompanying women of Ravana, however, reassured Sita of the nature of his threat, by expression of their lips, eyes and faces. Ravana commanded all his security women, watching over Sita, to do the needful to coax Sita to agree to his wishes. And with that, Ravana went back to his palace.

At an opportune moment, Hanuman made sweet speech within the hearing of Sita, extolling story of Rama leading to abduction of Sita and subsequent search efforts of Vanara. Sita was overjoyed. Sita informed Hanuman as to how Ravana was going to kill her after two months. Hanuman disclosed his identity as the minister of Sugriva and presented Rama's ring to Sita in order to strengthen her confidence in him. Hanuman offered to carry her on his back to Rama however Sita declined the offer and urged Hanuman to bring Rama to her. Sita gave him a precious jewel, as proof of their meeting and Hanuman placed it on his finger as he prepared to set out on his return journey.

Hanuman decided to ascertain the strength of Ravana and his army and thus began destruction of royal garden. Ravana sent series of warriors – Kinkars, Jambumali, five additional generals and Prince Aksha. Hanuman killed them all. This is when Ravana sent Indrajit who bound Hanuman using *Brahmastra* and brought him to Ravana.

Hanuman was wonderstruck to behold the splendor and personality of Ravana. Hanuman asked Ravana to restore Sita to Rama. Ravana ordered his commanders to put Hanuman to death, however, Vibhishan, younger brother of Ravana, intervened and urged Ravana to desist from killing Hanuman by pointing out that Hanuman was an envoy and killing him was not appropriate.

Commanders of Ravana, at his order, wrapped up the tail of Hanuman, soaked it in oil and then lighted it up while parading Hanuman through the city of Lanka. Hanuman escaped while he was being paraded through the city of Lanka, then he burnt part of the city, met Sita one more time and prepared himself to return to Vanara party, on the other side of the ocean.

Spring Season

The lunar month of Ashwin was over when Vanara party left the valley of Swayamprabha. They resumed their search and when, after some time, they were resting due to exhaustion, Sampati showed up. Some more time went by when they took Sampati to the seashore where Sampati performed final rites for his brother - Jatayu.

After this, they journeyed towards Lanka and reached on the northern shore of the ocean. I conjectured that Hanuman was in Lanka on 27 August 12209 BCE (Margashirsha full moon). Accordingly, Hanuman returned to Kishkindha after mid-September 12209 BCE.

The lunar month of Ashwin and the season of spring were already in vogue when Vanara party was searching through the valley of Swayamprabha [122-124]. Thus, it appears to be the season of late spring/Grishma when Hanuman visited Lanka. This assertion is corroborated by numerous and extensive descriptions of the spring season [139-143]. In addition, following observations corroborate time of Hanuman visiting Lanka as that of spring and early summer.

Error Elimination – Experiment 53

Analogy of Second month of Spring – Month of Madhava[144]

Valmiki employs analogy of second month (solar month of Indian calendar) of spring (Madhava) in describing sleeping women of Ravana in his gynaeceum. This is of course only an analogy and by itself, it does not signify much. However, in the context of numerous descriptions of the spring, it is relevant. At a minimum, it corroborates with the time of Hanuman's visit to Lanka.

लता नां माधवे मासि फुल्ला नां वायु सेवनात
अन्योन्य माला ग्रथितं सं सक्त कुसुमो च्च यं

व्यतिवेष्टितसुस्कन्थमन्योन्यभ्रमराकुलं
आसीद्वनमिवोद्धृतं स्त्रीवनं रावणस्य तत

Solar months of ancient Indian calendar are as follows: Madhu & Madhava (Vasanta season), Shukra & Shuchi (Grishma season), Nabha &

Nabhasya (Varsha season), Isha & Urja (Sharad season), Saha & Sahasya (Hemant season), Tapa & Tapasya (Shishir season).

Error Elimination – Experiment 54

Hanuman in Lanka – Time of Ashoka Flowers[145, 146]

Hanuman saw Ravana's bed decorated with wreaths of Ashoka flowers[145]. Hanuman noticed Sita seated by the Ashoka tree which was covered with flowers. Ashoka trees are known to exhibit flowers during the months of February through April in our times (early spring – early summer).

Presence of Ashoka flowers during Hanuman's visit to Lanka corroborate the time of his visit as that of late spring through early summer. Descriptions of *Ashoka-vana* also corroborate the timing of spring/late spring when Hanuman visited Lanka [147, 148].

Time of Full Moon

I have asserted that the time of Hanuman visiting Lanka was around the full moon. I want to split corroborative evidence for this assertion into two categories.

The first category has actual descriptions of the nights on or near the full moon day and the second category has analogies involving full moon.

While evidence from both categories can be used, and should be used as corroborative evidence, reader must realize that the evidence from the first category offers higher degree of corroboration.

Error Elimination – Experiment 55

Hanuman in Lanka – Time of Full Moon

After reaching Lanka, Hanuman waited until the sunset[136] before entering the city of Lanka. As he waited for sun to set, the bright moon appeared on the horizon[149].

This observation corroborates the timing of Hanuman visiting Lanka aroud the full moon day. The descriptions of the moon, of the same night, when moon reached the zenith, also leave no doubt about the timing of full moon, when Hanuman was in Lanka[150].

Error Elimination – Experiment 56

Hanuman in Lanka – Analogies of Full Moon

Numerous analogies of full moon are interspersed throughout Valmiki Ramayana descriptions of Hanuman's time in Lanka [151-161].

Time of Lunar Eclipse

My proposal for timing of Hanuman in Lanka, around 27 August 12209 BCE is specifically based on plausible references to lunar eclipse when Hanuman was in Lanka. This would make timing of Hanuman's visit to Lanka as that of late Grishma season. Numerous analogies refer to the lunar eclipse.

Error Elimination – Experiment 57

Hanuman in Lanka – Time of Lunar eclipse [162-167]

Multiple analogies of specifically lunar eclipse abound in Valmiki Ramayana when it describes Hanuman's visit to Lanka [162-167]. Voyager simulation shows that there was a lunar eclipse on 27 August 12209 BCE and was visible at the city of Lanka.

Duration of Hanuman's visit to Lanka

Total duration of Hanuman's visit to Lanka can be ascertained, albeit approximately and tentatively, with the help of few observations.

Day 1

He entered Lanka and walked through the capital in search of Sita. It was the time of spring in Lanka[135]. Hanuman reached Lanka and waited until the sunset before entering the city of Lanka[136]. This was day one of Hanuman in Lanka.

Hanuman searched through Lanka for Sita and he could not locate her even when half of the night was over[168].

Day 2

Finally, Hanuman located Sita in the *Ashoka-vana* during the night. He was keenly observing *Ashoka-vana* that was filled with trees in blossom and was looking for an opportunity to see Sita more closely, while the night was over. Towards the close of the night (morning), he heard chanting from the dwellings of Brahmanas who were well versed in six *Shastras* and in conducting *Yajna* and other rituals[169].

Hanuman saw Ravana approach Sita, along with his wives and servants. Ravana coaxed Sita to marry him. Hanuman patiently waited for an opportune moment. The day went by and he thought to himself that somehow he had to make contact with Sita by the end of upcoming night[170].

Day 3

Hanuman began singing the story of Rama. Sita heard it however initially she felt she might have simply heard it in her dream. Soon, she saw Hanuman who resembled the sun on the eastern horizon[171]. This appears to be the early morning of the next day.

After Hanuman-Sita conversation, Hanuman decided to ascertain strength of Ravana army and began destroying Ravana's pleasure gardens. This appears to be the morning of the same day. Hanuman climbed up to the top of a sanctuary and he appeared like a second sun just risen[172]. Hanuman defeated many of Ravana's commanders and Hanuman is compared with the rising sun with all its splendor[173]. Prince Aksha, his chariot and armor, on his way to Hanuman, was also compared with brilliant rays of the sun and the moon[174].

Day 4

After Hanuman burnt part of Lanka, he briefly met with Sita and then left the city of Lanka. It appears that he flew back to Vanara party, early morning, the next day. That day would be Day four.

Timing of Hanuman's return to Vanara Party

Since Hanuman was in Lanka for only four days, timing of his return from Lanka is essentially same as that of his timing of visiting Lanka. Valmiki Ramayana describes the sky when Hanuman was returning from

Lanka and provides corroborative evidence for my proposed timeline.

Error Elimination – Experiment 58

Hanuman returning from Lanka – View of the sky [175]

Hanuman left from Lanka early morning. This appears to be the day, two to four days removed (and after) from the full moon day. Valmiki describes the sky as follows.

The moon appeared attractive similar to a white water-lily, the sun appeared like a crane (Karandava bird) while nakshatras Pushya and Shravana like swans. Nakshatra Punarvasu appeared like a big fish, Mars appeared like a crocodile. Airavata appeared like an island and nakshatra Swati like a swan[175].

What these descriptions tell us is that in the early morning, when Hanuman flew from Lanka, portion of the sky – from nakshatra Punarvasu through nakshatra Shravana, was visible. Full moon-like moon was also visible and so was Mars. Let's see if these descriptions can corroborate for 27 August 12209 BCE. The actual day of Hanuman returning from Lanka is 2-3 days after the full moon day. This means I had to test this scenario for 29-30 August 12209 BCE.

Vartak has interpreted 'Airavata' as referring to the portion of the sky that represents 'Scorpio', i.e. nakshatras Anuradha through Moola, where the astral landscape (of Scorpio) can be perceived as the trunk of an elephant. I accept his interpretation. All that is described (with exception of actual *yogatara* of Shravana - Altair) can be corroborated for 29-30 August 12209 BCE.

Let's evaluate Ramayana observations for the day of 30 August 12209 BCE, three days after the full moon day of 27 August. Just before the sunrise, at 5:50 AM, the bright moon (three days after the full moon day) was in the area of Pushya, Mars was next to Pushya and the area of the sky from nakshatra Punarvasu through nakshatra Jyeshtha was visible. We had to wait for another hour – 6:50 AM, before the sun was above the horizon and still another hour before area of Shravana could be visible.

Two other grahas, not mentioned by Valmiki, Venus and Jupiter, were also visible. Of course we can talk of only those things that are mentioned. Even then I wondered why Valmiki may not have mentioned Venus and Jupiter in his descriptions of the sky. I noticed in Voyager simulation that Jupiter was in perfect or near perfect conjunction with star Magha (Regulus) and this could explain why mention of Jupiter might have been missed. Of course this remains my pure speculation.

We will revisit this observation, again, when we look at efforts of Shri Pushkar Bhatngar. We will able to have additional plausible corroboration of this observation for our timeline.

No logical reason for non-mention of Venus can be suggested.

Hanuman returns from Lanka	30 August 12209 BCE
Astral Body	**Right Ascension**
Nakshatra Punarvasu (Pollux)	18 hr 46 min
Nakshatra Pushya (Altarf)	19 hr 35 min
Nakshatra Magha (Regulus)	21 hr 16 min
Nakshatra Swati (Arcturus)	23 hr 17 min
Naskhatra Shravana (Altair)	7 hr 25 min
Moon	19 hr 51 min
Mars	20 hr 48 min
Jupiter	21 hr 15 min
(Venus)	3 hr 50 min
Sun	4hr 55 min

Summary of Plausible Eclipses in Ramayana

Ramayana Incident	Type of Eclipse	Time of Eclipse	Separation Angle
(Description & Date)	Solar/Lunar	(Peak)	(per simulation)
Khara-Rama battle (28 March 12210 BCE)	Solar Eclipse	7:44 PM	2.132
Vali-Vadha (22 September 12210 BCE)	Solar Eclipse	5:52 AM	1.182
Hanuman in Lanka (27 August 12209 BCE)	Lunar Eclipse	5.25 AM	2.092

15

KISHKINDHA TO LANKA

निरुत्साहस्य दीनस्य शोकपर्याकुलात्मनः |
सर्वार्थी व्यवसीदन्ति व्यसनं चाधिगच्छति || ६||

The efforts of one who is unenthusiastic, weak and immersed in sor-row cannot bring out any good. He immerses in grief and meets with disaster.

(Valmiki Ramayana – Yuddha 2:6)

Hanuman returned to the Vanara party on the northern seashore and entire party returned to Kishkindha. Soon Rama gave orders to Vanara leaders and the Vanara-army to depart for Lanka. Rama left from Kishkindha, for Lanka, on 29-30 September 12209 BCE.

Error Elimination – Experiment 59

Leaving Kishkindha- Time of Departure[176]

अस्मिनन्मुहूर्ते सुग्रीव प्रयाणमभिरोचये
युक्तो मुहूर्तो विजय प्राप्तो मध्यं दिवाकर:
उत्तरा फल्गुनी हृद्य श्वस्तु हस्तेन योक्ष्यते
अभिप्रयाम सुग्रीव सर्वानीकसमावृता:

The nakshatra of the day was Uttara Phalguni and Rama suggests that they leave that very day (or on the next day when nakshatra was

Hasta) from Kishkindha.

Calculating from the timing of Hanuman in Lanka, and then allowing ~30 days of time period for Hanuman to return to Kishkindha and the Vanara army to get ready for Lanka, I conjectured 29-30 September 12209 BCE as the time when Rama, along with the Vanara army, left for Lanka.

Duration of Journey: Kishkindha to Lanka

While it is relatively easy to define the boundaries on the duration of journey from Kishkindha to Lanka, it is indeed challenging to determine the exact duration of the journey from Kishkindha to seashore, and also the duration of their stay at the seashore.

I could make a case for Rama and his Vanara army still on their way to seashore, at least for a month, after they left Kishkindha.

Error Elimination – Experiment 60

On the way to Lanka
Conjunctions of Moon & Sun, with Jupiter and Venus[177]

कपिभ्यामुह्यमानौ तौ शुशुभते नरर्षभौ
महद्भ्यामिव संस्पृष्टौ ग्राहाभ्यां चन्द्रभास्करौ

Valmiki provides an analogy of the sun & the moon having conjunctions with two major grahas in describing the scene of Angada and Hanuman carrying Laxman and Rama on their shoulders, respectively.

Rama & Laxmana on shoulders on Hanuman & Angada	25 October 12209 BCE
Astral Body	Right Ascension
Moon (Full Moon)	20 hr 55 min
Jupiter	20 hr 55 min
Sun	8 hr 57 min
Venus	8 hr 50 min

Jupiter and Venus are not specifically mentioned, however, interestingly, translator of GP edition suggests them to be Jupiter and Venus. Such a conjunction, assuming identification of two major grahas with Jupiter/Venus is valid, could be seen on 24-25 October 12209 BCE. The sun was in conjunction with Venus while the moon (full moon) was in conjunction with Jupiter. This was the full moon of the lunar month of Magha. The time was that of Varsha (rainy) season.

Error Elimination – Experiment 61

On the way to Lanka
Additional astronomy observations[178]

Laxman describes multiple omens of this time period.

All directions appeared clear and the sun was shining brightly. Venus was shining with its bright light. Dhruva (BrahmaRashi), the very bright pole star, along with *Saptarshi* (seven sages) could be seen shining clearly[4]. Star Trishanku - Acrux (star named after King Trishanku, born in Ikshvaku dynasty and Rama's ancestor) was shining in the front (south) along with his minister (another prominent star next to star Trishanku). Nakshatra Vishakha, nakshatra of Ikshvaku dynasty, was free from any evil influence. On the other hand, nakshatra Moola, nakshatra of Rakshasa (Nairukta) race, was being afflicted by a Comet (Comet Laxman) and its bright tail of light. This is certainly bad omen for Rakshasa race and indicates their destruction[5].

The comet was at its lowest magnitude (brightest) around 10 September 12209 BCE.

I have already discussed two specific Ramayana observations [4-5] in estimating Ramayana millennium (13th Millennium BCE).

Observations of Venus and also of nakshatra Vishakha are too generic to comment. All I can say is that Venus was visible and that nakshatra Vishakha had no evil grahas (Saturn or Mars) in its vicinity during Rama's march to Lanka. Star Trishanku (Acrux) and its companion stars were above the southern horizon, and thus were visible at night.

Exciting Digression: Migration of Agastya to the South

Bright star of Agastya (Canopus) was conspicuous by its absence-both in the sky but also in the Valmiki Ramayana descriptions! This is because, I assert that star Agastya (Canopus) had attained a position close to the South Celestial Pole (SCP) and thus was not visible from latitudes in India, in 12000 BCE. Star Agastya (Canopus) would have been barely visible (just above horizon) from Colombo (Sri Lanka), in 12000 BCE.

Thus, if the story of sage Agastya crossing Vindhya and naming of star Agastya (Canopus) based on the bright star (Canopus) observed by sage Agastya is true, then I estimate the timing of sage Agastya crossing Vindhya long time before Ramayana (12000 BCE), and specifically before 16000 BCE, and more likely sometime around 25000 BCE through 20000 BCE.

I have added a note on the timing (and the rationale) of sage Agastya migrating to the south, at the end of this book (Appendix B).

Kishkindha to Seashore

The Vanara army traveled through the day and the night[179], in southern direction. They walked along the Sahya mountain range and then the Malaya mountain range[180]. The timing of their march appears to be that of late Grishma/early Varsha season, as trees were covered with blossom and fruits[181], forests full of honey while lakes and rivers were filled with aquatic flowers [182-183].

First they crossed the Sahya mountain range, then the Malaya mountain range and finally the Mahendra mountain range. Soon they arrived at the southern seashore[184].

Rama and the Vanara army climbed down from the Mahendra and sought out most excellent woodland adjoining the sea for their camp[185]. Rama and party had already anticipated the problem of crossing the ocean and thus asked everyone to camp there while remaining alert for covert enemy attacks[186]. Sugriva and Laxman organized the camp and the entire Vanara army looked like a second glorious sea[187]. The leaders of Vanara army began surveying the sea, while days and nights went by[188]. The Vanara army remained stationed comfortably on the seashore[189]. While it is difficult to estimate the exact duration of Vanara army at the seashore, it appears that they were at the seashore for a long time[190].

While Rama and his Vanara party were meditating on ways to cross the ocean; Ravana, in Lanka, held consultations with his ministers. Ravana and his team were certainly surprised by the deeds of Hanuman (his destroying Lanka and killing many of Ravana's brave warriors). Ravana appears to have an efficient espionage network for he was well aware of the movement of Rama and his Vanara army towards Lanka[191]. When Ravana asked for the advice of his ministers, all of them indulged in self-praise and tried to inspire confidence in Ravana. His general, Prahasta, vowed to kill Rama while Vibhishan, Ravana's younger brother, suggested returning Sita to Rama and thus save Lanka. Ravana ordered Prahasta, his general, to make adequate arrangements for the defense of Lanka and to inform Kumbhakarna of the whole situation. Vibhishan requested Ravana to return Sita to Rama. Ravana was annoyed to hear such words and castigated Vibhishan with harsh words.

Vibhishan, along with his four ministers, approached Rama on the other side of the ocean in no time[192] via air [193, 194]. After deliberations with key Vanara members, Rama decided to accept Vibhishan on his team. Rama assured Vibhishan of latter's safety, upon which Vibhishan descended to the ground, along with his four ministers[195].

Hanuman and Sugriva approached Vibhishan to seek advice for means to cross the ocean[196]. Vibhashan's advice appears to be vague, at least as narrated in Valmiki Ramayana, for all Vibhishan seemed to have said is that king Sagar, ancestor of Rama, had successfully dealt with the sea in the past and Rama should able to accomplish the same[197]. However joint interpretation of Vibhishan's words, by Laxman and Sugriva, makes it amply clear that Vibhishan had also suggested building a bridge over the ocean[198].

In Lanka, Shardula - one of Ravana's spies, who had seen Vanara army up close, approached Ravana and informed the arrival of huge Vanara army that was comfortably camped on the other side of the ocean[199]. Ravana sent Shuka with a task of approaching Sugriva with the aim of creating dissension among Rama's party, upon which Shuka flew to Vanara camp, approached Sugriva and delivered Ravana's message, while still in the air[200]. However Vanara warriors sprang up quickly into the air and brought Shuka down and the latter was only freed at Rama's intervention. When immunity was granted, Shuka preferred to become airborne again and continued his communication while still in the air[201]. It appears that while Shuka's torture, at the hands of Vanara ended, he was still kept by Rama in captivity[221].

The ocean remained highly turbulent. Rama sat down meditating for three days and nights[202]. Rama felt frustrated at the situation and he began throwing arrows at the ocean[203]. Laxman rushed to Rama, held his bow and requested Rama to control his anger and to find a noble and durable solution to the problem[204].

Nala-Setu

It appears that the ocean had become calm by now and Vanara Nala approached Rama, and comforted Rama with his skills at bridge-building. Nala also explained his reasons for not speaking of his skills until now. Nala suggested to Rama that the construction of the bridge should begin and Rama gave appropriate orders to Vanara army[205].

Vanara tore up rocks and trees from nearby forests and dragged them to the sea. They filled the sea with trees and shrubs[206]. Vanara army dug up huge rocks and transported them by means of mechanical means, and as they hurled the rocks into the sea, the rocks fell down, and the water rose up in the sky. Vanara army drew up strings (in order to stabilize these fillers – rocks/shrubs/trees) [207].

Nala constructed *Nala-setu*, the extensive bridge, a hundred yojana long, in the heart of the sea. The entire bridge was built by Vanara army. Some held staffs (for measuring the length and breadth of the bridge) while others collected the material. Parts of the bridge were constructed of reeds, logs and trees that were covered with blossom. A tumultuous sound arose from the rocks that were being hurled into the sea [208].

On the first day of construction, Vanara army completed 14 yojana and on the second day they completed 20 yojana. They completed 21 yojana on the third day, 22 yojana on the fourth day and with 23 yojana on the fifth day, they completed the construction of *Nala-setu*[209]. *Nala-setu* across the sea, constructed by Nala, looked charming like the Milky Way in the sky[210].

The Vanara army crossed the bridge to the other side, by taking long and short leaps, in no time[211]. Vibhishan, along with his four ministers, stood on the southern side to protect the bridge while Vanara army was crossing it[212]. Rama and Laxman crossed the bridge in the company of Sugriva[213]. The Vanara army camped on the southern shore and the area was abundant in roots and fruits[214].

Seashore to Lanka

Rama told Laxman to arrange Vanara army in various formations and prepare them to march towards Lanka through the regions of trees with fresh fruits and fresh water[215].

The winds were blowing, and the earth was quaking. Mountain peaks were shaking and trees were falling. Fierce clouds let loose showers while emitting harsh sounds and blazing sun was showering intense heat[216]. Rama told Laxman that they should march towards Lanka, at full speed, that very day[217]. The Vanara army looked exceptionally charming like an autumnal full moon night presided over by the moon and illuminated by bright stars[218].

They moved in formations, protected on all sides by specific leaders of Vanara and marched towards Lanka[219]. Soon they reached Lanka[220]. When movement of Vanara army appeared satisfactory, Rama ordered to let Shuka, Ravana's spy, set free, upon which Shuka sought presence of Ravana[221].

Shuka informed Ravana of Vanara army constructing the bridge across the ocean and their arrival in Lanka. Ravana commanded Shuka and Sarana - his minsisters, to enter Vanara army ranks and collect information[222]. Shuka and Sarana entered the Vanara army ranks that were stationed on the summits of mountains of Lanka[223]. They were detected and captured by Vibhishan. Rama set them free, upon which they went to Ravana, described the details of Vanara army and suggested that Ravana hand over Sita to Rama.

In his message to Ravana, Rama suggested (threatened) that Vanara army would attack Lanka, the very next day[224]. In reality, it appears that it would be 2-3 days more before the actual attack began. Ravana went to the roof of his palace, along with Shuka and Sarana, to survey the Vanara army. Ravana snubbed Shuka and Sarana for praising commanders of Vanara army, and then dispatched Shardula for espionage. Shardula returned and presented his own assessment of Vanara army. Ravana came to know of Rama's taking position near the mountain Suvela.

Ravana approached Sita, accompanied by Vidyujjiva. Vidyujjiva was expert in conjuring tricks, and presented her with counterfeit head of Rama, upon which Sita burst into a wail. Fortunately Ravana was abruptly called away. Ravana prepared his forces, after consultations with his ministers, for the war against Rama and the Vanara army.

Sarama reassured Sita that Rama was indeed alive and asked her not to be afraid. Sarama offered to go visit Rama secretly and deliver message of Sita. In turn, Sita requested Sarama to find out specific plans of Ravana. Sarama indeed found out the plans of Ravana and communicated them back to Sita. Malyavan requested Ravana to make peace with Rama however Ravana derided Malyavan, held consultations with ministers and asked Prahasta, his commander-in-chief, to guard four main gates against the attack of Vanara army. Then, Ravana retired to his palace.

Vibhishan informed Rama of Ravana's arrangement; the information gathered by Vibhishan's four ministers. Rama provided detailed instructions to Vanara commanders for storming the four gates of Lanka, and then he climbed mount Suvela with his army. Rama surveyed Lanka, from the top of mount Suvela, as sun sank below the horizon, reddening the evening twilight sky which was then illuminated by the full moon[225]. The night set in and Rama happily spent the night, along with the Vanara commanders and army, on the top of mount Suvela.

Having spent the night on the summit of mount Suvela, the commanders of Vanara army entered the parks and gardens[226], which were laden with blossom [227, 228], on the outskirts of Lanka. Rama was amazed to see the beauty of Lanka. Along with Sugriva, Rama then ascended the top of mount Suvela[229]. Rama caught sight of Ravana perched on the top of latter's palace. Infuriated Sugriva sprang from Suvela towards Ravana. Sugriva and Ravana engaged each other in fight, however soon Sugriva returned to Rama. Rama was not pleased with daring but reckless act of Sugriva and warned Sugriva of not repeating similar acts again. Rama positioned Vanara generals at the four gates and instructed them to attack when he signaled. Rama dispatched Angada to Ravana, as a final attempt, for reconciliation. Angada flew to Ravana[230] however returned with the news of no change in stance on the part of Ravana. Soon the war began.

Duration of the War

Valmiki Ramayana presents evidence for the beginning of the War, some 2-3 days after the full moon day. It also presents evidence for the end of War, with Rama killing Ravana, on *Amawasya* day. Other than these observations for the beginning and the end of War, there are few, if any, references that clearly allow us to estimate the duration and also to predict timings of specific war incidents.

Duration of the War appears to be of less than 15 days, and more likely of 13 days. Dr. P V Vartak have assumed the duration of War equal to 13 days.

Since I have shown that Rama was at the *ashram* of Bharadwaj on Vaishakha Shuddha 5 and he met with Bharata, the day after, on Vaishakha Shuddha 6, I could estimate that the War began on Chaitra Krishna Tritiya and ended on Chaitra *Amawasya*. This means that the war began on 25 December 12209 BCE and ended on 6 January 12208 BCE.

16

THE WAR & RAMA'S RETURN TO AYODHYA

य: स्वपक्षं परित्यज्य परपक्षं नीषेवते
स स्वपक्षे क्षयं याते पच्छात्तैरेव हन्यते

He who abandons his own side and joins adversary is killed by the very adversary, after his own kinsmen are destroyed by them.

(Valmiki Ramayana – Yuddha 87:16)

Day 1

The war began. The blast of conches and the roll of the drums and leonine roar of Vanara fighters accompanied by trumpeting of elephants, neighing of horses, clatter of chariot wheels and shout of Rakshasa made the earth, the sea and the air tremble. A terrible conflict ensued between Vanara and Rakshasa and soon it left mire of flesh and blood.

The fighting was indeed tiring and warriors were longing for the sunset to occur[231]. Soon, the sun set on the western horizon and the night began[232]. This appears to be the end of the first day of war, however, the fighting continued into the night[233]. In fact, the fight continued into the late night[234]. The day was 25 December 12209 BCE.

Day 2

Towards the end of the night (close to the morning of the next day), Indrajit employed his conjuring tricks and bound Rama and Laxmana[235] and then began piercing them with pointed arrows. Rama and Laxman fell to the ground[236]. Indrajit thought that the two brothers – Rama and Laxman - were dead, and thus entered Lanka.

Hanuman and other Vanara commanders surrounded Rama and Laxman and guarded their bodies on the battlefield, while in Lanka, Ravana commanded Rakshasa women to take Sita to the battlefield via Pushpak. The plan was executed, and Sita burst into tears when she looked at fallen bodies of Rama and Laxmana[237]. Soon Rama returned to consciousness but felt sad at the plight of Laxman.

Valmiki Ramayana presents an analogy of the setting sun and I have interpreted it to mean, possibly, the end of the second day of war[238]. In due course, even Laxman returned to consciousness. The Vanara army reached the gates of Lanka and the time appears to be that of mid-night[239] (at the end of the second day of war).

Vanara army made tumultuous noise and hearing this, Ravana sent his ministers to verify the cause of joyous mood in Vanara camp. Ministers informed presence of Rama and Laxman in good condition. Ravana felt overwhelmed with anxiety and commanded Dhumraksha to head to the battlefield and destroy Rama.

Dhumraksha mounted a chariot driven by donkeys and set forth through the western gate of Lanka where Hanuman had taken up his stand. The rain god poured down blood (water) and earth shook, while winds blew adversely with thunder like roar, and the fight continued through the darkness[240]. It is not clear if the darkness is due to the heavy rain and clouds or due to it being the time of night. Dhumraksha fought bravely however in the end was killed by Hanuman. Rakshasa army re-entered Lanka.

Ravana sent Vajradamshtra, who was skilled in conjuring tricks, to the battlefield. He left Lanka through the southern gate where Angada was stationed with his Vanara army. Another fight ensued and the earth glowed like an autumnal night[241]. This appears to be end of day two. Angada killed Vajradamshtra and Rakshasa army fled back to Lanka.

The day was 26 December 12209 BCE.

Day 3

Ravana sent Akampana, a brave and mighty commander, and he caused much destruction, however, in the end, was killed by Hanuman.

It is difficult to determine the exact time of Akampana's arrival on the battlefield. I have assigned it to day three based on the fact that 'darkness' on the battlefield is described as due to the dust[242].

Enraged to hear the news of Akampana's death, Ravana intently looked at his ministers and then proceeded, during early part of the day[243], to inspect all the fortified posts around the city of Lanka.

This day was 27 December 12209 BCE.

Day 4

Ravana sent Prahasta, his commander-in-chief, to fight against Rama and his army. Prahasta left with many powerful warriors- Narantaka, Kumbhahanu, Mahanad and Samunnata and as he proceeded towards the battlefield, clouds showered blood (water) on the chariot of Prahasta and also drenched all the marching army[244]. Nila killed Prahasta. Rakshasa army fled to Lanka.

This day was 28 December 12209 BCE.

Day 5

Ravana decided to go to the battlefield and ordered his commanders to prepare for the fight. Two analogies of 'newly risen sun' as Ravana prepared to enter the battlefield led me to conjecture that this could be the next day (Day five) of the war [245, 246]. Analogy of early morning cloud made me conjecture this timing to be that of early morning of that day[247].

Various commanders of Vanara army including Sugriva, Hanuman, Nila, Rama and Laxman fought with Ravana. The fighting continued for a long time, however, in the end Rama defeated Ravana. Rama told Ravana to rest by returning to Lanka. Ravana, his vanity and joy crushed, took this opportunity and returned to Lanka.

Ravana called his ministers and began recalling past warnings and curses heaped upon him by many personalities. He ordered his commanders to guard the four gates of the city with extra vigilance, and asked his ministers to rouse Kumbhakarna from his sleep. This seems to be the end of day five.

This day was 29 December 12209 BCE.

Day 6

Ravana's ministers roused Kumbhakarna with great efforts and then returned to Ravana. In time, Kumbhakarna woke up from his bed and walked towards the royal palace of Ravana. Ravana warned Kumbhakarna of Vanara prowess and skill of Rama, and urged Kumbhakarna to destroy Vanara army.

Kumbhakarna asked Ravana to relax and promised him destruction of Vanara army. Kumbhakarna told Ravana that he would drive fear of Ravana, similar to the sun dispersing the darkness of night[248]. I conjectured that this conversation might have occurred in the early hours of the morning of the sixth day.

Kumbhakarna fought bravely and caused significant damage to the Vanara army. As the day came to an end, Sugriva caused harm to Kumbhakarna and Kumbhakarna resembled like an evening cloud[249]. Later on, Laxman covered the armor of Kumbhakarna and made it disappear with his arrows, similar to the wind that disperses evening clouds[250] and Kumbhakarna shown like the sun with its rays being screened by clouds[251]. In the end, Rama killed Kumbhakarna. Ravana lamented over the death of Kumbhakarna.

This day was 30 December 12209 BCE.

Day 7

Many brave warriors of Ravana – Narantaka, Devantaka, Trishira, Mahodara and Mahaparshwa went to the battlefield. They fought bravely, however, in the end were killed by various warriors on Rama's side.

This day was 31 December 12209 BCE.

Day 8

Atikaya fought bravely and caused huge damage, however, in the end was killed by Laxman. Ravana's eyes were filled with copious tears at the news of enormous losses on his side.

Indrajit, Ravana's son, consoled his father and vowed to kill the Vanara army. Indrajit reached the battlefield with huge army. Indrajit caused enormous damage to Vanara army, defeated many of its leaders and finally hurt Rama and Laxman, with the help of *Brahmastra*. Then Indrajit returned to Lanka.

Vibhishan tried his best to restore confidence among Vanara commanders. Hanuman joined Vibhishan in this task. Many in Vanara army were affected due to assault of Indrajit and also due to the effect of

Brahmastra.

As the night arrived, Vibhishan and Hanuman, with torches in their hands, began walking around the battlefield, looking for survivors[252]. They saw key Vanara warriors stuck down on the battlefield – Sugriva, Angada, Nila, Sharabha, Gandhamandana, Sushena, Vegadarshi, Mainda, Nala, Jyotirmukha, Dwivida and others. By the end of the day (evening) huge Vanara army was affected due to effects of *Brahmastra*[253].

Hanuman, accompanied by Vibhishan, began to search for Jambavan[254]. Vibhishan noticed Jambavan and asked the latter about his injuries. Jambavan told Vibhishan that he could only hear Vibhishan's voice but could not see him, and eagerly asked Vibhishan if by luck Hanuman had survived this ordeal. Vibhishan was surprised that Jambavan inquired specifically the well being of Hanuman, instead of Rama, Laxman, Sugriva and others. Jambavan replied that if Hanuman had survived, then that meant Vanara army would be intact, on the other hand, if Hanuman had fallen prey to Indrajit's attack, then all Vanara were as good as dead, even if alive. Hanuman approached Jambavan and clasped his feet. Jambavan asked Hanuman to fly to Himalaya in a hurry and then approach mount Kailas via mount Rishabha and bring specific herbs[255]. In the middle of that night, Hanuman took off for Himalaya[256].

This day was 1 January 12208 BCE.

Day 9

Hanuman reached the mountain, and since he could not recognize specific herbs, he uprooted many of them and returned to Lanka by early morning[257]. All Vanara warriors, even those severely wounded, were healed due to the application of those herbs, as if awake from the sleep at the end of night (morning) [258].

It appears that this entire day was consumed in recovery of injured Vanara warriors. I assert this because Valmiki Ramayana refers to setting of the sun[259], before Vanara army attacked the city of Lanka.

Vanara army attacked the city of Lanka at night[260] and another big fight ensued. Lanka was ablaze and while the city of Lanka was burning, ocean looked charming like the sea of red water. Ravana became furious and sent Kumbha and Nikumbha along with Yupaksha, Shonitaksha, Prajagnha and Kampana to fight against the Vanara army.

Both armies were fighting at night[261]. They held torches in their hands. The light of the moon and of the stars, along with light from their torches, irradiated the sky. The moonlight, the splendors of ornaments worn by fighters and light of shining grahas/stars lit fighting warriors of both sides[262].

Angada killed Kampana and Prajagnha while Dwivida killed Shonitaksha. Mainda killed Yupaksha while Sugriva killed Kumbha. Hanuman killed Nikumbha.

This day was 2 January 12208 BCE.

Day 10

Ravana could not control his anger as he heard of this destruction and sent Makaraksha, son of Khara. Rama killed Makaraksha.

Ravana asked Indrajit to go to the battlefield. Indrajit accepted the command, poured oblations into the sacred fire and ascended his chariot and rushed to the battlefield.

Valmiki Ramayana states that Indrajit brought darkness to the battlefield by implementation of his conjuring tricks. I have no way of corroborating or falsifying this statement of Ramayana. Rama and Laxman employed many powerful *astra* however Indrajit remained unaffected. On the other hand, Indrajit pierced Rama and Laxman with many arrows and the two princes looked like *Kimshuka* trees in blossom. Rama began to reflect on speedy means to put an end to Indrajit.

It appears that either Rama decided to stop the fight or Indrajit decided to take a break and returned to the city of Lanka[263]. It appears Indrajit had some interesting plans in mind. He came out of the city of Lanka via western gate, but this time he had illusory – living image of Sita on his chariot. Hanuman, along with the Vanara army, attacked Indrajit. Indrajit killed illusory Sita in front of Hanuman. Hanuman initiated a counter attack on Indrajit and in turn Indrajit began another attack on the Vanara army. Hanuman ordered his army to retreat and executed a successful retreat.

Noticing retreat of the Vanara army, Indrajit proceeded towards the sanctuary of Nikumbhila[264] with aim of pouring oblations into the sacred fire. He began pouring oblations into the fire. The fire resembled the evening sun[265]. This seems to be the time of the sunset on this day.

Hanuman approached Rama and informed him of Indrajit's killing Sita (illusory). Rama fainted. Laxman consoled Rama and prepared the latter for the action. Vibhishan told Rama of conjuring tricks practiced by Indrajit and assured him of Sita being still alive. Vibhishan also urged

Rama to send Laxman to the sanctuary of Devi Nikumbhila and fight with Indrajit before latter's 'Yajna' was completed.

Laxman arrived at the sanctuary of Nikumbhila, with the Vanara army. Hanuman, Angada and Vibhishan also accompanied Laxman. Vanara army approached Indrajit's army as one would penetrate darkness[266]. The Vanara army attacked Indrajit's army and a great fight began. Soon the Vanara army caused great fear among Indrajit's army men. The news reached Indrajit. Indrajit emerged from the dark woods[267], even though his Yajna was not complete. Exchange of hot words took place between Indrajit and Vibhishan, and also between Indrajit and Laxman, followed by fight between Indrajit and Laxman.

This day was 3 January 12208 BCE.

Day 11

Laxman, mounted on the shoulders of Hanuman, looked like the sun rising on the eastern horizon[268]. The fighting ensued and arrows thrown by Laxman, hitting the chest of Indrajit, looked like the rays of the sun[269]. The long fight continued throughout the morning[270].

Vibhishan took a position in the front, and also encouraged the Vanara army to fight. Laxman killed the charioteer of Indrajit and few Vanara fighters killed the horses of Indrajit's chariot. In spite of this, Indrajit continued a fierce fight. The sky was thickly covered with arrows and was shrouded in darkness[271]. The entire battlefield was enveloped in darkness and looked dreadful[272]. Soon the sun set behind the western horizon[273].

The fight continued into the night and it was difficult for the fighters to figure out who they were fighting with, and if they belonged to their own side or the other[274]. Soon, Laxman killed Indrajit and Rakshasa army fled in all directions, similar to rays of the sun disappearing when the sun sinks below the horizon[275]. Fallen Indrajit, that mighty warrior, looked like the sun whose rays have cooled down[276].

Laxman, Vibhishan and others approached Rama with the news of Indrajit's death. Rama was delighted and embraced Laxman. Rama also praised Vibhishan, Hanuman and Vanara warriors for fighting with Indrajit over the course of three days and night[277]. Rama asked Sushena to treat wounds of Laxman and other Vanara warriors.

This day was 4 January 12208 BCE.

Day 12

Ravana became grief stricken at the news of Indrajit's death. In his anger, he proceeded to kill Sita.

His intelligent minister, Suparshwa, stopped Ravana from such dastardly act and instead encouraged him to go into the battlefield and kill Rama. Suparshwa told Ravana to prepare himself for the fight on that day of Krishna Chaturdashi (Chaitra Krishna 14) and attain victory the next day, i.e. on the day of *Amawasya* (Chaitra *Amawasya*)[278].

Ravana accepted the advice of Suparshwa and withdrew to his palace, and then proceeded to the council chamber. Ravana asked his commanders to attack Rama and his Vanara army with all their might. Accordingly, Ravana's commanders went to the battlefield, however were killed and defeated by Rama and his Vanara army. Rakshasa women wept and lamented death of their husbands.

This day was 5 January 12208 BCE.

Day 13

Ravana marched to the battlefield, along with his generals. He exhibited tremendous valor against Vanara commanders and Rama's army. Sugriva responded to the attack and caused significant destruction of Rakshasa army. Sugriva killed Virupaksha and also Mahodara while Angada killed Mahaparshwa.

Ravana began his determined attack on the Vanara army and caused much damage. Laxman attempted to fight with Ravana. Ravana bypassed Laxman and approached Rama. Rama-Ravana Yuddha began for the second time. In the meantime, Laxman also attacked Ravana and in turn Ravana threw javelin at Laxman. The javelin pierced Laxman and he fell to the ground. Rama felt despondent to see the plight of Laxman however Rama had no option but to continue the fight with Ravana. Laxman regained consciousness under the treatment of Sushena, with the help of herbs brought in by Hanuman, second time, from mount Mahodaya[279]. Rama was pleased to see Laxman back to normal and expressed his resolution to kill Ravana before the sunset[280].

Ravana attacked Rama, sitting in another chariot, and the fight resumed. Matali, charioteer of Indra, arrived at the scene with Indra's chariot to assist Rama[281]. The fighting went on and Rama severely wounded Ravana. Ravana's charioteer removed Ravana from the battlefield. Ravana regained his strength and then reproached the charioteer for removing him from the battlefield. Charioteer explained the rationale, for his actions, in sweet words, and then drove the chariot back to the battlefield.

Sage Agastya approached Rama and asked him to recite 'Aditya Hridaya' which Rama did and felt supremely exhilarated. Rama asked Matali to be on his guard as the fighting continued. Fierce fighting between Rama and Ravana continued unabated[284]. Matali reminded Rama of *astra* given by sage Agastya[285]. Rama charged the astra with mystic spell and discharged at Ravana. It pierced the heart of Ravana and Ravana fell to the ground.

This day was 6 January 12208 BCE.

Let's look at corroborative evidence for the timing of Ravana-vadha, from Valmiki Ramayana.

Error Elimination – Experiment 62

Analogy of an eclipse + Mercury stood assailing Rohini[282]

व्यथिता वानरेन्द्राश्च बभूवुः सविभीषणाः

रामचन्द्रमसं दृष्ट्वा ग्रस्तं रावणराहुणा

प्राजापत्यं च नक्षत्रं रोहिणी शशिनः प्रियां

समाक्रम्य बुधस्तस्थौ प्रजानाम शुभावहः

The day was Amawasya. At 7:45 PM, Mercury and nakshatra Rohini (also Krittika) were on the western horizon. The observation corroborates well for 6 January 12208 BCE.

Error Elimination – Experiment 63

Mars assailing Vishakha – Nakshatra of Kosala[283]

कोसलानां च नक्षत्रं व्यक्तमिन्द्राग्निदैवतं

आक्रम्याङ्गारकस्तस्थौ विशाखामपि चाम्बरे

Mars was nowhere close to nakshatra Vishakha, on 6 January 12208 BCE. Nakshatra Vishakha and Mars were present in the night sky, however that would only provide weak corroboration (if at all).

I am going to speculate and I do want readers (and especially researchers) to take note of my speculation.

Mars was near nakshatra Ashlesha on 6 January 12208 BCE (only 2 nakshatra space away from nakshatra Punarvasu). Mars had gone retrograde and was stationed in the areas of nakshatras Punarvasu through Magha (space of four nakshatras) for seven months (June 12209 BCE – January 12208 BCE). When not in retrograde, Mars travels through one nakshatra within a period of ~20 days.

My speculation is that 'Vishakha' here might have referred to nakshatra Punarvasu. I reiterate that this is only a speculation and I am noting it down for the benefit of future researchers. I also want to note down information from this observation that also contradicts my speculation. Nakshatra of Kosala is described as one whose nakshatra – Devata is 'Indra-Agni'. We do know that 'Indra-Agni' is devata of nakshatra Vishakha and not of Punarvasu.

I had run into similar speculation (identification of 'Vishakha', in addition to traditionally accepted 'Vishakha' next to nakshatra Chitra, with that of Punarvasu) while researching astronomy observations of Mahabharata text. I had wondered, based on few specific observations of Mahabharata text, if nakshatra 'Punarvasu' was also called 'Vi-shakha' in ancient times.

Funeral of Ravana & Rama meeting Sita

Vibhishan burst into a lament. Rama comforted him and asked him to perform funeral rites of Ravana. Ravana's wives, led by Mandodari, ran to the battlefield and lamented. Vibhishan performed funeral rites of Ravana. Rama installed Vibhishan on the throne of Lanka and then sent a message to Sita through Hanuman. Hanuman delivered the message of Rama to Sita and then brought back her message to Rama. At the command of Rama, Vibhishan escorted Sita to Rama's presence. After listening to Rama's harsh words, Sita underwent 'Agni-Pariksha' and Agni restored her back to Rama. Rama accepted her.

Rama's return to Ayodhya

They all rested for the night and when the next day arrived[286], Vibhishan requested Rama to accept his hospitality, however, Rama expressed his desire to return to Ayodhya as soon as possible. Rama told Vibhishan of the long and arduous path taken by them to arrive at Lanka[287] and asked Vibhishan to explore ways for Rama to get back to Ayodhya by the fastest route.

Vibhishan assured Rama that Pushpak-Arial car, would indeed take them to Ayodhya within a course of a day[288]. Vibhishan had Pushpak ready and Rama/Laxman felt astonished to see the Pushpak[289]. Rama invited Vibhishan and Vanara leaders to accompany him to Ayodhya. They agreed, and when they all had taken their seats, Pushpak rose into the air[290]. Pushpak flew through the air while making big noise[291]. They stopped on the way at Kishkindha where key Vanara women also joined the party. Pushpak flew again and landed near the *ashram* of sage Bharadwaj, on Vaishakha Shuddha Panchami[6]. This day was 12 January 12208 BCE. Sage Bharadwaj told Rama to go to meet Bharata, the next day[292], i.e. on 13 January 12208 BCE.

Rama sent Hanuman to meet Bharata and to evaluate the situation. Hanuman met Guha and then Bharata, and informed them of the return of Rama. Hanuman told Bharata that Rama would meet him the next day, on the lunar day of Pushya[7, 8]. Bharata was overjoyed to hear the news and ordered to decorate the streets of Ayodhya before sunrise[293].

Rama arrived, via Pushpak, to Ayodhya (Nandigram), early next day[294]. Bharata rendered back the kingdom of Ayodhya to Rama and Rama was coroneted as a king[295].

Birth of Kusha & Lava

Rama returned to Ayodhya on Vaishakha Shuddha 6. The day was 13 January 12208 BCE. The Vanara leaders who had arrived with Rama to Ayodhya stayed in Ayodhya, enjoying royal dishes, roots and fruits. More than a month elapsed while they stayed[296]. This would mean they lived in Ayodhya at least until the end of Sharad season (end of Vaishakha).

Rama enjoyed their company and they (Vanara leaders) stayed further in Ayodhya. Valmiki Ramayana tells us that even two months of Shishir (winter) season were spent by them in Ayodhya[297]. This would mean that Vanara leaders stayed in Ayodhya through next two seasons- Hemant and Shishir, i.e. until the end of lunar month of Bhadrapada.

At this time, Rama gave permission to Vanara leaders to return to Kishkindha[298]. Rama also gave permission to Vibhishan to return to Lanka.

And when the winter had become a thing of the past[299] and the spring had arrived[300], Rama and Sita began enjoying in his Ashoka garden and this is the time when Rama noticed signs of Sita being pregnant[301]. This was sometime during the lunar months of Ashwin or

Kartika.

The above descriptions tell us that Rama and Sita were together from the lunar month of Vaishakha (second half of Sharad season). They lived in Ayodhya through seasons of Hemant (autumn), Shishir (winter) and Vasanta (spring). It was during the season of Vasanta that Rama noticed the signs of Sita being pregnant.

Valmiki Ramayana also tells us that it was the season of Varsha (rain) and nakshatra Shravana, when Lava and Kusha were born[306]. It also tells us that Shatrughna was present at the *ashram* of Valmiki, on his way to Mathura, when Lava and Kusha were born[305].

Rama told Shatrughna to wait in Ayodhya until the season of Grishma (summer) was over and then to kill Lavana when season of Varsha (rain) began[302]. We also know that Shatrughna spent only one month with Rama in Ayodhya, after Rama's instructions[302] and then left for Mathura[303]. This means Shatrughna lived in Ayodhya until the season of Grishma was over (14 September 12208 BCE), i.e. lunar month of Margashirsha/Pausha. This also means Lava and Kusha were born sometime during Lunar months of Pausha or Magha. Since they were born on nakshatra Shravana[306], we can estimate their plausible birth dates: 1 or 2 September 12208 BCE, 29 September 12208 BCE or 26 October 12208 BCE.

It may be possible to select more probable date for the birth of Kusha & Lava however it will require additional assumptions (beginning of rain with respect to the day of summer solstice in Ramayana times, definition of full term pregnancy, context in which mention of Shravana appears in the reference, etc.).

For example, if we assume beginning of rainy season some ~20 days ahead of the day of summer solstice (as is the case at present: Rain begins at the beginning of June in India), then 1 or 2 September 12208 BCE is more plausible date for the birth of Kush & Lava, since 14 September 12208 BCE was the day of summer solstice.

There is one additional reason why I have refrained from proposing one specific day for the birth of Kusha and Lava. This is due to the fact that reference to 'Shravana' could be simply referring to the position of the sun in nakshatra Shravana. The sun used to be in the area of nakshatra Shravana at the beginning of Varsha (rainy) season during Ramayana times (~12000 BCE). For additional explanation, please refer to my conjecture in <u>Error Elimination – experiment 68</u>, of next chapter on 'Conflicting Observations'. If valid, Kusha & Lava would be born during the ~15 day time interval at the beginning of rainy season, when the sun was in nakshatra Shravana (26 September – 10 October 12208 BCE).

Calculating backwards by ~ 9 months (32-40 weeks), we can estimate the timing of Rama-Sita conceiving Lava and Kusha, sometime during the lunar months of Vaishakha, Jyeshtha or Ashadha. All these lunar months are valid and plausible months as Rama and Sita were together and in Ayodhya during these lunar months.

Error Elimination – Experiment 64

Birth of Kusha & Lava during rainy night & Shravana Nakshatra[306]

तथ तस्य प्रहृष्टस्य शत्रुघ्नस्य महात्मन:

व्यतीता वार्षिकी रात्रि: श्रावणी लघुविक्रमा

Kusha and Lava were born during a rainy night on nakshatra Shravana[306]. They were born sometime during September-October 12208 BCE.

Rama-Katha *Gayana* by Lava & Kusha

Shatrughna killed Lavana and stayed in Madhupuri for 12 years (12208 BCE through 12196 BCE) [307]. After this he decided to visit Rama[308] and after seven days of journey, reached the *ashram* of Valmiki[309]. While Shatrughna was enjoying hospitality of Valmiki and after he had taken his meal and was resting, he heard the deeds of Rama, in a melodious form, accompanied with the sound of the musical instruments with proper beats[310].

Thus Valmiki composed Ramayana (Bala Kanda through Yuddha Kanda) by the year 12196 BCE.

17

CONFLICTING OBSERVATIONS

There is nothing more necessary to the man of science than its history and the logic of discovery... the way error is detected, the use of hypothesis, of imagination, the mode of testing.

- Lord Acton

Valmiki Ramayana text has few observations that are internally inconsistent, and this means a researcher of Ramayana must choose between these contradictory statements.

Valmiki Ramayana text has few other observations that may or may not be internally inconsistent, however, these observations, if accepted as is, definitely conflict with my proposed timeline of Ramayana.

One must address such conflicting observations, conflicting internally or otherwise, and I have addressed them without making such distinction.

Those researchers who employed inductive reasoning in determining the timing of Ramayana were still expected to analyze all the available evidence and 'justify' it, at a minimum, for their proposed timeline. The fact that these researchers have not done so tells us that even their claim of inductive reasoning, although faulty for any scientific investigation, is not valid. What they seem to have done is looked at few observations, selectively rather than randomly (both are erroneous and faulty approaches), which appear to corroborate, at least in their mind, their proposed timeline. These researchers have ignored other observations, which would have falsified their theory and their proposed timeline, instantaneously.

While I have commented above on the problem of inductive reasoning and the nonsense of selective (random or otherwise) observations in the context of Ramayana, my comments apply equally well, even more so, to the works of Mahabharata researchers.

The approach of analyzing observations, either selectively or randomly, employed by these researchers (with the exception of Dr. Vartak), to test against the predictions of a given theory are erroneous. While the approach of testing random observations deserves the blame of 'ignorance'; testing of selective observations is even worse. The latter approach deserves the blame not only of ignorance and of deliberate manipulation but also of non-scientific vices: inconsistency, contradictions and in some cases outright tautology. This much criticism would suffice for now. I will analyze and provide criticism for the work of individual researchers in the next few chapters.

We should also recognize that these issues are not limited to research of Ramayana and Mahabharata, but applies equally to researches of entire ancient Indian narratives.

Let's return to the parts of Ramayana story in order to understand the context of conflicting observations of Ramayana.

Ages of Rama & Sita at the Time of their Wedding

Sage Vishwamitra came to king Dasharatha, to ask for assistance of Rama when Rama turned 16 years old[22]. Rama, along with Laxman, traveled with Vishwamitra for next four days and then protected *Yajna* of sage Vishwamitra for six days. Sage Vishwamitra asked Rama & Laxman to accompany him to attend *Yajna* of king Janaka. They reached Mithila, capital of king Janaka, in few days. Rama broke the *Shiva-Dhanushya* the very next day, and in few days all four brothers, Rama, Laxman, Bharata and Shatrughna, were wedded to the daughters of king Janaka (& king Kushadhwaja). Rama and party returned to Ayodhya and they spent a time of up to one year, happily, in Ayodhya.

During their *Vanavas*, as soon as they left mount Chitrakuta, Rama, Laxman and Sita visited the *ashram* of sage Atri & his wife Anusuya. Sita mentioned to Anusuya that her father (King Janaka) felt anxiety and decided to marry Sita when she became of age suitable for union with her husband[312]. This essentially tells us that Sita was of almost the same age as that of Rama, since Rama himself was 16 years old when he married Sita.

Ages of Rama & Sita when they left for *Vanavas*

When Rama turned 17 years old[64], king Dasharatha decided to coronate Rama. Gorresio's text of Valmiki Ramayana refers to Rama being 18 years old[311]. This is the same time Rama, Laxman and Sita left for '*Vanavas*' for 14 years.

Duration of Sita's stay in Ayodhya before she left for Vanavas

Since Rama was 16 years old when he married and left for the forest (*Vanavas*) when he turned 17, Sita essentially lived in Ayodhya for a year. This is corroborated by an observation from Valmiki Ramayana[313].

Conflicting Observation # 1

Duration of Sita's stay in Ayodhya: One Year or 12 Years?

Against this evidence, Valmiki Ramayana has few references where Rama's (and that of Sita's) age is stated to be markedly different than stated above. For example, in her conversation with Ravana at Panchavati, before he took her away to Lanka, Sita tells Ravana that she lived in Ayodhya, after marrying Rama, for 12 years and then in 13th year, king Dasharatha decided to coronate Rama and it is at this time she left for the forest along with Rama & Laxamana[314].

Sita repeats the same theme, when talking to Hanuman in Lanka, of her living in Ayodhya for 12 years and then in 13th year, king Dasharatha decided to coronate Rama[316]. The specific verses are repeated, as if essentially borrowed (references 314 & 316).

Error Elimination – Experiment 65

Duration of Sita's stay in Ayodhya before she left for Vanavas

Valmiki Ramayana has references which state that Rama was 16 years old when sage Vishwamitra came to Ayodhya asking for Rama's assistance[22]. Sita is described as age when she could have physical and romantic relationship with Rama, before and at the time of her marriage to Rama[312]. Rama was 17/18 year old at the time of his scheduled coronation and this is when he left for the forest (*Vanavas*), along with Sita and Laxman [64, 311]. This makes it abundantly clear that

Sita lived in Ayodhya, after her wedding, for approximately one year before she left for the forest (*Vanavas*).

Against this evidence, references of Sita living in Ayodhya for 12 years[314, 316, 317] are indeed conflicting. To resolve this conflict, let's look at the exact words of these conflicting references:

From Aranya Kanda[314]:

उषित्वा द्वादश समा इक्ष्वाकूणां निवेशने

भुज्जाना मानुपान्भोगान्सर्वकामसमृद्धिनी

तत्र त्रयोदशे वर्षे राजाऽमन्त्रयत प्रभुः

अभिषेचयिन्तु रामं समेतो राजमन्त्रिभिः

And from Sundara Kanda [316, 317]:

समा द्वादश तत्राहं राघवस्य निवेशने

भुज्जाना मानुपान्भोगान्सर्वकामसमृद्धिनी

तत्रत्रयोदशे वर्षे राज्येनेक्ष्वाकुनन्दनं

अभिषेचयिन्तु राजा सोपाध्यायः प्रचक्रमे

Dr. P V Vartak has suggested that the original word 'masa' (months) must have been written as 'sama (years), essentially a transliteration error. I accept this suggestin of Dr. Vartak.

Of course once the errornerous word (sama) was interpreted as referring to 'years' instead of 'months' the second verse naturally referred to year 13 (more likely added in later editions) to make sense of the previous verse that mentioned 12 years. And what was erroneously transliterated in Aryanyakanda was essentially repeated in Sundarakanda.

Interestingly, while BORI critical edition (CE) refers to 12 years in SundarKanda[317], in its selection of verses in Aranyakanda[315], it only refers to one year! To make this point clear, I quote the orignal below:

AranyaKanda CE 45:4-5

संवत्सरं चाध्युषिता राघवस्य निवेशने

भूज्जाना मानुपान्भोगान्सर्वकामसमृद्धिनी

ततः संवत्सरादूर्ध्वं सममन्यत मे पतिं

अभिषेचयिन्तु रामं समेतो राजमन्त्रिभिः

Let us look at the works of other researchers to see how they have resolved these conflicting observations.

There are, to the best of my knowledge, four specific attempts, besides mine, to determine the timing of Ramayana: (1) Vartak, (2) SRS, (3) Pushkar Bhatnagar and (4) Yardi.

Pushkar Bhatnagar and SRS have accepted these references of Sita living in Ayodhya for 12 years (instead of ~ 12 months), however, they have not bothered to explain the conflict these references create for other references from Valmiki Ramayana [64, 311]. Yardi's work, while excellent in exploring cultural and sociological elements of Ramayana, is extremely naïve and superficial as it relates to determing the timing of Ramayana. Yardi has not considered even a single observation of astronomy (or chronology or seasons) evidence from Valimiki Ramayana in proposing his timeline. Yardi is thus saved from the trouble of dealing with conflicting observations. Ignorance is the bliss indeed!

Vartak suggested and accepted 'transliteration error' of 'masa' and 'sama' and thus his interpretation of the word is same as mine, i.e. as months (and not years), however, he has gone on another tangent in interpreting 'Dwadashah' to mean 20 and not 12 months! I will address this specific issue of 12 vs. 20 months when I analyze and provide criticism of Dr. Vartak's theory and proposal, in Chapter 18.

Conflicting Observation # 2

Ages of Rama and Sita when they left for Vanavas

In Aranyakanda[318]:

मम भर्ता महातेजा वयसा पंच विंशक:
अष्टा दश हि वर्षाणि मम जन्मनि गण्यते

Sita states that Rama was 25 years old and she was 18 years old, at the time of Rama's scheduled coronation and when they left for the forest (Vanavas) [318]. Corresponding reference from BORI critical edition states that Rama was 25 years old, however, is silent on the age of Sita[319].

In Aranya kanda (BORI CE) [319]:

मम भर्ता महातेजा वयसा पंचविंशक:
रामेति प्रथितो लोके गुणवान्सत्यवाक्षुचि:

विशालाक्षो महाबाहुः सर्वभूतहिते रतः

There is one more observation where Maricha states to Ravana[330]:

इति एवं उक्तो धर्मात्मा राजा दशरथः तदा

प्रत्युवाच महाभागं विश्वामित्रम महामुनिं

ऊन द्वादश वर्षो अयं अकृत अस्त्रः च राघवः

कामं तु मम यत सैन्यं मया सह गमिष्यति

BORI Critical edition version of this observation states Rama to be 16 year old (and not 12 year old)[331]:

इत्येवमुक्तो धर्मात्मा राजा दशरथस्तदा

प्रत्युवाच महाभागं विश्वामित्रं महामुनिं

ऊन षोडश वर्षोऽयमकृतास्त्रश्च राघवः

कामं तु मम यत्सैन्यं मया सह गमिष्यति

बधिष्यामि मुनिश्रेष्ठ शत्रुं तव यथेप्सितं

Error Elimination – Experiment 66

Ages of Rama and Sita when they left for *Vanavas*

I want readers to recollect the problem stated in Error Elimination – Experiment 65 and my solution to that problem. Once readers understand how 12 months turned into, erroneously, 12 years, we are ready to solve the problem of the age of Rama equal to 25 years and that of Sita equal to 18 years when they left for the forest (*Vanavas*).

Assuming Rama was 25 years and Sita was 18 years old at the time of Rama's scheduled coronation, that would mean Rama was 13 (25-12= 13) years old and Sita was 6 (18-12 = 6) years old at the time of their wedding. Such a conclusion is inconsistent with Valmiki Ramayana references of Rama being 16 year old at the time of Vishwamitra seeking his assistance[22], or Rama being 17/18 year old at the time of his scheduled coronation [64, 311]. Such conclusion is also inconsistent with Sita's statement that she was of age suitable for physical union with her husband, before and at the time of her wedding[312]. In addition, When Sita, along with her sisters (Urmila, Mandavi and Shrutakirti), reached

Ayodhya, after the wedding, all of these princesses, without exception, happily enjoyed life with their respective husbands in their private apartments[329]. This is also consistent with Sita and her sisters of being mature age.

GP commentator states that Marich has minimized the age of Rama to 12 to impress upon Ravana the extraordinary might of Rama even at that tender age. Deliberate attempt or not, Rama being 12 year old at the time of Vishwamitra's request for assistance is inconsistent with all other references we have analyzed.

I want to bring it to the attention of readers and Ramayana researchers, without suggesting any causality, that all references when Rama is described as very young (12 year old) at the time of Vishwamitra requesting his assistance, have Lanka connection. For example, first Marich told this to Ravana at the former's *ashrama*[330], then Sita told this to Ravana in Panchavati[318] and finally Sita told this to Hanuman at *Ashoka-vana* in Lanka [316, 317].

Pushkar Bhatnagar and SRS have accepted references of Sita living in Ayodhya for 12 years [314, 316] and Rama being 25 year old [318, 319] and Sita being 18 year old[318] at the time of Rama's scheduled coronation, however, they have not bothered to explain the contradiction it poses for other relevant references from Valmiki Ramayana [22, 64, 311].

Conflicting Observation # 3

Lunar months of Varsha season

On the Indian subcontinent, in our times, rainy season begins from the tail end of Grishma and lasts until early part of Sharad season, and up to the end of Sharad season, depending on the geographical location.

Valmiki Ramayana describes the rainy season of four months. Three references of Valmiki Ramayana allude to the beginning of rainy season on Shravana[320] and ending it on Kartika[321]. Rama asked Sugriva to enjoy the four months of rainy season in Kishkindha and in the company of his loved ones, and to begin search for Sita as soon as rainy season was over.

Rama and Laxman lived in the cave, outside Kishkindha, during this time. Rama describes heavy rainfall and its effects, and states that the then lunar month was that of Bhadrapada (Prosthapada) [322]. Rama also recounts how Bharata, his younger brother, would have taken vows for the rainy season, while staying outside Ayodhya at Nandigram, during Ashadha[323].

Let's build a picture of rainy season based on this information from Valmiki Ramayana. Interpreting these references at face value [320-323], we can say that lunar month of Shravana was the first month of rainy season and lunar month of Bhadrapada was the peak of rainy season, and that rainy season lasted from lunar month of Shravana through lunar month of Kartika.

In our times (2000 CE), rainy season begins in India during the lunar month of Jyeshtha and ends at the end of the lunar month of Bhadrapada.

A season would shift by approximately one lunar month every 2000 years due to the 'precession of equinoxes'. This means we must go backwards by 4000 years (~2000 BCE) in order to have a shift of 2 lunar months. Thus, instead of Jyeshtha-Bhadrapada (2000 CE), we would have had Shravana-Kartika (2000 BCE) as the four lunar months of rainy season.

These Valmiki Ramayana observations [320-323] conflict with the timing of Ramayana proposed by this author (12200 BCE), SRS (10500 BCE), Vartak (7300 BCE) and Bhatnagar (5100 BCE). I may mention that with the exception of Dr. Vartak, no other Ramayana researcher has understood the implications of 'precession of equinoxes' for their proposed timeline and its alignment with seasons, as described in Valmiki Ramayana.

Mr. Yardi remained blissfully unaware of the conflict posed by above Valmiki Ramayana observations of rainy season [320-323]. These observations do corroborate the timing of ~1500 BCE, proposed by Yardi. I may mention that this is the only set of observations, from Valmiki Ramayana, that corroborate timeline proposed by Yardi.

Error Elimination – Experiment 67

Lunar Months of Rainy Season

Whatever is the origin and logic of these [320-323] observations, the observations are in direct conflict with all other astronomical, chronological and seasonal observations of Valmiki Ramayana. I have shown that Ramayana was before Mahabharata, in chapter 3, and I have also shown that Mahabharata War happened in 5561 BCE, in my book on the dating of the Mahabharata War. Even more important is the lower limit of 4500 BCE (based on Arundhati-Vasistha observation of Mahabharata text) on the timing of Mahabharata War.

Therefore, if one insists on validating lunar months of Shravana through Kartika as the only time of rainy season during Ramayana, one is left with only other option of speculating that Ramayana occurred during the previous round of 'precession of equinoxes', i.e. during ~28000 BCE, when rainy season would have aligned with lunar months of Shravana through Kartika. Of course, number of observations discussed in *__Error Elimination Experiments 1 through 66__* would falsify any such timeline – 2000 BCE, 28000 BCE or any other timeline in antiquity that aligns rainy season with lunar months of Shravana through Kartika. In short, if taken at a face value, we have <u>an unsolvable problem</u>.

We have to look elsewhere for the answer.

Error Elimination – Experiment 68

Lunar Months of Rainy Season

It would be too easy and simplistic to make a case for 'interpolation' for these references [320-323] of Valmiki Ramayana. The problem with such approach is that one enters slippery slopes in a hurry (figuratively speaking) and it is impossible to come back. My approach in this case would be to make it clear to readers and researchers that these specific references [320-323] are not only incompatible with my proposed timeline, but also with rest of the evidence/observations of Valmiki Ramayana. I also want to make it clear that with the exception of timeline proposed by Yardi (1500 BCE), these observations are indeed incompatible with proposed timelines of SRS, Vartak and Bhatnagar.

However, before moving on to the next conflicting observation, I want to suggest a conjecture and leave it to the readers and future researchers to determine its plausibility.

In our times (2000 CE), the rainy season is described (in India) in the language of astronomy mile posts using two distinct methods. One method, already discussed, is to describe the rainy season using position of the full moon with respect to background nakshatras, i.e. lunar months. The other method is to describe the rainy season based on position(s) of the sun with respect to the background nakshatras.

For example, in Indian state of Maharashtra, the pre-monsoon rain is called 'मृगाचा पाऊस (Mrigacha Paus)'. This is because during this time (i.e. pre-monsoon) the sun is near nakshatra Mrigashirsha (मृगशीर्ष).

Local farmers (in konkan area of Maharashtra, India) very much talk of rain in this language of nakshatra of the sun. For example, these farmers wish to have little rain (i.e. not too much rain) when nakshatra is Ardra (nakshatra next to Mrigashirsha in sun's journey), while rain during nakshatra Hasta is considered auspicious for good harvest (corresponding to lunar month of Bhadrapada).

Before I make my conjecture, let me present the actual observations of rainy seasons from Valmiki Ramayana.:

Beginning of rainy season[320]:

पूर्वोऽयं वार्षिको मास: श्रावण: सलिलागम:
प्रवृत्ता: सौम्य चत्वारो मासा वार्षिकसंज्ञिता:

End of rainy season[321]:

कार्तिके समनुप्राप्ते त्वं रावणवधे यत
एष न: समय: सौम्य प्रविश त्वं स्वमालयं
अभिषिच्चस्व राज्ये च सुहृद: सम्प्रहर्षय

Peak of rainy season[322]:

मासि प्रौष्ठपदे ब्रम्ह ब्राम्हणानां विवक्षतां
अयमध्यायसमय: सामगानामुपस्थित:

I conjecture that the word 'masa' was used in the sense of duration (~30 days) and/or time, and words such as 'Shravana', 'Kartika' and 'Proshthpada' as referring to nakshatra of the sun for designating beginning, end and peak of rainy season, respectively, as is also done in our times. The remaining observation of Bharata making his vows on 'Ashadha' simply refers to nakshatara Ashadha (not unlike Nakshatra Mrigashirsha) as the time of pre-monsoon season.

If my conjecture is valid, not only it solves the unsolvable (no matter what) problem of incompatibility of these [320-323] obsevations with the rest of Ramayana observations, but also corrborate them well for my proposed timeline of late 13th Millennium BCE!

I want readers to recall that in 13th Millennium BCE, the point of summer solstice was near nakshatra Shravana, and counting four months, beginning with the day of summer solstice, the sun would have traveled from nakshatra Shravana[320] through nakshatras Purva & Uttara

Bhadrapada[322] and finally to the area of nakshatra Krittika[321], to mark the end of rainy season. Of couse during the time of pre-monsoon, the sun would have been in the region of nakshatras Purva & Uttara Ashadha[323].

This interpretation corroborates well with my proposed timeline. I should re-emphasize that the traditional interpretation of these Ramayana references of rainy season [320-323] not only conflicts with all existing proposals (except that of Mr. Yardi) but also conflicts with rest of the observations of Valmiki Ramayana.

There is additional evidence within ancient Indian literature in support of my conjecture (nakshatras as referring to the positions of the sun and not the moon, in describing rainy season), however elaboration of that evidence necessitates detailed exposition. I do intend to discuss this additional evidence in future editions of this book.

Conflicting Observation # 4

Ravana's limit of 12 Month for Sita to make up her mind

Ravana took away Sita from Panchavati (Nashik) sometime during the Vasanta (spring) season, and after reaching Lanka housed Sita comfortably in his palace. He gave instructions to those looking after her to provide anything she demanded.

Ravana coaxed Sita to become his wife in every possible way. When Sita did not yield, he ordered Rakshasa women to take Sita to *Ashokavana* and intimidate her. Ravana continued coaxing Sita but with no desired outcome. This is when he finally gave her ultimatum that he would give her a time limit of 12 months, and threatened to kill her at the end of this period if she did not yield to his wishes[326]. Again we do not have specific information to estimate when exactly Ravana gave this ultimatum to Sita.

The problems we have to solve are:

(1) When exactly Ravana gave this ultimatum of 12 months to Sita

(2) And if Ravana indeed followed up on his threat or not

(3) And if Rama could rescue Sita before the time limit of this ultimatum expired.

Error Elimination – Experiment 69

Ravana's limit of 12 Month for Sita to make up her mind

Even after threatening with ultimatum of 12 months, Ravana did not give up on alternate means of coaxing Sita for he instructed Rakshasa women looking after Sita to win over her confidence and also try to co-ax her by recourse to fearful threats but also coax her with soft language[327].

Later on, when Hanuman visited Lanka, Hanuman witnessed Ravana visiting Sita in *Ashoka-vana*, coaxing her to yield to his desires and when Sita did not respond, reminded her that time limit for his ultimatum of 12 months would expire in two months[328].

Hanuman was in Lanka on 27 August 12209 BCE and thus we can estimate the timing of Ravana declaring his ultimatum of 12 months, to be around September/October 12210 BCE. Let's see if this estimate appears feasible.

We know that Ravana-Khara fight near Panchavati occurred on 28 March 12210 BCE and first dual between Sugriva and Vali took place on 21 September 12210 BCE. We also have good evidence to assume the timing of Ravana taking away Sita, from Panchavati, was that of spring season. Spring equinox was on 17 June 12209 BCE, which also means Ravana took away Sita during May-July 12209 BCE. This also corroborates well with the rest of proposed timeline. This answers one of the three problems related to Ravana's ultimatum of 12 months.

It was not until 6 January 12208 BCE that Rama could rescue and free up Sita, per my proposed timeline. Per my proposal, additional 4-5 months (and not just two months[328]) expired, from the time Hanuman met Sita, before Rama could rescue Sita.

And thus answer is big 'NO' on both counts to second and third problems, i.e. Ravana did not follow up on his threat of killing Sita after the expiry of 12 month time limit and Rama did not rescue Sita before this so called time limit set by Ravana.

Let's look at what other researchers have to say about this problem. Dr. Vartak has analyzed this issue in detail and while his proposed timing (7300 BCE) and his proposed season for taking away of Sita (Hemant season as opposed to my proposal of Vasanta) are different than mine, in the end he has reached similar conclusions for problem #2 and #3, i.e. Ravana did not follow up on his threat and Rama did not rescue Sita before this so called limit set by Ravana. All remaining researchers – SRS,

Bhatnagar and Yardi have shown no awareness of this problem. Naturally they have said nothing related to this problem.

Conflicting Observation # 5

Interpretation of a passage from Kishkindha Kanda[124]

वयम अश्वायुजे मासि काल संख्या व्यवस्थिता:
प्रस्थिता: सो~पि चातीत: किमत: कार्यमुत्तरम

GP edition Interpretation:

Bound by a time limit we sallied forth in the month of Ashwin. That month too has passed. What should be done after this?

This interpretation of GP edition directly contradicts not only Valmiki Ramayana descriptions of four months of rainy season (Shravana through Kartika), but also contradicts entire Kishkindha kanda narration where it is clear that Rama, Laxman and Sugriva did not begin their search for Sita until the four months of rainy season were over [324, 325]. In fact some time had gone by, after four months of rainy season, when Vanara parties finally arrived in Kishkindha and search for Sita began in all directions.

Of course additional analysis and criticism of this GP edition interpretation is not possible since the interpreter has taken no firm position on the alignment of lunar months with that of rainy season for the timing of Ramayana.

Error Elimination – Experiment 70

Translation of a passage from Kishkindha Kanda[124]

Dr. Vartak has accepted this interpretation and translation of GP edition, i.e. "Vanara party had begun their search for Sita during the lunar month of Ashwin". This would mean Vanara party had begun their search, per proposal of Vartak - 7300 BCE, at the beginning of rainy season! This directly contradicts not only Vartak's own chronological narration but also the chronological narration of Valmiki Ramayana.

While Vartak recognized the problem of lunar month of Ashwin and problem of seasons as described in Valmiki Ramayana, other researchers – Bhatnagar, SRS and Yardi have shown complete lack of awareness of this problem posed by the chronological narrations of Valmiki Ramayana, for their own timelines.

My Interpretation:

वयम अश्वायुजे मासि काल संख्या व्यवस्थिता:

प्रस्थिता: सो~पि चातीत: किमत: कार्यमुत्तरम

Vayam –us, we; ashwayuje masi –Lunar month of Ashwin, kalasamkhya vyavasthitha – based on proper calculations of time, prasthitta – departed, departure, sipichatit – that, kimat – what, karaymuttarmam – next to do

By proper calculations from the time of our departure, now is the lunar month of Ashwin and even that month too has passed. What should we do now?

I have shown, in Chapter 13, how my interpretation is consistent not only with word to word translation of this passage but also with remaining chronological narratives (e.g. season of spring and long elapsing of time) of Valmiki Ramayana, and of course, my proposed timeline.

This observation poses problems for proposals of Vartak and Bhatnagar either per GP edition (and their own) interpretation or per my interpretation.

Conflicting Observation # 6

Exalted grahas at the time of Rama-Janma[18]

Bala Kanda of Valmiki Ramayana described the *Graha-sthithi (planetary positions)*, at the time of Rama's birth as follows:

ततो यज्ञे समाप्ते तु ऋतू नाम षट समत्ययु:

तत: च द्वादशे मासे चैत्रे नावमिके तिथौ

नक्षत्रे अदिती दैवत्ये स्व उच्छ संस्थेषु पंचसु

ग्रहेषु कर्कटे लग्ने वाक्पता इंदुना सह

Translation:

After completion of Yajna and when six seasons had elapsed, then in

the 12th month, i.e. during the lunar month of Chaitra, on the 9th day, on nakshatra Punarvasu (Nakshatra Devata-Aditi) and when five grahas were in exalted state, Rama was born. Jupiter and the moon were in some specific combination with nakshatra Pushya (or area of zodiac Cancer). Karka was ascendant.

The observation makes it clear that the lunar day (*Tithi*) was Chaitra Shuddha 9 and nakshatra Punarvasu. Jupiter was together with the moon, and since nakshatra was Punarvasu, it is reasonable to expect the moon near Gemini/Cancer. The five grahas were described as exalted, however, neither the details of specific five grahas mentioned nor the definition of their being exalted.

Various translators and researchers have interpreted this 'exalted nature of grahas' per astrology conventions in <u>our times</u>. According to this convention, combination such as **Sun in Aries, Mars in Capricorn, Jupiter in Cancer, Venus in Pisces and Saturn in Libra is considered an exalted combination.**

Let's see to what extent this evidence is corroborated by various proposals. Vartak, Bhatnagar, SRS and this author have proposed specific days for the birth of Rama. Yardi has proposed a broad timeline of~1500 BCE with no specific dates for incidents of Ramayana.

SRS Proposal:

SRS have proposed 17 January 10205 BCE as the day of Rama-Janma. SRS state that they calculated this date based on Vedanga Jyotisha.

Voyager simulation tells us that the day is off by six days if we have to match this day, per description of Valmiki Ramayana, for Chaitra Shuddha 9. We can make this correction of six days (only for the sake of comparison) and now the day of Rama-Janma, per SRS proposal, would be 11 January 10205 BCE.

On this day, the sun was at the border of Aries and Pisces, Mars was in Cancer, Jupiter was at the border of Gemini and Taurus, Venus was at the border of Aries and Pisces and finally Saturn was in Capricorn. Considering that the observations were made visually, the sun can be taken as exalted (near Aries) and Venus can also be taken as exalted (near Pisces). Thus out of five grahas, two can be shown to be exalted. In addition, Jupiter can be interpreted to be close to the moon.

It is not clear if SRS have recognized the problem of this observation for their timeline. All we can say is that the graha positions for the day of Rama-Janma, proposed by SRS, <u>do not</u> corroborate with Ramayana observation.

Vartak Proposal:

Vartak has proposed 4 December 7323 BCE as the day of Rama-Janma. Voyager simulation tells us that the day was <u>way off</u> from the day of Chaitra Shuddha 9.

First and foremost, there appears to be an error on the part of Dr. Vartak in calculating 4 December 7323 BCE as the day of Chaitra Shuddha 9. Voyager simulation shows this to be the lunar month of Magha, some two months away from the month of Chaitra.

After going through hoops and loops for a few days, I realized that Dr. Vartak has employed Gregorian calendar (and not Julian calendar) system as reference system for his work on Ramayana (on the other hand, he employed Julian calendar for his work on Mahabharata). The two systems would have a gap of ~ 58 days between them, for the time period of 7300 BCE, proposed timing for Ramayana by Dr. Vartak.

We will have to keep this in mind while analyzing proposal of Dr. Vartak. Researchers who may want to compare my work with that of Vartak's should also keep this fact in mind.

On 4 December 7323 BCE (per Gregorian calendar), the sun was on the border of Aries and Pisces (still in Pisces), Mars was in Taurus, Jupiter was in Gemini, Venus was in Taurus and Saturn was in Scorpius. While Dr. Vartak claims to have all five grahas exalted, per the definition of astrology, reality is that only one graha (the sun) can be considered exalted (after giving his timeline some benefit of doubt) for the day of 4 December 7323 BCE.

Our conclusion is that the planetary positions for the day of Rama-Janma, proposed by Dr. Vartak, <u>do not</u> corroborate with Ramayana observation.

Bhatnagar Proposal:

Bhatnagar has proposed 10 January 5114 BCE as the day of Rama-Janma. On this day the sun was on the border of Aquarius and Pisces – still in zone of Aquarius and thus nowhere close to Aries, Mars was at the border of Taurus and Aries – still in zone of Aries and thus nowhere close to Capricorn, Jupiter was in Leo, but closer to Virgo than Cancer and thus cannot be considered in Cancer, Venus was in Pisces and closer to Aquarius and indeed should be considered exalted, and Saturn was in Scorpius and close to zone of Libra (but not in Libra). Moon is only 7 day old as opposed to desired (9 days old).

The error in the position of the moon could be due to the lack of correction in 'Delta T' required, as one goes back in antiquity, but not employed by all astronomy simulation software. I also think that, possibly, the timing is off by one month, i.e. the day of Chaitra Shuddha 9 would have been on 9 February 5114 BCE, instead of 10 January 5114 BCE, as claimed by Pushkar Bhatnagar.

Voyager simulation tells us that this date is off by around a month. We can make this correction and now the day would be 9 February 5114 BCE.

Even per this modified timing (9 February 5114 BCE), the sun was in Pisces, Mars was in Taurus, Jupiter was in Leo, Venus was in Pisces and Saturn was in Scorpius and close to zone of Libra (but not in Libra).

We have to conclude that the planetary positions for the day of Rama-Janma, proposed by Pushkar Bhatnagar, do not corroborate with Ramayana observation.

Thus no existing proposal for the timing of Rama-Janma can be shown to corroborate Ramayana observation of 'exalted grahas'. We

My Proposal:

I have proposed day of 29 November 12240 BCE for the day of Rama-Janma. On this day, the sun was in Pisces, Mars was at the border of Pisces and Aquarius, Jupiter was in Sagittarius, Venus was in Capricorn and Saturn was in Sagittarius.

The planetary positions for the day of Rama-Janma, proposed by me, do not corroborate with this Ramayana observation.

It is critical that readers recognize one important difference. Dr. Vartak and Pushkar Bhatnagar have accepted modern definition/interpretation for 'exalted combination of grahas' and they failed to corroborate it (in spite of their claims to contrary) for their proposed timing of Rama-Janma. I have neither accepted nor rejected modern definition/interpretation of 'exalted planetary combination'.

Thus no existing proposal for the timing of Rama-Janma can be shown to corroborate Ramayana observation of 'exalted grahas'. We are left with the following choices: (1) Propose another day for the Rama's birth (and that also means, another set of dates for remaining incidents of Ramayana), (2) Suggest/search for alternate definition/interpretation for 'exalted planetary combination' or (3) Accept that this specific Ramayana observation cannot be corroborated (not unlike Ramayana observations of rainy season).

Error Elimination – Experiment 71

Exalted grahas at the time of Rama-Janma[18]

I had to make corrections, before testing, to original proposed dates of all researchers (SRS, Vartak and Bhatnagar). While confusion with proposal of Dr. Vartak was due to the fact he employed Gregorian calendar in his calculations, corrections required for the proposal of Bhatnagar (even to test on his terms!) were more likely due to inferior quality of astronomy software he employed. I could not make any meaningful comments for the presence of errors in calculations of SRS.

I encourage able astronomers to check and re-check my calculations for all proposed dates (SRS, Vartak, Bhatnagar and mine).

I have proposed my alternate explanation for 'exalted state of grahas' in Chapter 8 (Error elimination-experiment 8).

Where to search for the combination of Exalted Grahas

Valmiki has only referred to five grahas and them being in exalted state/positions. He has not stated the definition of 'exalted' or for that matter which five grahas he was referring to. Even then, there may be some researchers (and readers) who may feel strong conviction about this observation. I would encourage them to search for such combination(s) within the Epoch of Ramayana (10,000 BCE – 17500 BCE). Of course they may, out of curiosity, want to explore other time intervals, e.g. around 5114 BCE, 7300 BCE, 1500 BCE and so on. The point is that they must back their conviction by action otherwise it is only an empty conviction.

I emphasize this point because I do come across many Indians who mean well and are sincere, who would ask me to test one thing or the other, as if they are providing me great help, while forgetting that the work of this kind demands actions (not just empty suggestions or mouse clicking in front of the computer and/or punching few keys on a Smartphone) and that research of ancient Indian history is not a spectator's sport.

18

THEORY & PROPOSAL OF P V VARTAK

Of course, the individual scientist may wish to establish his theory rather than to refute it. However, if he does not himself examine his favorite theory critically, others will do so for him. The only results which will be regarded by them as supporting the theory will be the failures of interesting attempts to refute it – failures to find counter-examples where such counter-examples would be most expected in the light of the best of the competing theories.

- Karl Popper

'Vastav Ramayana' of Dr. P V Vartak, written in 1978 CE, is a classic. It is been translated in English as 'A Realistic Approach to the Valmiki Ramayana'. His book covers multiple aspects of Ramayana, however, my focus, in this chapter, is on the analysis and criticism of Vartak's proposal for the timing of Ramayana.

I have said what I wanted to say about Dr. Vartak and his research, in my previous book. Dr. Vartak's proposed timeline, for the Mahabharata War, fell within the Epoch of Arundhati, and I began to test his timeline to either validate or falsify his proposal. While I could show that a better timeline can be proposed for the pre-war (and post-war) incidents of Mahabharata, his 18 day timeline of the Mahabharata War stood the test of rigorous testing involving more than 200 astronomy observations. And while I did revise the date for the Bhishma Nirvana - passing away of Bhishma, it was Dr. Vartak who had meticulously collected relevant astronomy and chronological references from the text of Mahabharata, which in turn allowed me to eliminate remaining errors.

In case of Ramayana, the timeline I have proposed (12200 BCE) is separated by some 5000 years from the timeline proposed (7300 BCE) by Dr. Vartak. I would not have dared to attempt researching on the timing of Ramayana, in the absence of his research, and in the absence of the awareness of his methodology. I should also mention that at least on two occasions, during his research, as documented in his book, he came close to proposing a time interval that I have established in Chapter 6 of this book. I have read his 'Vastav Ramayana' multiple times over the last decade.

With that preamble, let's begin with his theory.

Theory of Dr. P V Vartak

His theory, as far as the theory of visual observations of the sky is concerned, is same as that of my theory (see Chapter 2). However, he has invoked other theories (e.g. astrological *Dristhi* of a specific graha on specific Nakshatra). I have limited myself to the theory of 'visual observations' of the sky.

Dr. Vartak has employed descriptions of seasons not only in his work on the timing of Ramayana but also on the timing of Mahabharata, as clues, in determining the timing of many instances within these epics. My usage of the technique to gain insights from descriptions of seasons, rains, eclipses and analogies of such, is inspired by his work.

Dr. Vartak and I agree on the timing of 18 days of the Mahabharata War: 16 October – 2 November 5561 BCE and thus we agree on the lower bound for the timing of Ramayana, i.e. Ramayana occurred sometime before 5561 BCE.

I encourage all readers to read his (original 'Vastav Ramayana' in Marathi or its translation) to understand intricacies of his arguments and to comprehend his approach to his proposed timeline of Ramayana.

Do keep in mind that while Dr. Vartak has used the Julian calendar while proposing the timing of Mahabharata War, he has employed the Gregorian calendar, as reference calendar, when proposing the timing of Ramayana.

This is especially critical to keep in mind if you are curious and enthusiastic enough to test alternate proposals of researchers. By the way, this is the only way to become familiar with a specific proposal and able to determine a better proposal from multiple available efforts.

Many western researchers are perplexed by the ability of Indian researchers to propose specific days for the specific instances of ancient events (e.g. Ramayana or Mahabharata). While the ability of Indian researchers is to be appreciated, such marvels had been possible because of (1) Luni-solar Indian calendar, (2) Meticulous and accurate astronomy observations going back for more than 25000 years, and (3) creative means (allegory, methphor) employed by ancient Indian sages to document these observations via composition of Samhitas and conducting of *Yajna* and other rituals.

Indian Lunar Months & Precession of Equinoxes

Dr. Vartak has defined 7300 BCE as the approximate time interval of Ramayana. Let's us understand the correlation between Indian lunar months and corresponding seasons for 7300 BCE.

In 7300 BCE, the point of summer solstice was between nakshatras Chitra and Vishakha, the point of fall equinox was near nakshatra Shravana, the point of winter solstice was near nakshatra Ashwini and the point of spring equinox was near nakshatra Pushya. Speaking in the language of Indian lunar months, this meant, peak of winter occurred during the lunar months of Chaitra/Vaishakha, middle of spring (Vasanta) occurred during the month of Shravana, season of Varsha (rain) began during the month of Ashwin and middle of Sharad season occurred during the month of Pausha.

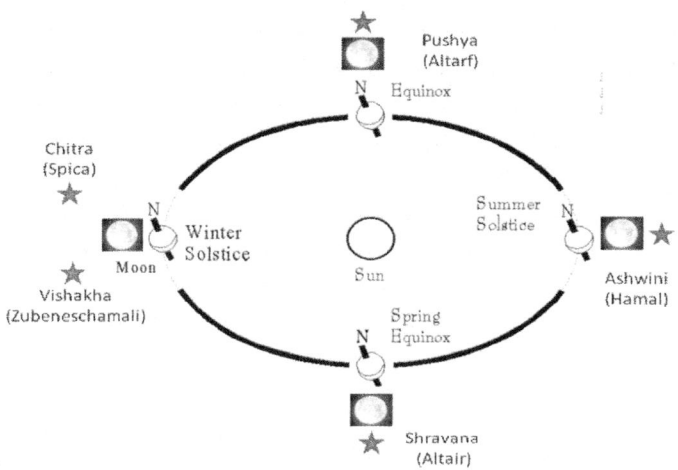

Rama- Janma & Rama's scheduled Coronation

The time of Rama Janma[18] and his coronation 17 years after his birth[2] occurred on Chaitra Shuddha 9 and the time was that of forests full of blossom[2], peacocks dancing in the rain[9] and the time of Sharad season [10-14, 21].

Against these descriptions of Valmiki Ramayana, consider dates for Rama Janma (4 December 7323 BCE) or for scheduled coronation of Rama (29 November 7306 BCE), proposed by Dr. Vartak.

On 4 December 7323 BCE, the sun is 11 days away from the day of winter solstice and thus it is the end of Hemant season. On 29 November 7306 BCE, the moon is 11 days old and near Magha. We will apply correction of few days to 26 November 7306 BCE when the moon is eight days old and near nakshatra Punarvasu. On this day, the sun is 20 days away from the day of winter solstice and thus it is the end of Hemant season.

Dr. Vartak indeed recognized that the lunar month of Chaitra, for his proposed time period of 7300 BCE, coincided with the beginning of (and thus peak of) winter. However he is mute on its lack of corroboration with Valmiki Ramayana descriptions when forests are full of blossom[2] or peacocks dancing in the rain[9] or this being the time of Sharad season [10-14, 21]. Dr. Vartak's proposed timing of Chaitra (peak of winter) does not corroborate, and rather contradicts, Valmiki Ramayana descriptions of the lunar month of Chaitra.

Valmiki Ramayana states that five grahas were exalted at the time of Rama Janma. It does not say what the 'exalted' meant and thus is open to interpretation. Dr. P V Vartak and Shri Bhatnagar have interpreted this to mean five grahas – Sun in Aries, Mars in Capricorn, Jupiter in Cancer, Venus in Pisces and Saturn in Libra. I have already covered my criticism of claims of Dr. Vartak regarding corroboration (or lack thereof) of his proposed day of Rama-Janma and observation of 'exalted grahas' of Ramayana.

Rama's Coronation: Positions of Sun, Mars & Rahu

Valmiki Ramayana observation is as follows[15]:

अवष्टब्धं च मे राम नक्षत्रं दारूणग्रहैः
आवेदयन्ति दैवज्ञाः सूर्यानअंगारकराहु भि

Dr. Vartak proposed 29 November 7306 BCE as the day of scheduled coronation of Rama. We will have to make small correction (even to test the proposal on his terms!) for 'Delta T" error to modify this date to 26/27 November 7306 BCE.

Dr. Vartak has interpreted this observation to mean that the sun, Mars and Rahu (node of the moon) were together. Difference of 2-3 days (26 or 29 November) will not make a difference for positions of Sun, Mars or Rahu. Voyager simulation shows that the sun and the node of moon were together and their position was between nakshatras Uttara Bhadrapada and Revati. On the other hand, Mars was near nakshatra *Mrigashirsha* and thus does not corroborate with this observation. Vartak calculated position of Rahu near nakshatra Vishakha and position of Mars near nakshatra Dhanistha. One of the nodes of moon was indeed at Chitra and thus near Vishakha (remember, node of the moon is not a point but rather, justifiably so, area of the sky at any given time). We have already seen that another node was between Uttara Bhadrapada and Revati and thus easily corroborates this observation of the sun and Rahu being together.

Vartak has invoked the theory of astrological *Drishthti* to explain why Rahu and Mars were also together with the sun on this day. Problem of astrological Drishthi is that once one begins, there is no stopping, and anything anywhere can be explained.

Dr. Vartak has mentioned one more interesting observation related to coronation of Rama. As they are ready to leave for the forest, Sita tells Rama[21]: (Ayodhya GP 26:9, CE 23:8)

अद्य बार्हस्पत: श्रीमान्युक्त: पुष्यो न राघव
प्रोच्यते ब्राह्मणै: प्राज्ञै: केन त्वमसि दुर्मना:

Sita refers to this day of scheduled coronation of Rama as an auspicious day when propitious Pushya day (nakshatra Pushya) has come along with day of Brihaspati. Since nakshatra Devata of Pushya is Brihaspati, Sita might be simply referring to this connection. We can see many instance of this in Valmiki Ramayana (e.g. nakshatra Vishakha being referred to along with additional attribute/adjective of nakshatra of Indra & Agni). In any case Vartak has conjectured this mention of Brihaspati as referring to 'Thursday' (day of Brihaspati) and thus Guru-Pushya yoga.

27 November 7306 BCE was Thursday and nakshatra was Pushya. I

have interpreted and corroborated this observation in Error Elimination – Experiments 6-8. While interpretation of Vartak regarding day of scheduled coronation of Rama being 'Brihaspati-day' (Thursday) and nakshatra Pushya may be open to interpretation, all I want to state is that my proposed day for scheduled coronation of Rama 20 December 12222 BCE was also Thursday.

Day of *Vanavas-Gaman*: Planetary positions

Dr. Vartak proposed 29 November (adjusted 27 November) 7306 BCE for the day of Rama's *Vanavas-gaman*. Valmiki Ramayana describes the scene in the sky[339]. The description is extremely generic, however Vartak has done impressive job of interpreting it.

Trishanku (Crux), Mars, Jupiter, Mercury along with Vishakha cornered the Moon.

The moon was near Pushya (26/27 November) and can be visualized being cornered by setting Mars or rising Jupiter and also by nakshatra Vishakha. Mercury was visible in the morning sky (not when the moon was in the sky) and thus my conjecture is that Valmiki has simply mentioned some of the visible grahas of that time. Saturn was also in the sky, next to the moon, however, since it is not mentioned, we will not say anything about it.

Sage Vishwamitra arrives in Ayodhya

All four princes- Rama, Laxman, Bharata & Shatrughna were studying various disciplines and soon they became experts. When they were enriched with wisdom and adorned with virtues, modesty, knowledge and far-sightedness[333], king Dasharatha deliberated with his family priests and relatives about the marriage of the princes[334]. When king Dasharatha was discussing this very subject, great sage Vishwamitra arrived at his palace[335].

I have conjectured this time to be that of Rama (and his brothers) completing 16 years and thus the time of Chaitra Shuddha 9. Dasharatha does mention Rama to be of merely 16 years old in his conversation with sage Vishwamitra[22]. I have shown corroboration of Valmiki Ramayana observations (chronological and astronomical) of Rama's leaving with sage Vishwamitra from Ayodhya, leading to the day of Rama's wedding in Mithila.

It is then interesting that Dr. Vartak conjectured the timing of Vishwamitra's arrival to be that of Vasanta/Grishma. Vartak offers two points in support of his conjecture:

(1) When Tataka arrived to attack Rama, plentiful dust rose in the air (or she raised plentiful dust) and she perplexed both princes, Rama and Laxman, with a huge cloud of dust for sometime[336]. Vartak combines this description with the fact that Tataka-vana was a dense forest with trees[337].

(2) *Vartak asserts that Yajna* usually took place during Vasanta (spring season) [338].

Dr. Vartak's observations [336, 337] would form a good corroborative evidence for his conjecture (season of spring/summer) if he could have established his conjecture with other independent evidence. Otherwise, these Valmiki Ramayana observations[336, 337] are no evidence for timing of Spring/Summer. It would equally apply to most of the year, with the exception of the time of heavy rain. His second point that *Yajna*s usually took place during Vasanta (spring) season is also problematic. The specific reference of Valmiki Ramayana he quotes simply states that when another season of Vasanta (spring) begun, king Dasharatha felt an urge to do *Yajna*. While it is reasonable to expect that *Yajna*s occurred throughout the year, in the absence of specific evidence, I have shown how the timing of *Yajna*s, at least their ending occurred in Sharad season (Error Elimination – Experiments, 12, 16 and 17)

Duration of Sita's stay in Ayodhya

I have dealt with the issue of duration of Sita's stay in Ayodhya, i.e. whether she stayed for one year of 12 years, in Chapter 17 – Conflicting Observations.

Dr. Vartak has shown why Sita's stay in Ayodhya for one year makes sense and why the argument for Sita's stay in Ayodhya for 12 years leads to contradictions. I agree with Dr. Vartak that Sita stayed in Ayodhya, before leaving to the forest, for one year. I have also shown that a time interval from 4/5 January 12223 BCE (Rama-Sita wedding) and 20/21 December 12223 BCE (Rama-Sita leaving for the forest) had 12 full moons. Thus Sita did live in Ayodhya for a year, after her wedding, before leaving for the forest.

On the other hand, Dr. Vartak has proposed 7 April 7307 BCE as the day of Rama-Sita wedding and 29 November 7306 BCE as the day of leaving for the forest. This adds up to a time interval of ~20 months. To corroborate this time interval of 20 months, instead of 12 months, Vartak has interpreted 'Dwa-dasha' as referring to 2 x 10 = 20, as opposed to 12.

Interestingly corresponding references from BORI Critical editon[315], also found in Gorresio's edition[313], do not employ the word 'Dwa-dasha' at all.

संवत्सरं चाध्युषिता राघवस्य निवेशने

भुञ्जाना मानुषान्भोगान्सर्वकामसमृद्धिनी

तत: संवत्सरादूर्ध्वं सममन्यत मे पतिं

अभिषेचयिन्तु रामं समेतो राजमन्त्रिभि:

And thus while interpretation of 'Dwa-dasha' equal to 12 or 20 may be debated, word 'Samvatsar' definitely means ~12 months and thus this observation would contradict Vartak's proposal of Sita living in Ayodhya for 20 months. I should also mention that during his conversations with Ravana, Maricha also uses the word 'Dwa-dasha'[330], this time describing age of Rama, albeit deliberately underestimated, and the appropriate interpretation of the word would be 12 (years), and not 20 (years) as suggested by Dr. Vartak's interpretation. I encourage readers and other researchers to identify other instances of 'Dwa-dasha' from Valmiki Ramayana.

Still the question as to why Vartak selected the timing of 10 March 7307 BCE, for sage Vishwamitra visiting king Dasharatha, remains unanswered. In addition, this assumption of his has neither removed any conflicting issues in the timeline of Ramayana, nor has it led to growth of knowledge, of Ramayana, in any way.

Day of Rama-Sita Wedding

If Rama was born on 4 December 7323 BCE and if sage Vishwamitra came to king Dasharatha on 10 March 7307 BCE, then Dasharatha's statement that Rama was merely 16 years old (or to be very specific as pointed out by Vartak – 15.75 years old) should have been rather merely 15 years old (or to be specific 15:25 years old). This makes Rama ~15.5 years old at the time of his wedding (7 April 7307 BCE).

Hanuman meets Sita in Lanka

Hanuman met Sita in Lanka and based on chronological narrative of Valmiki Ramayana, it was the time of late Vasanta/Grishma. Dr. Vartak proposed 1 September 7292 BCE when Hanuman entered Lanka, 2 September when Hanuman met Sita, and 3 September when Hanuman returned from Lanka. Let's test his proposed timeline. We may have to shift the date by one day each to correct for error of 'Delta T'. The timeline will shift to 31st August - 2nd September 7292 BCE. 1st September 7292 BCE was indeed a full moon day and day of lunar eclipse and eclipse was visible throughout the night.

The sun was 15 days away from point of fall equinox. That makes this full moon day middle of the first month of Sharad season. Even if we allow for descriptions of Vasanta(spring) season as proxy for descriptions of Sharad (pre-autumn) season, as indeed there are many similarities between the two seasons (Sharad and Vasanta), the proposed timeline of Vartak completely contradicts chronological narrative of Valmiki Ramayana. According to Valmiki Ramayana, Vanara parties had not even arrived in Kishkindha when four months of rainy season, which included two month of Sharad season, had elapsed. Vanara parties arrived in Kishkindha after this time and then they left in search of Sita.

While other parties returned to Kishkindha, the southern search party continued their search, in spite of realizing that they had missed the one month deadline set by Sugriva. They were searching for Sita, from the beginning of Hemant (autumn) season and through Shishir (winter) season, until middle of Vasanta (spring) season. Hanuman went to Lanka at the end of Vasanta (spring) season and more likely during Grishma (summer).

Ravana's limit of 12 Months for Sita to make up her mind

Even after threatening with ultimatum of 12 months, Ravana did not give up other means of coaxing Sita for he instructed Rakshasa women looking after Sita to win over her confidence and also try to coax her by recourse to fearful threats but also with soft words[327].

Later on when Hanuman visited Lanka, he witnessed Ravana visiting Sita in Ashoka-vana, coaxing her to yield to his desires and when Sita did not respond, reminded her that time limit for his ultimatum of 12 months would expire in 2 months[328].

1st September 7292 BCE, proposed day of Hanuman meeting Sita in

Lanka, per Dr. Vartak, was the middle of the first month of Sharad season. This is the time Sita tells Hanuman that she has 2 months left from the total time limit of 12 months set by Ravana. If we go backwards by 10 months (12-2), we arrive at the Hemant season of the previous year. Dr. Vartak has conjectured that Ravana took away Sita during the season of Hemant. His timeline then corroborates at least this one chronological detail of Valmiki Ramayana, i.e. abduction of Sita by Ravana. I should emphasize that the corroboration is only internally consistent with Dr.Vartak's own proposed timeline. Dr. Vartak's proposal of Hanumn in Lanka during the Sharad season contradicts numerous observations of Valmiki Ramayana. His proposed timeline does contradict rest of astronomy, chronology and seasonal evidence of Valmiki Ramayana.

Dr. Vartak reached conclusions similar to that of mine regarding Ravana's threat to kill Sita at the end of 12 month duration set by him, i.e. Ravana did not follow up on his threat and Rama did not rescue Sita before this so called limit set by Ravana.

To be factually correct, I should say that my conclusion for the above two aspects related to Ravana's time limit of 12 months agrees with that of Dr. Vartak's, since it was Dr. Vartak who did his work many years before my work.

Hanuman's Return from Lanka

Dr. Vartak proposed 3 September 7292 BCE for the day of Hanuman returning from Lanka. Valmiki Ramayana observations of the sky describe area from nakshatra Punarvasu through nakshatra Shravana. Voyager simulation shows a wonderful view of the sky at 6 AM. Nakshatra Punarvasu is on the western horizon and area of nakshatra Shravana (except *Yogatara* of Shravana, which was still below the eastern horizon) was visible. Mars was in the sky near nakshatra Jyeshtha. Vartak has described position of Mars closer to nakshatra Pushya. Vartak has interpreted the word 'Mahagraha' to mean 'crocodile'. Jupiter is below the eastern horizon. Venus and Saturn are up in the eastern sky and visible before the sunrise. Since we can talk only of those observations mentioned, we can say that the sky view corroborates well with the description of Ramayana.

I want to emphasize that asking questions of the kind - "If Saturn and Venus were also visible in the sky, how come they are not mentioned"- are relevant however they do not have impact on corroboration of a prediction with the available evidence. This is because all we can talk of is what is mentioned.

Ramayana description of the sky during Hanuman's return from Lanka does corroborate with the timing proposed by Dr. Vartak.

Day of Rama's return to Ayodhya from Lanka

Dr. Vartak proposed 6 December 7292 BCE for the day of Rama's return, from Lanka, to Ayodhya. Since he identified it with Chaitra Shuddha 6, we will make small correction of 2 days, due to 'Delta T' error' and the adjusted day would be 4 December 7292 BCE.

The nakshatras on 6 December or 4 December were Shravana and Uttara Ashadha, respectively. This is nowhere close to nakshatra Pushya as described in Valmiki Ramayana. Dr. Vartak did recognize this error. In fact it was him who identified this observation of 'Pushya' related to return of Rama, form Lanka, to Ayodhya.

Dr. Vartak did not adjust his corresponding timeline for *Ravanavadha* or for arrival of Rama in Ayodhya, even though he acknowledged the required correction of one lunar month related to timing of *Ravanavadha* and return of Rama to Ayodhya.

We will adjust this date for his timeline: The new date, corresponding to Vaishakha Shuddha 6, would be 19 December 7292 BCE.

I want to emphasize that I am adjusting these dates as if he would have (or should have) done it. Adjustment of dates simply allows us to test his proposal better. The bigger conclusion that his timeline is off by some 5000 years (12000 BCE vs. 7000 BCE) is still valid.

Timeline of the War

Since we adjusted the timing of Rama'a arrival in Ayodhya (from Lanka) and since Rama killed Ravana on *Amawasya* day and left immediately for Ayodhya, we would also have to adjust Vartak's proposed timeline for the War. His proposed timeline runs from 3 November through 15 November 7292 BCE. The adjusted timeline would run from, with reference to *Amawasya* day closest to 19 December 7292 BCE and going backwards, 1 December through 13 December 7292 BCE.

This would still be a wrong date for Ramayana by ~5000 years. All I did is tried to match the time of the lunar month, per his suggestion and also per the relevant observations of Valmiki Ramayana. The point being, Dr. Vartak himself would have made these corrections. These are local corrections of few days, and they do not change the bigger conclusion, i.e. disagreement between my proposal of 12200 BCE and Dr. Vartak's proposal of 7300 BCE.

Ravana-vadha: Mercury attacking Rohini

Valmiki Ramayana describes day of Ravana-vadha, when Mercury could be seen attacking Rohini. On 13 December 7292 BCE, the sun was near Ashwini, Mercury was west of the sun and thus this adjusted date for the last day of the War (and of Ravana-vadha) does not corroborate observation of Valmiki Ramayana.

Dr. Vartak's original date for last day of War – 15 November 7292 BCE, also, does not corroborate this observation of Valmiki Ramayana. On 15 November, the sun was near nakshatra Uttara Bhadrapada and Mercury was between nakshatras Shatabhishaj and Purva Bhadrapada, and thus was nowhere close to nakshatra Rohini.

Setting Sun near Pushya, during season of Hemanta[3]

Ramayana text refers to the setting of the Sun near Nakshatra Pushya (Aranya Kanda), during the season of Hemant (autumn).

निवृत्ताकाशशयनाः पुष्यनिता हिमारुणाः
शीता वृद्धतरायामास्त्रियामा यान्ति साम्प्रतम

This observation is capable of pinpointing a broad time interval of 11500 BCE – 17500 BCE, which interestingly enough, coincides with the conclusion drawn from Ramayana observation for month of Chaitra and it coinciding with season of flowers.

Since the observation of the sun setting near nakshatra Pushya, during the season of Hemant, is a visual observation, one may make a case for extending this period further. One may assert that nakshatra Pushya would have been visible at the western horizon, immediately after the setting of the Sun. While determining specific amount of separation between the sun and nakshatra Pushya could be anyone's guess, what we can comfortably state is that the separation of nakshatra Pushya from the position of the setting sun (during season of Hemet) does not need to be more than 30 degrees, i.e. nakshatra Pushya east of the setting sun by 30 degrees. This assumption would bring the time of this observation to as late as 11500 BCE.

Dr Vartak did interpret, at least initially, correctly and thus estimated a time period around 13160 BCE. However, another observation, and its erroneous interpretation, led Vartak to discard above estimate of ~13000 BCE for the timing of Ramayana.

Potential positions of Nakshatra Pushya(☆) with respect to Sun's position
Season of Hemanta (Autumn)

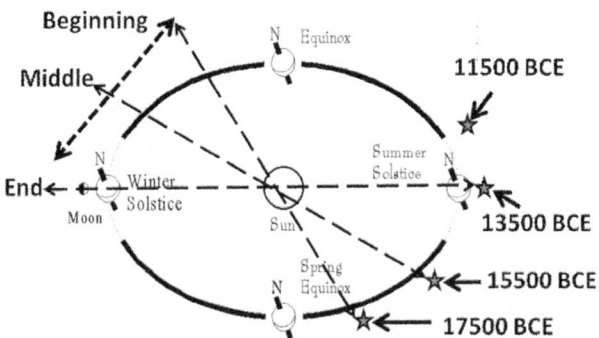

This other observation [4,130] was the mention of Star Abhijit (Vega). After meeting Sampati, Valmiki Ramayana tells us that Vanara party began their search further south with the assistance of star Abhijit as guide (Error Elimination- Experiment 52). We have seen that Abhijit was the North Pole star during 10,000 BCE-14,000 BCE (Error Elimination – Experiment 3).

Vartak argued that Abhijit was described as 'shining brightly' in the Valmiki Ramayana[130] and thus position of Abhijit cannot be close to the point of celestial North Pole. This was a grave error on the part of Dr. Vartak.

Nakshatra Abhijit can be near the point of North Celestial Pole and also 'shine brightly'. In fact, the position of Abhijit near the point of Celestial North Pole, makes it accessible, as reference for determining directions and thus during travel, throughout the year.

Instead of straightforward interpretation of Pushya[3] but also of Abhijit [4,130], Vartak made an erroneous conjecture, convenient to his timeline, namely that Laxman observed nakshatra Pushya right over his head, when the sun was setting on the western horizon. This shifted the position of Pushya by 90^0 instantaneously! Only problem is that, such an interpretation is not only wrong, but also any attempt such as this, brings the entire discipline of Archeo-astronomy into troubled waters. In an instance, Vartak shifted the timing for the interpretation of this observation[3] by ~6000 years!

This was one of the two instances of how Vartak had reached a plausible time interval of Ramayana (13000 BCE), but decided in favor of another time interval (7300 BCE), driven by other considerations.

Shravana *Ganana* of Vishwamitra

Dr. Vartak quotes two references from the Mahabharata. One of these two references state that ancient to the times of Mahabharata, a Shravana (nakshatra) based calendar existed, i.e. Shravana was considered the first nakshatra. The reference also states that this system of 'Shravana-*ganana* was initiated by sage Vishwamitra[340]. The second reference refers to 'Shravana' as the first Naksahtra[341] (GP version) or 'Shravishtha –Dhanishtha' as the first Nakshatra[342] (CE version).

Let's begin with the 'Shravishtha-Dhanishtha' version of second reference. I have shown in Chapter 5 of my book – When did the Mahabharata War Happen? : The Mystery of Arundhati', how and why Dhanishtha (Shravistha) became the first nakshatra. The timing of this incident was around 14602 BCE.

Approximately 1000 years after the above incident (after 14602 BCE), the point of summer solstice moved to nakshatra Shravana and the timing of this incident was 13268 BCE. My conjecture is that this is the time of sage Vishwamitra who demanded the correction required, i.e. to change the status of Shravana as the first nakshatra, instead of Dhanishtha.

This conjecture of mine not only explains the meaning of **prati-srushti** created by sage Vishwamitra with Shravana-*Ganana*, but also determines the timing of sage Vishwamitra, and possibly that of king Trishanku[340].

Vartak interpreted these references [340, 341], in the context of his proposed timing of 7300 BCE (for Ramayana) by stating that sage Vishwamitra initiated counting of nakshatras from the beginning of fall equinox, instead of existing method of their counting from the beginning of spring equinox. Vartak could assign the time for this correction, based on his interpretation, to ~7500 BCE (7849 BCE).

To do this, however, he was forced to interpret the beginning of Nakshatra-*ganana* with two different cardinal points. Vartak had assumed the point of winter solstice as the first point of Nakshatra *ganana*, in defining the broader timeline of Ramayana. However, with this reference of 'Shravana' [340, 341], and his related explanation of *'prati-srushti'* of sage Vishwamitra, Dr. Vartak was forced to assume the beginning of Nakshatra –ganana, based on the point of spring equinox.

Dr. Vartak recognized and acknowledged this contradiction.   Dr. Vartak explained the reason for this contradictory choice by stating that, had he not assumed 'spring equinox' as the first point – in his explanation of **Prati-srushti**, Vishwamitra and Nakshatra Shravana reference from Mahabharata; his proposed time, per his explanation – with assuming winter solstice as the first point- would have led him to time period of 14000 BCE!

Although Dr. Vartak reached this conclusion – plausible time of Ramayana near 14000 BCE- in a tortuous fashion and in combination with numerous conjectures for which he could not provide independent evidence (e.g. Vishwamitra's Prati-srushti meant Vishwamitra initiating Nakshatra-*Ganana* from 180^0 opposite cardinal point), this was the second instance where he proposed a time period that would have matched with my proposed time interval.

There is no rationale whatsoever for this twisting and turning of Dr. Vartak. I have already explained (Chapter 5 of the book –When did the Mahabharata War Happen?) why Dhanishtha was assigned the first Nakshatra status in 14602 BCE.

Let's roll forward another 1000 years and the time had arrived to assign first status to Nakshatra Shravana (13268 BCE). This was the time of sage Vishwamitra who assisted king Trishanku[340]. By 12000 BCE, and thus by the time of Ramayana (12200 BCE) the point of summer solstice was near nakshatra Uttara Ashadha. May be that is the reason why Bharata would take his vows for the four months of rainy season on nakshatra Ashadha[323], first nakshatra of his time!

Four months of Rainy Season

In India, the time of summer solstice coincides with the beginning of rainy season (monsoon). The rainy season began with the lunar month of *Magha* for my proposed timeline of Ramayana (12200 BCE). The rainy season began with the lunar month of Ashwin for timeline of Ramayana (7300 BCE) proposed by Dr. Vartak. Valmiki Ramayana refers to Shravana as the first month of rainy season[320].

We have already seen that if we accept Valmiki Ramayana statement of the beginning of rainy season, specifically its identification with the lunar month of Shravana, then the logical inference is that Ramayana happened either in 2000 BCE, 28000 BCE or in further antiquity separated by ~26000 years (orbital period of precession of equinoxes). We have seen why 2000 BCE does not make sense and anyone making such a claim has onus to corroborate numerous astronomy, chronology and seasonal observations of Valmiki Ramayana.

Dr. Vartak conjectured this reference of Shravana to be the first month of rainy season, or Kartika to be the last month of rainy season, as interpolation in later times, possibly around 2000 BCE. Interpolation or not, I have shown that these Ramayana references of rainy season contradict numerous internal references from Valmiki Ramayana. I have also suggested an alternate solution.

Let's get back to the proposal of Dr. Vartak. Let's see how the first month of the rainy season for his timeline, i.e. lunar month of Ashwin, contradicts not only his own proposed timeline but also numerous observations of Valmiki Ramayana.

Valmiki Ramayana states that Rama waited on the outskirts of Kishkindha for the four months of rainy season [324, 325]. This would mean Rama waited until the end of lunar month of Pausha, after which he sent Laxman to Sugriva. Eventually Vanara parties arrived in Kishkindha and then left in search of Sita in all directions, with an assigned time limit of one month. This would mean Sugriva had given them a time limit of at least up to the end of lunar month of Magha, and more likely until middle or end of lunar month of Phalgun. However, Valmiki Ramayana has numerous references of the southern Vanara party worried that the timeline set by Sugriva had expired. On the other hand, per Dr. Vartak's proposal, Hanuman was already in Lanka, on the full moon day of Pausha! This contradicts numerous observations of Kishkindha kanda but also of rest of Valmiki Ramayana.

The season, per proposal of Dr. Vartak, based on the position of the sun, would be the early part of Sharad season! This also contradicts with observations of Valmiki Ramayana.

Dr. Vartak suggested a possible correction to such a bizarre scenario by stating that Rama may not have waited until the end of rainy season, but only until the end of the first month of Sharad (end of the third month of rainy season). This does not solve the problem either because this modification, assuming acceptable, still does not explain either south Vanara party complaining of missing Sugriva's deadline or Hanuman in Lanka on the full moon day of Pausha!

Dr. Vartak missed the descriptions of changing seasons as southern Vanara party searched for Sita. This led him to propose a compact timeline for the events of Vali-vadha through Hanuman in Lanka. This in turn led to contradiction of his timeline with observations of Valmiki Ramayana.

Interpretation of a passage from Kishkindha Kanda[124]

वयम अश्वायुजे मासि काल संख्या व्यवस्थिताः
प्रस्थिताः सो~पि चातीतः किमतः कार्यमुत्तरम

GP edition Interpretation:

Bound by a time limit we sallied forth in the month of Ashwin. That month too has passed. What should be done after this?

This interpretation of GP edition directly contradicts not only Valmiki Ramayana descriptions of the four months of rainy season (Shravana through Kartika), but also contradicts entire Kishkindha kanda narration where it is clear that Rama, Laxman and Sugriva did not begin their search for Sita until the four months of rainy season were over [324, 325]. In fact some time had gone by, after four months of rainy season, when Vanara parties finally arrived in Kishkindha and search for Sita began in all directions.

Dr. Vartak has accepted interpretation and translation of GP edition, i.e. "Vanara party had begun their search for Sita during the lunar month of Ashwin". This would mean the Vanara parties had begun their search, per proposal of Vartak - 7300 BCE, at the beginning of rainy season! This directly contradicts not only Vartak's own chronological narrative and but also chronological narrative of Valmiki Ramayana.

In addition, irrespective of the interpretation and significance of the lunar month of Ashwin, Ramayana descriptions of the arrival of Vasanta (spring) season while the southern Vanara party was still searching for Sita, tells us that they were searching for Sita through the seasons of Hemant (autumn), Shishir(winter) and Vasanta (spring). These descriptions are consistent with their nagging worry which was repeated numerous times that the time limit set by Sugriva had expired long ago. Vanara party was searching for Sita even through the season of Vasanta (spring) and only towards the end of Vasanta (spring) season Hanuman was in Lanka. This is consistent with descriptions of Vasanta (spring) season when Hanuman was in Lanka.

On the other hand, per timeline proposed by Dr. Vartak, Hanuman had found Sita before the four months of rainy season were over.

Conclusion

We have seen that Ramayana observations employed by Dr. Vartak in developing his proposal for the Ramayana era <u>do not</u> corroborate his proposed timeline, even according to his own interpretation (e.g. definition of exalted state of grahas).

Dr. Vartak's proposal is internally (and only internally) consistent on <u>only</u> two points:

(1) Timing of abduction of Sita and corresponding conversation between Hanuman and Sita (in Lanka)
(2) Duration of Sita's stay in Ayodhya.

In addition, he methodically eliminated the confusion related to the age of Rama (and Sita) at the time of Rama's scheduled coronation. He also undertook a tedious task of collecting observations, of astronomy and of seasons, from Valmiki Ramayana and made an attempt to test as many of these observations as he could.

Valmiki Ramayana references of astronomy, seasons and chronological observations, not employed by Dr. Vartak, decisively falsify his proposed timeline. Additional references, interpreted erroneously (lunar month of Chaitra, sun setting on Pushya during the season of Hemant) by Dr. Vartak, when interpreted in a consistent fashion, decisively place a lower limit of ~11,000 BCE on the timing of Ramayana – some 4000 years earlier than the timing proposed by Dr. Vartak.

Final Remarks

I was fortunate in that I studied works of many great scientists – Kepler, Galileo, Fresnel, Newton, Einstein, Bohr, Wigner and many more. I also read their biographies. I was fortunate to study works of Karl Popper, Vinoba Bhave and Joseph Campbell. I am also fortunate that I studied works of Dr. Vartak. And by luck, I could make small contributions of my own – to the timing of Mahabharata War, two years ago, and to the timing of Ramayana, in this book.

Research conducted by Dr. Vartak, specifically as it relates to antiquity of Indian civilization, is of high quality. Rarely I come across works of this quality in my readings of antiquity of ancient civilizations, be it through the research in areas of astronomy, archeology, genetics or anthropology. He is 80 years old and continues to research in numerous areas while revising his existing works, in the light of newfound information.

In his book on the dating of Mahabharata – 'Swayambhu', he had attempted testing astronomy observation of Arundhati and Vasistha[126] in multiple ways. He was not happy with the outcome and suggested astronomy community (as early as 1971 CE) to test that observation.

I became aware of AV (Arundhati-Vasistha) observation in 1995 CE, began testing in 1997 CE, persevered for 12+ years, and by luck, succeeded in solving the problem of AV observation during the summer of 2009 CE. This work of mine became the precursor for my previous book on Mahabharata War.

In his book on dating of Ramayana - 'Vastav Ramayana', Dr. Vartak had provided three such clues for the benefit of future researchers:

(1) One observation[1] from Valmiki Ramayana, interpretation of which would lead to a plausible time of one million years in antiquity for the timing of Ramayana.

(2) One observation of a comet that was afflicting nakshatra Moola, when Rama was ready for his march to Lanka, from Kishkindha. Dr. Vartak could not corroborate this observation, however, recognized the plausible but immense value of this observation and thus requested astronomy experts to research this observation[5]. I did test this observation and readers know the outcome.

(3) Dr. Vartak recognized the contradiction in his interpretation of the rationale for designating first Nakshatra, based on observation from Taittiriya Samhita vs. based on observation(s) from Mahabharata [340-342]. Dr. Vartak interpreted first observation (Taittiriya Samhita) by assuming winter solstice as the point of first nakshatra while he interpreted his second observation (Mahabharata) by assuming spring equinox as the point of first nakshatra. He recognized the contradiction and stated his rationale in making this second choice (in case of dating of Ramayana) since he could not find other relevant evidence to go back as far as 14000 BCE as the time of Ramayana. He suggested researchers to study this time interval and to check if relevant evidence can be obtained.

I have explained my methodology and how testing of specific observations from Valmiki Ramayana led me to a broad interval of 10,000 BCE -17,500 BCE, for the plausible timing of Ramayana. Vartak had come close to predicting a timeline identical to my propsed timeline, while interpreting another observation[3] from Valmiki Ramayana.

Once I defined this broad time interval of 7500 years for the plausible timing of Ramayana millennium, and after making numerous failed attempts to narrow down my search to a specific millennium (or century), I made a bold and desperate move to take help of 'comet' observation[5] from Valmiki Ramayana. I ran cumbersome simulation for months, in search of this comet, and by luck, could able to define 13th Millennium BCE as the millennium of Ramayana. My Mahabharata research went on for 12+ years and was benefited by work of Dr. Vartak. My Ramayana research took more than five years. My Ramayana research has benefited from the work of Dr. Vartak's work and also from my past experience of researching Mahabharata.

Readers of my Mahabharata book often wonder what kept me going for 12+ years in search of an 'impossible' explanation for AV observation. My answer is that it was the faith in the words of Vyasa. In case of Ramayana, my answer is that it was the faith in the words of Valmiki. On the other hand, it was the faith in the works and methodology of Dr. Vartak that attracted me to Archeo-astronomy.

I digressed, but the point I want to make about Dr. Vartak is that, he remains scientific and methodical in his work. His approach is deductive and only ventures into 'inductive' speculation when all other efforts do not lead to any progress or to a corroboration of his theory. Whenever he ventures into inductive logic, he recognizes its limitations and clearly states them. He encourages other researchers to analyze and test his theories and proposals.

I summarize his research philosophy, as I understand it, in words of Albrecht Durer:

But I shall let the little I have learnt go forth into the day in order that someone better than I may guess the truth, and in his work may prove and rebuke my error. At this I shall rejoice that I was yet a cause whereby such truth has come to light.

19

THEORY & PRPOSAL OF PUSHKAR BHATNAGAR

If we are uncritical we shall always find what we want: we shall look for, and find, confirmations, and we shall look away from, and not see, whatever might be dangerous to our pet theories.

- Karl Popper

Late Shri Pushkar Bhatnagar proposed timing for various incidents in Rama's life. He summarized his findings in a book 'Dating the Era of Lord Rama'.

Recently Saroj Bala, along with Kulbhushan Mishra, published a book 'Historicity of Vedic and Ramayana Eras: Scientific Evidences from the Depths of Oceans to the Heights of Skies'. In it, Saroj Bala and coauthor argue for the timing of Ramayana, as proposed by Pushkhar Bhatnagar. I will limit my comments to work of Pushkar Bhatnagar however my criticism would equally apply to Saroj Bala's acceptance of Bhatnagar's Ramayana timeline.

Bhatnagar has certainly put a lot of efforts and we must appreciate his efforts. Unfortunately his Ramayana investigation is naïve and innocent. The approach is, unfortunately, very much inductive (सूतावरून स्वर्ग), as opposed to deductive (युक्तिवाद). I would encourage all to read his book and then compare it's methodology with my work.

The fact that his proposal is inaccurate/wrong/erroneous on multiple grounds should not be seen as its biggest drawback. After all, many great minds have been wrong. Rather the biggest problem of his approach is the use of wrong methodology. It is difficult to say whether his use of software or his manual calculations deceived him. It is hard for us to figure out the reasons for the confidence he felt in his findings, in spite of the fact that what he is claiming to be the planetary situation, for a given instance of Ramayana, is far from the truth, as can be verified by anyone using decent astronomy software.

Of course the problem is intrinsic to the methodology of inductive reasoning. Inductive reasoning, by nature, gets into verbose argumentation, since its main feature is that of justification. As the evidence, to be explained for a given incident/phenomena, piles up; inductive reasoning becomes more inconsistent, more contradictory and tautological. This is the reason why inductive approach is that of presenting selective evidence that appears to prop up a given theory or proposal. The very approach is unscientific.

Theory of Pushkar Bhatnagar

While he never clearly states his theory, it appears to be similar to my theory, i.e. astronomy observations of Ramayana. On the other hand his background assumptions are different (e.g. the timing of Mahabharata War). It is not clear if he accepted timeline of Mahabharata War around ~3000 BCE, only because it was convenient for his proposed timeline of Ramayana. Accepting (even insisting) that Mahabharata War occurred after 5000 BCE is a necessity for his proposal since accepting my timeline of Mahabharata War (5561 BCE) automatically falsifies his proposal for the timing of Ramayana.

Indian Lunar Months & Precession of Equinoxes

We may want to refer to Chapters 4/5 of this book. This will allow us to understand why Shri Pushkar Bhatnagar's proposal falls short of corroborating any observations of Valmiki Ramayana.

He claims to have understood the phenomenon of 'Precession of Equinoxes'. Unfortunately, his comprehension of the phenomenon of 'Precession of Equinoxes' is a mixed baggage, and in the final analysis a disaster for his research.

He certainly understood the loose correspondence between Indian lunar months (e.g. Chaitra, Vaishakha, Jyeshtha, etc.) and the months of Gregorian/Julian Calendar. Thus he states, correctly, that while the lunar month of Chaitra coincides with March-April in our times (2000 CE), in 5000 BCE (some 7000 years ago) the lunar month of Chaitra coincided with December/January.

This approximate shift of 3 months is due to two reasons. First, it is purely due to the phenomenon of 'precession of equinoxes' which would shift 'median lunar *Tithi*' by one day every 71 years. Thus for 7000 years, we should observe a shift of 7000/71 ~ 100 days. The second reason for this shift is due to the slight difference in length of time between Julian and Gregorian calendars.

Important point for our analysis of Shri Bhatnagar's research is that, while he understood this shift for correspondence between Indian lunar months and months of Julian/Gregorian calendar, he <u>completely missed</u> the implication of 'precession of equinoxes' for the shift in season for a given lunar month. A season would shift by one lunar month approximately every 2000 years due to the 'precession of equinoxes'.

No wonder Shri Bhatnagar is assuming lunar month of Chaitra to be that of spring (Vasanta), even in 5000 BCE, while the reality is that lunar month of Chaitra coincided with the peak of winter (interphase of Hemant and Shishir seasons) during 5000 BCE. During the period of 5000 BCE, lunar months coincided with six seasons as follows:

Chaitra-Vaishakha	Shishir (winter)
Jyeshtha –Ashadha	Vasanta (spring)
Shravana-Bhadrapada	Grishma (summer)
Ashwin-Kartika	Varsha (rain)
Margashirsha –Pausha	Sharad (pre-Autumn)
Magha-Phalgun	Hemant (autumn)

I have shown that in year 5561 BCE, time of the Mahabharata War, the point of summer solstice coincided with nakshatra Hasta (one nakshatra before Chitra), which also meant lunar month of Chaitra was the beginning of winter season (Shishir). In another 500 years (~5000 BCE), the point of summer solstice would have moved by only 7-8 degrees and thus the month of Chaitra would still be the first month of winter season.

Let's keep this correlation in mind as we analyze proposal of Shri Bhatnagar.

Rama- Janma & Rama's scheduled Coronation

The time of Rama Janma[18] and his coronation 17 years after his birth[2] occurred on Chaitra Shuddha 9 and the time was that of forests full of blossom[2], peacocks dancing in the rain[9] and the time of Sharad season [10-14, 21].

Against this descriptions of Valmiki Ramayana, consider dates for Rama Janma (10 January 5114 BCE) or for the scheduled coronation of Rama (4/5 January 5089 BCE), proposed by Shri Bhatnagar.

On 10 January 5114 BCE, the sun was 16 degrees away from the point of winter solstice (i.e. winter solstice would occur 16 days after this day) and on 4/5 January 5089 BCE, the sun was 21 degrees away from the point of winter solstice (i.e. winter solstice would occur 21 days after this day). Therefore Valmiki Ramayana observations of season, at the time of Rama-Janma, do not corroborate with the proposed timing of Bhatnagar.

We have already seen, in Chapter 17, how astronomy observations of five grahas in exalted state, at the time of Rama-Janma, per very definition accepted by Shri Bhatnagar, do not corroborate with proposed timing of Shri Bhatnagar.

Age of Rama at the time of leaving for *Vanavas* (Exile)

Shri Bhatnagar has claimed Rama's age to be equal to 25 and Sita's age equal to 18 at the time of Rama's scheduled coronation and subsequent leaving for the *Vanavas*. He has also claimed that Sita lived in Ayodhya, after her marriage to Rama, for 12 years before leaving for the Vanavas. I have already shown how such a claim leads to numerous contradictions. I have dealt with this issue in my chapter on Conflicting observations (Error Elimination – Experiments 65 & 66) and I won't repeat the explanation here. On the other hand, Shri Bhatnagar has not bothered to explain related and conflicting observations.

Rama's Coronation: Positions of Sun, Mars & Rahu

Valmiki Ramayana observation is as follows[15]:

अवष्टब्धं च मे राम नक्षत्रं दारूणग्रहैः
आवेदयन्ति दैवज्ञाः सूर्यानअंगारकराहु भि

Shri Bhatnagar has interpreted this to mean that the sun, Mars and Rahu (node of the moon) were together (within one nakshatra space). On 5 January 5089 BCE, the sun was between nakshatras Shatabhishaj and Purva Bhadrapada. Rahu is rather a region in the space and not point and the position of this node was at nakshatra Shatabhishaj. Thus the sun and Rahu can be considered together. On the other hand, Mars is between nakshatras Hasta and Uttara Phalguni and thus nowhere close to the sun and/or Rahu. Thus this Ramayana observation does not corroborate with proposal of Shri Bhatnagar.

I have interpreted and corroborated this observation in Error Elimination – Experiments 6-8.

Time of Khara-Rama fight

Shri Bhatnagar proposed that Khara-Rama fight took place sometime after the first month of Hemant (autumn) season and before the beginning of Vasanta (spring) season and that there was a solar eclipse on this day.

Shri Bhatnagar proposed 7 October 5077 BCE as the day of Khara-Rama fight. Let's test this prediction. There was no solar eclipse on 7 October 5077 BCE. However, I realized that most of the proposed dates by Shri Bhatnagar are off by ~ 2 days, and I conjectured that this could be due to inability of astronomy software, used by him, to take into account 'Delta T' correction. We would compensate for this correction (so as to enable further testing and criticism of his theory and proposal) and now we do have a solar eclipse, albeit in the morning and not in the afternoon/evening as claimed by Shri Bhatnagar (and required per evidence of Valmiki Ramayana) on 5 October 5077 BCE. Mars was also in the middle of the sky, at least in the morning when the solar eclipse began. We should keep in mind that it is not easy to predict exact timing (or angle) of an eclipse, thousands of years into antiquity.

We would have accepted this evidence as rather good corroboration of this Ramayana incident. Unfortunately, the sun was 24 days away from the point of fall equinox and that meant this was the beginning of Sharad (pre-autumn) season and not the end of Hemant season as demanded and claimed by evidence of Valmiki Ramayana and also by Shri Bhatnagar.

I have summarized and corroborated observations related to Khara-Rama fight in Error Elimination – Experiments 23-28.

Vali-vadha

Shri Bhatnagar proposed that Rama killed Vali, during the second

194

dual between Vali and Sugriva, at the beginning of the rainy season and that there was a solar eclipse, during morning, on that day.

Shri Bhatnagar proposed 3 April 5077 BCE as the day of *Vali-vadha*. Let's test this prediction. There was no solar eclipse on 3 April 5077 BCE. However if we test it in the vicinity of 3 April, we find that there was indeed a solar eclipse on 11 April 5077 BCE. This gap of 8 days cannot be explained by lack of 'Delta T' correction alone. This probably points to the faulty astronomy software he might have employed. In any case, we will test it for 11 April 5077 BCE, since at least there was a solar eclipse on this day, and it appears to have begun in the morning.

We would have accepted this evidence, albeit with little hesitation, as corroboration of *Vali-vadha*, for date proposed by Shri Bhatnagar.

Wait a minute. You guessed it! Unfortunately, the sun was 19 days away from the point of spring equinox and that meant it was the beginning of Vasanta (spring) season and not the beginning of the rainy season as required per evidence of Valmiki Ramayana (and per claim of Shri Bhatnagar).

I have summarized and corroborated observations related to Vali-vadha in Error Elimination – Experiments 34-39.

Hanuman meets Sita in Lanka

Shri Pushkar Bhatnagar proposed that Hanuman met Sita, in Lanka, sometime during the lunar months of Kartika/Margashirsha and on the full moon day.

Shri Bhatnagar asserts this to be the time of late Sharad/early Hemant and that there was a lunar eclipse on this day. This assertion of Bhatnagar directly contradicts with the evidence of Ramayana. Valmiki Ramayana describes the timing of Hanuman visiting Lanka (and meeting Sita) to be that of the spring season.

Valmiki Ramayana does provide numerous analogies of 'full moon becoming free from Rahu' in this context and thus if one can confirm a lunar eclipse for one's proposed timeline of Hanuman meeting Sita, it would be a wonderful corroboration. However, absence of a lunar eclipse, for a given proposal, is not a falsification of that proposal, as long as other conditions are corroborated. This is a subtle but very critical distinction and I want readers to understand it in full before proceeding further.

Shri Bhatnagar proposed 12 September 5076 BCE as the day when Hanuman met Sita in Lanka. Let's test his prediction. 12 September

5076 BCE was not a full moon day. We can check in the vicinity and find that 9 September was indeed a full moon day. It appears that there was a lunar eclipse. However, the lunar eclipse occurred and was over before the moonrise in Lanka and thus was not visible to anyone in Lanka. We may still give a benefit of doubt (to Bhatngar proposal) and accept this as at least a weak corroboration, only for the aspect of 'lunar eclipse' reference of Ramayana

The problem with this proposed timing is that the day was 39 days after the day of summer solstice and thus at the peak of rainy season. Thus the time proposed by Shri Bhatnagar agrees neither with the season of Vasanta (spring) per descriptions of Valmiki Ramayana nor with the season of late Sharad/early Hemant, albeit erroneous, as proposed by Shri Bhatnagar.

I have summarized and corroborated observations related to Hanuman meeting Sita in Lanka, in Error Elimination – Experiments 53-57.

Hanuman's Return from Lanka

Shri Bhatnagar proposed that Hanuman left from Lanka on 14 September 5076 BCE, two days after he met Sita, and that Hanuman left from Lanka during the early morning.

First, we will have to adjust proposed date of Shri Bhatnagar, for Hanuman meeting Sita, from 12 September to 9 September, to match the day of full moon and 14 September in order for the position of moon to be close to nakshatra Punarvasu.

I want readers to understand that we are trying our best to make proposals of Shri Bhatnagar as valid as we can. In other words, we are trying our best to give his proposal a benefit of doubt, as much as we can. This would make stay of Hanuman in Lanka for up to five days, which is closer to my conjecture (based on Valmiki Ramayana references) than 'two days' of Shri Bhatnagar. If we assume 11 September (2 days after the full moon day, as proposed by Shri Bhatnagar) instead of 14 September, no significant difference occurs in the sky view, except that in case of 11 September, other nakshatras such as Krittika and Rohini also become visible.

Valmiki Ramayana describes the view of the sky, as Hanuman left Lanka to cross the ocean, in a poetic manner. The portion of the sky from nakshatra Punarvasu through nakshatra Shravana is described.

Shri Bhatnagar states, correctly, that this entire portion of the sky cannot be visible at any given time and thus conjectured that this also alludes to the traveling time of Hanuman while crossing the ocean. This is very logical and should be considered as his original contribution to Ramayana research.

Shri Bhatnagar summarizes Valmiki Ramayana description:

The Moon was like lotus while Sun appeared like a crane. In the sky, Pushya and Shravana Nakshatras were seen like swans. Punarvasu appeared like a big fish. Mars and the large graha (Jupiter), the elephant of Indra – Airavata, Island and the Swati Nakshatra were seen to be moving like a Swan.

On 14 September 5076 BCE, the phase of the moon is that of four days after the full moon day and the position of the moon is near naskshatra Punarvasu. This corroborates well with the descriptions of the sky. On the other hand, since the sun is near nakshatra Vishakha, only naskshatras Punarvasu through Swati would be visible. The portion of the sky from nakshatra Swati through nakshatra Shravana, as described in Valmiki Ramayana, would not be visible at all due to the glare of the sun. Of course, once we realize that this is a poetic description, we can conjecture that Valmiki would have imagined half of the visible (potentially visible) sky beginning with nakshatra Punarvasu and up to the region of nakshatra Shravana. While this could be true, we must recognize that Mars and Jupiter, per summary of Shri Bhatnagar, are simply nowhere to be found in the sky. Mars and Jupiter are near nakshatra Jyeshtha and thus would not have been visible at all in the morning, since the sun was near nakshatra Vishakha and would be on the horizon, long before Mars and Jupiter came up on the horizon.

I have already commented (Hanuman meets Sita in Lanka) on the mismatch between season of Valmiki Ramayana (spring) with actual season for the proposal of Shri Bhatnagar (rainy), but not recognized to be so by him, since he is thiking this time to be that of Sharad/Hemant.

While timing proposed by Shri Bhatnagar does not corroborate with the sky view of Valmiki Ramayana at the time of Hanuman's return from Lanka, Shri Bhatnagar translation did provide me with a surprising gift.

In Error Elimination-Experiment 58, I wrote:

Two other grahas, not mentioned by Valmiki, Venus and Jupiter are also visible. Of course we can talk of only those things that are mentioned. Even then I wondered why Valmiki may not have mentioned Venus and Jupiter in his descriptions of the sky. I noticed in Voyager simulation that Jupiter was in perfect or near perfect conjunction with Star Magha (Regulus) and this could explain why mention of Jupiter might have been missed. Of course this remains my pure speculation. No logical reason for non-mention of Venus can be suggested.

I had accepted the translation of GP edition. Vartak had also translated 'Mahagraha' to mean crocodile. Both meanings of Mahagraha (Crocodile or great graha) are valid. The recognition of Jupiter by Shri Bhatnagar makes my corroboration even stronger. Let's recall that Jupiter was in close conjunction with nakshatra Magha, and in the sky and visible, for my proposed timing of Hanuman returning from Lanka.

Hanuman meets Rama

Shri Bhatnagar proposed that Rama left from Kishkindha, along with Vanara-army on 19 September 5076 BCE. This would mean Bhatnagar is claiming that southern Vanara search party, along with Hanuman, traveled the distance from southern shore (Rameshwaram) to Kishkindha (Hampi/Bellary in Karnataka) in less than 5 days!

While it is true that Valmiki Ramayana talks of flying ability among Vanara, not all Vanara could fly. In addition, there is no mention of Vanara party returning to Kishkindha flying. In fact there are descriptions of them taking rest on the way and spending time at Sugriva's garden where they feasted on honey and became inebriated. Besides, Shri Bhatnagar is not accepting existence of flying Pushpak, so it is reasonable to assume that he is not accepting flying Vanara. I leave it to readers to figure out if it is possible for Vanara party to walk a distance from Rameshwaram to Hampi/Bellary in 5 days. As a reference, I may mention that current distance via national/state highways, using the shortest route, is over 900 kilometers, which would mean ~200 kilometers of walking per day!

Kishkindha to Lanka – Astronomy observations

Shri Bhatnagar has not provided specific duration for Rama's journey from Kishkindha to Lanka and thus we cannot analyze or provide criticism for this portion of his Ramayana proposal.

Taking this as a broad time period of 19 September through 21 November 5076 BCE, let's see to what extent we can corroborate timeline proposed by Shri Bhatnagar. Shri Bhatnagar summarizes Valmiki Ramayana description:

Venus has gone on the back side, Saptarshi are visible brightly and they are moving around the pole star. Trishanku – our ancestor (Trishanku refers to the constellation CRUX) is brightly visible in the front. The Moola Nakshatra, which protects the Rakshasa, is being inflicted with Dhumra-Ketu (node).

The correct translation of 'Dhuma-Ketu' is 'Comet' and not 'node' as claimed by Shri Bhatnagar. Let's test this description for the proposed timing of Shri Bhatnagar. Venus could be seen during this period in the morning while star Trishanku could not have been seen until 10 October 5076 BCE. No Dhuma-ketu (comet) was observed during this period of three months. Thus, Ramayana observations are not corroborated by the proposed timeline of Shri Bhatnagar.

First day of the War

Shri Bhatnagar proposed 21 November 5076 BCE as the first day of the War. This day is 1-2 days before *Amawasya*! This is interesting because Valmiki Ramayana is rich with specific references for the beginning of the war to be near the full moon day. Shri Bhatnagar's proposal is in direct contradiction with observations of Valmiki Ramayana.

Last day of the War

Shri Bhatnagar has proposed 4 December 5076 BCE as the last day of the War. This is the day Rama killed Ravana. The day appears to be 10th or 11th day of Shuddha Paksha and Shri Bhatnagar agrees with this identification/validation of the moon's phase. This is in direct conflict with evidence of Ramayana. Valmiki Ramayana alludes to the last day of the War as that of *Amawasya* and thus the last day of War, proposed by Shri Bhatnagar contradicts observations of Valmiki Ramayana.

Shri Bhatnagar states that "No descriptions of astronomical bodies are available to ascertain specific days of the War".

It is true that there are not many astronomy observations, besides observations of the phases of the moon at the beginning and at the end of the War. However there is indeed an observation of 'Mercury attacking Rohini' on the last day of the War[282] and I have shown how this observation corroborates with my proposed timeline.

In case of Shri Bhatnagar's proposal, Mercury is near nakshatra Shatabhishaj, on 4 December 5076 BCE and thus nowhere near nakshatra Rohini. As a result, Ramayana evidence fails to corroborate proposed last day of the War by Bhatnagar.

Arrival from Lanka at the *Ashram* of Sage Bharadwaj

Shri Bhatnagar proposed 29 December 5076 BCE as the day when Rama arrived at the *ashram* of sage Bharadwaj, from Lanka. Shri Bhatnagar claimed this day to be that of Shuddha 5 (lunar *Tithi*). We will have to make a slight correction (of 2 days) to adjust the phase of the moon to match this *Tithi* and the adjusted day (for the sake of testing) would be 27 December 5076 BCE.

Valmiki Ramayana states that Rama met Bharata, at Nandigram/Ayodhya, the next day and the nakshatra of the day was Pushya. Nakshatra for Shri Bhatnagar's proposed date of 27 December (or 29 December) 5076 BCE is Ashwini (or Rohini) and thus the Nakshatra of the next day would be Bharani (or Mrigashirsha). Thus Shri Bhatnagar's proposal does not corroborate observations of Valmiki Ramayana, either related to arrival of Rama, from Lanka, at the *ashram* of sage Bharadwaj or Rama-Bharata meet the very next day.

Observations not considered by Shri Bhatnagar

There are numerous observations from Valmiki Ramayana, astronomical and chronological in nature, that are not employed or evaluated by Shri Bhatnagar. These observations do not corroborate the timeline proposed by him. On the other hand, observations, specifically from Chapter 6 of this book that define upper and lower bounds on the timing of Ramayana, falsify proposal of Shri Bhatnagar.

Mahabharata War & Kali-Yuga

Shri Bhatnagar discusses archeological and geological evidence for his timeline. He also discusses the timing of Mahabharata War and of Kali-Yuga. I would encourage readers to read my book —'When did the Mahabharata War happen? The Mystery of Arundhati' for detailed discussion of astronomy evidence of Mahabharata text and how that can be employed to predict the timing of Mahabharata War. The book also falsifies any and all claims, made after 4500 BCE, for the timing of Mahabharata War.

Conclusion

We have seen that Ramayana observations employed by Shri Bhatnagar in developing his proposal do not corroborate his proposed timeline, even according to his own interpretation (e.g. definition of exalted state of grahas).

Shri Bhatnagar failed to explain his logic of selecting references that allude to older age of Rama (and Sita) at the time of Rama's scheduled coronation, and fails to explain how such a selection is consistent with the rest of chronological, sociological and physiological accounts, related to Rama and Sita, as described in Valmiki Ramayana.

Valmiki Ramayana references of astronomy, seasons and chronological observations, not employed by Shri Bhatnagar, decisively falsify his proposed timeline. In fact, Valmiki Ramayana references discussed in chapter 6 decisively place a lower limit of ~11,000 BCE on the timing of Ramayana – some 6000 years earlier than the timing proposed by Shri Bhatnagar.

Brief note on life and work of Shri Pushkar Bhatnagar

Late Shri Pushkar Bhatnagar is to be congratulated for his courage to attempt a difficult task, the task of determining the timing of Ramayana. While so much is written about Ramayana within and outside academia, no one from academia, worth his/her salt (or without) have dared to do what Shri Bhatnagar attempted. He worked for the Indian Revenue Service and was diagnosed with cancer as early as 1991 CE. In spite of his health, he worked tirelessly on this project and published his work in 2004 CE.

When I tested his proposal few years ago, I wrote to Mr. Pushkar Bhatnagar about my findings. After few attempts of mine to contact him, his daughter wrote me back with the inevitable news of his sad demise. While I was not aware of it, he was fighting cancer for some time.

Since Saroj Bala is taking forward the work of Late Shri Bhatnagar, I request her to consider my analysis and criticism of his work, and a rebuttal of my work, in her future publications.

One has to do a work of this kind to realize the amount of time and efforts it consumes, while looking after the necessities of life. Only through the recognition of the errors of past researchers, on whose shoulders we stand, we can perhaps see farther.

20

THEORIES & PROPOSALS
OF
SRS & YARDI

There is nothing more necessary to the man of history than its science and the logic of discovery... the way error is detected, the use of hypothesis, of imagination, the mode of testing.

- Nilesh Oak

We will look at, in brief, two efforts, besides that of Dr. Vartak and Shri Bhatnagar, on the dating of Ramayana. These two attempts also serve us well to illustrate why a researcher (or believer) merely stating a timing for Ramayana (or any other historical incident) – in Treta yuga, about a million years ago, in 10,000 BCE or 1500 BCE is never enough, but a researcher must state how he arrived at such a time period and what evidence led him to such an inference.

The First proposal is by three authors, who proposed dates for three distinct instances of Ramayana, but did not bother to tell us how they arrived at it. This work is a good illustration of why a sincere attempt that is not backed by theory or that does not explain the logic behind its discovery does not lead to the growth of knowledge.

The second proposal is by Mr. M R Yardi (Yardi hereafter). His work, specifically on the dating of Ramayana, is a good illustration of nonsensical methodology employed by Indologists, from India and from around the world, during past 300 years in researching history of India. Anyone interested in ancient history of India should not be content in knowing the dates proposed by so called 'experts' and 'scholars' but should treat them as a conjecture, or a working hypothesis, that must be tested against the basic criteria of logic of discovery, use of hypothesis and its consistency, simplicity, falsifiability and testability.

SRS

In 2002 CE, Three authors- Dr. S P Sabarathnam, N P Ramadurai and V Sundaram (SRS hereafter) published a book 'Ancient History of India through Astronomy'. It was edited by N Mahalingam and was published by International Society for the Investigation of Ancient Civilizations, Chennai.

I could not obtain a copy of this book, in spite of my multiple efforts. Therefore I am not familiar with their theory and how they arrived at their proposed timing of Ramayana. All it says is that they used *Vedanga Jyotisha* for actual calculations.

This limits me to simply test specific dates proposed by them against the internal observations of Valmiki Ramayana. This also means I can test only those instances for which they have mentioned the dates. I have gathered this information with the help of many kind friends. Most of this information is based on reviews written for the book.

They have proposed dates for Rama's birth, Ravana's death and Rama's coronation, after returning to Ayodhya.

Day of Rama-Janma

SRS have proposed 17 January 10205 BCE as the day of Rama-Janma. They do not tell us how they arrived at their prediction. Let's test this date against the descriptions of Valmiki Ramayana. Rama was born on Chaitra Shuddha 9 and on Punarvasu Nakshatra.

Voyager simulation tells us that the *Tithi* on 17 January was Chaitra Shuddha 12. We will adjust it by 3/4 days to 12 January 10205 BCE, to match with Ramayana description. This error is more likely due to lack of 'Delta T' correction.

I have already discussed lack of corroboration of SRS proposed timing of Rama-Janma with astronomy descriptions of Ramayana.

Ravana-Vadha

SRS proposed 8 January 10167 BCE as the day of *Ravana-Vadha*. A simple math would tell us that this incident occurred when Rama was

~38 years old, which also means SRS are assuming that Rama was 25 years old when he left for the forest. SRS assumption, regarding the age of Rama (and Sita) is thus identical to one made by Shri Bhatnagar. We have already seen how this assumption is erroneous. Reader can always refer to Error Elimination – Experiments 65 & 66.

Valmiki Ramayana tells us that the day was *Amawasya* and Mercury was seen attacking nakshatra Rohini. Voyager simulation shows this day to be the fourth day of Shuddha Paksha. We will go backward by ~4 days (for the sake of testing) to match it with the day of *Amawasya*. This adjusted day would be 4 January 10167 BCE. The day had possible solar eclipse late in the day which would corroborate analogies of Rahu afflicting the sun on the last day of the War. Mercury was too close to the sun and also near nakshatra Revati, i.e. nowhere close to nakshatra Rohini and thus does not corroborate with Valmiki Ramayana description of Mercury attacking Rohini.

Rama's return to Ayodhya and Coronation

SRS proposed 15 January 10167 BCE as the day of Rama's return to Ayodhya and his coronation. Since they have not given additional details, it is impossible to know how they estimated this day. All we can do is test it to see if the nakshatra of the day was Pushya and *Tithi* - either Shuddha 6 or Krishna 6, as described in Valmiki Ramayana.

Since we adjusted SRS date of *Ravana-vadha* by 4 days, we will give benefit of doubt to SRS and see if moving their proposed date by few days allow us to match with *Tithi* (6th lunar day) and nakshatra (Pushya).

Voyager simulation tells us that January 11, 10167 BCE aligned with nakshatra Pushya (moon near Pushya) and it was Chaitra or Vaishakha Shuddha 7/8. SRS have not mentioned their theory however if we assume their theory to be same as my theory, i.e. visual observations of the sky, then we can say that this day of Rama's coronation corroborates Valmiki Ramayana descriptions.

Reader must understand that the corroboration of SRS proposal is valid for only lunar day (*Tithi*) observation of Ramayana, albeit after adjustment of few days. Otherwise, SRS proposed timing of Ramayana fails to corroborate observations of Ramayana.

Corroboration of SRS Proposal for Seasons of Valmiki Ramayana

It must be said that broader time interval (end of 11th millennium

BCE and beginning of 10th millennium BCE) selected by SRS does fall, albeit at the one end, within the broader time interval defined by me in Chapter 6. This is the reason why seasonal descriptions of Valmiki Ramayana are corroborated by proposal of SRS.

I request SRS to expand their work further and propose specific dates or time intervals for remaining incidents of Valmiki Ramayana. I request readers to do the same.

Conclusion

SRS have proposed dates for only three specific instances of Ramayana. I checked multiple Ramayana observations (e.g. comet near nakshatra Moola, Mercury near Rohini, Sun & Mars together during Rama-Janma and during scheduled coronation of Rama) for proposed timing of Ramayana by SRS, and on all counts, the observations do not corroborate with their proposed timeline.

Yardi

Mr. M. R. Yardi wrote 'Epilogue of Ramayana' and my analysis and criticism of his work is based on the contents of that book. Yardi also reminds us, correctly, that the critical edition (in this case critical edition of Ramayana prepared by BORI-Pune) of any work gives only a reliable text which existed at a particular time, depending on the dates of the earliest manuscripts available. Yardi refers to a statistical study which resulted in identification of six different styles of writing Ramayana. However, it is not clear from the book itself what study he is referring to. I encourage readers to bring it to my attention if they are aware of what Yardi might be referring to.

This book of less than 250 pages has lot of information related to Ramayana and its multiple narratives, influence of various cultures on modified narratives of Ramayana in faraway places such as Indonesia, China and Japan.

Unfortunately, Yardi has given a naïve and superficial treatment when it comes to the dating of Ramayana. Since the book you are holding is focused on dating of Ramayana, we will limit our discussion to Yardi's effort on the dating of Ramayana.

In his introduction, Yardi states that Valmiki must have lived at least two centuries (!) before Vaishampayana, Vaishampayana being the author of original Mahabharata. I fail to see the logic of two centuries. Next, Yardi describes the timing of Vaishampayana as that of 10th century BC (~1000 BCE). He does not elaborate how he arrived at the timing of Vaishampayana. On this basis, Yardi places Valmiki around 1200 BCE! No evidence of any kind is provided in support of above statements.

I quoted Yardi's thoughts from introduction of his book, in the above paragraph, to make readers aware of things to come. Most of his inferences, if not all, regarding dating of Ramayana (or any other document for that matter) are good illustration of his humongous confusion of logic and tautology. He has readily employed casual (no evidence offered in its support) opinions of researchers as evidence when it suited his whim. Add to this confusion, additional confusion arising from 'Absence of evidence = Evidence of Absence'.

For example, consider this. He writes:

The date of Harivamshkar can be determined from the internal evidence in Harivamsha and a terracotta find from Sugh assigned to the second century BC. The latter contains an art depiction of Krishna learning Brahmi alphabet at the *Ashrama* of Guru Sandipani'. This fact is, however, not mentioned in the critical edition of the Mahabharata (BORI), but only in the Harivamsha (Vishnu Parva 79:3). So this fixes the date of Harivamsha and its author as second century BC.

A reader without any knowledge of archeology or Harivamsha or Mahabharata should able to interpret above evidence in a straightforward manner, i.e. story of Krishna learning at *ashram* of sage Sandipani existed in second century BCE. That is all that can be inferred from the above narration of Mr. Yardi. This narration of his, in any way, does not lead to the conclusion about the original writing of Harivamsha or its author to second century BCE.

In another instance, Mr. Yardi employs evidence of the type presented above and does reach a correct conclusion. In his words,

It thus seems that by at least the third century A.D., the Uttarakanda had come to be regarded as an integral part of Valmiki Ramayana.

However such joy remains short-lived. He reverts to confused logic that is mixed with opinions of others, but treats as if it is evidence. Let's follow him in his words:

As regards Sauti, there is **direct astronomical evidence** to show that **he could not have lived prior to 450 BC**. According to B. B. Dikshit, the winter solstice in the Vedanga Jyotisha period used to take place at the beginning of Dhanishtha. At present (2000 CE)

its place is near Purva Ashadha. It must, therefore, be taking place near the Shravana in some former age. Dikshit read 'Shravanadini rikshani'[341] (from Mahabharata) **and thought that although it was not so stated explicitly, the very expression 'shravanadini' conveyed that the winter solstice began in the Shravana Nakshatra.** However, according to the critical edition, the correct reading is 'shravishthadini rikshani'[342], where 'Shravishtha' is only another name for 'Dhanishtha'. Sauti, however, mentions that Vishwamitra, in creating a parallel world[340], arranged for **the winter solstice** to begin in Shravana. This new arrangement came into vogue according to Dikshit's calculations by about 450 BC (**emphasis mine**)

A casual reader would be impressed by the first statement that claims to have produced '**direct astronomical evidence**'. On the other hand, a simple analysis of the material in its support would tell us that what is construed as 'direct astronomical evidence' is but confused interpretation of another researcher. This other researcher – B. B. Dikshit – has assumed 'winter solstice' without telling us his rationale. Now it is possible that B B Dikshit has indeed done that, in which case it becomes responsibility of the author (Mr. Yardi) to explain the rationale of original author. I may mention that text of Mahabharata [340-342] does not anywhere refer to 'winter solstice'.

Fortunately, Mr. Yardi does derive logical conclusion, although based on erroneous inference about the timing of Sauti, that Ramayana was composed earlier than 450 BCE.

Mr. Yardi also lists views of various 'experts' which are interpreted by naïve and careless people as 'established truth'. I have seen them quoted in discussions – be it on blogs, lectures, discussion forums or social gatherings. Here is an illustration from this book of Mr. Yardi:

Diverse views have been expressed regarding the dating of Valmiki's original Ramayana. With the exception of Weber, who placed its date as the 3rd or 4th century A.D., Jacobi, Keith & MacDonnell suggested that the core of Ramayana was composed before 500 B.C. More recent dates have been postulated by Bulcke (end of 4th century BC), Gonda (4th century BC) and Guruge (before 3rd century BC). Two eminent archaeologists H D Sankalia and B B Lal have expressed contrary views regarding the date of original Ramayana. While Sankalia says that it might go back to a period between 1500 and 1000 BC, B B Lal states that it is posterior to the original Bharata of Vaishampayana.

The most common theme, among above views about the timing of Valmiki's original Ramayana, is characteristic lack of evidence or rationale for their views. Fortunately, Mr. Yardi examines few for us:

Sankalia states that the uppermost limit of Ramayana cannot be earlier than the beginning of the Iron Age in India, since he (Sankalia) thought it impossible to date the first introduction of iron in Northern India, and particularly in Uttar Pradesh and Bihar before 800 BCE. And since Ramayana mentions iron, it cannot be (actual happening or writing of it) before 800 BCE.

Let's understand the problem of such logic. First and foremost, Sankalia confused the absence of evidence with evidence of absence. Secondly, if iron was not found in India before 800 BCE and Ramayana has mention of iron, what made him still date Ramayana sometime between 1500 BCE and 1000 BCE?

Here is why one should be careful in not equating absence of evidence with evidence of absence. It is illogical and wrong. Fortunately, we have a good story to illustrate this very point. Consider what happened after Sankalia made that statement. For example, recently (2003 CE) excavations in Northern India (UP) have found iron artifacts that were shown to be as old as 1800 BCE. This is a good illustration of why assertions based on absence of evidence are illogical and unscientific and outright dangerous for research of any kind, and especially for areas where one has to depend on whatever evidence is available, e.g. ancient history.

If a researcher is not careful, he can reach wrong conclusions in a hurry. For example, this evidence of iron artifacts in 1800 BCE can be a corroborative evidence for some historical incident, that mentions iron, that is been dated, by independent means, to say 1800 BCE. However, identification of iron artifacts in UP for a period of 1800 BCE cannot be used as evidence to prove that something <u>did not happen</u> prior to 1800 BCE which mentions iron.

If any credit can be given to Yardi, as it relates to the dating of Ramayana, it is this: He reached a conclusion that Ramayana occurred before Mahabharata! Rest of his attempt to date Ramayana is nonsensical, chaotic and illogical. I would encourage curious readers to read his chapter on dating of Ramayana from the book 'Epilogue of Ramayana', in the original.

21

RAMAYANA DIARY

इदमाख्यानमायुष्यं सौभाग्यं पापनाशनम
रामायणं वेदसमं श्राद्धेषु श्रावयेद बुधः

Narration of Ramayana bestows longevity, enhances fortune, dispels sins and, is truly equal to Veda. (That is why) The wise recite it.

(Valmiki Ramayana – Uttara 111:4)

The ultimate aim of the quest must be neither release nor ecstasy for oneself, but the wisdom and the power to serve others.

- Joseph Campbell

Rama, son of king Dasharatha, was born on 29 November 12240 BCE, during the lunar month of Chaitra, on nakshatra Punarvasu and *Tithi* of Chaitra Shuddha Navami. Laxman, Bharata and Shatrughna, his brothers were also born around this time. Kausalya gave birth to Rama, Sumitra gave birth to Laxman and Shatrughna, and Kaikayi gave birth to Bharata. As they grew, they were trained in all the arts desired of a princely conduct.

When Rama (and his brothers) turned 16, king Dasharatha began discussing the subject of marriage of his sons, with his ministers and relatives. This is when sage Vishwamitra arrived at the palace of king Dasharatha and asked Dasharatha for assistance of Rama for 10 days.

Rama completed 16 years, per lunar *Tithi*, on 3 December 12224

BCE. Sage Vishwamitra arrived in Dasharatha's court on 4 December and left Ayodhya, with Rama and Laxman, on 5th December 12224 BCE.

They walked for about 12 miles along the bank of Sharayu. Sage Vishwamitra taught 'Bala' and 'Atibala' *vidya* to Rama on this day. They stayed on the bank of Sharayu for the night. This was the day of 5 December 12224 BCE.

Next morning, on 6 December 12224 BCE, they continued their journey and arrived at the confluence of rivers Sharayu and Ganga. They reached a hermitage by the evening and spent their night most comfortably.

Next day, on 7 December 12224 BCE, they crossed river Ganga in the morning and entered *Tataka-vana*. After some time Tataka came running at them and Vishwamitra ordered Rama to kill Tataka. Rama killed Tataka. They spent the night at *Tataka-vana*.

Next morning, on 8 December 12224 BCE, sage Vishwamitra congratulated Rama on his accomplishment and imparted Rama the knowledge of various *astras* (missiles). At the end of this day they arrived at *Siddhashrama*- their final destination where Rama and Laxman had to guard the *Yajna* for the next six days and nights. They slept at *Siddhashrama*.

In the early morning, on 9 December 12224 BCE, after ablutions, Rama and Laxman stood in front of sage Vishwamitra. The sages of *Siddhashrama* explained to Rama and Laxman, their duties of guarding the *Yajna*, day and night, for six days. Rama and Laxman did a great job of guarding the *Yajna* for the six days and nights (9-14 December 12224 BCE). On the sixth day, Marich and Subahu attacked the *Yajna* ground. While Marich was thrown away (made him run away?) by arrow of Rama, Laxman killed Subahu. The *Yajna* was completed, without hindrance, and sage Vishwamitra felicitated both brothers as he offered his evening prayers. This was the day of 14 December 12224 BCE.

Next day, on 15 December 12224 BCE, both brothers, after a good night's rest, were refreshed. Sage Vishwamitra told them about the upcoming *Yajna* of king of Mithila and suggested that the two princes should accompany sage Vishwamitra and his companions to Mithila. They left for Mithila with many carts and after traveling a long distance, spent their night on the bank of river Shona. Sage Vishwamitra and two princes continued to converse into the late night and when half of the night was over, the moon slowly rose in the sky.

Next morning, on 16 December 12224 BCE, they all got up early and proceeded on their journey. They reached river Ganga by noon. Sage

Vishwamitra told two brothers numerous stories related to river Ganga. They decided to stay on the bank of river Ganga as evening approached.

Next day, on 17 December 12224 BCE, they decided to cross river Ganga. They saw the city of Vishala and sage Vishwamitra educated the two princes on its history.

They spent the night at Vishala and proceeded towards Mithila, the next day. They reached *ashram* of Ahilya. This was on 18 December 12224 BCE. On this very day, they reached Mithila. Hearing the news of the arrival of sage Vishwamitra, king Janaka came in a hurry to welcome the party. King Janaka told the party that the *Yajna* would continue for 12 more days, i.e. until 30 December 12224 BCE.

Next morning, on 19 December 12224 BCE, king Janaka invited sage Vishwamitra and the two princes to his court. Rama lifted the *Shiva-Dhanushya* on this day. King Janaka expressed his wish to offer Sita to Rama in marriage and asked permission of sage Vishwamitra to send messengers to Ayodhya.

Messengers of Janaka took three days to reach Ayodhya (20-23 December 12224 BCE). King Dasharatha's advisors suggested that they leave for Mithila the next day. King Dasharatha left for Mithila, along with his army, the next day (24/25 December) and reached Mithila, after a journey of 4 days, on 29 December12224 BCE. The moment king Janaka heard of Dasharatha's arrival, he set about preparing for latter's reception. King Janaka told Dasharatha, on this day (29 December) that they would decide the muhurta (auspicious time) of Rama-Sita wedding, next day, i.e. on 30 December12224 BCE, as soon as his *Yajna* was concluded. Both parties spent the night happily.

Next morning, on 30 December 12224 BCE, after completing the final rites of his *Yajna*, King Janaka asked Shatananda, his family priest, to invite king Kushadhwaja of Samkasha, king's brother. Messengers were dispatched on horses and king Kushadhwaja arrived in Ayodhya, with his family, on or before 1-2 January 12223 BCE. Janaka and Kushadhwaja decided to offer their 3 other daughters – Urmila, Mandavi and Shrutakirti to Laxman, Bharata and Shatrughna.

King Janaka sat down, with Dasharatha and Kushadhwaja, to decide the muhurta for the wedding. This day was either 1 or2 January 12223 BCE and nakshatra was Magha. They decided to perform the wedding on nakshatra Uttara Phalguni, 3 days from that day, i.e. on 4 or 5 January 12223 BCE. This was the day of Vaishakha Shuddha 11 or 12.

Rama-Sita wedding, as well as weddings of Rama's three brothers took place on 4 or 5 January 12223 BCE. Next day, i.e. on 5 or 6 January

12223 BCE, sage Vishwamitra left for his own hermitage and king Dasharatha proceeded, along with his sons and newlywed daughter-in-laws, towards Ayodhya.

Newlywed couples spent their time in romantic association with their respective spouses, in the comfort of their own private residences. A year went by. Rama was soon going to turn 17 and Dasharatha thought of Rama's coronation on the throne of Ayodhya. However, Kaikayi, one of Dasharatha's queens, changed the course of history and in turn Rama had to leave for the *Vanavas* (forest-stay) for 14 years. Rama left for the forest, along with Sita and Laxman, on 20/21 December 12223 BCE.

King Dasharatha sunk in despair and could not control his grief. Dasharatha remained in sad mood and died around the midnight of sixth day, from the day Rama left for the forest. This day was 25/26 December 12223 BCE. Residents of Ayodhya came to know of their king's death the next morning, i.e. 26/27 December 12223 BCE.

Sage Markandeya and other sages urged Vasistha, on 26/27 December, to install any of the princes on the throne immediately. Since Laxman had left with Rama and Bharata and Shatrughna were at their maternal uncle's place, sage Vasistha dispatched the messengers, to capital of Kekaya, to fetch Bharata and Shatrughna, in a hurry.

The messengers left immediately and reached Kekaya capital by the fastest route. They reached Kekaya capital by 29 December 12222 BCE. Bharata & Shatrughna left Kekaya capital on 30 December 12222 BCE and after a journey of seven days, arrived in Ayodhya on 5 January 12222 BCE.

Bharata performed 11th and 12th day rituals, related to the death of king Dasharatha, on 6th and 7th January 12222 BCE, respectively. Sage Vasistha asked Bharata to accept the throne on the 14th day (from the death of king Dasharatha), i.e. on 9 January 12222 BCE. Bharata rejected the request of sage Vasistha and rather offered to spend 14 years in place of Rama, in the forest.

Bharata ordered construction of roads and camps suitable for army and members of royal family to travel from Ayodhya to bank of Ganga. The construction began in earnest. Soon construction was completed and Bharata left in search of Rama on 26 January 12222 BCE, around the time of full moon day of Vaishakha and during the season of Sharad (pre-autumn). Bharata and his army camped at Shrigaverapura, a place ruled by Guha, and then traveled to the hermitage of sage Bharadwaj. Bharata met sage Bharadwaj and then traveled further in search of Rama. This was the timing of late Sharad season.

After a long search, Bharata could locate whereabouts of Rama. Bharata met Rama on the *Amawasya* day of the lunar month of Ashadha. The day was 10 April 12222 BCE. On the very next day, on the first day – *Pratipada*- of lunar month of Shravana (11 April 12222 BCE), Bharata asked for sandals of Rama. This was the peak of winter season (Shishir), i.e. middle of winter season. Bharata left Chitrakuta and returned to Ayodhya by the end of spring season.

Soon, Rama left Chitrakuta, along with Sita and Laxman, and visited many sages and their residences. They roamed through the Dandakaranya for many years and then arrived at the *ashram* of sage Agastya. Sage Agastya instructed Rama about divine missiles and suggested that Rama go and stay at Panchavati, on the bank of river Godavari. Rama, Sita and Laxman left for Panchavati, met Jatayu on the way, and soon settled in Panchavati.

They lived happily in Panchavati for a long time, and another season of Hemant (autumn) arrived. Shurpanakha, sister of Ravana, visited Rama, at Panchavati, around this time. Shurpanakha felt infatuation towards Rama and expressed her wish to marry him and went on to attack Sita. Laxman loped the nose and ears of Shurpanakha and she ran away with pain and anger to her brother Khara. Khara sent his 14 men to punish Rama and Rama killed them all. Shurpanakha approached Khara for the second time. Khara and Dushana marched towards Panchavati with a huge army. This day was 28 March 12210 BCE. The time was that of Shishir (winter) season. Long fight ensued and Rama defeated Khara and his army. Rama also killed Dushana, Trishira and Khara.

Surviving Rakshasa warrior – Akampana, traveled to Lanka to disclose this news to Ravana. Ravana became extremely angry went to the *ashram* of Marich and requested latter's help in punishing Rama. Marich described prowess of Rama and advised Ravana to refrain from doing anything to Rama. In deference to the advice of Marich, Ravana returned to Lanka. Seeing no response from Ravana, Shurpanakha went to Lanka and scolded Ravana for his inaction. Ravana went to Marich for the second time and convinced Marich for his assistance. Ravana and Marich arrived at Panchavati.

Marich assumed a remarkable and attractive form of a deer, with the help of his conjuring skills, and began moving about near Rama's residence in Panchavati. Sita noticed this golden deer and asked Rama to capture it. This was the season of Vasanta (spring). Laxman did judge this golden deer to be a trick and Rama did not disagree with Laxman.

However Rama still decided to go after the golden deer and after chasing it for a while finally killed it. Marich uttered a cry, before dying, in a voice resembling that of Rama. Sita could hear it at her residence and insisted that Laxman should leave her and go help Rama. Laxman was confident of Rama's prowess and loyal to his promise (to Rama) of guarding Sita, and thus did not agree to her suggestion. However Sita became upset and said many undeserving words to Laxman, upon which he left in search of Rama.

All along Ravana was waiting for an opportunity and as soon as Laxman left in search of Rama, Ravana approached Sita and tried to entice her with praise and sweet words. When Sita refused, he lifted her forcefully. Hearing Sita's cry for help, Jatayu ran for her help, fought with Ravana but was severely injured. Ravana left, along with Sita for Lanka. This was the season of spring and thus sometime during May-July 12210 BCE.

Ravana lodged Sita, initially, in a royal palace with attendants, and ordered all attendants to be most pleasing to Sita and look after her every need. Ravana tried to woo Sita by various means, however, when unsuccessful in wooing Sita, he sent her to *Ashoka-vana* and assigned a time limit of 12 months for acceptance of his proposal (to marry him) and threatened her with death if the proposal was not accepted by Sita within the time limit.

Back in Panchavati, Rama met Laxman and both of them rushed back to their residence only to find that Sita had disappeared. They began searching for Sita in earnest and met Jatayu on the way. Jatayu informed them that Ravana had abducted Sita. They continued searching for Sita, ran into Kabandha. Kabandha advised them to make an alliance with Sugriva and also informed them of directions to Rishyamukha Hill and Lake Pampa. Rama and Laxman visited sage Shabari, on their way to Rishyamukha, at the *ashram* of sage Matanga and then proceeded to Lake Pampa.

Sugriva saw them from the top of Rishyamukha and not knowing who they were, sent Hanuman to ascertain the purpose of Rama and Laxman to arrive near Rishyamukha – his residence. Rama and Sugriva met, decided to form an alliance and Sugriva requested Rama to get rid of Vali, Sugriva's elder brother.

Still uncertain of Rama's strength, Sugriva ascertained strength of Rama in a shrewd fashion and when satisfied went to Kishkindha, and challenged Vali for a dual. As planned, Rama sat hidden behind a tree.

The dual between Vali and Sugriva began however Rama could not hit Vali with an arrow, since Vali and Sugriva looked alike. Rama could not be certain of identity of Vali. Seeing no action from Rama, Sugriva lost heart and ran away from the combat. This first fight took place in the late afternoon and just before the sunset. The day was 21 September 12210 BCE.

Sugriva was upset. Rama explained his dilemma to discouraged Sugriva and encouraged Sugriva to seek another encounter with Vali. This time, Laxman uprooted blossomed Gajapushpi creeper and tied it around the neck of Sugriva for identification. Vali and Sugriva began their second dual. This time, Rama struck Vali with an arrow and Vali fell to the ground. This second fight occurred in the morning, the very next day after the first fight. The day was 22 September 12210 BCE. This was the end of Grishma (summer) season and the season of Varsha had just begun.

Vali scolded Rama in harsh language, however recognizing that his own death was inevitable, requested Rama to take care of Angada. Tara, wife of Vali, rushed to the place where Vali had fallen. Sugriva was crowned a king and Rama told Sugriva and others to wait until the four months of rainy season were over, before initiating search for Sita. Rama retired, along with Laxman, to mount Prasravana, on the outskirts of Kishkindha.

When the four months of rainy season (Varsha and Sharad) elapsed and seeing no action from Sugriva, Rama sent Laxman to Kishkindha to remind Sugriva of latter's promise. Sugriva ordered his companions to summon all Vanara parties to Kishkindha. Over a period of next several days and weeks, hordes of Vanara arrived in Kishkindha.

Sugriva met Rama, along with his key Vanara commanders and gave specific orders to Vanara search parties. He sent search parties in all four directions and gave them a time limit of one month to return to Kishkindha.

The search for Sita began sometime after 13 January 12209 BCE, when season of Sharad was over. All parties began their search sometime in the season of Hemant (autumn) and all were back to Kishkindha within the time limit set by Sugriva, except the search party that was headed south.

Hanuman, Nila and Angada were key Vanara warriors of the southern search party. They began the search for Sita sometime during the season of Hemant (autumn) and they began scouring places that were difficult to access. They walked through the regions, rich in fruits and roots.

As their search continued, season of Shishir (winter) commensed. The search party found it difficult to obtain food. The trees had no flowers, fruits or even leaves. Soon the time appointed by Sugriva, for searching of Sita, expired. The search party continued their search, beyond the time limit set by Sugriva. They reached south-western summit of the mountain. Eventually, the exhausted search party reached a valley-Rikshbila-difficult to access. Overcome by hunger, thirst and exhaustion, they entered the valley.

They found the valley filled with climbers and creepers and many birds whose limbs were laden with pollen. This is then the timing of early spring (Vasanta). After walking through the valley for some distance they arrived at the place of Swayamprabha. The place was spring season personified. Naga and Karnika trees were in blossom and trees had fruits and honeycombs. Vanara party dined on fruits and roots.

Hanuman narrated their story to Swayamprabha and how they had already went beyond the time limit set by Sugriva before even they arrived at her place. Swayamprabha provided Vanara party with directions to get out of the valley and Vanara party resumed their search.

Now Vanara party beheld the shore less ocean. When they sat exhausted on the hill, they were alarmed to see treetops of spring season heavy with flowers and enshrouded by numerous vines. It was indeed a season of spring.

Angada addressed members of the search party and stated that based on his calculations, from the time of their departure from Kishkindha, the current time was that of the lunar month of Ashwin and that month of Ashwin had also elapsed. This conversation took place sometime after mid-July of 12209 BCE (13 June-13 July 122209 BCE was the time of lunar month of Ashwin). This was the end of spring season.

By luck, the search party ran into Sampati, brother of Jatayu, and he informed them that Ravana had taken Sita to Lanka. With renewed vigor, Vanara party headed towards Lanka and soon reached the northern seashore. Crossing the ocean was indeed a challenge and individual Vanara described their flying strengths. Finally, Jambavan encouraged Hanuman to take up the task. Hanuman agreed and climbed up to the top of mount Mahendra and readied himself to leap into the sea.

Hanuman swam across the ocean, entered Lanka and began searching for Sita through various palaces and gardens of Lanka. Eventually Hanuman located Sita in *Ashok-vana*. Sita told Hanuman that Ravana had given her time limit of 12 months to yield to Ravana's wishes and that only two months of that time limit were remaining. Hanuman was in Lanka during 27-30 August 12209 BCE and this was the time of late Grishma (summer). Ravana had abducted Sita sometime during the spring season of the previous year. This means Ravana had set a time limit of 12 months for Sita to yield to his wishes, only after Sita was in Lanka for a while. Thus Ravana set the time limit of 12 months for Sita sometime in the lunar month of Magha (previous year), i.e. sometime during October-November of 122210 BCE.

Hanuman comforted Sita and promised to take her message to Rama. Before leaving Lanka, Hanuman decided to ascertain the strength of Ravana army. He provoked Ravana's men by destroying Ravana's pleasure gardens. Ravana sent series of men to fight Hanuman however Hanuman killed them all. Indrajit caught Hanuman and took him to Ravana. Ravana ordered his men to burn the tail of Hanuman. As Hanuman was taken around through the streets of Lanka, he escaped and began burning Lanka. He met Sita briefly and then left for the northern shore of the ocean. This time Hanuman flew back and the time was that of the early morning and the day was 30 August 12209 BCE.

Hanuman reached the northern shore, and all members of search party left for Kishkindha. They approached Kishkindha with great speed and reached sometime before 29 September 12209 BCE. Rama and his Vanara army left from Kishkindha on nakshatra Uttara Phalguni (or Hasta). They traveled day and night, and after a long journey arrived at the northern seashore. The Vanara army camped at the seashore and Rama, along with Laxman and key Vanara leaders began deliberation on means of crossing the ocean.

While Rama was deliberating on means of crossing the ocean, Ravana held consultations with his ministers in Lanka. Vibhishan, younger brother of Ravana, repeatedly requested Ravana to return Sita to Rama however Ravana did not like his advice and castigated him with harsh words. Vibhishan approached Rama, along with his four ministers, and Rama decided to accept Vibhishan. Vanara leaders asked Vibhishan for his advice on means to cross the ocean.

In Lanka, Shardula - one of Ravana's spies, informed Ravana of arrival of Vanara army on the northern seashore and their being camped on the seashore. Ravana sent Shuka with the aim of causing dissention within Rama's team. Shuka arrived at Rama's camp. Vanara warriors caught Shuka and held him captive.

The ocean remained highly turbulent. Rama sat down for three nights and days meditating on ways to cross the ocean. He felt frustrated and began throwing arrows at the ocean but was calmed down by Laxman. Nala, one of the Vanara commanders, approached Rama and expressed his ability and willingness to build a bridge across the ocean.

The bridge was completed in five days and then Vanara army crossed the bridge and camped on the southern side of the ocean. Then they moved in formations, protected from all sides, towards Lanka, and settled near mount Suvela. The city of Lanka was surrounded by the Vanara army. This was the peak of Sharad (pre-autumn) season.

At this time, Rama let Shuka free. Shuka returned to Ravana. Ravana ordered his ministers, Shuka and Sarana, to enter Vanara army ranks and collect information. Shuka and Sarana were detected and captured by Vibhishan. Rama set them free, upon which they returned to Ravana and described impressive details of the Vanara army.

The Vanara army entered parks and gardens of Lanka which were laden with blossom. Rama had his Vanara army ready to attack through the four gates of Lanka, and then sent Angada to Ravana. Angada returned to Rama with the message of no change of attitude from Ravana. Soon the war began. The first day of War was 25 December 12209 BCE, three days after the full moon day.

The war continued for almost a fortnight (24 December 12209 BCE – 7 January 12208 BCE). Rama killed Ravana on the last day of the War. Final rights of Ravana, meeting between Rama and Sita and coronation of Vibhishan took place over the next few days and then Rama flew towards Ayodhya through Pushpak Vimana, along with Sita, Laxman, Sugriva, Vibhishan, Hanuman and key Vanara leaders. They took a break at Kishkindha where key Vanara ladies joined them and then all headed for the *ashram* of sage Bharadwaj and reached there on 12 January 12208 BCE. Rama and Bharata met at Nandigram, near Ayodhya, the very next day, on 13 January 12208 BCE and Rama's coronation took place this very day. This was the end of Sharad (pre-autumn) season.

Vanara leaders stayed in Ayodhya and enjoyed the hospitality of Rama while another month elapsed. They spent additional time in Ayodhya even through the two months of Shishir (winter) season. At this time, Rama gave permission to the Vanara leaders and also Vibhishan to return to Kishkindha and Lanka, respectively.

Shishir (winter) season became a thing of the past and the spring arrived. Rama and Sita began enjoying their time together and while sitting in their *Ashoka-vana*, Rama noticed the signs of Sita being pregnant. Rama asked Laxman, in response to the gossip among the residents of Ayodhya, to take Sita to the forest and leave her near the *ash-*

ram of Valmiki. Sita began living in the *ashram* of Valmiki.

Shatrughna pledged to kill Lavana and Rama told Shatrughna to wait until the season of Grishma (summer) was over and then to head for Mathura and kill Lavana. Accordingly when season of Grishma (summer) elapsed and season of Varsha (rain) began, Shatrughna left Ayodhya and rested for a night at the *ashram* of Valmiki, on his way to Mathura, and that is when Sita gave birth to two boys- Kusha and Lava.

Shatrughna proceeded to Mathura, the next day, killed Lavana and established Mathura. He was busy in establishment and ruling of Mathura for 12 years. Shatrughna decided to visit Ayodhya, stopped on his way at the *ashram* of Valmiki and had an opportunity to listen to 'Ramayana', sung to the tunes of musical instruments. This was sometime in year 12196 BCE.

22

A BETTER THEORY

In order that a new theory should constitute a discovery or a step for-ward it should conflict with its predecessor – that is to say, it should lead to at least some conflicting results. This means, from a logical point of view, that it should contradict its predecessor: it should over-throw it. In this sense, progress in science – or at least striking pro-gress – is always revolutionary.

- Karl Popper

Overview of Existing Proposals

There are, to the best of my knowledge, four proposals for the timing of Ramayana. SRS tell us that they employed *Vedanga Jyotisha* and pre-sent dates for only three instances from Ramayana (~10200 BCE) and provide no explanation whatsoever how they arrived at it. Shri M R Yardi thinks Ramayana happened sometime around 1300 BCE, based on naïve logic that can be not be termed even remotely rational, empirical or scientific. Shri Pushkar Bhatnagar began with the present and went backwards, looking for planetary positions at the time of Rama Janma, as described in Valmiki Ramayana, but also as interpreted by Shri Bhatnagar, and proposed 5114 BCE. Dr. P V Vartak employed similar, but not identical, approach like that of Shri Bhatnagar and looked for a time when planetary positions, supposedly, matched with those de-scribed at the time of Rama Janma. Of course Dr. Vartak began with the year of Mahabharata War (5561 BCE) as the lower bound for the timing of Ramayana, and proposed 7300 BCE.

We have seen that proposed timing of SRS cannot be corroborated with observations of Valmiki Ramayana. In addition, numerous observations of Valmiki Ramayana falsify their proposed date rather easily.

Attempt by Shri Yardi is naïve at best and ridiculous at worst. His proposed timing of ~1300 BCE is falsified by Mahabharata timing of 5561 BCE and also by numerous observations of Valmiki Ramayana. Two observations of Valmiki Ramayana, which contradict all other evidence of Valmiki Ramayana, related to lunar months of rainy season, corroborate ad hoc timing of 1300 BCE proposed by Shri Yardi. Of course Shri Yardi himself was unaware of that. Even if he would have become aware of these observations, he would not have dared to mention them, since that would have also forced him to look at rest of astronomy, chronology and seasons observations of Valmiki Ramayana. These additional observations would have shown their incompatibility for 1300 BCE.

Attempt by Shri Pushkar Bhatnagar stressed looking at positions of grahas that match, supposedly, the descriptions of grahas at the time of Rama Janma. We have seen how positions of grahas for his proposed day of Rama-Janma (10 January 5114 BCE) match neither positions claimed by Shri Bhatnagar nor descriptions of Valmiki Ramayana. Mahabharata timing of 5561 BCE falsifies proposal of Shri Bhatnagar. Numerous observations of Valmiki Ramayana also falsify proposed timing of Ramayana by him.

Dr. Vartak looked at genealogical tables of ancient kings, similarity and difference between social aspects of Rig-Veda, Ramayana and Mahabharata, astronomy evidence, seasonal descriptions and evolutionary traits. His approach in narrowing down to a specific date of Rama Janma was similar to that of Shri Bhatnagar. On two occasions, Dr. Vartak came close to proposing a timeline that would have matched broader timeline proposed by this author (10,000 BCE – 17,500 BCE). Dr. Vartak did recognize the conflict of Valmiki Ramayana descriptions of seasons for his proposed timeline. On the other hand, other researchers did not even comprehend this challenge for their timeline.

Valmiki Ramayana descriptions of seasons (e.g. Chaitra as the month of flowers and of blooming forests with peacocks and rain, southern search party searching for Sita through seasons of Hemant, Shishir and Vasanta, time of spring when Hanuman visits Lanka and many such instances), are not corroborated for proposal of Vartak, Bhatnagar or

Yardi.

Let's consider my theory and proposed timing of Ramayana.

My Theory

My theory has two theses.

1. All astronomy observations are visual observations of the sky
2. Ramayana author employed analogies of corresponding seasons, descriptions of nature (flowers, trees, rain, clouds, tides, stormy sea, etc.,), sky views and planetary configurations while describing the incidents of Ramayana.

Ramayana: My Proposed Timeline

1. Birth of Dasharatha ~ 12300 BCE.
2. Dasharatha performs Putra-Kameshthi *Yajna*: December 12241 BCE- January 12241 BCE.
3. Rama- Janma (Birth of Rama): 29 November 12240 BCE.
4. Arrival of sage Vishwamitra in Ayodhya: 4 December 12224 BCE.
5. Rama & Laxman kill Tataka: 7 December 12224 BCE.
6. Arrival at *Siddhashrama*: 8 December 12224 BCE
7. Rama & Laxman protect *Yajna* of Vishwamitra: 9-14 December 12224 BCE.
8. Leaving for Mithila and day of late night conversations: 15 December 12224 BCE.
9. Arrival at city of Vishala: 17 December 12224 BCE.
10. Rama meets Ahilya at latter's *ashram*: 18 December 12224 BCE.
11. Arrival in Mithila: 18 December 12224 BCE.
12. Rama lifts Shiva-Dhanushya: 19 December 12224 BCE.
13. King Dasharatha arrives in Mithila: 29 December 12224 BCE.
14. King Janaka completes *Yajna*: 30 December 12224 BCE.
15. Wedding day of Rama-Sita decided: 1 or2 January 12223 BCE.
16. Rama-Sita Wedding: 4/5 January 12223 BCE.
17. Rama's scheduled coronation: 20/21 December 12223 BCE.
18. Rama's Vanavas-gaman: 20/21 December 12223 BCE.
19. Death of Dasharatha: 25/26 December 12223 BCE.
20. Messenger's traveling to Kekaya capital: 27-29 December 12223 BCE.

21. Bharata's journey from Kekaya capital to Ayodhya: 30 December 12223 BCE – 5 January 12222 BCE.
22. Bharata performs 11th & 12th day rituals for Dasharatha: 6th and 7th January 12222 BCE.
23. Sage Vasistha requests Bharata to accept the throne of Ayodhya: 9 January 12222 BCE.
24. Bharata leaves Ayodhya to meet Rama: 26 January 12222 BCE.
25. Bharata meets Rama at Chitrakuta: 10 April 12222 BCE.
26. Bharata asks for Sandals of Rama: 11 April 12222 BCE.
27. Rama & Khara fight: 28 March 12210 BCE.
28. Ravana abducted Sita from Panchavati: May-July 12210 BCE
29. Ravana set time limit for Sita to yield to his wishes: Sometime during October-November 12210 BCE.
30. Vali-Sugriva fight-1st round: 21 September 12210 BCE.
31. Vali-Sugriva fight- 2nd round: 22 September 12210 BCE.
32. Rama-Laxman lived outside Kishkindha: 22 September-13 January 12209 BCE.
33. Vanara search parties leave Kishkindha: After 13 January 12209 BCE.
34. Angada's frustration during search of Sita: Mid-July 12209 BCE.
35. Hanuman in Lanka: 27-30 August 12209 BCE.
36. Hanuman flying back from Lanka: 30 August 12209 BCE.
37. Rama & Vanara army leave for Lanka, from Kishkindha: 29 September 12209 BCE.
38. Building & Construction of Nala-Setu: Sometime during 8 Decemer-18 December 12209 BCE.
39. Rama & Vanara Army on Mountain Suvela: 22 December 12209 BCE.
40. The War: 24 December 12209 BCE – 7 January 12208 BCE.
41. Rama at the *ashram* of sage Bharadwaj: 12 January 12208 BCE
42. Rama meets Bharata: 13 January 12208 BCE.
43. Rama's coronation: 13 January 12208 BCE.
44. Vanara leaders & Vibhishan return, from Ayodhya to Kishkindha and Lanka, respectively: Sometime after 17 May 12208 BCE.
45. Rama sends Sita to *ashram* of Valmiki (through Laxman): May-July 12208 BCE.
46. Birth of Kusha & Lava: September/October 12208 BCE.
47. Completion of Ramayana (as sung by Kusha & Lava to Rama in Ayodhya): 12196 BCE.

My Key Contributions

- My theory proceeds from a simple, almost trivial, unifying idea that all astronomy observations of Valmiki Ramayana are visual observations of the sky.

- My theory is independently testable. Anyone can access astronomy software such as Voyager 4.5™, follow through my book and test each Valmiki Ramayana observation.

- Two observations of Valmiki Ramayana – (1) Lunar month of Chaitra and (2) Sun setting on Nakshatra Pushya during the season of Hemant (autumn), define a time interval of 7000 years (10500 BCE-17500 BCE) for the plausible timing of Ramayana.

- Plausible time interval, thus defined, not only provided rational explanation for two additional observations of Valmiki Ramayana – (1) BrahmaRashi as bright pole star and (2) Lunar month of Ashwin aligning with season of spring, but also led to additional corroboration and further narrowing down of this plausible time interval of Ramayana (10500 BCE – 14500 BCE).

- My theory and corresponding proposed timeline asserts, independently, occurrence of Ramayana before Mahabharata.

- My proposal corroborates observation of comet near nakshatra Moola. In addition, this observation became crucial observation (not unlike Arundhati-Vasistha observation of Mahabharata) for determining the timing of other Ramayana incidents.

- My proposal establishes plausible connection between Indra-Dhwaja festival of Ramayana and *'Gudhi-Padava'* festival (Maharashtra) in our times. If true, this would also mean the festival was connected with the season of spring and ancient Indians maintained the timing of festival, against the changing lunar months due to the precession of equinoxes, for more than 14000 years.

- All past researchers have assumed that incidents beginning with arrival of Shurpanakha at Panchavati and ending with killing of Ravana, took place over a period of one year. I have shown this to be inconsistent with Valmiki Ramayana observations of seasons and other chronology observations and have shown this period to be that of ~2 years.

- My timeline explains the phenomenon of 'creation of *Prati-srushti'* by sage Vishwamitra, defines a specific time when sage

Vishwamitra undertook that task and his rationale. This interpretation also puts in perspective 'Fall of Abhijit'. The incident of 'Fall of Abhijit' is no longer to be seen as some stray astronomy observation in remote antiquity.

- My timeline of Ramayana places a lower limit of ~12000 BCE on the migration of sage Agastya to the southern India.
- My proposed timeline corroborates seasonal descriptions of Valmiki Ramayana:
  1. Lunar month of Chaitra as month of flowers and of blooming forests
  2. Lunar month of Ashwin coinciding with the season of spring
  3. Khara-Rama fight during the season of winter
  4. Bharata arriving at Chitrakuta during the season of winter
  5. Abduction of Sita during the season of spring
  6. Searching of Sita by southern search party for a long time through the seasons of Hemant, Shishir, Vasanta and Grishma
  7. Hanuman visiting Sita in Lanka during the season of spring
  8. Vanara leaders and Vibhishan staying in Ayodhya through the seasons of Hemant and Shishir
  9. Birth of Kusha-Lava at the beginning of Varsha season and their being conceived during the season of Sharad/Hemant

Observations explained by previous Theories

Shri Bhatnagar has determined dates for three instances of Ramayana, (1) Khara-Rama fight [94-95, 98-100], (2) Killing of Vali by Rama [108-112] and (3) Hanuman visiting Sita in Lanka [150-167], based on Valmiki descriptions of the solar eclipses for first two instances and based on the Lunar eclipse for Hanuman's visit to Sita in Lanka. Dr. Vartak is mute on the point of eclipses for these three instances. In fact Dr. Vartak has not proposed specific dates for Khara-Rama fight and killing of Vali.

First and foremost we should understand that unless there is clear mention of 'eclipse', we cannot assume that there was indeed an eclipse. If there are indirect references to an eclipse and if a researcher can demonstrate that there was an eclipse for his proposed timeline, then it can be considered as good corroboration of evidence. On the other hand, if explicit reference of eclipse does not exist, absence of an eclipse cannot be seen as falsification of a specific proposal.

I have shown, for my proposed timeline, that there were indeed solar eclipses during Khara-Rama fight and during killing of Vali and a lunar eclipse when Hanuman visited Sita in Lanka.

Dr. Vartak has interpreted observation of the sun setting on nakshatra Pushya during the season of Hemanta[3], in a decidedly false manner. The observation is straightforward and while the duration of Hemant (autumn) season would be of two months and thus position of the sun could vary over 60^0, Dr. Vartak has interpreted it to mean addi-tional 90^0 away from plausible position of Pushya (with respect to the sun). This he did to coerce a corroboration of this observation for his proposed timeline of 7300 BCE. While a position of nakshatra Pushya, separated by 15^0 to 30^0 can be conceived easily and would be reasona-ble (visual observation), anything beyond this separation would defeat the very purpose of such observation in predicting a time interval. Dr. Vartak indeed realized this and had commented that only reason he did not interpret this observation in a straightforward manner was due to such interpretation leading to a timeline of ~13000 BCE. He felt this time interval was too far in antiquity and thus he was forced to interpret it in a fashion to suit his proposed timeline of ~7300 BCE.

I have shown that this observation[3] leads to a time interval of 11500 BCE-17500 BCE for the plausible timing of Ramayana.

Dr. Vartak and Shri Bhatnagar have claimed to have five grahas in exalted positions during their proposed day of Rama Janma. I have shown that this is not the case for their proposed day of Rama Janma. In fact, no researcher, including myself, has shown five grahas to be in exalted positions for their respective proposals of Rama Janma.

Observations NOT explained by previous Theories

Four observations [2-4, 124] that defined the Epoch of Ramayana (10,000 BCE – 17,500 BCE) were not explained and/or understood by any of the past researchers. No wonder the Epoch of Ramayana eluded them.

Dr. Vartak did understand the straightforward interpretation of Pushya[3] observation, but decided to interpret it differently. Dr. Vartak recognized importance of 'Comet near nakshatra Moola' observation[5] and although he could not test it or validate it for his proposal, he re-quested future researchers to study it. I have done exactly that and also shown it to be a crucial observation in determining specific time period of ~30 years within 7500 years long Epoch of Ramayana.

Valmiki Ramayana is rich in descriptions of seasons, beginning with Rama Janma and ending with Kusha-Lava Janma. While it describes tim-ing of Rama-Janma as that of blooming forests and dancing peacocks and rainclouds, it describes timing of Kusha-Lava Janma as that of early rain. It describes cold Hemant (autumn) season in Panchavati and beautiful Vasanta (spring) season when Hanuman visited Sita in Lanka. It also describes South Vanara party, searching for Sita, through changing seasons of Hemant, Shishir, Vasanta and Grishma. Valmiki Ramayana describes these seasons via direct descriptions but also via analogies. My proposed timeline corroborated 200+ such observations of seasons (their descriptions/analogies) from Valmiki Ramayana. I have described the details of such observations under 'Ramayana – My auxiliary Hypothesis' below.

How to Judge: Introduction of an Auxiliary hypothesis

In my book on the dating of Mahabharata, besides key statement of my theory viz. all astronomy observations are visual observations of the sky, I had introduced two auxiliary hypotheses: (1) Mahabharata astronomers had access to telescopic vision/instruments that could observe objects not visible to the naked eye and (2) Mahabharata author had embedded astronomy observations (eclipses, phases and positions of the moon, etc.) in the form of analogies in describing war scenes.

While all readers were thrilled by astronomy interpretations of Arundhati-Vasistha, planetary positions and motions; many did not grasp the importance of my auxiliary hypotheses and some even felt that corroboration shown by me, between positions and phases of the moon and positions of warriors, was farfetched. We have to look for the origin of such impressions in the misunderstood and misinformed role of auxiliary hypotheses.

Inductive methodology wants to limit auxiliary hypotheses for exactly opposite reasons why scientific methodology (deductive methodology) wants to limit them.

We should remember that only those auxiliary hypotheses are acceptable whose introduction does not diminish the degree of testability or testability of system in question, but, on the contrary, increases it. If the degree of falsifiability is increased, then introducing the auxiliary hypothesis has actually strengthened the theory. The system now rules out more than it did previously. It prohibits more. The introduction of an auxiliary hypothesis should always be regarded as an attempt to construct a new system; and this new system should always be judged based on if constitutes a real advance in our knowledge of the world.

Examples of acceptable auxiliary hypotheses are the hypothesis of telescopic vision or analogies of astronomy landscape to war scenes, in the context of Mahabharata war. This is because the hypothesis of telescopic vision corroborated three instances of seven planetary formations, presence of Neptune near nakshatra *Purva Bhadrapada*, presence of Haley's comet near nakshatra *Pushya* and presence of Pluto near nakshatra *Krittika*. The hypothesis of analogies of astronomy landscape (phases and positions of the moon) with that of war scenes, not only corroborated numerous observations related to lunar *Tithis* for 18 days of the Mahabharata War – phases and positions of the moon and lunar eclipse, but also falsified all proposals that claimed to have beginning of the Mahabharata War removed from the day of *Amawasya*.

Examples of unsatisfactory/unacceptable auxiliary hypotheses include 'cometary theory' of Prof. Narahari Achar or Prof. Mohan Gupta, theory of 'indicative power' of Prof. Mohan Gupta, theory of 'astrological Drishthi' of Dr. P V Vartak or Prof. Raghavan and the theory of 'statistical fitting of planetary positions' by Prof. Ananad Sharan.

Ramayana: My Auxiliary hypothesis

My theory in determining the timing of Ramayana has two statements. The second statement is an auxiliary hypothesis, stated as follows:

Ramayana author employed analogies of corresponding seasons, descriptions of nature (flowers, trees, rain, clouds, tides, stormy sea, etc.,), sky views and planetary configurations while describing the incidents of Ramayana.

My proposed timeline corroborates all seasons as described in Valmiki Ramayana and summarized under key contributions of this chapter. However there are many more observations of seasons in Valmiki Ramayana that are not connected to a specific incident.

I developed a scheme to test corroboration/compatibility/consistency of these observations for my proposed Ramayana timeline as follows:

1. I listed all (as many as I could) observations from Valmiki Ramayana that had descriptions of seasons.
2. I noted down the season, based on the description/analogy of Valmiki Ramayana observation in one column and based on my proposed timeline in another column

3. Two possibilities existed for a match between Valmiki Ramayana observation and my proposed timeline: If timeline per my proposal agreed with descriptions/analogy of Valmiki Ramayana, I marked such agreement as 'corroborated'. If timeline per my proposal disagreed with descriptions/analogy of Valmiki Ramayana, I marked such disagreement as 'Not corroborated'.

4. I identified 225+ descriptions/analogies of seasons in Valmiki Ramayana.

Analysis of these 225+ descriptions/analogies of seasons from Valmiki Ramayana text shows excellent corroboration with my proposed timeline. The table below shows illustration of how this data was analyzed and compared against my proposed timeline.

(Ramayana Reference) (Gita Press Edition)	Season Ramayana description/Analogy	Season Per my proposal	Agreement Yes/No
Bala 22:22-33	Sharad	Shard	Yes
Ayodhya 3:36-37	Sharad	Sharad	Yes
Ayodhya 93:10	Varsha (end of Grishma)	Sharad	No
Aranya 42:31	Vasanta	Vasanta	Yes
Aranya 44:7	Sharad	Vasanta	No
Kishkindha 1:1-10	Late Vasanta/Grishma	Late Vasanta/Grishma	Yes
Kishkindha 1:91	Vasanta	Vasanta	Yes
Kishkindha 28:66	Varsha	Varsha	Yes
Kishkindha 30:1-63	Sharad	Sharad	Yes
Sundar 2:2	Vasanta	Vasanta	Yes
Sundar 66:13	Sharad	Vasanta	No
Yuddha 12:14	Sharad	Sharad	Yes
Yuddha 24:37	Vasanta	Sharad	No
Uttara 39:26-30	Shishir	Shishir	Yes
Uttara 42:1-15	Vasanta	Vasanta	Yes

There were 16 instances (16 out of 225+) where seasons according to my proposed timeline conflict with descriptions/analogies of seasons from Valmiki Ramayana. All these 16 instances fell into a unique category where season of spring/autumn, per my proposed timeline, had description/analogy from Valmiki Ramayana that were exactly opposite, i.e. season of spring (per my timeline) had corresponding description/analogy of autumn (per Valmiki Ramayana) and vice versa.

I want to bring it to the attention of reader that there are indeed many similarities between two seasons of spring and autumn, especially in the context of Indian subcontinent. Both seasons are marked by days and nights of equal length, pleasant weather, clear skies, inflorescence, flowers, fruits, honey and festive times.

All remaining 225+ seasonal descriptions/analogies of Valmiki Ramayana corroborated my proposed timeline. This is an excellent example of an acceptable auxiliary hypothesis since it led to an increase in degree of testability, falsifiability and also growth of our knowledge for seasons during Ramayana and their correspondence with lunar months.

Information, Truth & Falsity Content

Significant misunderstanding also exists, among readers and researchers alike, about the role of observations- i.e. is it a must that we test all observations or is it ok to test few selected observations? I will repeat what I wrote in my previous book, to clarify this point.

A theory that corroborates more information is a better theory where information refers to set of observations that lead to the growth of knowledge, *ceteris paribus*.

Let C (a) be the content of observation 'a' and C (b) be the content of observation 'b'

$$C (a) < C (ab) > C (b)$$

A theory that corroborates both 'a' and 'b' is better than a theory that corroborates 'only a' or 'only b'. All theories under comparison should use identical set of observations in evaluating corroborative (truth) and contradictory (falsity) content, i.e., critical tests of observations. A theory with higher truth content and lower falsity content is better theory than other theories whose truth content is lower and falsity content is higher.

Measurement of information, truth and falsity content becomes more useful when comparing two or more theories, and especially for two different predictions (e.g. multiple proposals for the timing of Ramayana). I have listed all Ramayana observations and tested them for corroboration, conflict resolution and falsification.

(Additional) Requirements of a Better theory

All explanations of astronomy observations from Ramayana are derived from a simple hypothesis of visual observations of the sky. No astrological '*Drishthi*' and no astrological definitions of 'exalted' grahas! This is the simple, new and powerful unifying hypothesis. My auxiliary hypothesis is equally consistent with the primary hypothesis. I have shown my theory to be consistent, or free from contradictions with not only astronomy observations but also with chronological observations and descriptions of seasons.

Dr. P V Vartak and Shri Pushkar Bhatnagar claimed to have five grahas in 'exalted' positions, per definitions of astrology, for their proposed day of Rama-Janma. Unfortunately claims of both Dr. Vartak and Shri Bhatnagar are wrong and we have already shown the evidence. In addition, Valmiki Ramayana descriptions of seasons contradict proposals of Dr. Vartak, Shri Bhatnagar and Shri Yardi. Four Ramayana observations [2-4, 124] that define broader Epoch of Ramayana falsify proposals of all Ramayana researchers. Any proposal for the timing of Ramayana must corroborate Ramayana observation of 'comet near nakshatra Moola'[5] around the time of Rama and Vanara army leaving for Lanka, from Kishkindha. None of the four proposals we investigated (SRS, Vartak, Bhatnagar, Yardi) corroborate this observation for their timeline.

Conclusion

I do not claim my work to be the final word on this subject. Fortunately deductive methodology enables a methodical way to test one's theory/proposal and thus corroborate or falsify the findings.

Imagination has its place in formulation and proposal of a theory, however testing/experiments provide the verdict on the corroboration or the falsification of a theory.

In words of Sir Karl Popper:

Although I believe that in the history of science it is always the theory and not the experiment, always the idea and not the observation, which opens up the way to new knowledge, I also believe that it is always the experiment which saves us from following a track that leads nowhere: which helps us out of the rut, and which challenges us to find a new way.

I must make it clear that while not a final word on this subject, I do claim my work to be the best, and my theory/proposal to be the better theory/proposal, among five proposals (SRS, Vartak, Bhatnagar-Bala, Yardi and Oak) put forward to determine the timing of Ramayana.

23

IMPLICATIONS, PREDICTIONS & NEW PROBLEMS

"We need not try to make history out of legend, but we ought to assume that beneath much that is artificial or incredible there lurks something of fact."
    - C Leonard Woolley

Superior theory explains more, and is better tested. Every worthwhile new theory raises new problems and frankly the worth of a new theory can be measured by new problems, i.e. problems of an ever-increasing depth and an ever-increasing fertility. The most lasting contribution to the growth of scientific knowledge that a new theory can make is the new problems, which it raises.

World Civilizations

I showed in my previous book that the Mahabharata civilization (5561 BCE) turns out to be the earliest, based on dates proposed for other civilizations, e.g. Egyptian, Sumerian, Babylonian, Mayan or Inca civilizations. Archeological research on Sindhu-Sarasvati (Indus) civilization has pushed timing of this civilization as far back as 7000 BCE.

Research presented in this book pushes the date for the earliest civilization to 13th millennium BCE (Ramayana). We should also realize that there is documented genealogy of at least 64 generations before Rama and numerous other ancient Indian history (besides Ramayana and Mahabharata) to be still explored.

Dating of Veda

In my previous book, I wrote:

Mahabharata observations (Fall of Abhijit) allude to the events of the ancient past as far back as 14500 B.C. and 22500 B.C. The Mahabharata text contains references, which indicate Veda and Ramayana predating the Mahabharata. Although exact timing of Ramayana is uncertain, what is certain is that Ramayana occurred long before the Mahabharata war. Ramayana and Mahabharata, both contain references to Veda. The Mahabharata War, as a chronological marker, pushes the timing of Ramayana and that of Veda, in further antiquity.

Although I began my research on Ramayana with the timing of Mahabharata (5561 BCE) as the lower bound, I have shown that a time interval of 10000 BCE-17500 BCE can be inferred for plausible timing of Ramayana from internal astronomy observations of Ramayana. The timing of Ramayana in 13th millennium BCE (12240 BCE- 12196 BCE), as a chronological marker, pushes the timing of Veda (Rig-Veda, Yajur-Veda, Sama-Veda), in further antiquity, since Ramayana mentions existence of all three of them. We must remember that Vyasa (5561 BCE) did edit all Vedas and thus the timing of edited (possibly what we have today) version of Vedas is that of Mahabharata (~5561 BCE).

The occurrence of Ramayana in 13th millennium BCE and specific reference of 'BrahmaRashi' as referring to North Pole Star, corroborate 'Fall of Abhijit' observation and also explains the significance of another observation from Mahabharata - 'creation of *Prati-srushti*' by sage Vishwamitra. We no longer have to look at 'Fall of Abhijit' (14602 BCE) as some isolated instance in antiquity.

River Sarasvati

Two rivers, Sutlej and Yamuna, responsible for the grand status of river Sarasvati in Rig-Veda times (i.e. composition of Rig-Veda), have already separated from Sarasvati in Ramayana times[346]. Yamuna has already merged with Ganga[347]in Ramayana times. Thus we may have to go back in further antiquity in search of the grand Sarasvati of Rig-Veda, i.e. before 13th millennium BCE. This assertion is consistent with evidence from Valmiki Ramayana and also with findings of Francfort's research team. Francfort's research concluded that actual large paleocourses (of Sarasvati) of the river have been dry since the early Holocene period or even earlier. It is important to recognize that pre-

Harappan settlements exist from 3700 BCE. Early Holocene refers to time interval 10000 BCE – 7000 BCE.

Studies done by Clift, et al, have shown, based on U-Pb Zircon dating, that river Yamuna flowed westwards and into river Sarasvati before 47000 BCE. This means river Yamuna was not flowing eastward and/or merging with Ganga, before 47000 BCE. On the other hand Ramayana refers to eastward flowing of river Yamuna in many places and also merging of Yamuna with Ganga. We thus have 47000 BCE as the upper limit on the timing of Ramayana, from purely geological evidence and thus anyone claiming occurrence of Ramayana more than 50,000 BP (before Present) has an obligation to explain this discrepancy (absence of eastward flowing Yamuna) for their timeline!

Out of India (OIT) Migrations

Indo-Aryan speaking civilizations such as Mitanni were established in Northern Syria and South-eastern Turkey by 1500 BCE. Many other civilizations from this region have allusions to them migrating from the east. These civilizations need to be studied in the context of newly established Ramayana (and also Mahabharata) timeline. These could be, but not necessarily, post Mahabharata migrations to the west.

King Pururava had two sons from Urvashi, Ayu and Amawasu. Ayu migrated to the east and his descendants were known as Kuru-Panchala and Kashi-Videhas. Amawasu migrated to the west and his descendants were known as Gandharas (Afganistan), Parsu (Persia) and Arrattas (western Iran). King Pururava is listed as descendant of Ila, and Ila is listed as descendant of Manu.

It is true that genealogy of kings lists only prominent kings. Still, with limited list of kings available, the Pandavas are listed after a gap of 55+ descendants of king Pururava, from the line of Ayu (Kuru-Panchalas). As a result one has to search for Amawasu migration, long before the Mahabharata War.

Genealogy of Ikshvaku dynasty shows that there were 28 kings between Rama and Brihadbala. Brihadbala was contemporary of Mahabharata and fought from Kaurava side and was killed during the Mahabharata War. This would make time of king Pururava (55-28 = 27) some 27+ generations before Rama. We must remember that genealogy of kings can provide only approximate (and only corroborative evidence) and thus we need more reliable evidence to determine the timing(s) of OIT migrations.

During the time of Ramayana, we observe westward expansion. Shatrughna went west (from Ayodhya) to Mathura and established that place over a period of 12 years. Bharata went to Northwest India – Gandharva Pradesh (Afghanistan, NW Pakistan), along with his sons – Taksha and Pushkal, defeated Shailush, and established Takshashila and Pushkalavati over a period of five years.

Sindhu-Sarasvati Civilization

Ramayana period of 13th millennium makes Sindhu-Sarasvati civilization a post Ramayana civilization. All phases of Sindhu-Sarasvati civilization, including early food producing era of 7000 BC (Mehagarh Phase I) are post Ramayana settlements.

Domestication of Horses (& Elephants)

This is what I wrote in my previous book:

While I do not accept lack of evidence for domestication of horses as evidence against my Mahabharata timeline, I consider my theory and proposed timeline of the Mahabharata War untenable if it could be proved that domesticated horses did not exist in India during 6th millennium B.C. In fact my timeline demands presence of domesticated horses in India long before 6th millennium B.C. Since nothing can be 'proved' per say, I am rather predicting existence of domesticated horses (in India) definitely around 5561 B.C., long time before the earliest date proposed (4000 B.C.) for domestication of horses and that too only outside India by traditional scholarship. In fact I am predicting existence of domesticated horses long before 5561 B.C., based on my assertion of Ramayana before Mahabharata, and Vedas before Ramayana and the fact that Mahabharata, Ramayana and Vedas have descriptions of domesticated horses, Ashwamedha sacrifice and horse drawn chariots.

Valmiki Ramayana describes Ayodhya of king Dasharatha as a place crowded with horses and elephants. Ayodhya had horses of excellent breed born from areas of Kamboja, Bailika, Vanayu and elephants of high breed such as Iravata and of three classes- Bhadra, Mandra and Mirga, from Vindhya and Himalaya mountains[348].

In the light of 13th millennium BCE as the timing of Ramayana, I would state that my timeline demands presence of domesticated horses in India long before 13th millennium BCE and thus I am predicting existence of domesticated horses (in India) definitely during 13th millennium BCE, thousands of years earlier than proposed date of 4000 BCE by traditional scholarship.

Invention of Writing

Ramayana and Mahabharata texts preserve numerous details of empirical astronomical observations of their times and those of further antiquity with respect to Ramayana and Mahabharata. Ability of these ancient civilizations to document empirical data amazes me.

I conjecture that writing skills existed long before 3500 BCE, the date accepted as invention of writing by traditional scholarship. I do not know where to look for such evidence or the type of empirical evidence that will convince us of the antiquity of writing skills.

Rig-Veda, Ramayana and Mahabharata contain indirect allusions to the existence of writing nevertheless I desire independent evidence. We have mention of names of warriors engraved on arrows in the Mahabharata text and name of Rama engraved on arrows in the Ramayana text.

New & Existing Problems

This book is focused on determining the timing of Ramayana. However, there is another set of observations, e.g. Pushpak Vimana and its ability to fly from Lanka (Candy) to Ayodhya in one day, ability of Hanuman to fly with great speed, mystic missiles and such. What we read in Valmiki Ramayana, in such instances, is the outcome of that technology but no background information whatsoever. In effect, we have too many unknowns. Thus, while we can conjecture and even offer suggestions, our theories will remain untested theories until we device ingenious experiments to test them. Until then our discussion will remain inconclusive.

Valmiki Ramayana contains many subjects that raise many problems for our understanding of Ramayana times, when viewed through our biases towards ancient civilizations.

My goal is to list few of these problems and thus have a ready list for future researchers. Let's make a list of these problems. Recognize that the list is only illustrative in nature and numerous additional problems can be listed.

(1) Location, rationale for building of Nala-Setu and challenges of finding remnants of Nala-setu in our times.

(2) Knowledge of geography in Ramayana times: Sugriva demonstrates amazing knowledge of not only Indian subcontinent but also many parts of the world. On the other hand, Valmiki's narrative exhibits inferior knowledge for the southern Indian geography, specifically related to descriptions of 'Vindhya' mountain ranges.

(3) 13th Millennium: Elephants with four, three and two tusks, status of Sarasvati and other rivers, weather and monsoon pattern in Indian subcontinent

(4) Kumbhakarna and his sleeping disorder

(5) Corroboration of Treta Yuga with the timing of Ramayana: Timing of Ramayana after Rig, Yajur and Sama Veda but before Mahabharata

(6) Corroboration and meaning of big numbers in Ramayana: e.g., Dasharatha of 77000 years, Rama ruling for 10000 years

(7) Corroboration of numerous incidents of Ravana's life: Superimposition of Time and place

(8) Who were Vanara, Rikshas, Gridhas and Garudas?

(9) Pushpak Vimana, counterpart of modern airplane, that was capable of carrying good number of people from Lanka to Ayodhya, a distance of ~1500 miles within a day.

(10) Valmiki Ramayana talks of many having an ability to fly: Vanara – Hanuman, Sugriva, Angada, Gridha- Sampati, Rakshasa: Vibhishan, his ministers, Ravana's espionage team- Shuka, Sarana, Ravana's son-Indrajit, etc., If all residents of Lanka did not have ability to fly, how did they cross the ocean?

(11) How did Valmiki gather information of the instances that occurred away from Ayodhya?

(12)Rakshasa were experts in conjuring tricks – Golden Deer, Indrajit bringing Sita like person to the battlefield, Indrajit fighting while invisible to others, Vidyujjiva creating human like masks of Rama and Laxman to show Sita.

(13)What made Hanuman and Angada carry Rama and Laxman on their shoulders during the journey or while fighting with Ravana army?

(14) What is the significance of planned *Yajna* of Indrajit at Nikumbhi, which according to Vibhishan, if completed, would have turned detrimental to Rama and his Vanara army?

(15) Chariot of Indra and Matali- sudden appearance from where?

(16) Sanjivani plants

I have researched first 8 problems and I will soon publish this work, as a separate book. The book wil also discuss similar problems from the Mahabharata. Dr. P V Vartak has discussed many of these problems in his book 'Vastav Ramayana' and I encourage readers to read his book in the original (Marathi) or its translation.

Myth of a theory that explains everything

If one dreams of a theory that explains not only when Ramayana happened but also the mystery behind Pushpak Vimana, flying ability of Hanuman, Sampati, Jatayu, Angada, Sugriva, Vibhishan and his ministers, members of Ravana's spy team, conjuring abilities of Rakshasa, invisibility of Indrajit during the war, efficacy of Sanjivani plants that healed injuries of Rama, Laxman and Vanara and many such things of Valmiki Ramayana, we cannot certainly blame such an individual. We all would want to see such a theory.

In scientific language, we will call such a theory, a theory with highest level of universality. Why don't we have such theories – in physics, chemistry, biology, evolution, geology, genetics or history? The reason we don't have such theories with high level of universality because such theories are too far removed from the level reached by the testable science of the day and for that very reason may give rise to a 'metaphysical system'.

For example, a proposal of Ramayana occurring about a million years in antiquity is based on series of metaphysical statements.

(1) Valmiki Ramayana refers to time of Rama as that of after Krita/Satya Yuga.

(2) There are numerous statements in other ancient Indian litera-ture that refers to Rama's time as that of Treta Yuga.

(3) We have numerous theories of Yuga, about their definition and their length coupled with confusion of 'divine' vs. 'human' years.

(4) We have few interpretations for 'divine' or 'human' years.

While only one set of such theories lead us to a time period of one million years for the timing of Ramayana, we have no means to test this proposition, i.e. theories of Yuga. We do not have accurate astronomy simulations that will allow us to test planetary positions one million years into antiquity.

Let's consider Ramayana observations of elephants with four, three and two tusks [344, 345]. If we want to set/design a crucial experiment to test this hypothesis, then we will need, as a first approximation, a well corroborated theory such as my theory/proposal in this book. At the same time, we will also need something new – something new that can be tested, which in this case won't come from the field of astronomy, but rather from the field of evolution, genetics, archeology and geology. Thus the system will not be considered metaphysical. In this case, this new experiment, irrespective of its final outcome, will be considered a new advance towards the growth of knowledge.

Similar logic would also apply to other observations of Ramayana. For example, to understand the rationale for location (or construction method in building) of Nala-Setu, our experiment would include knowledge of changes in the sea level, changes in the bottom of sea level, mechanism of earth crust and/or tectonic displacement along the border of Sri Lanka/India during, before and after 13th millennium BCE.

Corroboration of descriptions for world geography, as narrated by Sugriva, would require knowledge of sea levels in 13th millennium BCE and also knowledge of anthropological and geological realities of the areas mentioned by Sugriva.

This may explain why a link with the science of the day is as a rule es-tablished by those theories which are proposed in an attempt to meet the current problem situations, i.e. current difficulties, contradictions and falsifications. For example, problem of Pushpak Vimana is more relevant and amenable to possible tests since 20th century CE (i.e. after availability of flying Airplanes) than in say 16th century CE.

Path of Science

One who truly understands this scientific process will immediately recognize that merit of a specific theory is always to be judged in the context of another theory, one's own or those of others.

Discussion of a theory in the absence of another theory or without the context of a specific problem is futile. This is because science is not a system of certain well established statements, nor it is a system that steadily advances towards a state of finality. Although it can neither attain truth nor probability, the striving for knowledge and the search for truth are still the strongest motives of scientific discovery.

Bold ideas, unjustified anticipations and speculative thoughts are our only means for interpreting nature and history. We must hazard them to win our prize. As Novalis said, "Theories are like nets, those who cast may catch." Those among us who are unwilling to expose their ideas to the hazard of refutation do not take part in the scientific game.

In words of Sir Karl Popper:

The old scientific ideal of absolutely certain, demonstrable knowledge has proved to be an idol. The demand for scientific objectivity makes it inevitable that every scientific statement must remain *tentative forever*. It may indeed be corroborated, but such corroboration is relative to other statements, which, again, are tentative. Only in our subjective experiences of conviction, in our subjective faith, can we be 'absolutely certain'.

Appendix A

ORIGIN OF WEEKDAY NAMES

By

Sudarshan Bharadwaj & Nilesh Nilkanth Oak

The nomenclature of the weekdays is similar across multiple cultures. The weekdays in many European languages are named after the Sun, Moon, Mars, Mercury, Jupiter, Venus, and Saturn, respectively.

For example, the weekdays in English are: Sunday, Monday, Tuesday, Wednesday, Thursday, Friday, and Saturday. Of these, Sunday, Monday, and Saturday are readily recognizable as being named after the Sun, Moon, and Saturn, respectively. Tuesday is derived from "Tiv's day," which is named after the Norse god of single combat, Tyr. Wednesday is derived from "Woden's day," Thursday from "Thor's day," and Friday from "Freya's day." Among the Norse gods and goddesses, Tyr is identified with Mars, Woden with Mercury, Thor with Jupiter, and Freya with Venus. This nomenclature is also similar to that in Northern European languages such as Danish, Dutch, or Swedish. Similarly, the weekdays in French, Italian, and Spanish are named, for the most part, after the Roman days of the Sun, Moon, Mars, and so on to Saturn.

European sources attribute the nomenclature of the weekdays to the Greeks or the Babylonians. However, there is scant evidence for these claims, and the claims are mostly based on conjectures, circular logic and uninformed opinions.

We will look at four sets of explanations, two ancient Indian texts on astronomy and two from individual scientists/researchers from last two centuries.

Aryabhatiya & Surya Siddhanta

Both are well known, most referred and most esteemed. Like many Indian classical works, they are poems in the Sanskrit language.

Not trivial works by any means, they cover cosmology, planetary motions, eclipses, conjunctions, star positions, risings/settings, mathematics, geography, instrumentation and model-making. Both of them are not conventional textbooks in the sense that they are too succinct and somewhat cryptic for a rank beginner. They are rather meant as a concise aid to instruction for the experienced teacher.

While both works share commonalities, **Surya Siddhanta** is much older. **Aryabhatiya** appears to be from fifth century CE. In his excellent work, Anil Narayanan (see selected bibliography) has shown that while **Surya Siddhanta** has been updated several times (last update as recently as 580 CE), possibly the actual epoch was as far back as 7300 BCE-7800 BCE, in antiquity.

Aryabhatiya

To date, the best explanation for this particular ordering of the weekdays and their association with various grahas comes from a verse in the Aryabhatiya, composed by the Indian mathematician and astronomer Aryabhatta (**Aryabhatiya, Kala-Kriya Pada, Verse, 16**):

सप्तैते होरेशा: शनैश्चराद्या यथाक्रमं शीघ्रा: |
शीघ्रक्रमाच्च्तुर्था भवन्ति सूर्योदयाद् दिनपा: | |

The (above mentioned – mentioned in previous verse) seven Grahas beginning with Saturn, which are arranged in the order of increasing velocity, are the lords of the successive hours. The Grahas occurring fourth in the order of increasing velocity are the lords of the successive days, which are reckoned from Sunrise (in Lanka).

(Sanskrit word 'Graha' is generally translated as 'planets' in astronomical context. This is a mistake. The meaning of 'graha' is 'one that grasps'. Thus, in the astronomical context, the word 'graha' means an astral object that grasps another astral object (e.g. 'Graha' approaching a nakshatra – a visual delusion, of course). It also means an astral body that exerts attractive force on the earth.)

What we have above is a 'mnemonic device'. The original form or explanation can be understood or explained in few different ways.

The lords of the twenty-four hours (with hours being measured from sunrise at Lanka) are: Saturn, Jupiter, Mars, Sun, Venus, Mercury, Moon, Saturn, Jupiter, Mars, Sun, Venus, Mercury, Moon, Saturn, Jupiter, Mars, Sun, Venus, Mercury, Moon, Saturn, Jupiter, Mars, respectively, and the lords of the seven days are: Saturn, Sun, Moon, Mars, Mercury, Jupiter, Venus, respectively.

The lord of the day is the lord of the first hour of that day, the day being measured from sunrise.

Surya Siddhanta

Surya Siddhanta has similar explanation **(Bhugoladhyaya -78)**

मन्दादध: क्रमेण स्युश्चतुर्था दिवसाधिप:
होरेशा सूर्यतनयादधोध: क्रमशस्तथा

Starting from the Saturn downward, the fourth graha is called the lord of the day. The graha starting from the Saturn successively down-wards are the lords of the hour.

Another way to understand this explanation is shown in the table:

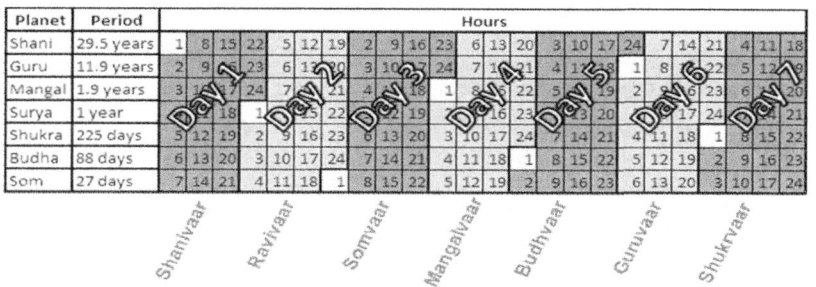

Planet	Period	Hours																						
Shani	29.5 years	1	8	15	22	5	12	19	2	9	16	23	6	13	20	3	10	17	24	7	14	21	4	11	18
Guru	11.9 years	2	9	16	23	6	13	20	3	10	17	24	7	14	21	4	11	18	1	8	15	22	5	12	19
Mangal	1.9 years	3	10	17	24	7	14	21	4	11	18	1	8	15	22	5	12	19	2	9	16	23	6	13	20
Surya	1 year	4	11	18	1	8	15	22	5	12	19	2	9	16	23	6	13	20	3	10	17	24	7	14	21
Shukra	225 days	5	12	19	2	9	16	23	6	13	20	3	10	17	24	7	14	21	4	11	18	1	8	15	22
Budha	88 days	6	13	20	3	10	17	24	7	14	21	4	11	18	1	8	15	22	5	12	19	2	9	16	23
Som	27 days	7	14	21	4	11	18	1	8	15	22	5	12	19	2	9	16	23	6	13	20	3	10	17	24

Shanivaar   Ravivaar   Somvaar   Mangalvaar   Budhvaar   Guruvaar   Shukrvaar

Shri Suhas Gurjar of Jyotrividya Parisamshta-Pune made one of the authors aware of this **Aryabhatiya** reference. He also provided an explanation. It is summarized in the table below: Shri Gurjar has made it intuitive by using 6 AM as a proxy for the sunrise. Weekday is named after the 'graha' corresponding to 6 AM of that day, beginning with Shani (Saturn) and thus Saturday.

आकाशातील दृश्य गतीच्या चढत्या क्रमाने ग्रह/ सूर्य	शनीवार	रवीवार	सोमवार	मंगळवार	बुधवार	गुरूवार	शुक्रवार
शनि	६ १३ २०	३ १० १७	२४ ७ १४ २१	४ ११ १८	१ ८ १५ २२	५ १२ १९	२
गुरू	७ १४ २१	४ ११ १८	१ ८ १५ २२	५ १२ १९	२ ९ १६ २३	६ १३ २०	३
मंगळ	८ १५ २२	५ १२ १९	२ ९ १६ २३	६ १३ २०	३ १० १७ २४	७ १४ २१	४
सूर्य (रवी)	९ १६ २३	६ १३ २०	३ १० १७ २४	७ १४ २१	४ ११ १८ १	८ १५ २२	५
शुक्र	१० १७ २४	७ १४ २१	४ ११ १८ १	८ १५ २२	५ १२ १९ २	९ १६ २३	६
बुध	११ १८ १	८ १५ २२	५ १२ १९ २	९ १६ २३	६ १३ २० ३	१० १७ २४	७
चंद्र (सोम)	१२ १९ २	९ १६ २३	६ १३ २० ३	१० १७ २४	७ १४ २१ ४	११ १८ १	८

Sudarshan Bharadwaj did exhaustive search for the origins of week-day names. He found that as of November 2013, there are no other rational explanations for the order of weekdays (i.e. other than **Aryabhatiya**) anywhere in the world. Of course there is no dearth of explanations however they share a common theme. All of these re-maining explanations are convoluted and circular in nature, claiming the origin, arbitrarily, to Babylonians or Greeks, based on opinions, conjectures and speculations however with characteristic lack of factual evidence.

The only rational explanation for the nomenclature of the weekdays comes from an Indian source. No other culture provides any reason for why a particular graha (planet) is associated with a particular day of the week. Only the Indian Jyotish (Hora-shastra) provides the rationale, and not some folk-lore reason, but rather an astronomical one.

Hindu concept of seven day week is much older and has other asso-ciated astronomical issues. In Judaism, seven day week is taken for granted without any introspection. There is no development of ideas or background on the issue, which indicates that this concept was bor-rowed, ready-made, from another culture. Judaism is not the only cul-ture to do so. Other cultures have also done this. All of them have sev-en day week. And none of them have any associated astronomy with it to decide why it should be seven days and which day corresponds to which planet (or deity) and rationale for the sequence.

We are asserting that ancient cultures of Europe/Africa/Arabia (Greece, Rome, Egypt, Babylonia, etc.) were not aware of the true ra-tionale behind naming and sequence of week days. We are asserting that western civilization to this day is not aware of the true rationale behind naming and sequence of week days. These assertions are based on the evidence as of November 2013. Of course, we are not denying the possibility of discoveries of old manuscripts among above mentioned cultures that refers to ancient Indian explanation for the naming of weekdays.

One of the authors searched the internet and Wikipedia, exhaustively, for any and all references in this context. We also saved screenshots of these Wikipedia searches (as of November 2013). Reader must be aware that information on Wikipedia is dynamic and while Wikipedia is a decent source of information for numerous non-controversial subjects; when it comes to subjects of critical importance (philosophy, original research, appropriation and digestion of ideas) Wikipedia is, as Rajiv Malhotra puts it, "a sinister force behind the deceptive mask of fairness and level playing field." Readers may visit www.rajivmalhotra.com to know more about original and groundbreaking work of Rajiv Malhotra.

Sir Oliver Lodge (1893 CE)

And before someone jumps and claims that Europe was aware of this true rationale by the time of Copernicus, Kepler, Galileo and Newton; let me refer them to the explanation offered by Sir Oliver Lodge (Pioneers of Science, Macmillan & Co, 1893, pages 17-19).

Lodge states that seven grahas were known: Moon, Mercury, Venus, Sun, Mars, Jupiter, Saturn and states that they were supposedly ordered in this sequence due to their distance from the earth. He also mentions that at times the sun was thought to be nearer than Mercury or Venus. He states that Mars, Jupiter and Saturn were placed in that order because that is the order of their apparent motions, and it was natural to suppose that the slowest moving bodies were furthest off.

The explanation for the sequence of days (beginning with Sunday) is similar to one offered by Aryabhatta, however without the comprehension of its true rationale. It is not clear if Lodge is referring to the order of grahas round the circle counterclockwise, as the method of astrologers of his day, or his own way of explaining it. The method works, however, I want to emphasize that Lodge has not shown awareness of the underlying rationale and explanation of Aryabhatta.

And while on the subject I want to make another observation. Lodge states that science of Greek was remarkable, at least in some areas. However he laments that it largely based on what has **proved** to be a wrong method of procedure, viz. **the introspective and conjectural**, rather than **the inductive and experimental** (I suppose the correct method in Lodge's opinion) (**emphasis mine**).

Unfortunately, both Greeks and Lodge missed the correct method, although each of them shared an element of it, viz. ***conjectural and experimental***.

He summarizes the procedure for weekeday names using the following diagram.

Dr. P V Vartak

Available ancient Indian literature is vast, in spite of the fact that much has been lost. No wonder likes of Dr. P V Vartak, who has done much original research and much of it based on astronomy observations, still missed either **Surya Siddhanta** or **Aryabhatiya** references for the rationale of weekday names.

In his words (A Realistic Approach to the Valmiki Ramayana, Blue Bird, 2008, pages 302-306),

The Sun was held as *atman* and the Moon was held as the *manas,* the first name given to the weekeday from the Sun, e.g. Aditya. The next day was named after the Moon, e.g. Soma. Then they (sages) gave alternate names, once from the Moon and once from the Sun. This means they selected grahas alternately from the external and the internal group. After Monday, they took Mangal (Mars) from the external group, then Budha (Mercury) from the internal, then Guru (Jupiter) from external, then Shukra (Venus) from internal, then Shani (Saturn) from the external.

The point I want to make is that if we have an existing order, one can always retrofit an explanation that may be arbitrary and still logical. This could be proposal of European astrologers, Sir Oliver Lodge or Dr. P V Vartak.

Division of Day in 24 Parts

Nilesh Oak did exhaustive search for the origins of division of the day into 24 hours and found that online references full of conjectures and speculations, but little evidence.

Internet search produced the following that is worth mentioning:

Our 24-hour day comes from the ancient Egyptians who divided day-time into 10 hours they measured with devices such as shadow clocks, and added a twilight hour at the beginning and another one at the end of the day-time. Night-time was divided in 12 hours, based on the observations of stars. The Egyptians had a system of 36 star groups called 'decans' — chosen so that on any night one decan rose 40 minutes after the previous one. In the Egyptian system, the length of the 'day-time' and 'night-time' hours were unequal and varied with the seasons. In summer, day-time hours were longer than night-time hours while in winter the hour lengths were the other around.

We were aware of multiple time measurement systems in Indian astronomy but could not think of any system that divided the day into 24 parts. This is crucial for explanation of 'mnemonic devices' provided by *Aryabhatiya* and *Surya Siddhanta*. While both of them provided measurement system of time, the division of the day into 24 parts was not suggested. Ancient Indian literature does present multiple time measurement systems and existence of a system that divided a day into 24 parts is intuitive for a civilization that has Luni-solar calendar, 12 months, six seasons, etc. That is all fine. But did we have documented evidence of such?

Srimad Bhagavad Purana, Skandha 3, Adhyaya 11, Shlok 1-14 provided one such evidence. It presents time measurement system as follows:

1 Ahoratra (day & night)	= 8 Prahar	= 24 hours
1 Aha= 1 ratra	= 4 Prahar	= 12 hours
6 or (7) Nadika (Danda)	= 1 Prahar	= 3 hours
2 Nadika (danda)	= 1 Muhurta	= 60 minutes
15 Laghu	= 1 Nadika	= 30 minutes
15 Kashtha	= 1 Laghu	= 2 minutes (120 Seconds)
5 Kshana	= 1 Kashtha	= 8 seconds

3 Nimesh	= 1 Kshana	= 1.6 seconds
3 lav	= 1 Nimesh	= 0.53 seconds
3 Vedha	= 1 lav	= 0.17 seconds
100 Truti	= 1 Vedha	= 0.056 seconds
3 Trasarenu	= 1 Truti	= 0.00056 seconds
3 Anu	= 1 Trasarenu	= 0.00019 seconds
2 Paramanu	= 1 Anu	= 0.000063 seconds
1 Paramanu		= 0.000032 seconds

We want to make few observations:

1. While we were aware of ancient Indian time measurement system where: '1 AhoRatra (24 hour day) = 30 Muhurtas' and thus '1 Muhutra= 48 minutes', the above time measurement system from Srimad Bhagavad Purana refers to '1 Muhurta = 60 minutes = 1 hour = 1 hora'.

2. This is then not unlike the difference between US and UK Gallon: same unit of measurement (Muhurta) with different magnitude (60 min vs. 48 min). Three significantly different sizes are in current use: Imperial gallon (~4.546 L), US gallon (~3.79 L) and US Dry gallon (~4.40 L).

3. The fact that 6 or 7 Nadika corresponds to 1 Prahar, also means 24-28 Nadika corresponded to 1 Aha (daylight). This flexibility appears to be result of changing length of the day (and night) between 12-14 hours, with changes in the season. Flexibility in the length of daytime (sunlight) is useful for civic purposes (not unlike 'daylight saving time' adjustments).

4. The system of dividing a day into 24 parts called 'hora' seems to be relevant only in consideration with the theory of week days and astrology. Otherwise astronomy works seem to employ different time units.

5. Above observations point to the fact that this system of time measurement described in *Srimad Bhagavad Purana* was suitable for both astronomy and astrology purposes, for the astronomy timekeeping and also for the civic timekeeping.

6. Varahamihira has suggested Sanskrit origin of 'hora' by explaining that the word is 'coined' by taking the middle portion of the word 'a**hora**tra', leaving out 'a' and 'tra'.

Appendix B

SAGE AGASTYA'S MIGRATION TO THE SOUTH

Valmiki Ramayana tells us that sage Agastya and his descendants were already well settled in southern India. This means sage Agastya had moved to the southern India definitely before 12300 BCE.

Proposal of K D Abhyankar

K D Abhyankar published a note in Current Science (Vol. 89, No. 12, 25 December 2005) where he argued for sage Agastya migration to southern India around 4000-5000 BCE. His claim directly contradicts with my assertion for the presence of the sage Agastya(s) in southern India during and before 12300 BCE. The purpose of this brief note of mine is to provide criticism of K D Abhyankar's claim.

K D Abhyankar begins with Puranic story. In his words:

The Puranic story tells us that the Vindhya Mountain tried to compete with the Himalayas in height by becoming taller and taller. People became afraid that it may obstruct the path of the sun; so they approached sage Agastya who was the Guru (teacher) of the Vindhya. As Agastya arrived, the Vindhya Mountain prostrated before him in reverence. The sage said that he was going south and that the mountain should lie prostrated till he returned. But the sage never returned thus laying the Vindhya flat for ever.

Abhyankar goes on to interpret this tale as an allegory to the actual crossing of the Vindhya, by sage Agastya, for the first time in history. Abhyankar also tells us his conjecture that when sage Agastya crossed the Vindhya and came to the southern India, he would have been the first northerner to see the star Canopus and hence the star was named after him (Agastya), not unlike Megellanic clouds in the southern sky are named after the navigator Magellan, who first saw them as he sailed southwards.

I do not want to get into the discussion of the 'truth claim' of Abhyankar's Agastya story. Rather, objective of this note is,

(1) To question his proposed timing, <u>assuming</u> his story of sage Agastya and his <u>rationale</u> for nomenclature of star Canopus as Agastya is valid.

(2) To show that, <u>assuming his story of sage Agastya and his rationale for nomenclature of star Canopus as Agastya is valid</u>, the timing of sage Agastya crossing Vindhya has to go back definitely before 17000 BCE, and more likely to the time interval of 19,000 BCE- 25,000 BCE.

We will assume the identical criteria employed by Abhyankar in his proplsal of 4000BCE-5000 BCE timeline for the migration of sage Agastya to the southern India. He writes:

If we assume that for a star to be visible at a place its altitude at the meridian passage should be at least 5^0.

Abhyankar tested for the visibility of star Agastya (Canopus) from various Indian locations and came to the conclusion that " star Agastya was not visible from any part of India before 10,000 BCE". In fact this (10,000 BCE) is the time when it became visible at Kanyakumari (southern tip of India). Later on, it became visible in the Vindhya region around 5200 BCE. Abhyankar states that if one makes 8^0 (and not 5^0) meridian altitude as the criterion for visibility, then the date of sage Agastya (migration) would be shifted to about 4000 BCE.

This is how Abhyankar proposed 5000 BCE-4000 BCE time interval as the probable epoch of sage Agastya crossing the Vindhya mountain range. We will first estimate the plausible epoch of sage Agastya crossing the Vindhya mountain, ceteris paribus, and then come back to explain why there is such a huge gap between our proposal and that of Abhyankar.

Let's begin with the mutually agreed facts. Abhyankar admits that star Agastya was not visible from any part of India before 10,000 BCE. Abhyankar also recognizes the visibility (and lack of visibility) of star Agastya as a cyclic phenomena (related to 'precession of equinoxes') that will repeat after every ~26000 years.

Proposal of Nilesh Nilkanth Oak

I have made a case for Ramayana to have occurred in 12200 BCE and thus during Ramayana times, star Agastya could not have been visible anywhere from India.

We have an interesting case of corroboration of this fact. I say interesting because the evidence (corroboration) is of a 'negative' kind! Valmiki Ramayana talks of star Trishanku (Crux), a prominent star in the southern part of the sky. Valmiki Ramayana also talks of sage Agastya, multiple times, however, is silent on star Agastya. I assert that this is due to the fact that star Agastya (Canopus) was not visible from India, during Ramayana times.

I should also add that there is a plausible reference to visibility of star Agastya, in Mahabharata (Vana Parva), during the exile of Pandavas. The exact location for this plausible observation is hard to decipher. I do want to point out though that star Agastya was indeed above horizon in northern India during 5561 BCE, the timing of Mahabharata War confirmed by this author.

Since sage Agastya was already in the southern India in Ramayana times and assuming conjecture for the nomenclature of star Agastya (Canopus) of Abhyankar is true, we will have to go back in further antiquity (before 12200 BCE) to search for the timing of Agastya migration to the south.

I simulated the altitude (at meridian) of star Agastya (Canopus) for Bhopal, India (near Vindhya). As we simulate the sky, going back in antiquity, star Canopus touches the horizon (from below) around 17,000 BCE. If we want to match 5^0 or 8^0 altitudes suggested by Abhyankar, we are looking at a time interval of 19,000 BCE through 25,000 BCE when star Agastya was at those altitudes.

Of course, star Agastya would have been visible in southern India, much later than 17000 BCE. For example, star Agastya had altitude of 5^0 with respect to Kanyakumari (southern tip of India) around 17,000 BCE. Star Agastya was on the horizon (zero altitude) at Kanyakumari around 14,000 BCE. This then sets the lower limit for Agastya migration to the south.

The question arises: Why did Abhyankar missed his timing by more than 10,000 years? Abhyankar missed his timing because he stuck to baseless assumptions of Mahabharata timing (1200 +/- 1000 BCE or 2300 BCE, as he puts it) and further groundless assumption of 2000 year difference between Mahabharata and Ramayana (thus, he assumed

Ramayana around 4000 BCE or 5000 BCE)!

Comprehension & Comparision of Multiple Proposals

If my only purpose was to show how Abhyankar is wrong in his esti-mation of the timing of sage Agastya's southern migration, I would have never written this note. Many readers and researchers struggle in com-prehending a given theory. They do lot worse when they have to decide on a better theory, from the available theories. Part of this confusion is due to their desire for a 'proved' or 'established' theory. Thus, when new theory shakes the faith held by readers and researchers in an exist-ing theory; instead of taking the path of critical discussion, their natural reaction, at least for majority of them, is that of anger. I mean anger at the new theory that destroyed the foundations of existing theory (and its consequences). While we can only guess at the root cause of this anger, I conjecture that it originates from the pessimism that sets in due to the falsification of their cherished theory.

My hope is that both readers and researchers, alike, recognize that it is possible to choose a better theory and/or proposals between availa-ble alternatives.

The issue is best summarized by Sir Karl Popper:

The position between optimism and pessimism which I am trying to establish may be briefly described as follows: I agree with the pessimists that there is no justification for the claim of any particular theory or assertion to be true. Thus there is no justification of any claim to know, including the claims of scientific knowledge. But this merely means that all knowledge, including scientific knowledge, is hypothetical or conjectural: it is uncertain, fallible. This certainly does not mean that every assertion is as good as any other competing assertion. For we can discuss our various competing assertions, our conjectures, critically; and the result of the critical discussion is that we find out why some among the competing conjectures are better than others.

Accordingly, I agree with the optimists that our knowledge can grow, and can pro-gress; for we can sometimes justify the verdict of our critical discussion when it ranks certain conjectures higher than others.

A verdict of this kind always appraises our conjectures or theories from the point of view of their approach to truth: although we cannot justify any claim that a theory is true, we can sometime give good reasons for asserting that one theory is better than another, or even than all its competitors. In this way our knowledge can grow, and sci-ence can progress.

Selected Bibliography

1. Vartak, P. V., 'Wastav Ramayana, Pune
2. Oak, Nilesh Nilkanth, 'When did the Mahabharata War Happen? The Mystery of Arundhati (2011)
3. Vartak, P. V., Swayambhu, Pune (1996)
4. Vaidya, C. V. 'Epic India, or, India as described in the Mahabharata and the Ramayana'
5. Francfort, Henri-Paul, "Evidence for Harappan Irrigation system in Haryana and Rajasthan'", Eastern Anthropologist (1992) 45:87-103
6. Valmiki Ramayana, English Translation, Gita Press, Gorakhpur
7. Valmiki Ramayana, Critical edition by BORI-Pune
8. Popper, Karl, Conjectures and Refutations
9. Popper, Karl, The Logic of Scientific Discovery
10. Popper, Karl, The Poverty of Historicism
11. Clift, P. D. et al, "U-Pb zircon dating evidence for a pleistocene Sarasvati River and capture of the Yamuna River", Geology, 2012
12. Bhatnagar, Pushkar, 'Dating the era of Lord Ram'
13. Yardi, M. R., 'Epilogue of Ramayana'
14. Shukla, K. S. (& Sarma, K. V.) "Arybhatiya of Aryabhata (critically edited), Indian National Science Academy, 1976
15. Lodge, Oliver, Pioneers of Sciene, MacMillan &Co., 1893 (pages 17-19)
16. Abhyankar, K. D., "Folklore and Astronomy: Agastya a sage and a star", Current Science, Vol 89, No 12, 25 December 2005
17. Dikshit, S. B., "History of Indian Astronomy", Govt of India Press, 1969
18. Narayanan, A, 'Dating the Surya Siddhanta using computational simulation of proper motions and ecliptic varation, IJHS, 45.4 (2010), 455-476
19. Narayanan, A, 'The pulsating Indian epicycle of the Sun, IJHS, 46.3 (2011), 411-425
20. Vartak, P. V, 'A Realistic Approach to the Valmiki Ramayana' Blue Bird, 2008, (pages 302-306)
21. A C Bhaktivedanta Swami Prabhupada, 'Srimad Bhagvatam' (one volume edition) 1982 (pages 515-518)

VALMIKI RAMAYANA REFERENCES

1.
Bala GP 39:4-5, CE 38:4-5
शङ्करश्वशुरो नाम हिमवानचलोत्तमः ।
विन्ध्यपर्वतमासाद्य निरीक्षेते परस्परम् ॥ ४॥

तयोर्मध्ये प्रवृत्तोऽभूद्यज्ञः स पुरुषोत्तम ।
स हि देशो नरव्याघ्र प्रशस्तो यज्ञकर्मणि ॥ ५॥

2.
Ayodhya GP 3:4.CE 3:4
चैत्रः श्रीमानयं मासः पुण्यः पुष्पितकाननः ।
यौवराज्याय रामस्य सर्वमेवोपकल्प्यताम् ॥ ४॥

3.
Aranya GP 16:12, CE 16:12
निवृत्ताकाशशयनाः पुष्यनीता हिमारुणाः ।
शीता वृद्धतरायामास्त्रियामा यान्ति साम्प्रतम् ॥ १२॥

4.
Yuddha GP 4:48, CE 4:48
ब्रह्मराशिर्विशुद्धश्च शुद्धाश्च परमर्षयः ।
अर्चिष्मन्तः प्रकाशन्ते ध्रुवं सर्वे प्रदक्षिणम् ॥ ४३॥

5.
Yuddha GP 4:51-52, CE 4: 46-47
नैरृतं नैरृतानां च नक्षत्रमभिपीड्यते ।
मूलं मूलवता स्पृष्टं धूप्यते धूमकेतुना ॥ ४६॥
सरं चैतद्विनाशाय राक्षसानाम् उपस्थितम् ।
काले कालगृहीतानां नक्षत्रं ग्रहपीडितम् ॥ ४७॥

6.
Yuddha GP 124:1, CE 112:1
पूर्णे चतुर्दशे वर्षे पञ्चभ्यां लक्ष्मणाग्रजः ।
भरद्वाजाश्रमं प्राप्य ववन्दे नियतो मुनिम् ॥ १॥

7.
Yuddha GP 125:24, CE 113:22
पञ्चमीमद्य रजनीमुषित्वा वचनान्मुने: ।
भरद्वाजाभ्यनुज्ञातं द्रक्ष्यस्यद्यैव राघवम् ॥ २२॥

8.
Yuddha GP 126:54, CE 114:45
तं गङ्गां पुनरासाद्य वसन्तं मुनिसन्निधौ ।
अविघ्नं पुण्ययोगेन श्वो रामं द्रष्टुमर्हसि ॥ ४५॥

9.
Ayodhya GP 2.17, CE 2:13
इति ब्रुवन्तं मुदिताः प्रत्यनन्दन्नृपा नृपम् ।
वृष्टिमन्तं महामेघं नर्दन्तमिव बर्हिणः ॥ १३॥

10.
Ayodhya GP 3:36-37, CE 3:20-21
तेन विभाजिता तत्र सा सभाभिव्यरोचत ।
विमलग्रहनक्षत्रा शारदी द्यौरिवेन्दुना ॥ २०॥

तं पश्यमानो नृपतिस्तुतोष प्रियमात्मजम् ।
अलङ्कृतमिवात्मानमादर्शतलसंस्थितम् ॥ २१॥

11.
Ayodhya GP 7:31,
मन्थराया वच: श्रुत्वा शयनात् सा शुभानना
उत्तस्थौ हर्षसम्पूर्णा चन्द्रलेखेव शारदी

12.
Ayodhya GP 15:32, CE 13:26
शारदाभ्रघनप्रख्यं दीसं मेरुगुहोपमम् ।
दामभिर्वरमाल्यानां सुमहद्भिरलङ्कृतम् ॥ २६॥

13.
Ayodhya 19:37
उचितं च महाबाहुर्न जहौ हर्षमात्मवान
शारद: समुद्तीर्णांशुश्चन्द्रस्तेज इवात्मजं

14.
Ayodhya GP 44:31, CE 39:16
निशम्य तल्लक्ष्मणमातृवाक्यं
रामस्य मातुर्नरदेवपत्न्याः ।
सद्यः शरीरे विननाश शोकः
शरद्रतो मेघ इवाल्पतोयः ॥ १६॥

15.
Ayodhya GP 4:18, CE 4:18
अवष्टब्धं च मे राम नक्षत्रं दारुणैर्ग्रहैः ।
आवेदयन्ति दैवज्ञाः सूर्याङ्गारकराहुभिः ॥ १८॥

16.
Ayodhya GP 10:11
स कैकेय्या गृहं श्रेष्ठं प्रविवेश महायशा:
पांडुराभमिवाकाश राहुयुक्तं निशाकर

17.
Ayodhya GP 15:3, CE 13:3
उदिते विमले सूर्ये पुष्ये चाभ्यागतेऽहनि ।
अभिषेकाय रामस्य द्विजेन्द्रैरुपकल्पितम् ॥ ३॥

18.

Bala 18:8-9

ततो यज्ञे समाप्ते तु ऋतू नाम षट् समत्ययुः
ततः च द्वादशे मासे चैत्रे नावमिके तिथौ
नक्षत्रे अदिती दैवत्ये स्व उच्छ्व संस्थेषु पंचसु
ग्रहेषु कर्कटे लग्ने वाक्पता इंदुना सह
प्रोद्यमाने जगन्नाथम् सर्व लोक नमस्कृतम्
कौसल्या अजनयत रामं सर्व लक्षण संयुतम्
विष्णो अर्ध महाभागम् पुत्रं ऐक्वाकु नन्दनम्
लोहिताक्षम् महाबाहु रक्त ओष्टम् दुंदुभी स्वनम्

19.

Bala GP 8:24

तासां तेनातिकान्तेन वचनेन सुवर्चसां
मुखपद्मान्यशोभन्त पद्मानीव हिमात्यये

20.

Bala GP 16:25, CE 15:23

हर्षरश्मिभिरुद्योतं तस्यान्तःपुरमाबभौ ।
शारदस्याभिरामस्य चन्द्रस्येव नभोऽंशुभिः ॥ २३॥

21.

Ayodhya GP 26:9, CE 23:8

अद्य बार्हस्पतः श्रीमान्युक्तः पुष्यो न राघव
प्रोच्यते ब्राह्मणैः प्राज्ञैः केन त्वमसि दुर्मनाः

22.

Bala GP 20.2, CE 19:2

ऊनषोडशवर्षो मे रामो राजीवलोचनः ।
न युद्धयोग्यतामस्य पश्यामि सह राक्षसैः ॥ २॥

23.

Bala GP 19:5, CE 18:5

व्रते मे बहुशश्चीर्णे समाप्त्यां राक्षसाविमौ ।
मारीचश्च सुबाहुश्च वीर्यवन्तौ सुशिक्षितौ ।
तौ मांसरुधिरौघेण वेदिं तामभ्यवर्षताम् ॥ ५॥

24.

Bala GP GP 19:4, CE 18:4

अहं नियममातिष्ठ सिद्ध्यर्थे पुरुषर्षभ ।
तस्य विघ्नकरौ द्वौ तु राक्षसौ कामरूपिणौ ॥ ४॥

25.

Bala GP19:18, CE 18:17

अभिप्रेतमसंसक्तमात्मजं दातुमर्हसि ।
दशरात्रं हि यज्ञस्य रामं राजीवलोचनम् ॥ १७॥

26.

Bala GP 22:11, CE 21:9

अध्यर्धयोजनं गत्वा सरय्वा दक्षिणे तटे ।
रामेति मधुरा वाणीं विश्वामित्रोऽभ्यभाषत ॥ ९॥

27.

Bala GP 22:13, CE 21:10

गृहाण वत्स सलिलं मा भूत्कालस्य पर्ययः ।
मन्त्रग्रामं गृहाण त्वं बलामतिबलां तथा ॥ १०॥

28.

Bala GP 22:23, CE 21:19

गुरुकार्याणि सर्वाणि नियुज्य कुशिकात्मजे ।
ऊषुस्तां रजनीं तत्र सरय्वां सुसुखं त्रयः ॥ १९॥

29.

Bala GP 23:1-2, CE 22:1-2

प्रभातायां तु शर्वर्यां विश्वामित्रो महामुनिः ।
अभ्यभाषत काकुत्स्थं शयानं पर्णसंस्तरे ॥ १॥

कौसल्या सुप्रजा राम पूर्वा सन्ध्या प्रवर्तते ।
उत्तिष्ठ नरशार्दूल कर्तव्यं दैवमाह्निकम् ॥ २॥

30.

Bala GP 23:5, CE 22:5

तौ प्रयाते महावीर्यौ दिव्यं त्रिपथगां नदीम् ।
ददृशाते ततस्तत्र सरय्वाः सङ्गमे शुभे ॥ ५॥

31.

Bala GP 23:21-22, CE 22:18-19

यथा अहम् अजपन् संध्याम् ऋषयः ते समाहिताः ।
तत्र वासिभिः आनीता मुनिभिः सुव्रतैः सह ॥ १-२३-२१
न्यवसन् सुसुखम् तत्र काम आश्रम पदे तथा ।
कथाभिरभिरामाभिरभिरामौ नृपात्मजौ । - यदवा -
कथाभिः अभि रामभिः अभि रमौ नृप आत्मजौ
रमयामास धर्मात्मा कौशिको मुनिपुङ्गवः ॥ १-२३-२२

32.

Bala GP 24:1, CE 23:1

ततः प्रभाते विमले कृताह्निकमरिन्दमौ ।
विश्वामित्रं पुरस्कृत्य नद्यास्तीरमुपागतौ ॥ १॥

33.

Bala GP 26:31-34, CE 25:20-22

एवम् उक्त्वा सुराः सर्वे जग्मुर् हृष्टा विहायसम् ॥ १-२६-३१
विश्वामित्रम् पूजयन् ततः संध्या प्रवर्तते ।
ततो मुनिवरः प्रीतः ताटका वध तोषितः ॥ १-२६-३२
मूर्ध्नि रामम् उपाघ्राय इदम् वचनम् अब्रवीत् ।
इह अद्य रजनीम् राम वसाम शुभ दर्शन ॥ १-२६-३३
श्वः प्रभाते गमिष्यामः तद् आश्रम पदम् मम ।
विश्वामित्रः वचः श्रुत्वा हृष्टो दशरथात्मजः ॥ १-२६-३४
उवास रजनीम् तत्र ताटकाया वने सुखम् ।

34.

Bala GP 27:1-3, CE 26:1-3

अथ तां रजनीमुष्य विश्वामित्रो महायशाः ।
प्रहस्य राघवं वाक्यमुवाच मधुराक्षरम् ॥ १॥

परितुष्टोऽस्मि भद्रं ते राजपुत्र महायशः ।
प्रीत्या परमया युक्तो ददाम्यस्त्राणि सर्वशः ॥ २॥

देवासुरगणान्वापि सगन्धर्वोरगानपि ।
यैरमित्रान्प्रसह्याजौ वशीकृत्य जयिष्यसि ॥ ३॥

तानि दिव्यानि भद्रं ते ददाम्यस्त्राणि सर्वशः |
दण्डचक्रं महादिव्यं तव दास्यामि राघव || ४||

धर्मचक्रं ततो वीर कालचक्रं तथैव च |
विष्णुचक्रं तथात्युग्रमैन्द्रं चक्रं तथैव च || ५||

वज्रमस्त्रं नरश्रेष्ठ शैवं शूलवरं तथा |
अस्त्रं ब्रह्मशिरश्चैव ऐषीकमपि राघव || ६||

35.
Bala GP 29:31-32, CE 28:20
कुमारौ एव तां रात्रिम् उषित्वा सुसमाहितौ |
प्रभात काले च उत्थाय पूर्वां संध्याम् उपास्य च || १-२९-३१
प्रशुची परम् जाप्यम् समाप्य नियमेन च |
हुत अग्निहोत्रम् आसीनम् विश्वमित्रम् अवन्दताम् || १-२९-३२
कुमारावपि तां रात्रिमुषित्वा सुसमाहितौ |
प्रभातकाले चोत्थाय विश्वामित्रमवन्दताम् || २०||

36.
Bala GP 30:4, CE 29:4
अद्य प्रभृति षड्रात्रं रक्षेत राघवौ युवाम् |
दीक्षां गतो ह्येष मुनिर्मौनित्वं च गमिष्यति || ४||

37.
Bala GP 31:1-2, CE 30:1-2
अथ तां रजनीं तत्र कृतार्थौ रामलक्ष्मणौ |
ऊषतुर्मुदितौ वीरौ प्रहृष्टेनान्तरात्मना || १||

प्रभातायां तु शर्वर्यां कृतपौर्वाह्णिकक्रियौ |
विश्वामित्रमृषींश्चान्यान्सहितावभिजग्मतुः || २||

38.
Bala GP 31:6-7, CE 30:6-7
मैथिलस्य नरश्रेष्ठ जनकस्य भविष्यति |
यज्ञः परमधर्मिष्ठस्तत्र यास्यामहे वयम् || ६||

त्वं चैव नरशार्दूल सहास्माभिर्गमिष्यसि |
अद्भुतं च धनूरत्नं तत्र त्वं द्रष्टुमर्हसि || ७||

39.
Bala GP 31:17, CE 30:16
तं व्रजन्तं मुनिवरमन्वगादनुसारिणाम् |
शकटी शतमात्रं तु प्रयाणे ब्रह्मवादिनाम् || १६||

40.
Bala GP 31:19-20, CE 30:18-19
ते गत्वा दूरमध्वानं लम्बमाने दिवाकरे |
वासं चक्रुर्मुनिगणाः शोणाकूले समाहिताः || १८||

तेऽस्तं गते दिनकरे स्नात्वा हुतहुताशनाः |
विश्वामित्रं पुरस्कृत्य निषेदुरमितौजसः || १९||

41.
Bala GP 34:14-17, CE 33:14-17
गतोऽर्धरात्रः काकुत्स्थ कथाः कथयतो मम |
निद्रामभ्येहि भद्रं ते मा भूद्विघ्नोऽध्वनीह नः || १४||

निष्पन्दास्तरवः सर्वं निलीना मृगपक्षिणः |
नैशेन तमसा व्याप्ता दिशश्च रघुनन्दन || १५||

शनैर्वियुज्यते सन्ध्या नभो नेत्रैरिवावृतम् |
नक्षत्रतारागहनं ज्योतिर्भिरवभासते || १६||

उत्तिष्ठति च शीतांशुः शशी लोक्तमोनुदः |
ह्लादयन्प्राणिनां लोके मनांसि प्रभया विभो || १७||

42.
Bala GP 35:1-3, CE 34:1-3
उपास्य रात्रिशेषं तु शोणाकूले महर्षिभिः |
निशायां सुप्रभातायां विश्वामित्रोऽभ्यभाषत || १||

सुप्रभाता निशा राम पूर्वा सन्ध्या प्रवर्तते |
उत्तिष्ठोत्तिष्ठ भद्रं ते गमनायाभिरोचय || २||

तच्छ्रुत्वा वचनं तस्य कृत्वा पौर्वाह्णिकीं क्रियाम् |
गमनं रोचयामास वाक्यं चेदमुवाच ह || ३||

43.
Bala GP 35:7, CE 34:6
ते गत्वा दूरमध्वानं गतेऽर्धदिवसे तदा |
जाह्नवीं सरितां श्रेष्ठां दर्शुर्मुनिसेविताम् || ६||

44.
Bala GP 44:20, CE 43:19
एष ते राम गङ्गाया विस्तरोऽभिहितो मया |
स्वस्ति प्राप्नुहि भद्रं ते सन्ध्याकालोऽतिवर्तते || १९||

45.
Bala GP 45:3-5, CE 44:3-4
तस्य सा शर्वरी सर्वा सह सौमित्रिणा तदा |
जगाम चिन्तयानस्य विश्वामित्रकथां शुभाम् || ३||

ततः प्रभाते विमले विश्वामित्रं महामुनिम् |
उवाच राघवो वाक्यं कृताह्निकमरिन्दमः || ४||

46.
Bala GP 45.6, CE 44:5
गता भगवती रात्रिः श्रोतव्यं परमं श्रुतम् |
क्षणभूतेव सा रात्रिः संवृत्तेयं महातपः |
इमां चिन्तयतः सर्वां निखिलेन कथां तव || ५||

तराम सरितां श्रेष्ठां पुण्यां त्रिपथगां नदीम् |

47.
Bala GP 48:9, CE 47:9
ततः परमसत्कारं सुमतेः प्राप्य राघवौ |
उष्य तत्र निशामेकां जग्मतुर्मिथिलां ततः || ९||

48.
Bala GP 48:14-19, CE 47:14-19
हन्त ते कथयिष्यामि शृणु तत्त्वेन राघव |
यस्यैतदाश्रमपदं शप्तं कोपान्महात्मना || १४||

गौतमस्य नरश्रेष्ठ पूर्वमासीन्महात्मनः |
आश्रमो दिव्यसङ्काश सुरैरपि सुपूजितः || १५||

स चेह तप आतिष्ठद्दह्न्यासहितः पुरा |
वर्षपूगान्यनेकानि राजपुत्र महायशः || १६||

तस्यान्तरं विदित्वा तु सहस्राक्षः शचीपतिः |
मुनिवेषधरोऽहल्यामिदं वचनमब्रवीत् || १७||

ऋतुकालं प्रतीक्षन्ते नार्थिनः सुसमाहिते |
सङ्गमं त्वहमिच्छामि त्वया सह सुमध्यमे || १८||

मुनिवेषं सहस्राक्षं विज्ञाय रघुनन्दन |
मतिं चकार दुर्मेधा देवराजकुतूहलात् || १९||

49.

Bala GP 50:1-2, CE49:1-2

ततः प्रागुत्तरां गत्वा रामः सौमित्रिणा सह ।
विश्वामित्रं पुरस्कृत्य यज्ञवाटमुपागमत् ॥ १॥

रामस्तु मुनिशार्दूलमुवाच सहलक्ष्मणः ।
साध्वी यज्ञसमृद्धिर्हि जनकस्य महात्मनः ॥ २॥

50.

Bala GP 50:15, CE 49:14-15

धन्योऽस्म्यनुगृहीतोऽस्मि यस्य मे मुनिपुङ्गव ।
यज्ञोपसदनं ब्रह्मन्प्राप्तोऽसि मुनिभिः सह ॥ १४॥

द्वादशाहं तु ब्रह्मर्षे शेषमाहुर्मनीषिणः ।
ततो भागार्थिनो देवान्द्रष्टुमर्हसि कौशिक ॥ १५॥

51.

Bala GP 67:17, CE 66:17

आरोपयित्वा मौर्वीं च पूरयामास वीर्यवान् ।
तद्बभञ्ज धनुर्मध्ये नरश्रेष्ठो महायशाः ॥ १७॥

52.

Bala

GP 67:22-27, CE 66:22-27

जनकानां कुले कीर्तिमाहरिष्यति मे सुता ।
सीता भर्तारमासाद्य रामं दशरथात्मजम् ॥ २२॥

मम सत्या प्रतिज्ञा च वीर्यशुल्केति कौशिक ।
सीता प्राणैर्बहुमता देया रामाय मे सुता ॥ २३॥

भवतोऽनुमते ब्रह्मञ्शीघ्रं गच्छन्तु मन्त्रिणः ।
मम कौशिक भद्रं ते अयोध्यां त्वरिता रथैः ॥ २४॥

राजानं प्रश्रितैर्वाक्यैरानयन्तु पुरं मम ।
प्रदानं वीर्यशुल्काः कथयन्तु च सर्वशः ॥ २५॥

मुनिगुप्तौ च काकुत्स्थौ कथयन्तु नृपाय वै ।
प्रीयमाणं तु राजानमानयन्तु सुशीघ्रगाः ॥ २६॥

कौशिकश्च तथेत्याह राजा चाभाष्य मन्त्रिणः ।
अयोध्यां प्रेषयामास धर्मात्मा कृतशासनात् ॥ २७॥

53.

Bala GP 68.1, CE 67:1

जनकेन समादिष्टा दूतास्ते क्लान्तवाहनाः ।
त्रिरात्रमुषित्वा मार्गे तेऽयोध्यां प्राविशन्पुरीम् ॥ १॥

54.

Bala GP

68:18-19, CE 67:18-19

मन्त्रिणो बाढमित्याहुः सह सर्वैर्महर्षिभिः ।
सुप्रीतश्चाब्रवीद्राजा श्वो यात्रेति स मन्त्रिणः ॥ १८॥

मन्त्रिणस्तु नरेन्द्रस्य रात्रिं परमसत्कृताः ।
ऊषुः प्रमुदिताः सर्वे गुणैः सर्वैः समन्विताः ॥ १९॥

55.

Bala GP 69:1, CE 68:1

ततो रात्र्यां व्यतीतायां सोपाध्यायः सबान्धवः ।
राजा दशरथो हृष्टः सुमन्त्रमिदमब्रवीत् ॥ १॥

56.

Bala GP 69:7, CE 68:7

गत्वा चतुरहं मार्गं विदेहानभ्युपेयिवान् ।
राजा तु जनकः श्रीमाञ्श्रुत्वा पूजां अकल्पयत् ॥ ७॥

57.

Bala GP 69:12, CE 68:11-12

दिष्ट्या मे निर्जिता विघ्ना दिष्ट्या मे पूजितं कुलम् ।
राघवैः सह सम्बन्धाद्वीर्यश्रेष्ठैर्महात्मभिः ॥ ११॥

श्वः प्रभाते नरेन्द्रेन्द्र निर्वर्तयितुमर्हसि ।
यज्ञस्यान्ते नरश्रेष्ठ विवाहमृषिसंमतम् ॥ १२॥

58.

Bala

GP 69:16-19, CE 68:15-18

तद्धर्मिष्ठं यशस्यं च वचनं सत्यवादिनः ।
श्रुत्वा विदेहाधिपतिः परं विस्मयमागतः ॥ १५॥

ततः सर्वे मुनिगणाः परस्परसमागमे ।
हर्षेण महता युक्तास्ता निशाम् अवसन्सुखम् ॥ १६॥

राजा च राघवौ पुत्रौ निशाम्य परिहर्षितः ।
उवास परमप्रीतो जनकेन सुपूजितः ॥ १७॥

जनकोऽपि महातेजाः क्रिया धर्मेण तत्त्ववित् ।
यज्ञस्य च सुताभ्यां च कृत्वा रात्रिमुवास ह ॥ १८॥

59.

Bala GP 70:1-3, CE 69:1-3

ततः प्रभाते जनकः कृतकर्मा महर्षिभिः ।
उवाच वाक्यं वाक्यज्ञः शतानन्दं पुरोहितम् ॥ १॥

भ्राता मम महातेजा यवीयानतिधार्मिकः ।
कुशध्वज इति ख्यातः पुरीमध्यवसच्छुभाम् ॥ २॥

वार्याफलकपर्यन्तां पिबन्निक्षुमती नदीम् ।
साङ्काश्यां पुण्यसङ्काशां विमानमिव पुष्पकम् ॥ ३॥

60.

Bala GP 70:6, CE 69:5

शासनात्तु नरेन्द्रस्य प्रययुः शीघ्रवाजिभिः ।
समानेतुं नरव्याघ्रं विष्णुमिन्द्राज्ञया यथा ॥ ५॥

61.

Bala GP 70:8, CE 69:6

आज्ञया तु नरेन्द्रस्य आजगाम कुशध्वजः ॥ ६॥

62.

Bala GP 71:24, CE 70:24

मघा ह्यद्य महाबाहो तृतीये दिवसे प्रभो ।
फल्गुन्यामुत्तरे राजंस्तस्मिन्वैवाहिकं कुरु ।
रामलक्ष्मणयोरर्थे दानं कार्यं सुखोदयम् ॥ २४॥

63.

Bala GP 74:1-2, CE 73:1-2

अथ रात्र्यां व्यतीतायां विश्वामित्रो महामुनिः ।
आपृच्छ्य तौ च राजानौ जगामोत्तरपर्वतम् ॥ १॥

विश्वामित्रो गते राजा वैदेहं मिथिलाधिपम् ।
आपृच्छ्याथ जगामाशु राजा दशरथः पुरीम् ॥ २॥

64.

Ayodhya GP 20:45, CE 17:26

दश सस च वर्षाणि तव जातस्य राघव ।
अतीतानि प्रकाङ्क्षन्त्या मया दुःखपरिक्षयम् ॥ २६॥

65.

Bala GP 16:31

ततस्तु ताः प्राश्य तदुत्तमस्त्रियो
महीपतेरुत्तमपायसं पृथक्
हुताशनादित्यसमानतेजस
अचिरेण गर्भान् प्रतिपेदिरे तदा

66.

Bala GP 22:22-23, CE 21:18-19

ततो रामो जलं स्पृष्ट्वा प्रहृष्टवदनः शुचिः ।
प्रतिजग्राह ते विद्ये महर्षेर्भावितात्मनः ।
विद्यासमुदितो रामः शुशुभे भूरिविक्रमः ॥ १८॥

गुरुकार्याणि सर्वाणि नियुज्य कुशिकात्मजे ।
ऊषुस्तां रजनीं तत्र सरय्वां सुसुखं त्रयः ॥ १९॥

67.

Ayodhya GP 2:12, CE 2:10

तं चन्द्रमिव पुष्येण युक्तं धर्मभृतां वरम् ।
यौवराज्येन योक्तास्मि प्रीतः पुरुषपुङ्गवम् ॥ १०॥

68.

Ayodhya GP 3:41, CE 3:24

त्वया यतः प्रजाश्चेमाः स्वगुणैरनुरञ्जिताः ।
तस्मात्त्वं पुष्ययोगेन यौवराज्यमवाप्नुहि ॥ २४॥

69.

Ayodhya GP 4:1-2, CE 4:1-2

गतेऽथ नृपो भूयः पौरेषु सह मन्त्रिभिः ।
मन्त्रयित्वा ततश्चक्रे निश्चयज्ञः स निश्चयम् ॥ १॥

श्व एव पुष्यो भविता श्वोऽभिषेच्येत मे सुतः ।
रामो राजीवताम्राक्षो यौवराज्य इति प्रभुः ॥ २॥

70.

Ayodhya GP 4:21-22, CE 4:21-22

अद्य चन्द्रोऽभ्युपगतः पुष्यात्पूर्वं पुनर्वसुम् ।
श्वः पुष्य योगं नियतं वक्ष्यन्ते दैवचिन्तकाः ॥ २१॥

तत्र पुष्येऽभिषिञ्चस्व मनस्त्वरयतीव माम् ।
श्वस्त्वाहमभिषेक्ष्यामि यौवराज्ये परन्तप ॥ २२॥

71.

Ayodhya GP 4:33, CE 4:33

श्रुत्वा पुष्येण पुत्रस्य यौवराज्याभिषेचनम् ।
प्राणायामेन पुरुषं ध्यायमाना जनार्दनम् ॥ ३३॥

72.

Ayodhya GP 7:11, CE 7:7

श्वः पुष्येण जितक्रोधं यौवराज्येन राघवम् ।
राजा दशरथो राममभिषेचयितानघम् ॥ ७॥

73.

Ayodhya GP 8:9, CE 8:3

सुभगा खलु कौसल्या यस्याः पुत्रोऽभिषेक्ष्यते ।
यौवराज्येन महता श्वः पुष्येण द्विजोत्तमैः ॥ ३॥

74.

Ayodhya GP 57:26, CE 51:22

स तूष्णीमेव तच्छ्रुत्वा राजा विभ्रान्त चेतनः ।
मूर्छितो न्यपतद्भूमौ रामशोकाभिपीडितः ॥ २२॥

75.

Ayodhya GP 62:17, CE 56:14

वनवासाय रामस्य पञ्चरात्रोऽद्य गण्यते ।
यः शोकहतहर्षायाः पञ्चवर्षोपमो मम ॥ १४॥

76.

Ayodhya GP 63:4, CE 57:3

स राजा रजनीं षष्ठीं रामे प्रव्रजिते वनम् ।
अर्धरात्रे दशरथः संस्मरन्दुष्कृतं कृतम् ।
कौसल्यां पुत्रशोकार्तामिदं वचनमब्रवीत् ॥ ३॥

77.

Ayodhya GP 64.78, CE 58:57

तथा तु दीनं कथयन्नराधिपः
प्रियस्य पुत्रस्य विवासनातुरः ।
गतेऽर्धरात्रे भृशदुःखपीडितस्
तदा जहौ प्राणमुदारदर्शनः ॥ ५७॥

78.

Ayodhya GP 65:1, CE 59:1

अथ रात्र्यां व्यतीतायां प्रातरेवापरेऽहनि ।
बन्दिनः पर्युपतिष्ठंस्तत्पार्थिवनिवेशनम् ॥ १॥

79.

Ayodhya GP 71:18, CE 65:13-14

वनं च समतीत्याशु शर्वर्यामरुणोदये ।
अयोध्यां मनुना राज्ञा निर्मितां स ददर्श ह ॥ १३॥

तां पुरीं पुरुषव्याघ्रः सप्तरात्रोषितः पथि ।
अयोध्यामग्रतो दृष्ट्वा रथे सारथिमब्रवीत् ॥ १४॥

80.

Ayodhya GP 77:1, CE 71:1

ततो दशाहेऽतिगते कृतशौचो नृपात्मजः ।
द्वादशेऽहनि सम्प्राप्ते श्राद्धकर्माण्यकारयत् ॥ १॥

81.

Ayodhya GP 76:9, CE 70:9

विधवा पृथिवी राजंस्त्वया हीना न राजते ।
हीनचन्द्रेव रजनी नगरी प्रतिभाति माम् ॥ ९॥

82.

Ayodhya GP 79:1, CE 73:1

ततः प्रभातसमये दिवसेऽथ चतुर्दशे |
समेत्य राजकर्तारो भरतं वाक्यमब्रुवन् || १||

83.

Ayodhya GP 79:7-8, CE 73:7-8

ज्येष्ठस्य राजता नित्यमुचिता हि कुलस्य नः |
नैव भवन्तो मां वक्तुमर्हन्ति कुशला जनाः || ७||

रामः पूर्वो हि नो भ्राता भविष्यति महीपतिः |
अहं त्वरण्ये वत्स्यामि वर्षाणि नव पञ्च च || ८||

84.

Ayodhya

GP 82:1-2, CE 76:1-2

तामार्यगणसम्पूर्णां भरतः प्रग्रहां सभाम् |
ददर्श बुद्धिसम्पन्नः पूर्णचन्द्रां निशाम् इव || १||

आसनानि यथान्यायमार्याणां विशतां तदा |
अदृश्यत घनापाये पूर्णचन्द्रेव शर्वरी || २||

85.

Ayodhya GP 89:1-6, CE 83:1-6

व्युष्य रात्रिं तु तत्रैव गङ्गाकूले स राघवः |
भरतः कल्यमुत्थाय शत्रुघ्नमिदमब्रवीत् || १||

शत्रुघ्नोत्तिष्ठ किं शेषे निषादाधिपतिं गुहम् |
शीघ्रमानय भद्रं ते तारयिष्यति वाहिनीम् || २||

जाग्रमि नाहं स्वपिमि तथैवार्यं विचिन्तयन् |
इत्येवमब्रवीद्भ्रात्रा शत्रुघ्नोऽपि प्रचोदितः || ३||

इति संवदतोरेवमन्योन्यं नरसिंहयोः |
आगम्य प्राञ्जलिः काले गुहो भरतमब्रवीत् || ४||

कच्चित्सुखं नदीतीरेऽवात्सीः काकुत्स्थ शर्वरीम् |
कच्चिच्च सह सैन्यस्य तव सर्वमनामयम् || ५||

गुहस्य तत्तु वचनं श्रुत्वा स्नेहादुदीरितम् |
रामस्यानुवशो वाक्यं भरतोऽपीदमब्रवीत् || ६||

86.

Ayodhya GP 93:10, CE 87:10

मुञ्चन्ति कुसुमान्येते नगाः पर्वतसानुषु |
नीला इवात्रपापाये तोयं तोयधरा घनाः || १०||

87.

Ayodhya GP 112:20, CE 104:20

एवं ब्रुवाणं भरतं कौसल्यासुतमब्रवीत् |
तेजसादित्यसङ्काशं प्रतिपच्चन्द्रदर्शनम् || २०||

88.

Ayodhya GP 99:41, CE 93:40

ततः सुमन्त्रेण गुहेन चैव
समीयतू राजसुतावरण्ये |
दिवाकरश्चैव निशाकरश्च
यथाम्बरे शुक्रबृहस्पतिभ्याम् || ४०||

89.

Ayodhya GP 94:1-2, CE 88:1-2

दीर्घकालोषितस्तस्मिन्निगिरौ गिरिवनप्रियः |
विदेह्याः प्रियमाकङ्क्षन्त्वश्च चित्तं विलोभयन् || १||

अथ दाशरथिश्चित्रं चित्रकूटमदर्शयत् |
आर्यामममरसङ्काशः शचीमिव पुरन्दरः || २||

90.

Ayodhya GP 99:7, CE 93:6

ददर्श च वने तस्मिन्महतः सञ्चयान्कृतान् |
मृगाणां महिषाणां च करीषैः शीतकारणात् || ६||

91.

Ayodhya GP 114:12, CE 106:12

पुष्पनद्धां वसन्तान्ते मत्तभ्रमरशालिनीम् |
दुतदावाग्निविप्लुष्टां क्लान्तां वनलताम् इव || १२||

92.

Ayodhya GP 114:25-26

नहि राजत्ययोध्येयं सासारेवार्जुनी क्षपा
कदा नु खलु मे भ्राता महोत्सव इवागतः
जनयिष्यत्ययोध्यायां हर्ष ग्रीष्म इवाम्बुदः
तरुणैश्चारुवेषैश्च नरैरुन्नगामिभिः

93.

Aranya GP 16:1, CE 15:1

वसतस्तस्य तु मुखं राघवस्य महात्मनः |
शरद्व्यपाये हेमन्त ऋतुरिष्टः प्रवर्तते || १||

94.

Aranya GP 23:10-13, CE 22:10-12

नित्याशिवकरा युद्धे शिवा घोरनिदर्शनाः |
नेदुर्बलस्याभिमुखं ज्वालोद्गारिभिराननैः || १०||

कबन्धः परिघाभासो दृश्यते भास्करान्तिके |
जग्राह सूर्यं स्वर्भानुरपर्वणि महाग्रहः || ११||

प्रवाति मारुतः शीघ्रं निष्प्रभोऽभूदिवाकरः |
उत्पेतुश्च विना रात्रिं ताराः खद्योतसप्रभाः || १२||

95.

Aranya

GP 23:8-10, CE 22:8-9

बभूव तिमिरं घोरमुद्धतं रोमहर्षणम् |
दिशो वा विदिशो वापि सुव्यक्तं न चकाशिरे || ८||

क्षतजार्द्रसवर्णाभा सन्ध्याकालं विना बभौ |
खरस्याभिमुखं नेदुस्तदा घोरा मृगाः खगाः || ९||

96.

Aranya GP 29:23, CE 28:23

कामं बह्वपि वक्तव्यं त्वयि वक्ष्यामि न त्वहम् |
अस्तं गच्छेद्धि सविता युद्धविघ्नस्ततो भवेत् || २३||

97.

Aranya 23:13-14, CE 22:13

संलीनमीननविहगा नलिन्यः पुष्पपङ्कजाः |
तस्मिन्क्षणे वभ्युध विना पुष्पफलैर्द्रुमाः || १३||

98.
Aranya GP 23:34, CE 22:34

सा भीमवेगा समराभिकामा

सुदारुणा राक्षसवीर सेना ।

तौ राजपुत्रौ सहसाभ्युपेता

मालाग्रहाणामिव चन्द्रसूर्यौ ॥ ३४॥

99.
Aranya GP 25:5, CE 24:5

स तेषां यातुधानानां मध्ये रतो गतो खरः ।
बभूव मध्ये ताराणां लोहिताङ्ग इवोदितः ॥ ५॥

100.
Aranya GP 28:9, CE 27:9

शरजालावृतः सूर्यो न तदा स्म प्रकाशते ।
अन्योन्यवधसंरम्भादुभयोः सम्प्रयुध्यतोः ॥ ९॥

101.
Aranya GP 35:11, 13, CE 33:11,13

सशैलं सागरानूपं वीर्यवानवलोकयन् ।
नानापुष्पफलैर्वृक्षैरनुकीर्ण सहस्रशः ॥ ११॥
कदल्याढकिसम्बाधं नालिकेरोपशोभितम् ।
सालैस्तालैस्तमालैश्च तरुभिश्च सुपुष्पितैः ॥ १३॥

102.
Aranya GP 42:21-22, CE 40:18-19

प्रलोभनार्थं वैदेह्या नानाधातुविचित्रितम् ।
विचरन्गच्छते सम्यक्षाद्रलानि समन्ततः ॥ १८॥

रूप्यबिन्दुशतैश्चित्रो भूत्वा च प्रियदर्शनः ।
विटपीनां किसलयान्भक्त्वादन्यिचचार ह ॥ १९॥

103.
Aranya GP 44:9, CE 42:9

अथायतस्थे सुश्रान्तश्छायामाश्रित्य शाद्वले ।
मृगैः परिवृतो वन्यैरद्रात्प्रत्यदृश्यत ॥ ९॥

104.
Aranya GP 46:38, CE 44:36

ततः सुवेषं मृगया गतं पतिं

प्रतीक्षमाणा सहलक्ष्मणं तदा ।

निरीक्षमाणा हरितं ददर्श तन्

महद्वनं नैव तु रामलक्ष्मणौ ॥ ३६॥

105.
Aranya GP 49:30, CE 47:29

आमन्त्रये जनस्थानं कर्णिकारांश्च पुष्पितान् ।
क्षिप्रं रामाय शंसध्वं सीता हरति रावणः ॥ ३०॥

106.
Aranaya GP 56:23-25, CE 54:21-22

सीताया वचनं श्रुत्वा परुषं रोमहर्षणम् ।
प्रत्युवाच ततः सीतां भयसन्दर्शनं वचः ॥ २१॥

शृणु मैथिलि मद्वाक्यं मासान्द्वादश भामिनि ।
कालेनानेन नाभ्येषि यदि मां चारुहासिनि ।
ततस्त्वां प्रातराशार्थं सूदाश्छेत्स्यन्ति लेशशः ॥ २२॥

107.
Kishkindha
GP 12:16-17, CE 12:16-17

तं श्रुत्वा निनदं भातुः कुद्धो वाली महाबलः ।
निष्पपात सुसंरब्धो भास्करोऽस्ततटादिव ॥ १६॥

ततः सुतुमुल युद्ध वालिसुग्रीवयोरभूत् ।
गगने ग्रहयोर्घोरं बुधाङ्गारकयोरिव ॥ १७॥

108.
Kishkindha GP 14:10, CE 14:8

कृताभिज्ञान चिह्नस्त्वमनया गजसाह्वया ।

विपरीत इवाकाशे सूर्यो नक्षत्र मालया ॥ ८॥

109.
Kishkindha GP 15:3, CE 15:3

स तु रोषपरीताङ्गो वाली सन्ध्यातपप्रभः ।

उपरक्त इवादित्यः सद्यो निष्प्रभतां गतः ॥ ३॥

110.
Kishkindha GP 16:25, CE 16:23

तौ भीमबलविक्रान्तौ सुपर्णसमवेगिनौ ।

प्रवृद्धौ घोरवपुषौ चन्द्रसूर्याविवाम्बरे ॥ २३॥

111.
Kishkindha GP 17:3, CE 17:3

तस्मिन्निपतिते भूमौ हर्यृषाणां गणेश्वरे ।

नष्टचन्द्रमिव व्योम न व्यराजत भूतलम् ॥ ३॥

112.
Kishkindha GP 22:17, CE 22:17

इत्येवमुक्तः सुग्रीवो वालिना भातृसौहृदात् ।
हर्षं त्यक्त्वा पुनर्दीनो ग्रहग्रस्त इवोडुराट् ॥ १७॥

113.
Kishkindha GP 48:5-6, CE 47:5

ते भक्षयन्तो मूलानि फलानि विविधानि च ।
अन्वेषमाणा दुर्धर्षा न्यवसंस्तत्र तत्र ह ।
स तु देशो दुरन्वेषो गुहागहनवान्महान् ॥ ५॥

114.

Kishkindha GP 48:9-11, CE 47:7-9

यत्र यन्द्यफला वृक्षा विपुष्पाः पर्णवर्जिताः ।
निस्तोयाः सरितो यत्र मूलं यत्र सुदुर्लभम् ॥ ७॥

न सन्ति महिषा यत्र न मृगा न च हस्तिनः ।
शार्दूलाः पक्षिणो वापि ये चान्ये वनगोचराः ॥ ८॥

स्निग्धपत्राः स्थले यत्र पद्मिन्यः फुल्लपङ्कजाः ।
प्रेक्षणीयाः सुगन्धाश्च भ्रमरैश्चापि वर्जिताः ॥ ९॥

115.

Kishkindha GP 49:4, CE 48:4

कालब्ध नो महान्यातः सुग्रीवश्चोग्रशासनः ।
तस्माद्ध्वन्तः सहिता विचिन्वन्तु समन्ततः ॥ ४॥

116.

Kishkindha GP 50:4, CE 49:3

तेषां तत्रैव वसता स कालो व्यत्यवर्तत ॥ ३॥

आसेदुः तस्य शैलस्य कोटिम् दक्षिण पश्चिमाम् ।
तेषाम् तत्र एव वसताम् स कालो व्यत्यवर्तत ॥ ४-५-३

117.

**Kishkindha GP 50:9-10, 15-17
CE 49:7-8, 13-14**

गिरिजालावृतान्देशान्मार्गित्वा दक्षिणां दिशम् ।
क्षुत्पिपासा परीताश्च श्रान्ताश्च सलिलार्थिनः ।
अयकीर्णे लतायुक्तैर्दृशुस्ते महाबिलम् ॥ ७॥

ततः क्रौञ्चाश्च हंसाश्च सारसाश्चापि निष्क्रमन् ।
जलार्द्राश्चक्रवाकाश्च रक्ताङ्गाः पद्मरेणुभिः ॥ ८॥
अस्माच्चापि बिलाद्धसाः क्रौञ्चाश्च सह सारसैः ।
जलार्द्राश्चक्रवाकाश्च निष्पतन्ति स्म सर्वशः ॥ १३॥

नूनं सलिलयान्त्रं कूपो या यदि वा ह्रदः ।
तथा चेमे बिलद्वारे स्निग्धास्तिष्ठन्ति पादपाः ॥ १४॥

118.

Kishkindha GP 50:24-29, CE 49:19-22

ततस्तं देशमागम्य सौम्य वितिमिरं वनम् ।
दृदृशुः काञ्चनान्वृक्षान्दीप्तवैश्वानरप्रभान् ॥ १९॥

सालास्तालाश्च पुनागान्वक्कुभान्यञ्जुलान्धवान् ।
चम्पकान्नागवृक्षाश्च कर्णिकारांश्च पुष्पितान् ॥ २०॥

तरुणादित्यसङ्काशान्वैडूर्यमयवेदिकान् ।
नीलवैडूर्यवर्णांश्च पद्मिनः पतगावृताः ॥ २१॥

महद्भिः काञ्चनैर्वृक्षैर्वृत बालार्क सन्निभैः ।
जातरूपमयैर्मत्स्यैर्मैर्महद्भिश्च सकच्छपैः ॥ २२॥

119.

Kishkindha GP 50:32-37, CE 49:25-29

दृदृशुस्तत्र हरयो गृहमुख्यानि सर्वशः ।
पुष्पितान्फलिनो वृक्षान्प्रवालमणिसन्निभान् ॥ २५॥

काञ्चनभ्रमराश्चैव मध्नि च समन्ततः ।
मणिकाञ्चनचित्राणि शयनान्यासनानि च ॥ २६॥

महार्हाणि च यानानि दृदृशुस्ते समन्ततः ।
हैमराजतकांस्यानां भाजनानां च सञ्चयान् ॥ २७॥

अगरूणां च दिव्यानां चन्दनानां च सञ्चयान् ।
शुचीन्यभ्यवहार्याणि मूलानि च फलानि च ॥ २८॥

महार्हाणि च पानानि मध्नि रसवन्ति च ।
दिव्यानामम्बराणां च महार्हाणां च सञ्चयान् ।
कम्बलानां च चित्राणामजिनां च सञ्चयान् ॥ २९॥

120.

Kishkindha GP 53:2, CE 52:15

मयस्य माया विहित गिरिदुर्गे विचिन्वताम् ।
तेषां मासो व्यतिक्रान्तो यो राज्ञा समयः कृतः ॥ १५॥

121.

Kishkindha GP 53:3-4, CE 52:16-17

विन्ध्यस्य तु गिरेः पादे सम्प्रपुष्पितपादपे ।
उपविश्य महाभागाश्चिन्तामापेदिरे तदा ॥ १६॥

ततः पुष्पातिभारार्गॉल्लताशतसमावृतान् ।
द्रुमान्वासन्तिकान्दृष्ट्वा बभूवुर्भयशङ्किताः ॥ १७॥

122.

Kishkindha GP 53:5, CE 52:18

ते वसन्तमनुप्राप्तं प्रतिवेध्य परस्परम् ।
नष्टसन्देशकालार्था निपेतुर्धरणीतले ॥ १८॥

123.

Kishkindha GP 53:8, CE 52:20

शासनात्कपिराजस्य यथं सर्वे विनिर्गताः ।
मासः पूर्णो बिलस्थानां हरयः किं न बुध्यते ॥ २०॥

124.

Kishkindha GP 53:9,

वयम् अश्वायुजे मासि काल संख्या व्यवस्थिताः ।
प्रस्थिता सो ~ पि चातीत. किमत. कार्यमुत्तरम

125.

Kishkindha GP 16:37

इन्द्र ध्वज इव उद्धूत पौर्णे मास्याम् महीतले ।
अश्वयुक् समये मासि गत सत्त्वो विचेतनः ।
बाष्प संरुद्ध कण्ठस्तु वाली च आर्तं स्वरः शनैः ॥ ४-१६-३७

126.

MBH Bhishma GP 2:31, CE 2:31

या चैषा विश्रुता राजंस्त्रैलोक्ये साधुसंमता
अरुन्धती तथाप्येष वसिष्ठः पृष्ठतः कृतः ३१

127.

Kishkindha GP 53:13, CE 52:21

तस्मिन्नतीते काले तु सुग्रीवेण कृते स्वयम् ।
प्रायोपयेशन युक्तं सर्वेषां च यनौकसाम् ॥ २१॥

128.

Kishkindha GP 53:21, CE 52:29

तीक्ष्णः प्रकृत्या सुग्रीवः प्रियासक्तश्च राघवः ।
समीक्षा कृत कार्यास्तु तस्मिंश्च समये गते

129.

Kishkindha GP 57:16-17, CE 56:16-17

ते यय दण्डकारण्य विचित्य सुसमाहिताः ।
अज्ञानात्तु प्रविशः स्म धरण्या वियृत बिलम् ॥ १६॥

मयस्य माया विहित तद्विल च विचिन्वताम् ।
व्यतीतस्तत्र नो मासो यो राज्ञा सामयः कृतः ॥ १७॥

130.

Kishkindha GP 63:15, CE 62:15

अथ पवनसमानविक्रमाः

प्लवगवराः प्रतिलब्ध पौरुषाः ।

अभिजिदभिमुखां दिशं ययुर्

जनकसुता परिमार्गणोन्मुखाः ॥ १५॥

131.

Sundara GP 1:12-13, CE 1:11-12

स चचालाचलाश्चारु मुहूर्तं कपिपीडितः ।
तरुणा पुष्पिताग्राणां सर्वे पुष्पमशातयत् ॥ ११॥

तेन पादपमुक्तेन पुष्पौघेण सुगन्धिना ।
सर्वतः संवृतः शैलो बभौ पुष्पमयो यथा ॥ १२॥

132.

Sundara GP 1:46, 49, 51-55
CE 1:42, 45, 47-51

स मत्तकोयष्टिभकान्पादपान्पुष्पशालिनः ।
उद्वहन्नूरुवेगेन जगाम विमलेऽम्बरे ॥ ४२॥

सुपुष्पितार्बेर्बहुभिः पादपैरन्वितः कपिः ।
हनुमान्पर्वताकारो बभूवाद्भुतदर्शनः ॥ ४५॥

स नानाकुसुमैः कीर्णः कपिः साङ्कुरकोरकैः ।
शुशुभे मेघसङ्काशः खद्योतैरिव पर्वतः ॥ ४७॥

विमुक्तास्तस्य वेगेन मुक्त्वा पुष्पाणि ते दुमाः ।
अवशीर्यन्त सलिले नियृताः सुहृदो यथा ॥ ४८॥

लघुत्वेनोपपन्न तद्विचित्र सागरेऽपतत् ।
दुमाणा विविध पुष्प कपिवायुसमीरितम् ॥ ४९॥

पुष्पौघेणानुबद्धेन नानावर्णेन वानरः ।
बभौ मेघ इवोघन्वै विद्युद्गणविभूषितः ॥ ५०॥

तस्य वेगसमुद्धूतैः पुष्पैस्तोयमदृश्यत ।
ताराभिरभिरामाभिरुदिताभिरिवाम्बरम् ॥ ५१॥

133.

Sundara GP 1:116 CE 1:102

तिष्ठ त्वं हरिशार्दूल मयि विश्रम्य गम्यताम् ।
तदिदं गन्धवत्स्वादु कन्दमूलफल बहु ।
तदास्वाद्य हरिश्रेष्ठ विश्रान्तोऽनुगमिष्यसि ॥ १०२॥

134.

Sundara GP 1:211 CE 1:189

ततः स लम्बस्य गिरेः समृद्धे

विचित्रकूटे निपपात कूटे ।

सकेतकोद्दालकनालिकेरे

महाद्रिकूटप्रतिमो महात्मा ॥ १८९॥

135.

Sundara GP 2:2, 6-7, 9-13
CE 2, 6-7, 9-` 13

शाद्वलानि च नीलानि गन्धवन्ति यनानि च ।
गण्डवन्ति च मध्येन जगाम नगवन्ति च ॥ ६॥

शैलांश्च तरुसञ्चन्नान्वनराजीश्च पुष्पिताः ।
अभिचक्राम तेजस्वी हनुमान्प्लवगर्षभः ॥ ७॥

सरलान्कर्णिकारांश्च खर्जूरांश्च सुपुष्पितान् ।
प्रियालान्मुचुलिन्दांश्च कुटजान्केतकानपि ॥ ९॥

प्रियङ्गून्गन्धपूर्णांश्च नीपान्सप्तच्छदांस्तथा ।
असनान्कोविदारांश्च करवीरांश्च पुष्पितान् ॥ १०॥

पुष्पभारनिबद्धांश्च तथा मुकुलितानपि ।
पादपान्विहगाकीर्णान्पवनाधूतमस्तकान् ॥ ११॥

हंसकारण्डवाकीर्णा यापीः पद्मोत्पलायुताः ।
आक्रीडान्विविधान्रम्यान्विविधांश्च जलाशयान् ॥ १२॥

सन्ततान्विविधैर्वृक्षैः सर्वर्तुफलपुष्पितैः ।
उद्यानानि च रम्याणि ददर्श कपिकुञ्जरः ॥ १३॥

136.

Sundara GP 2:48-49 CE 2:46

इति संचिन्त्य हनुमान् सूर्यस्यास्तमयं कपिः ।
आचकांक्षे ततो वीरो वैदेह्या दर्शनोत्सुकः ॥ ५-२-४८

सूर्ये चास्तं गते रात्रौ देहं संक्षिप्य मारुतिः ।
वृषदंशकमात्रः सन् बभूवाद्भुतदर्शनः ॥ ५-२-४९

इति सञ्चिन्त्य हनुमान्सूर्यस्यास्तमयं कपिः ।
आचकाङ्क्षे तदा वीरा वैदेह्या दर्शनोत्सुकः ।
पृषदंशकमात्रः सन्बभूवाद्भुतदर्शनः ॥ ४६॥

137.

Sundara

GP 17:1-3 CE 15:1-3

ततः कुमुदषण्डाभो निर्मलं निर्मलः स्वयम् ।
प्रजगाम नभश्चन्द्रो हंसो नीलमिवोदकम् ॥ १॥

साचिव्यमिव कुर्वन्स प्रभया निर्मलप्रभः ।
चन्द्रमा रश्मिभिः शीतैः सिषेवे पवनात्मजम् ॥ २॥

स ददर्श ततः सीता पूर्णचन्द्रनिभाननाम् ।
शोकभारैरिव न्यस्ता भारेनौवमियाम्भसि ॥ ३॥

138.

Sundara GP 22:8-9 CE 20:8-9

द्वौ मासौ रक्षितव्यो मे योऽवधिस्ते मया कृतः ।
ततः शयनमारोह मम त्वं वरवर्णिनि ॥ ८॥

द्वाभ्यामूर्ध्वं तु मासाभ्यां भर्तार मामनिच्छतीम् ।
मम त्वां प्रातराशार्थमारभन्ते महानसे ॥ ९॥

139.

Sundara GP 4:5 CE 3:20

प्रविष्टः सत्त्वसम्पन्नो निशायां मारुतात्मजः ।
स महापथमास्थाय मुक्तापुष्पविराजितम् ॥ २०॥

140.

Sundara GP 14:2:26 CE 12:2-26

स तु संह्रष्टसर्वाङ्गः प्राकारस्थो महाकपिः ।
पुष्पिताग्रान्वसन्तादौ ददर्श विविधान्द्रुमान् ॥ २॥

सालानशोकान्भव्याश्च चम्पकाश्च सुपुष्पितान् ।
उद्दालकान्नागवृक्षांश्चूतान्कपिमुखानपि ॥ ३॥

अथामयणसञ्चन्ना लताशतसमावृताम् ।
ज्यामुक्त इव नाराचः पुप्लुये वृक्षवाटिकाम् ॥ ४॥

स प्रविष्य विचित्रां तां विहगैरभिनादिताम् ।
राजतैः काञ्चनैश्चैव पादपैः सर्वतोवृताम् ॥ ५॥

विहगैर्मृगसङ्घैश्च विचित्रा चित्रकाननाम् ।
उदितादित्यसङ्काशां ददर्श हनुमान्कपिः ॥ ६॥

वृता नानाविधैर्वृक्षैः पुष्पोपगफलोपगैः ।
कोकिलैर्भृङ्गराजैश्च मत्तैर्नित्यनिषेवितान् ॥ ७॥

प्रह्रष्टमनुजे काले मृगपक्षिसमाकुले ।
मत्तबर्हिणसङ्घुष्टं नानाद्विजगणायुताम् ॥ ८॥

मार्गमाणो वरारोहा राजपुत्रीमनिन्दिताम् ।
सुखप्रसुप्तान्विहगान्बोधयामास वानरः ॥ ९॥

उत्पतद्भिर्द्विजगणैः पक्षैः सालाः समाहताः ।
अनेकवर्णा विविधा मुमुचुः पुष्पवृष्टयः ॥ १०॥

पुष्पावकीर्णः शुशुभे हनुमान्मारुतात्मजः ।
अशोकवनिकामध्ये यथा पुष्पमयो गिरिः ॥ ११॥

दिशः सर्वाभिदावन्तं वृक्षषण्डगतं कपिम् ।
दृष्ट्वा सर्वाणि भूतानि वसन्त इति मेनिरे ॥ १२॥

वृक्षेभ्यः पतितैः पुष्पैरवकीर्णा पृथग्विपैः ।
ररा यसुधा तत्र प्रमदेव विभूषिता ॥ १३॥

तरस्विना ते तरयस्तरसाभिप्रकम्पिताः ।
कुसुमानि विचित्राणि ससृजुः कपिना तदा ॥ १४॥

निर्धूतपत्रशिखराः शीर्णपुष्पफलद्रुमाः ।
निःक्षिप्तवस्त्राभरणा धूर्ता इव पराजिताः ॥ १५॥

हनूमता येगवता कम्पितास्ते नगोत्तमाः ।
पुष्पपर्णफलान्याशु मुमुचुः पुष्पशालिनः ॥ १६॥

विहगैसङ्घैर्हीनास्ते स्कन्धमात्राश्रया द्रुमाः ।
बभ्रुरगमाः सर्वे मारुतेनेव निर्धुताः ॥ १७॥

विधूतकेशी युवतिर्यथा मृदितवर्णिका ।
निष्पीतशुभदन्तौष्ठी नखैर्दन्तैश्च विक्षता ॥ १८॥

तथा लाङ्गूलहस्तैश्च चरणाभ्यां च मर्दिता ।
बभ्रयाशोकवनिका प्रभग्नवरपादपा ॥ १९॥

महालतानां दामानि व्यधमत्तरसा कपिः ।
यथा प्रावृषि चिन्ध्यस्य मेघजालानि मारुतः ॥ २०॥

स तत्र मणिभूमीश्च राजतीश्च मनोरमाः ।
तथा काञ्चनभूमीश्च विचरन्दद्शे कपिः ॥ २१॥

वापीश्च विविधाकाराः पूर्णाः परमवारिणा |
महार्हमणिसोपानैरुपपन्नास्ततस्ततः ॥ २२॥

मुक्ताप्रवालसिकता स्फटिकान्तरकुट्टिमाः |
काञ्चनैस्तरुभिश्चित्रैस्तीरजैरुपशोभिताः ॥ २३॥

फुल्लपद्मोत्पलवनाश्चक्रवाकोपकूजिताः |
नत्यूहरुतसङ्घुष्टा हंससारसनादिताः ॥ २४॥

दीर्घाभिर्द्रुमयुक्ताभिः सरिद्भिश्च समन्ततः |
अमृतोपमतोयाभिः शिवाभिरुपसंस्कृताः ॥ २५॥

लताशतैरवतताः सन्तानकसमावृताः |
नानागुल्मावृतवनाः करवीरकृतान्तराः ॥ २६॥

141.
Sundara GP 14:35-40, 52
CE 12:35-40, 51

ये के चित्पादपास्तत्र पुष्पोपगफलोपगाः |
सच्छत्राः सवितर्दर्दिकाः सर्वं सौवर्णयदिकाः ॥ ३५॥

लतापतानैर्बहुभिः पर्णैश्च बहुभिर्युताम् |
काञ्चनीं शिशुपामेकां ददर्श स महाकपिः ॥ ३६॥

सोऽपश्यद्भूमिभागाश्च गर्तप्रस्रवणानि च |
सुवर्णवृक्षानपरान्ददर्श शिखिसंनिभान् ॥ ३७॥

तेषां द्रुमाणां प्रभया मेरोरिव महाकपिः |
अमन्यत तदा वीरः काञ्चनोऽस्मीति वानरः ॥ ३८॥

ता काञ्चनैस्तरुगणैर्मारुतेन च वीजिताम् |
किङ्किणीशतनिर्घोषां दृष्ट्या यित्समयमागमत् ॥ ३९॥

सुपुष्पिताग्रां रुचिरां तरुणाङ्कुरपल्लवाम् |
तामारुह्य महावेगः शिंशपां पर्णसंयुताम् ॥ ४०॥

एवं तु मत्वा हनुमान्महात्मा
प्रतीक्षमाणो मनुजेन्द्रपत्नीम् |
अवेक्षमाणश्च ददर्श सर्वं
सुपुष्पिते पर्णघने निलीनः ॥ ५२॥

142.
Sundara GP 15:3-14 CE 13:3-14

तां स नन्दनसङ्काशां मृगपक्षिभिरावृताम् |
हर्म्यप्रासादसम्बाधां कोकिलाकुलनिःस्वनाम् ॥ ३॥

काञ्चनोत्पलपद्माभिर्वापीभिरुपशोभिताम् |
बह्वासनकुथोपेतां बहुभूमिगृहायुताम् ॥ ४॥

सर्वर्तुकुसुमै रम्यैः फलवद्भिश्च पादपैः |
पुष्पितानामशोकानां श्रिया सूर्योदयप्रभाम् ॥ ५॥

प्रदीप्तामिव तत्रस्थो मारुतिः समुद्वैक्षत |
निष्प्रशाखा विहगैः क्रियमाणामिवासकृत् |
विनिष्पतद्भिः शतशश्चित्रैः पुष्पावतंसकैः ॥ ६॥

आमूलपुष्पनिचितैरशोकैः शोकनाशनैः |
पुष्पभारातिभारैश्च स्पृशद्भिरिव मेदिनीम् ॥ ७॥

कर्णिकारैः कुसुमितैः किंशुकैश्च सुपुष्पितैः |
स देशः प्रभया तेषां प्रदीप्त इव सर्वतः ॥ ८॥

पुंनागाः सप्तपर्णाश्च चम्पकोद्दालकास्तथा |
विवृद्धमूला बहवः शोभन्ते स्म सुपुष्पिताः ॥ ९॥

शातकुम्भनिभाः के चित्के चिदग्निशिखोपमाः |
नीलाञ्जननिभाः के चित्तत्राशोकाः सहस्रशः ॥ १०॥

नन्दनं विविधोद्यानं चित्रं चैत्ररथं यथा |
अतिवृत्तमियाचिन्त्यं दिव्यं रम्यं श्रिया वृतम् ॥ ११॥

द्वितीयमिव चाकाशं पुष्पज्योतिर्गणायुतम् |
पुष्परत्नशतैश्चित्रं पञ्चमं सागरं यथा ॥ १२॥

सर्वर्तुपुष्पैर्निचितं पादपैर्मधुगन्धिभिः |
नानानिनादैरुद्यानं रम्यं मृगगणैर्द्विजैः ॥ १३॥

अनेकगन्धप्रवहं पुण्यगन्धं मनोरमम् |
शैलेन्द्रमिव गन्धाढ्यं द्वितीयं गन्धमादनम् ॥ १४॥

143.
Sundara GP 18:6-9 CE 16:6-9

स सर्वाभरणैर्युक्तो बिभ्रच्छ्रियमनुत्तमाम् |
तां नगैर्विविधैर्जुष्टां सर्वपुष्पफलोपगैः ॥ ६॥

वृतां पुष्करिणीभिश्च नानापुष्पोपशोभिताम् |
सदामदैश्च विहगैर्विचित्रां परमाद्भुताम् ॥ ७॥

ईहामृगैश्च विविधैर्धृतां दृष्टिमनोहरैः |
वीथीः सम्प्रेक्षमाणश्च मणिकाञ्चनतोरणाः ॥ ८॥

नानामृगगणाकीर्णं फलैः प्रपतितैर्वृताम् |
अशोकवनिकामेव प्राविशत्सन्ततद्रुमाम् ॥ ९॥

144.

Sundara GP 9:64-65 CE 7:61-62

लतानां माधवे मासि फुल्लानां वायुसेवनात् ।
अन्योन्यमालाग्रथितं ससत्कुसुमोच्चयम् ॥ ६१॥

व्यतिवेष्टितसुस्कन्धमन्योन्यभ्रमराकुलम् ।
आसीद्वनमिवोद्भूतं स्रीयन्रावणस्य तत् ॥ ६२॥

145.

Sundara GP 10:4

जातरूपपरिक्षिप्तं चित्रभानो: समप्रभम्
अशोक मालां विततं ददर्श परमासनम्

146.

Sundara GP 25:6 CE 23:6

सा त्वशोकस्य विपुलां शाखामालाम्बद्ध पुष्पिताम् ।
चिन्तयामास शोकेन भर्तारं भग्नमानसा ॥ ६॥

147.

Sundara GP 16:25 CE 14:25

नैषा पश्यति राक्षस्यो नेमान्पुष्पफलद्रुमान् ।
एकस्थहृदया नूनं राममेवानुपश्यति ॥ २५॥

148.

Sundara GP 16:31 CE 14:31

अस्या हि पुष्पावनताग्रशाखाः
शोकं दृढं वै जनयत्यशोकाः ।
हिमव्यपायेन च मन्दरश्मिर्
अभ्युत्थितो नैकसहस्ररश्मिः ॥ ३१॥

149.

Sundara GP 2:57-58 CE 2:54-55

चन्द्रोऽपि साचिव्यमिवास्य कुर्वंस्
तारागणैर्मध्यगतो विराजन् ।
ज्योत्स्नाविताननेन वितत्य लोकम्
उत्तिष्ठते नैकसहस्ररश्मिः ॥ ५४॥

शङ्खप्रभं क्षीरमृणालवर्णम्
उद्गच्छमानं व्यवभासमानम् ।
ददर्श चन्द्रं स कपिप्रवीरः
पोप्लूयमानं सरसीव हंसं ॥ ५५॥

150.

Sundara GP 5:1-9 CE 5:1-7

ततः स मध्यं गतमंशुमन्तं
ज्योत्स्नावितानं महदुद्रमन्तम् ।
ददर्श धीमान्दिवि भानुमन्तं
गोष्ठे वृषं मत्तमिव भ्रमन्तम् ॥ १॥

लोकस्य पापानि विनाशयन्तं
महोदधिं चापि समेधयन्तम् ।
भूतानि सर्वाणि विराजयन्तं
ददर्श शीतांशुमथाभियान्तम् ॥ २॥

या भाति लक्ष्मीर्भुवि मन्दरस्था
तथा प्रदोषेषु च सागरस्था ।
तथैव तोयेषु च पुष्करस्था
रराज सा चारुनिशाकरस्था ॥ ३॥

हंसो यथा राजतपञ्जरस्थः
सिंहो यथा मन्दरकन्दरस्थः ।
वीरो यथा गर्वितकुञ्जरस्थश्
चन्द्रोऽपि बभ्राज तथाम्बरस्थः ॥ ४॥

स्थितः ककुद्मानिव तीक्ष्णशृङ्गो
महाचलः श्वेत इवोच्चशृङ्गः ।
हस्तीव जाम्बूनदबद्धशृङ्गो
विभाति चन्द्रः परिपूर्णशृङ्गः ॥ ५॥

प्रकाशचन्द्रोदयनष्टदोषः
प्रवृद्धरक्षः पिशिताशदोषः ।
रामाभिरामेरितचित्तदोषः
स्वर्गप्रकाशो भगवान्प्रदोषः ॥ ६॥

तन्त्री स्वनाः कर्णसुखाः प्रवृत्ताः
स्वपन्ति नार्यः पतिभिः सुवृत्ताः ।
नक्तञ्चराश्चापि तथा प्रवृत्ता
विहर्तुमत्यद्भुतरौद्रवृत्ताः ॥ ७॥

151.

Sundara GP 10:3 CE 8:2

तस्य चैकतमे देशे सोऽग्र्यमाल्यविभूषितम् ।
ददर्श पाण्डुरं छत्रं ताराधिपतिसन्निभम् ॥ २॥

152.

Sundara GP 10:31, 34, 48

CE 8:29, 32, 44

शशिप्रकाशवदना वरकुण्डलभूषिताः ।

अम्लानमाल्याभरणा ददर्श हरियूथपः ॥ २९॥

तासां चन्द्रोपमैर्वक्त्रैः शुभैर्ललितकुण्डलैः ।

विरराज विमानं तन्नभस्ताराग‍णैरिव ॥ ३२॥

अन्या कमलपत्राक्षी पूर्णन्दुसदृशानना ।

अन्यामालिङ्ग्य सुश्रोणी प्रसुप्ता मदविह्वला ॥ ४४॥

153.

Sundara GP 12:21, 13:13

CE 10:21, 11:13

नागकन्या वरारोहाः पूर्णचन्द्रनिभाननाः ।

दृष्टा हनूमता तत्र न तु सीता सुमध्यमा ॥ २१॥

सम्पूर्णचन्द्रप्रतिमं पद्मपत्रनिभेक्षणम् ।

रामस्य ध्यायती वक्त्रं पञ्चत्वं कृपणा गता ॥ १३॥

154.

Sundara GP 15:28-30 CE 13:27-29

पूर्णचन्द्रानना सुभ्रूं चारुवृत्तपयोधराम् ।

कुर्वन्ती प्रभया देवी सर्वा वितिमिरा दिशः ॥ २७॥

तां नीलकेशी बिम्बौष्ठीं सुमध्यां सुप्रतिष्ठिताम् ।

सीतां पद्मपलाशाक्षीं मन्मथस्य रतिं यथा ॥ २८॥

इष्टां सर्वस्य जगतः पूर्णचन्द्रप्रभाम् इव ।

भूमौ सुतनुमासीनां नियतामिव तापसीम् ॥ २९॥

155.

Sundara GP 18:14 CE 16:14

राजहंसप्रतीकाशं छत्रं पूर्णशशिप्रभम् ।

सौवर्णदण्डमपरा गृहीत्वा पृष्ठतो ययौ ॥ १४॥

156.

Sundara GP 28:11 CE 26:11

हा राम सत्यव्रत दीर्घबाहो

हा पूर्णचन्द्रप्रतिमानवक्त्र ।

हा जीवलोकस्य हितः प्रियश् च

वध्यां न मां वेत्सि हि राक्षसानाम् ॥ ११॥

157.

Sundara GP 30:7,10 CE 28:7,10

अहमाश्वासयाम्येनां पूर्णचन्द्रनिभाननाम् ।

अदृष्टदुःखां दुःखस्य न ह्यन्तमधिगच्छतीम् ॥ ७॥

मया च स महाबाहुः पूर्णचन्द्रनिभाननः ।

समाश्वासयितुं न्याय्यः सीतादर्शनलालसः ॥ १०॥

158.

Sundara GP 32:10 30:5

स्वप्नोऽपि नायं न हि मेऽस्ति निद्रा

शोकेन दुःखेन च पीडितायाः ।

सुखं हि मे नास्ति यतोऽस्मि हीना

तेनेन्दुपूर्णप्रतिमाननेन ॥ ५॥

159.

Sundara GP 36:39 CE 34:37

यथा सुनयने वल्गु बिम्बौष्ठं चारुकुण्डलम् ।

मुखं द्रक्ष्यसि रामस्य पूर्णचन्द्रमिवोदितम् ॥ ३७॥

160.

Sundara GP 37:1 CE 35:1

सीता तद्वचनं श्रुत्वा पूर्णचन्द्रनिभानना ।

हनूमन्तमुवाचेदं धर्मार्थसहितं वचः ॥ १॥

161.

Sundara GP 49:7 CE 47:7

नीलाञ्जनचय प्रख्यं हारेणोरसि राजता ।

पूर्णचन्द्राभयवक्त्रेण सबलाकमियाम्बुदम् ॥ ७॥

162.

Sundara GP 1:170 CE 1:154

तं दृष्ट्वा यदनान्मुक्तं चन्द्रं राहुमुखादिव ।

अब्रवीत्सुरसा देवी स्वेन रूपेण वानरम् ॥ १५४॥

163.

Sundara GP 1:196 CE 1:176

आस्ये तस्या निमज्जन्तं ददृशुः सिद्धचारणाः ।

ग्रस्यमानं यथा चन्द्रं पूर्णं पर्वणि राहुणा ॥ १७६॥

164.

Sundara GP 19:12-14 CE 17:11-13

आयतीमिव विध्वस्तामाज्ञां प्रतिहतां इव ।

दीसामिव दिशं काले पूजामपहृताम् इव ॥ ११॥

पद्मिनीमिव विध्वस्तां हतशूरां चमूम् इव ।

प्रभामिव तपोध्वस्तामुपक्षीणामिवापगाम् ॥ १२॥

वेदीमिव परामृष्टां शान्तामग्निशिखाम् इव ।

पौर्णमासीमिव निशां राहुग्रस्तेन्दुमण्डलाम् ॥ १३॥

165.

Sundara GP 29:7-8 CE 27:7-8

तस्याः पुनर्बिम्बफलोपमौष्ठं

स्वक्षिभ्रुकेशान्तमरालपक्ष्म ।

वक्त्रं बभासे सितशुक्लदंष्ट्रं

राहोर्मुखाच्चन्द्र इव प्रमुक्तः ॥ ७॥

सा वीतशोका व्यपनीततन्द्री
शान्तज्वरा हर्षविबुद्धसत्त्वा ।
अशोभतार्या वदनेन शुक्ले
शीतान्शुना रात्रिरियोदितेन ॥ ८॥

166.
Sundara GP 35:87 CE 33:78
चारु तच्चानन तस्यास्तामशुक्लायतेक्षणम् ।
अशोभत विशालाक्ष्या राहुमुक्त इयोड़ुराट् ।
हनूमन्त कपि व्यक्त मन्यते नान्यथेति सा ॥ ७८॥

167.
Sundara GP 36:5 CE 34:4
चारु तददनं तस्यास्तामशुक्लायतेक्षणम् ।
बभूव प्रहर्षोद्ग्रं राहुमुक्त इयोड़ुराट् ॥ ४॥

168.
Sundara GP 9:34 CE 7:31
परिवृत्तेऽर्धरात्रे तु पाननिद्रावशं गतम् ।
क्रीडित्योपरत रात्रौ सुष्वाप बलवत्तदा ॥ ३॥

169.
Sundara GP 18:1-2 CE 16:1-2
तथा विप्रेक्षमाणस्य यन पुष्पितपादपम् ।
विचिन्यतश्च वैदेही किं चिच्छेष निशाभवत् ॥ १॥

षड्ङ्गवेदविदुषा क्रतुप्रवरयाजिनाम् ।
शुश्राव ब्रह्मघोषाथ विरात्रे ब्रह्मरक्षसाम् ॥ २॥

170.
Sundara GP 30:12 CE 28:12
अनेन रात्रिशेषेण यदि नाभ्यास्यते मया ।
सर्वथा नास्ति सन्देहः परित्यक्ष्यति जीवितम् ॥ १२॥

171.
Sundara GP 31:19 CE 29:12
सा तिर्यगूर्ध्वं च तथाप्यधस्तान्
निरीक्षमाणा तमचिन्त्य बुद्धिम् ।
ददर्श पिङ्गाधिपतेरमात्यं
वातात्मजं सूर्यमिवोदयस्थम् ॥ १२॥

172.
Sundara GP 43:4
आरुह्य गिरिसम्काशम् प्रासादम् हरियूथपः ।
बभौ स सुमहातेजाः प्रतिसूर्य इवोदितः ॥ ५-४३-४

173.
Sundara GP 46:19-20 CE 44:17-18
ततस्तं दश्शुर्वीरा दीप्यमानं महाकपिम् ।
रश्मिमन्तमियोद्यन्तं स्वतेजोरश्मिमालिनम् ॥ १७॥

तोरणस्थ महावेग महासत्त्व महाबलम् ।
महामति महोत्साह महाकाय महाबलम् ॥ १८॥

ततः तम् दश्शुः वीरा दीप्यमानम् महाकपिम् ॥ ५-४६-१७
रश्मिमन्तम् इव उदयन्तम् स्व तेजो रश्मि मालिनम् ।
तोरणस्थम् महावेगम् महासत्त्वम् महाबलम् ॥ ५-४६-१८

174.
Sundara GP 47:3-6 CE 45:3-6
ततो महद्वालदिवाकरप्रभं
प्रतप्तजाम्बूनदजालसन्ततम् ।
रथां समास्थाय ययौ स वीर्यवान्
महाहरिं तं प्रति नैरृतर्षभः ॥ ३॥

ततस्तपःसङ्ग्रहसञ्चयार्जितं
प्रतप्तजाम्बूनदजालशोभितम् ।
पताकिनं रत्नविभूषितध्वजं
मनोजवाष्टाश्ववरैः सुयोजितम् ॥ ४॥

सुरासुराधृष्यमसङ्गचारिणं
रविप्रभं व्योमचरं समाहितम् ।
सतूणमष्टासिनिबद्धबन्धुरं
यथाक्रमावेशितशक्तितोमरम् ॥ ५॥

विराजमानं प्रतिपूर्णवस्तुना
सहेमदाम्ना शशिसूर्यवर्चसा ।
दिवाकराभं रथमास्थितस्ततः
स निर्जगामामरतुल्यविक्रमः ॥ ६॥

175.
Sundara GP 57:1-5 CE 45:1-4
सचन्द्रकुमुदं रम्यं सार्ककारण्डवं शुभम् ।
तिष्यश्रवणकदम्बमभ्रशैवलशाद्वलम् ॥ १॥

पुनर्वसु महामीनं लोहिताङ्गमहाग्रहम् ।
ऐरावतमहाद्वीपं स्वातीहंसविलोडितम् ॥ २॥

वातसङ्घातजातोर्मिं चन्द्रांशुशिशिराम्बुमत् ।
भुजङ्गयक्षगन्धर्वप्रबुद्धकमलोत्पलम् ॥ ३॥

ग्रसमान इवाकाश ताराधिपमिवालिखन् ।
हरन्निय सनक्षत्र गगन सार्कमण्डलम् ॥ ४॥

176.
Yuddha GP 4:3-5 CE 4:3-4
अस्मिन्मुहूर्ते सुग्रीव प्रयाणमभिरोचये ।
युक्तो मुहूर्ता विजयः पासो मध्य दिवाकरः ॥ ३॥

उत्तरा फल्गुनी ह्याद्य श्वस्तु हस्तेन योक्ष्यते ।
अभिप्रयाम सुग्रीव सर्वानीकसमायुताः ॥ ४॥

267

177.

Yuddha GP 4:42 CE 4:37

कपिभ्यामुह्यमानौ तौ शुशुभाते नरर्षभौ ।
महद्भ्यामिव संस्पृष्टौ ग्राहाभ्यां चन्द्रभास्करौ ॥ ३७॥

178.

Yuddha GP 4:47-53 CE 4:41-48

अनु वाति शुभो वायुः सेना मृदुहितः सुखः ।
पूर्णवल्गुस्वराश्चेमे प्रवदन्ति मृगद्विजाः ॥ ४१॥

प्रसन्नाश्च दिशः सर्वा विमलश्च दिवाकरः ।
उशना च प्रसन्नार्चिरनु त्वां भार्गयो गतः ॥ ४२॥

ब्रह्मराशिर्विशुद्धश्च शुद्धाश्च परमर्षयः ।
अर्चिष्मन्तः प्रकाशन्ते ध्रुव सर्व प्रदक्षिणम् ॥ ४३॥

त्रिशङ्कुर्वैमलो भाति राजर्षिः सपुरोहितः ।
पितामहवरोऽस्माकमिष्वाकूणां महात्मनाम् ॥ ४४॥

विमले च प्रकाशेते विशाखे निरुपद्रवे ।
नक्षत्रं परमस्माकमिष्वाकूणां महात्मनाम् ॥ ४५॥

नैरृतं नैरृतानां च नक्षत्रमभिपीड्यते ।
मूलं मूलवता स्पृष्ट धूप्यते धूमकेतुना ॥ ४६॥

सरं चैतद्विनाशाय राक्षसानाम् उपस्थितम् ।
काले कालगृहीताना नक्षत्र ग्रहपीडितम् ॥ ४७॥

179.

Yuddha GP 4:68 CE 4:53

सा स्म याति दिवारात्रं महती हरिवाहिनी ।
हृष्टप्रमुदिता सेना सुग्रीवेणाभिरक्षिता ॥ ५३॥

180.

Yuddha GP 4:70-71 CE 4:55

ततः पादपसम्बाधं नानामृगसमाकुलम् ।
सह्यपर्वतमासेतुर्मलयं च मही धरम् ॥ ५५॥
काननानि विचित्राणि नदीप्रस्रवणानि च ।
पश्यन्नपि ययौ रामः सह्यस्य मलयस्य च ॥ ५६॥

181.

Yuddha GP 4:53 CE 4:48

प्रसन्नाः सुरसाश्चापो वनानि फलवन्ति च ।
प्रयान्त्यभ्यधिक गन्धा यथर्तुकुसुमा द्रुमाः ॥ ४८॥

182.

Yuddha GP 4:59-60

वरीक्षोत्संति सर्वाणि संस्कृतूरीवरीतेवद् । मरांसि विमलव्यासि दुःसाक्षोर्णीयं पर्वतम् ॥ ५९ ॥
समान्यूपिमदेशांधि वनानि फलवन्ति च । वर्णेन च समन्ताय विश्वेश्वरश्च सावितत् ॥ ६० ॥

183.

Yuddha GP 4:72-91 CE 4:57-62

येवेल्लरिलक्षकैश्वलानकसोकान्तिमन्दुसारकान् । विनिश्वान्करवीराश्च भजन्ति स्म द्रुकब्माः ॥ ७२ ।।
मेवोकांच वरजार्थे इक्षन्ग्योश्चपादपान् । नम्वुकावलकादीर्गान्मनन्ति स्म द्रुकब्माः ॥ ७३ ।।

प्रस्तेरुप न रम्गेणु विचिकाः कानव्ठहृदः । वाचुष्टेशरचरिततम् सुगन्धर्विकच्छिन वालु ॥ ७४ ॥
वाक्तः सुल्कसर्वाणी याति चन्दनकौकसा । क्षष्टरैस्तुक्ष चित्रिरेणु मधुविष्णुं ॥ ७५ ॥
अर्चिक्षे वौस्रावुमरु चातुभिल्ट्षु विद्रुषिका । पात्रष्टमु मषुत्ते रेणुक्षोदुर्विमरेव पतिकः ॥ ७६ ॥
सूपदप्रवान्यार्णांक जादृयमान सैवहस्य । गिरिनिरेणु रम्येणु सर्वतो वहते संपर्वष्टिणया ॥ ७७ ॥
केलयक सिन्धुवारांक वर्षन्त्वाष मनोरमाः । माध्वयो नग्ससृष्टीच हृणयदुप्मान मुनिजुक्काः ॥ ७८ ॥
चिरिमिक्षा मणुक्ष्याय केर्तित्त वहुकालान । रक्षेबाखेलकवीष नमाष्टलाल पुप्षिकाः ॥ ७९ ॥
चूक्षा मेवाविखावीष कामितारायवा पुरिष्णाः । मुक्षुतिन्दार्थ्यवारीष विष्रदाः ग्रहवासमान ॥ ८० ॥
[वैता जालक्सनवर्षवन एकाः कुरक्सवसना ॥]
दिगाजलाःनिप्रभिय पूष्कला नक्ष्यरल्यवस्ता । नीलाचार्ष्ठाकथ सिरला अद्योतेखा पक्षवस्तवया ॥ ८१ ॥
मीरप्राणी इश्वरृतुः सर्वे पर्योध्यक्तीद्यनां । वाक्ष्यस्सिमिमिमिदी रम्यानु फलवानि अवैव यात ॥ ८२ ॥
पक्षवारदापुरिकाः कार्स्वविमेषियाः । प्रवेऽ क्रीकौ संर्वाणी कारावयमादियाः ॥ ८३ ॥
कोलेश्लाकुनि सितिः श्रार्विकम मयगरीते । व्याकौक वहुविरीरीदि संचकमानु समन्वता ॥ ८४ ॥
षरै तोकमिकोयं पुक्षे कुट्रीयोर्सक्तक्स्या । वारिकिषेदक्समास्या पुष्ठे रम्यजकश्ते जलवग्वा ॥ ८५ ॥
तस्य घ्यव्हुत्रे हुष्मान नाचादिजमच्यासल्वता । क्षाल्स्या विश्वेहम्वस्मान जलेश्रीपरितभ्यानत्वयो ॥ ८६ ॥
अब्योश्चे तरुष्मान स्प योवास्रष्या वानरुः । फलाश्समृघ्वपूर्वीनि मूल्यानि कुसुमानि च ॥ ८७ ॥
वैचष्ठूषोर्नराक्ष्यण पादच्यष् धरोकरः । द्रोणामात्रमक्षमणानि लम्बमानानि वनराः ॥ ८८ ॥
यषुः पिबन्तः छक्षमासते यर्पुनि मषुपिद्गमा । पादच्यानवभंजन्तो विकर्षन्तस्तथा लताः ॥ ८९ ॥
विरष्ष्यो गिरिराज्प्रयष्या ः क्षरवींथाः । इरोन्योऽन्ये तु कपयो नैरृत्तो मषुदर्पिताः ॥ ९० ॥
अन्ये इक्षान्वप्रवन्ते वैचृविवचारि चाफेर । बभूव वसुधा वैस्तु संपूर्णा हरिपुङ्गवैः ॥
यथा कमलकेदारैः पक्षेरिव वसुन्धरा ॥ ९१ ॥

चम्पकास्तिलकाश्चूतानशोकान्सिन्दुवारकान् ।
करवीराश्च तिमिशान्भञ्जन्ति स्म प्लवङ्गमाः ॥ ५७॥

फलान्यमृतगन्धीनि मूलानि कुसुमानि च ।
बुभुजुर्वानरास्तत्र पादपाना बलोत्कटाः ॥ ५८॥

द्रोणमात्रप्रमाणानि लम्बमानानि वानराः ।
ययुः पिबन्तो हृष्टास्ते मध्वनि मधुपिङ्गलाः ॥ ५९॥

पादपानयभञ्जन्तो विकर्षन्तस्तथा लताः ।
विधिमन्तो गिरिवरान्प्रययुः प्लवगर्षभाः ॥ ६०॥

वृक्षेभ्योऽन्ये तु कपयो नर्दन्तो मधुदर्पिताः ।
अन्ये वृक्षान्प्रपद्यन्ते प्रपतन्त्यपि चापरे ॥ ६१॥

बभूव वसुधा तैस्तु सम्पूर्णा हरिपुङ्गवैः ।
यथा कमलकेदारैः पक्षवैरिव वसुन्धरा ॥ ६२॥

184.

Yuddha GP 4:92-96 CE 4:63-67

महेन्द्रमथ सम्प्राप्य रामो राजीवलोचनः ।
अध्यारोहन्महाबाहुः शिखरं द्रुमभूषितम् ॥ ६३॥

ततः शिखरमारुह्य रामो दशरथात्मजः ।
कूर्ममीनसमाकीर्णमपश्यत्सलिलाशयम् ॥ ६४॥

ते सह्यं समतिक्रम्य मलयं च महागिरिम् ।
आसेदुरानुपूर्व्येण समुद्रं भीमनिःस्वनम् ॥ ६५॥

अयरुह्य जगामाशु वेलायनमनुत्तमम् ।
रामो रमयतां श्रेष्ठः ससुग्रीयः सलक्ष्मणः ॥ ६६॥

अथ धौतोपलतलां तोयौघैः सहसोत्थितैः ।
वेलामासाद्य विपुलां रामो वचनमब्रवीत् ॥ ६७॥

185.

Yuddha GP 4:97-102 CE 4:68:72

एते वयमनुप्राप्ताः सुग्रीव वरुणालयम् ।
इहेदानीं विचिन्ता सा या न पूर्वं समुत्थिता ॥ ६८॥

अतः परमतीरोऽयं सागरः सरितां पतिः ।
न चायमनुपायेन शक्यस्तरितुमर्णवः ॥ ६९॥

तदिहैव निवेशोऽस्तु मन्त्रः प्रस्तूयतामिह ।
यथेदं वानरबलं परं पारमवाप्नुयात् ॥ ७०॥

इतीव स महाबाहुः सीताहरणकर्शितः ।
रामः सागरमासाद्य वासमाज्ञापयत्तदा ॥ ७१॥

सम्प्राप्तो मन्त्रकालो नः सागरस्येह लङ्घने ।
स्वां स्वां सेनां समुत्सृज्य मा च कश्चित्कुतो व्रजेत् ।
गच्छन्तु वानराः शूरा ज्ञेयं छन्नं भयं च नः ॥ ७२॥

187.

Yuddha GP 4:103-109 CE 4:73-77

रामस्य वचनं श्रुत्वा सुग्रीव सहलक्ष्मणः । सेनां निवेशयत्तीरे सागरस्य दुमायुते ॥ १०२ ॥
विरराज समीपस्थे सागरस्य च तद्वलम् । मधुपाण्डुजलः श्रीमान्द्वितीय इव सागरः ॥ १०४ ॥
वेलावनमुपागम्य ततस्ते हरिपुङ्गवाः । विनिविष्टाः परं पारं काङ्क्षमाणा महोदधेः ॥ १०५ ॥
तेषां निविशमानानां सैन्यवर्धनहर्षिणाम् । अरुर्क्षीय महानादमर्णवस्य महाशुभे ॥ १०६ ॥
सा वानसृणां व्रजिनी सुग्रीवेणाभिपालिता । विभा निविष्टा महती रामशार्वराभवत् ॥ १०७ ॥
सा महार्णवमासाद्य हृष्टा वानरवाहिनी । वायुवेगसमाधूतं पश्यमाना महार्णवम् ॥ १०८ ॥
दूरपारमसंबाधं रक्षोगणनिषेवितम् । पश्यन्तो वरुणावासं निषेदुर्हरियूथपाः ॥ १०९ ॥

रामस्य वचनं श्रुत्वा सुग्रीवः सहलक्ष्मणः ।
सेना न्यवेशयत्तीरे सागरस्य दुमायुते ॥ ७३॥

विरराज समीपस्थे सागरस्य तु तद्वलम् ।
मधुपाण्डुजलः श्रीमान्द्वितीय इव सागरः ॥ ७४॥

वेलावनमुपागम्य ततस्ते हरिपुङ्गवाः ।
विनिविष्टः परं पारं काङ्क्षमाणा महोदधेः ॥ ७५॥

सा महार्णवमासाद्य हृष्टा वानरवाहिनी ।
वायुवेगसमाधूतं पश्यमाना महार्णवम् ॥ ७६॥

दूरपारमसंबाधं रक्षोगणनिषेवितम् ।
पश्यन्तो वरुणावासं निषेदुर्हरियूथपाः ॥ ७७॥

188.

Yuddha GP 4:110-111 CE 4:78-79

चण्डनक्रग्रहेयरं क्षपादौ दिवसक्षये । इक्ष्वतमिव देवीर्घृतयन्तदिव चोर्मिभिः ॥ ११० ॥
चन्द्रोदये समुद्धूतं प्रतिचन्द्रसमाकुलम् । क्ष्वानिल्मह्याव्राहैः कीर्ण तिमितिमिङ्गिलैः॥ १११ ॥

चण्डनक्रग्रहं घोरं क्षपादौ दिवसक्षये ॥
चन्द्रोदये समाधूतं प्रतिचन्द्रसमाकुलम् ॥ ७८॥

चण्डानिलमहाग्राहैः कीर्ण तिमितिमिङ्गिलैः ।
दीप्तभोगैरिवाकीर्ण भुजङ्गैर्वरुणालयम् ॥ ७९॥

189.

Yuddha GP 5:1-3 CE 5:1-3

सा तु नीलेन विधिवत्स्यारक्षा सुसमाहिता ।
सागरस्योत्तरे तीरे साधु सेना निवेशिता ॥ १॥

मैन्दश्च द्विविधश्चोभौ तत्र यानरपुङ्गवौ ।
विचेरतुश्च तां सेनां रक्षार्थं सर्वतो दिशम् ॥ २॥

निविष्टायां तु सेनायां तीरे नदनदीपतेः ।
पार्श्वस्थं लक्ष्मणं दृष्ट्वा रामो वचनमब्रवीत् ॥ ३॥

190.

Yuddha GP 5:5 CE 5:5

न मे दुःखं प्रिया दूरे न मे दुःखं हृतेति च ।
एतदेवानुशोचामि वयोऽस्या ह्यतिवर्तते ॥ ५॥

191.

Yuddha GP 6:16-18 CE 6:16-18

यानराणां हि वीराणां सहस्रैः परिवारितः ।
रामोऽभ्येति पुरीं लङ्कामस्माकमुपरोधकः ॥ १६॥

तरिष्यति च सुव्यक्तं राघवः सागरं सुखम् ।
तरसा युक्तरूपेण सानुजः सबलानुगः ॥ १७॥

अस्मिन्नेवङ्गते कार्ये विरुद्धे यानरैः सह ।
हितं पुरे च सैन्ये च सर्वे समन्त्र्यतां मम ॥ १८॥

192.

Yuddha GP 17:1 CE 11:1

इत्युक्त्वा परुषं वाक्यं रावणं रावणानुजः ।
आजगाम मुहूर्तेन यत्र रामः सलक्ष्मणः ॥ १॥

193.

Yuddha GP 17:2 CE 11:2

तं मेरुशिखराकारं दीप्तामिव शतह्रदाम् ।
गगनस्थं महीस्थास्ते दद्दशुर्वानराधिपाः ॥ २॥

194.

Yuddha GP 17:9-11 CE 11:7-9

शीघ्रं व्यादिश नो राजन्वधायैषां दुरात्मनाम् ।
निपतन्तु हताश्चैते धरण्यामल्पजीविताः ॥ ७॥

तेषां सम्भाषमाणानामन्योन्यं स विभीषणः ।
उत्तरं तीरमासाद्य खस्थ एव व्यतिष्ठत ॥ ८॥

उवाच च महाप्राज्ञः स्वरेण महता महान् ।
सुग्रीवं तांश्च सम्प्रेक्ष्य खस्थ एव विभीषणः ॥ ९॥

195.

Yuddha GP 19:1-2 CE 13:1-2

राघवेणाभये दत्ते सन्तो रावणानुजः ।
खात्पपातायनिं हृष्टो भक्तैरनुचरैः सह ॥ १॥

स तु रामस्य धर्मात्मा निपपात विभीषणः ।
पादयोः शरणान्वेषी चतुर्भिः सह राक्षसैः ॥ २॥

196.

Yuddha GP 19:28-29 CE 13:11-12

अब्रवीच्च हनूमांश्च सुग्रीवश्च विभीषणम् |
कथं सागरमक्षोभ्यं तराम वरुणालयम् || ११||

उपायैरभिगच्छामो यथा नदनदीपतिम् |
तराम तरसा सर्वे ससैन्या वरुणालयम् || १२||

197.

Yuddha GP 19:30-31 CE 13:13-14

एवमुक्तस्तु धर्मज्ञः प्रत्युवाच विभीषणः |
समुद्रं राघवो राजा शरणं गन्तुमर्हति || १३||

खानितः सगरेणायमप्रमेयो महोदधिः |
कर्तुमर्हति रामस्य ज्ञातेः कार्यं महोदधिः || १४||

198.

Yuddha GP 19:32-40 CE 13:

एवं विभीषणेनोक्ते राक्षसेन विपश्चिता |
प्रकृत्या धर्मशीलस्य राघवस्याप्यरोचत || १५||

स लक्ष्मण महातेजाः सुग्रीवं च हरीश्वरम् |
सत्क्रियार्थं क्रियादक्षः स्मितपूर्वमुवाच ह || १६||

विभीषणस्य मन्त्रोऽयं मम लक्ष्मण रोचते |
ब्रूहि त्वं सहसुग्रीवस्त्वापि यदि रोचते || १७||

सुग्रीवः पण्डितो नित्यं भवान्मन्त्रविचक्षणः |
उभाभ्यां सम्प्रधार्यार्थं रोचते यत्तदुच्यताम् || १८||

एवमुक्तौ तु तौ वीरावुभौ सुग्रीवलक्ष्मणौ |
समुदाचारं संयुक्तमिदं वचनमूचतुः || १९||

किमर्थं नो नरव्याघ्र न रोचिष्यति राघव |
विभीषणेन यत्कृतमस्मिन्काले सुखावहम् || २०||

अबद्ध्वा सागरे सेतुं घोरेऽस्मिन्वरुणालये |
लङ्का नासादितुं शक्या सेन्द्रैरपि सुरासुरैः || २१||

विभीषणस्य शूरस्य यथार्थं क्रियतां वचः |
अलं कालात्यय कृत्वा समुद्रोऽअयं नियुज्यताम् || २२||

एवमुक्तः कुशास्तीर्णे तीरे नदनदीपतेः |
संविवेश तदा रामो वेद्यामिव हुताशनम् || २३||

199.

Yuddha GP 20:1-5

ततो निषिद्धे ध्वजिनीं सुग्रीवेणाभिपश्चितया | ददर्श राससोऽभ्येव ह्यर्धूले नाम वीर्यवान् || १ ||
पारो राक्षसमस्य राघवस्य दुरात्मना | तं दृष्ट्वा स्त्रीसोऽज्वीर्यं वशिनम्य स राक्षः || ३ ||
आविश्य लङ्कां येन राममभिवदब्रवीत् | एष वै वानरश्रीवो लङ्कुं समभिवर्तते || ३ ||
भगवत्यामयेपच द्वितीय इव सागरः | पुत्रो दशरथस्येपी ज्यातस्यो राघवस्यणी || ४ ||
सेष्पो रक्तसेची सीतायाः पद्मानवी | एनौ सागरमस्यम संविविष्टौ वैदाछुवै || ५ ||

200.

Yuddha GP 20:13-14

स तेषां राक्षसेन्द्रेण संदिष्टो रजनीचरः | शुको विहंगमो भूत्वा तूर्णंधाषुख चाम्बरम् || १३ ||
स गत्वा दूरमध्वानमुपर्युपरि सागरम् | संस्थितो ह्याम्बरे वाक्यं धुग्रीवमिदमब्रवीत् || १४ ||

201.

Yuddha GP 20:20

स च पत्रलघुर्भूत्वा हरिभिर्दर्शितेऽभये
अन्तरिक्षे स्थितो भूत्वा पुनर्वचनमब्रवीत

202.

Yuddha GP 21:10-11, CE 14:1

तस्य रामस्य सुप्तस्य कुश आस्तीर्णे मही तले |
नियमादप्रमत्तस्य निशास्तिस्रोऽतिचक्रमुः || ६-२१-१०
स त्रिरात्रोषितस्तत्र नयज्ञो धर्मवत्सलः |
उपासत तदा रामः सागरं सरितां पतिम् || ६-२१-११
तस्य रामस्य सुप्तस्य कुश्ठास्तीर्णे महीले । नियमादप्रमत्तस्य निशास्तिस्रोऽतिचक्रमुः ॥ १० ॥
स त्रिराषोपितस्तत्र नयझो धर्मवत्सलः । उपासत तदा रामः सागरं सरितां पतिम् ॥ ११ ॥

तस्य रामस्य सुप्तस्य कुशास्तीर्णे महीतले |
नियमादप्रमत्तस्य निशास्तिस्रोऽतिचक्रमुः || १||

203.

Yuddha GP 21:25-26

एवमुक्त्वा धनुष्पाणिं क्रोधविस्फारितेक्षणः
बभूव रामो दुर्धर्षं युगान्ताग्निरिव ज्वलन्
सम्पीडय च धनुर्धारं कम्पयित्वा शरैर्जगत्
मुमोच विशिखानुग्रान्व्रजानिव शतक्रतुः

204.

Yuddha GP 21:33-34

ततस्तु तम् राघव मुग्रवेगम् |
प्रकर्षमाणम् धमरप्रमेयम् |
सौमित्रिरुत्पत्य विनिःश्वसन्तम् |
मामेति चोक्त्वा धनुरालंलम्बे || ६-२१-३३
एतद्विनापि ह्युदधेस्तवार्य |
सम्पत्स्यते वीरतमस्य कार्यम् |
भवद्विधाः क्रोधवशम् न यान्ति |
दीर्घम् भवान्पश्यतु साधुवृत्तम् || ६-२१-३४

205.

Yuddha GP 22:45-54, CE 15:8-14

अयं सौम्य नलो नाम तनुजो विश्वकर्मणः |
पित्रा दत्तवरः श्रीमान्प्रतिमो विश्वकर्मणः || ८||

एष सेतुं महोत्साहः करोतु मयि वानरः |
तमहं धारयिष्यामि तथा ह्येष यथा पिता || ९||

एवमुक्त्वोदधिर्नष्टः समुत्थाय नलस्ततः |
अब्रवीद्वानरश्रेष्ठो वाक्यं रामं महाबलः || १०||

अहं सेतुं करिष्यामि विस्तीर्णं वरुणालये |
पितुः सामर्थ्यमास्थाय तत्त्वमाह महोदधिः || ११||

मम मातुर्वरो दत्तो मन्दरे विश्वकर्मणा |
औरसस्तस्य पुत्रोऽहं सदृशो विश्वकर्मणा || १२||

न चाप्यहमनुक्तो वै प्रब्रूयामात्मनो गुणान् |
काममद्यैव बध्नन्तु सेतुं वानरपुङ्गवाः || १३||

270

ततो निसृष्टरामेण सर्वतो हरियूथपाः ।
अभिपेतुर्महारण्यं दृष्ट्वा शतसहस्रशः ॥ १४॥

206.
Yuddha GP 22:55-59 CE 15:15-18

ते नगान्नगसङ्काशाः शाखामृगगणर्षभाः ।
बभञ्जुर्जानरास्तत्र प्रचक्रुश्च सागरम् ॥ १५॥

ते सालैश्चाश्वकर्णैश्च धवैर्वंशैश्च वानराः ।
कुटजैरर्जुनैस्तालैस्तिकलैस्तिमिशैरपि ॥ १६॥

बिल्वकैः सप्तपर्णैश्च कर्णिकारैश्च पुष्पितैः ।
चूतैश्चाशोककृक्षैश्च सागरं समपूरयन् ॥ १७॥

समूलांश्च विमूलांश्च पादपान्हरिसत्तमाः ।
इन्द्रकेतूनिवोद्यम्य प्रजह्रुर्हरयस्तरुन् ॥ १८॥

207.
Yuddha GP 22:60-62 CE 15:19

हस्तिमात्रान्महाकायाः पाषाणांश्च महाचलाः । पर्वतांश्च समुत्पाट्य यन्त्रैः परिवहन्ति च ॥ ५६ ॥
वस्तिप्रमाणैर्भवर्णः क्षरद्भा जलस्यूद्धतैः । सैलैरलर्त्यै चाकाशमसावास्तदा चाकाशैः पुनः ॥ ५७ ॥
सहुर्त्ते क्षोभयामाश्चुर्निर्वेशः समयन्तः । तूयराणान्ये महद्भस्ति शौर्यवे क्षायवोयान्ति ॥ ५८ ॥

208.
Yuddha GP 22:63-67 CE 15:20-21

दशयोजनविस्तीर्णं शतयोजनमायतम् ।
नलश्चक्रे महासेतुं मध्ये नदनदीपतेः ॥ २०॥

शिलानां क्षिप्यमाणानां शैलानां तत्र पात्यताम् ।
बभूव तुमुलः शब्दस्तदा तस्मिन्महोदधौ ॥ २१॥

209.
Yuddha GP 22:68-72

कृत्वा मथंनेमहा योजनानि पर्पूर्यं । बह्लीन्वलक्ष्यासगिर्ससरमार्गः पुगह्वे ॥ ६४ ॥
द्विश्यैव सर्वेकड्डा योजनानि तु त्रियद्धिः । कृतानि दर्शर्गेन्पैं भीमकायैर्महाबलैः ॥ ६५ ॥
अह्ना तृतीयेन तथा योजनानि तु सागरे । तरसा पर्वताकारैर्वानरैर्णवलचित्तेन च ॥ ६६ ॥
चतुर्थेन तथा चाह्ना द्वाविंशतिपरापि चैं । योजनानि महावेगैः कृतानि त्वरितेन्नेः ॥ ६७ ॥
पञ्चमेन तथा चाह्ना प्रष्टैः शिष्कारिभिः । योजनानि यथोक्तान्सुवेलेप्यैत्युपक्रियाचिक्रय चैं ॥ ६८ ॥

210.
Yuddha GP 22:73-74, 79 CE 15:22, 26

स नलेन कृतः सेतुः सागरे मकरालये ।
शुशुभे सुभगः श्रीमान्स्वातीपथ इवाम्बरे ॥ २२॥

विशालः सुकृतः श्रीमान्सुभूमिः सुसमाहितः ।
अशोभत महासेतुः सीमन्त इव सागरे ॥ २६॥

211.
Yuddha GP 22:77-78 CE 15:24-25

आप्लवन्तः प्लवन्तश्च गर्जन्तश्च प्लवङ्गमाः ।
तमचिन्त्यमसह्यं च अद्भुतं लोमहर्षणम् ।
ददृशुः सर्वभूतानि सागरे सेतुबन्धनम् ॥ २४॥

तानि कोटिसहस्राणि वानराणां महौजसाम् ।
बध्नन्तः सागरे सेतुं जग्मुः पारं महोदधेः ॥ २५॥

212.
Yuddha GP 22:80-81 CE 15:27

ततः परे समुद्रस्य गदापाणिर्विभीषणः ।
परेषामभिघातार्थमतिष्ठत्सचिवैः सह ॥ २७॥

213.
Yuddha GP 22:84-85 CE 15:28-29

अग्रतस्तस्य सैन्यस्य श्रीमान्नामः सलक्ष्मणः ।
जगाम धन्वी धर्मात्मा सुग्रीवेण समन्वितः ॥ २८॥

अन्ये मध्येन गच्छन्ति पार्श्वतोन्ये प्लवङ्गमाः ।
सलिले प्रपतन्त्यन्ये मार्गमन्ये न लेभिरे ।
के चिद्वैहायस गताः सुपर्णा इव पुप्लुवुः ॥ २९॥

214.
Yuddha GP 22:86-87 CE 15:30-31

घोषेण महता घोषं सागरस्य समुच्छ्रितम् ।
भीममन्तर्दधे भीमा तरन्ती हरिवाहिनी ॥ ३०॥

वानराणां हि सा तीर्णा वाहिनी नल सेतुना ।
तीरे निविविशे राज्ञा बहुमूलफलोदके ॥ ३१॥

215.
Yuddha GP 23:1-3

निमित्तानि निमित्तज्ञो दृष्ट्वा लक्ष्मणपूर्वजः ।
सौमित्रिं सम्परिष्वज्य इदं वचनमब्रवीत्
परिगृह्योदकं शीतं वनानि फलवन्ति च
बलौघं संविभज्येमं व्यूह्य तिष्ठेम लक्ष्मण
लोकक्षयकरं भीमं भयं पश्याम्युपस्थितं
प्रबर्हणं प्रवीराणामृक्षवानररक्षसाम्

216.
Yuddha GP 23:4-5

वाताश्च कलुषा वान्ति कम्पते च वसुंधरा
पर्वताग्राणि वेपन्ते पतन्ति च महीरुहाः
मेघा क्रव्यादसंकाशा परुषाः परुषस्वना
क्रूरा क्रूरं प्रवर्षन्ति मिश्रं शोणितबिन्दुभिः

217.
Yuddha GP 23:13-14

क्षिप्रमद्यैव दुर्धर्षां पुरीं रावणपालितां
अभियाम जवेनैव सर्वैर्हरिभिरावृताः
इत्येवमुक्त्वा धन्वी स रामः संग्रामधर्षणः
प्रतस्थे पुरतो रामो लङ्कामभिमुखो विभुः

218.
Yuddha GP 24:1

सा वीरसमिती राज्ञा विराज व्यवस्थिता
शशिना शुभनक्षत्रा पौर्णमासीव शारदी

219.
Arrangments of Vanara Army
Yuddha GP 24:14-18

शत्रवः कपिसेनां वा वकत्रादाव वीर्यवान् । अङ्गुरः सह मीकेन खिट्टेदुरसि दुर्जयः ॥ १४ ॥
खिट्टेज्ञानरचेष्टिन्या बानरोपसयवाहन्। औदित्वो दक्षिणं पार्श्वपुन्या वैष बाकर ॥ १५ ॥
गन्धदनरसैन दुर्षपसादनम् गन्धमादन । खिट्टेदंनरवन्दिन्वा सैन्यं पश्चविधिष्ठिः ॥ १६ ॥
मूर्ध्नि स्वात्यारस्वदं पैसो लक्ष्मणेन समन्वितम् । जाम्बवांश्च सुषेणश्च वेगदर्षी च बाकर ॥ १७ ॥
कास्त्रस्य महासेनाः कुप्तिं रक्षन्तु ते कच । जयन्तं कपिसेनाया कपिराग्रेव्धेरसतु ॥ १८ ॥
पश्चार्धिमव श्वेकस्य प्रभेवास्तलेसमा इव ॥

271

220.
Yuddha GP 24:20
प्रगृह्य गिरिश्रृंगाणि महतश्च महीरुहान
आसेदुर्वानरा लंकाम् मिमर्दयिषवो रणे

221.
Yuddha GP 24:22-24
ततो रामो महातेजाः सुग्रीवमिदमब्रवीत
सुविभक्तानी सैन्यानि शुक एष विमुच्यतां
रामस्य तु वचः श्रुत्वा वानरेंद्रो महाबलः
मोचयामास तं दूतं शुकं रामस्य शासनात
मोचितो रामवाक्येन वानरैश्च निपीडितः
शुकः परमसंत्रस्तो रक्षोऽधिपमुपागमत

222.
Yuddha GP 25:1-8 CE 16:1-8
सबले सागरं तीर्णे रामे दशरथात्मजे ।
अमात्यौ रावणः श्रीमानब्रवीच्छुकसारणौ ॥ १॥

समग्रं सागरं तीर्णं दुस्तरं वानरं बलम् ।
अभूतपूर्वं रामेण सागरे सेतुबन्धनम् ॥ २॥

सागरे सेतुबन्धं तु न श्रद्दध्यां कथं चन ।
अवश्यं चापि सङ्ख्येयं तन्मया वानरं बलम् ॥ ३॥

भवन्तौ वानरं सैन्यं प्रविश्यानुपलक्षितौ ।
परिमाणं च वीर्यं च ये च मुख्याः प्लवङ्गमाः ॥ ४॥

मन्त्रिणो ये च रामस्य सुग्रीवस्य च संमताः ।
ये पूर्वमभिवर्तन्ते ये च शूराः प्लवङ्गमाः ॥ ५॥

स च सेतुर्यथा बद्धः सागरे सलिलार्णवे ।
निवेशश्च यथा तेषां वानराणां महात्मनाम् ॥ ६॥

रामस्य व्यवसायं च वीर्यं प्रहरणानि च ।
लक्ष्मणस्य च वीरस्य तत्त्वतो ज्ञातुमर्हथ ॥ ७॥

कश्च सेनापतिस्तेषां वानराणां महौजसाम् ।
एतज्ज्ञात्वा यथातत्त्वं शीघ्रमगन्तुमर्हथ ॥ ८॥

223.
Yuddha GP 25:10-12 CE 16:10-12
ततस्तद्वानरं सैन्यमचिन्त्यं लोमहर्षणम् ।
सङ्ख्यातुं नाध्यगच्छेतां तदा तौ शुकसारणौ ॥ १०॥

तत्स्थितं पर्वतायेषु निदेषु गुहासु च ।
समुद्रस्य च तीरेषु वनेष्पवनेषु च ॥ ११॥

तरमाणं च तीर्णं च तर्तुकामं च सर्वशः ।
निविष्टं निविशच्चैव भीमनादं महाबलम् ॥ १२॥

224.
Yuddha GP 25:24-25 CE 16:20-21
श्वःकाले नगरीं लङ्कां सप्राकारां सतोरणाम् ।
राक्षसं च बलं पश्य शरैर्विध्वंसितं मया ॥ २०॥

घोरं रोषमहं मोक्ष्ये बलं धारय रावण ।
श्वःकाले वज्रवान्वज्रं दानवेष्विव वासवः ॥ २१॥

225.
Yuddha GP 38:19 CE 29:17
ततोऽस्तमगमत्सूर्यः सन्ध्यया प्रतिरञ्जितः ।
पूर्णचन्द्रप्रदीपा च क्षपा समभिवर्तते ॥ १७॥

226.
Yuddha GP 39:1 CE 30:1
तां रात्रिमुषितास्तत्र सुवेले हरिपुङ्गवाः ।
लङ्कायां ददृशुर्वीरा वनान्युपवनानि च ॥ १॥

227.
Yuddha GP 39:2-9, 12, 17 CE 30:2-9, 13, 18
समसौम्यानि रम्याणि विशालान्यायतानि च ।
दृष्टिरम्याणि ते दृष्ट्वा बभूवुर्जातविस्मयाः ॥ २॥

चम्पकाशोककपुंनागसालतालसमाकुला ।
तमालवनसञ्चन्ना नागमालासमावृता ॥ ३॥

हिन्तालैर्जुनैर्नीपैः सप्तपर्णैश्च पुष्पितैः ।
तिलकैः कर्णिकारैश्च पटालैश्च समन्ततः ॥ ४॥

शुशुभे पुष्पिताग्रैश्च लतापरिगतैर्द्रुमैः ।
लङ्का बहुविधैर्दिव्यैर्यथेन्द्रस्यामरावती ॥ ५॥

विचित्रकुसुमोपेतै रक्तकोमलपल्लवैः ।
शाद्वलैश्च तथा नीलैश्चित्राभिर्वनराजिभिः ॥ ६॥

गन्धाढ्यान्यभिरम्याणि पुष्पाणि च फलानि च ।
धारयन्त्यगमास्तत्र भूषणानीव मानवाः ॥ ७॥

तच्चैत्ररथसङ्काशं मनोज्ञं नन्दनोपमम् ।
वनं सर्वर्तुकं रम्यं शुशुभे षट्पदायुतम् ॥ ८॥

नत्यूहकोयष्टिभकैर्नृत्यमानैश्च बर्हिभिः ।
रुतं परभृतानां च शुश्रुवे वननिर्झरे ॥ ९॥

तेषां प्रविशतां तत्र वानराणां महौजसाम् ।
पुष्पसंसर्गसुरभिर्ववौ घ्राणसुखोऽनिलः ॥ १३॥

शिखरं तु त्रिकूटस्य प्रांशु चैकं दिविस्पृशम् ।
समन्तात्पुष्पसञ्चन्नं महाराजतसंनिभम् ॥ १८॥

228.
Yuddha GP 39:25
नानाविहगसंघुष्टां नानामृगनिषेवतां
नानाकुसुमसंपन्नाम् नानाराक्षससेवितां

229.

Yuddha GP 40:1

ततो रामः सुवेलार्गं योजनद्वयमण्डलम् ।
उपारोहत्ससुग्रीवो हरियूथैः समन्वितः ॥ ६-४०-१

230.

Yuddha GP 41:73-74 CE 31:62-63

इत्युक्तः स तु तारेयो रामेणाक्लिष्टकर्मणा ।
जगामाकाशमाविश्य मूर्तिमानिव हव्यवाट् ॥ ६२॥

सोऽतिपत्य मुहूर्तेन श्रीमाद्रावणमन्दिरम् ।
ददर्शासीनमव्यग्रं रावणं सचिवैः सह ॥ ६३॥

231.

Yuddha GP 43:46 CE 33:46

विदार्यमाणा हरिपुङ्गवैस्तदा
निशाचराः शोणितदिग्धगात्राः ।

पुनः सुयुद्धं तरसा समाश्रिता
दिवाकरस्यास्तमयाभिकाङ्क्षिणः ॥ ४६॥

232.

Yuddha GP 44:1 CE 34:1

युध्यतामेव तेषां तु तदा वानररक्षसाम् ।
रविरस्तं गतो रात्रिः प्रवृत्ता प्राणहारिणी ॥ १॥

233.

Yuddha GP 44:2 CE 33:2

अन्योन्यं बद्धवैराणां घोराणां जयमिच्छताम् ।
सम्प्रवृत्तं निशायुद्धं तदा वारणरक्षसाम् ॥ २॥

234.

Yuddha GP 44:16 CE 33:15

सा बभूव निशा घोरा हरिराक्षससाहारिणी ।
कालरात्रीव भूतानां सर्वेषां दुरतिक्रमा ॥ १५॥

235.

Yuddha GP 44:34-39 CE 34:29-30

भीज्ष्वीलनाथः पायो रावणी रणगर्भितः । बेहारपपरो वीरो रामिधं कोवगर्छितम् ॥ ११ ॥
अश्यो निहितानुबाणान्मुखोचावनिवर्षकः । रीर्व न कृष्ठवर्ण चैव पोरेनौगवैः शरैः ॥ १४ ॥
विधैर समरे हृद्रः सर्वगेष्ठ रीप्यवी । मायया संक्रमलस मोहयाप्यावयी युधि ॥ १५ ॥
अद्यद्ः सर्वभूतानां कूटयोधी निशाचरः । वयनं प्रदर्भन चातरी रामकृष्णी ॥ १६ ॥
जो तेन पुरुषव्याघी कुद्रेनार्थिविरिः शरैः । सरसाधिर्गैवी वीरो तदा भेजन वानरा ॥ १७ ॥
प्रधावकास्तु पद्म न प्रकस्थो वार्धिर्दू राक्षसराक्षपुत्रः ।
मायां मयोऽके समुपाजगाम बध्न्व शौ रामसुती हैरात्मा ॥ १८ ॥

236.

Yuddha GP 45:18 CE 35:18

तौ सम्प्रचलितौ वीरौ मर्मभेदेन कर्शितौ ।
निपेततुर्महेष्वासौ जगत्यां जगतीपती ॥ १८॥

237.

Yuddha GP 47:11-18 CE 37:11-17

तस्य तद्वचनं श्रुत्वा रावणस्य दुरात्मनः ।
राक्षस्यस्तास्तथेत्युक्त्वा प्रजग्मुर्यत्र पुष्पकम् ॥ ११॥

ततः पुष्पकमादाय राक्षस्यो रावणाज्ञया ।
अशोकवनिकास्थां तां मैथिलीं समुपानयन् ॥ १२॥

तामादाय तु राक्षस्यो भर्तृशोकपरायणाम् ।
सीतामारोपयामासुर्विमानं पुष्पकं तदा ॥ १३॥

ततः पुष्पकमारोप्य सीतां त्रिजटया सह ।
रावणोऽकारयल्लङ्कां पताकाध्वजमालिनीम् ॥ १४॥

प्राघोषयत हृष्टश्च लङ्कायां राक्षसेश्वरः ।
राघवो लक्ष्मणश्चैव हताविन्द्रजिता रणे ॥ १५॥

विमानेनापि सीता तु गत्वा त्रिजटया सह ।
ददर्श वानराणां तु सर्वं सैन्यं निपातितम् ॥ १६॥

प्रहृष्टमनसश्चापि ददर्श पिशिताशनान् ।
वानरांश्चापि दुःखार्तान्रामलक्ष्मणपार्श्वतः ॥ १७॥

238.

Yuddha GP 49:15 CE 39:15

शयानः शरतल्पेऽस्मिन्त्स्वशोणितपरिप्लुतः ।
शरजालैश्चितो भाति भास्करोऽस्तमिव व्रजन् ॥ १५॥

239.

Yuddha GP 50:65 CE 40:64

ततस्तु भीमस्तुमुलो निनादो
बभूव शाखामृगयूथपानाम् ।

क्षये निदाघस्य यथा घनानां
नादः सुभीमो नदतां निशीथे ॥ ६४॥

240.

Yuddha GP 51:33-34 CE 41:33

ववर्ष रुधिरं देवः सञ्चचाल च मेदिनी ।
प्रतिलोमं ववौ वायुर्निर्घातसमनिःस्वनः ।
तिमिरौघावृतास्तत्र दिशश्च न चकाशिरे ॥ ३३॥

241.

Yuddha GP 53:31

हारकेयूरवस्त्रैश्च शस्त्रैश्च समलंकृता
भूमिर्भाति रणे तत्र शारदीव यथा निशा

242.

Yuddha GP 55:18-22, CE 43:15-19

रजश्चारुणवर्णाभं सुभीममभवद्दशम् ।
उद्धृतं हरिरक्षोभिः संस्रोध दिशो दश ॥ १५॥

अन्योन्यं रजसा तेन कौशेयोद्धूतपाण्डुना ।
संवृतानि च भूतानि दृदृशुर्न रणाजिरे ॥ १६॥

न ध्वजो न पताकावा वर्म वा तुरगोऽपि वा ।
आयुधं स्यन्दनं वापि दृदृशे तेन रेणुना ॥ १७॥

शब्दश्च सुमहांस्तेषां नर्दतामभिधावताम् ।
श्रूयते तुमुले युद्धे न रूपाणि चकाशिरे ॥ १८॥

हरीनेव सुसङ्क्रुद्धा हरयो जघ्नुराहवे ।
राक्षसाश्चापि रक्षांसि निजघ्नुस्तिमिरे तदा ॥ १९॥

243.

Yuddha GP 57:2 CE 45:2

स तु ध्यात्वा मुहूर्तं तु मन्त्रिभिः संविचार्य च ।
पुरीं परिययौ लङ्कां सर्वान्गुल्मानवेक्षितुम् ॥ २॥

244.

Yuddha GP 57:36-37 CE 45:35-38

अन्तरिक्षात्पपातोल्का वायुश्च परुषो ववौ ।
अन्योन्यमभिसंरब्धा ग्रहाश्च न चकाशिरे ॥ ३५॥

ववर्षू रुधिरं चास्य सिषिचुश्च पुरःसरान् ।
केतुर्मूर्धनि गृध्रोऽस्य विलीनो दक्षिणामुखः ॥ ३६॥

सारथेर्बहुशश्चास्य सङ्ग्राममवगाहतः ।
प्रतोदो न्यपतद्धस्तात्सूतस्य हयसादिनः ॥ ३७॥

निर्याण श्रीश्च यास्यासीद्धास्वरा च सुदुर्लभा ।
सा ननाश मुहूर्तेन समे च स्खलिता हयाः ॥ ३८॥

245.

Yuddha GP 59:14 CE 47:14

योऽसौ गजस्कन्धगतो महात्मा
नवोदितार्कोपमतामवक्त्रः ।
प्रकम्पयन्नागशिरोऽभ्युपैति ह्य्
अकम्पनं त्वेनमवेहि राजन् ॥ १४॥

246.

Yuddha GP 59:17 CE 47:17

योऽसौ नवार्कोदिततामचक्षुर्
आरुह्य घण्टानिनदप्रणादम् ।
गजं खरं गर्जति वै महात्मा
महोदरो नाम स एष वीरः ॥ १७॥

247.

Yuddha GP 59:18 CE 47:18

योऽसौ हयं काञ्चनचित्रभाण्डम्
आरुह्य सन्ध्याभ्रगिरिप्रकाशम् ।
प्रासं समुद्यम्य मरीचिनद्धं
पिशाच एषाशनितुल्यवेगः ॥ १८॥

248.

Yuddha GP 63:52

यदि चेन्द्राद् भयं राजन् यदि चापि स्वयम्भुवः
ततोऽहं नाशयिष्यामि नैशं तम इवांशुमान

249.

Yuddha GP 67:91

अमर्षाच्छोणितोद्वारी शुशुभे रावणानुजः
निलाञ्जनचयप्रख्यःससंध्य इव तोयदः

250.

Yuddha GP 67:103

अथास्य कवचं शुभ्रं जाम्बूनदमयं शुभं
प्रच्छादयामास शरैः संध्याभ्रमिव मारुतः

251.

Yuddha GP 67:104

निलाञ्जनचयप्रख्यः शरैः कांचनभूषणैः
आपीड्यमानः शुशुभे मेघैः सूर्य इवांशुमान

252.

Yuddha GP 74: CE 61:7

तावुभौ युगपद्वीरौ हनूमद्राक्षसोत्तमौ ।
उल्काहस्तौ तदा रात्रौ रणशीर्षे विचरतुः ॥ ७॥

253.

Yuddha GP 74:12 CE 61:12

सप्तषष्टिर्हताः कोट्यो वानराणां तरस्विनाम् ।
अह्नः पञ्चमशेषेण वल्लभेन स्वयम्भुवः ॥ १२॥

254.

Yuddha GP 74:13 CE 61:13

सागरौघनिभं भीमं दृष्ट्वा बाणार्दितं बलम् ।
मार्गते जाम्बवन्तं स्म हनूमान्सविभीषणः ॥ १३॥

255.

Yuddha GP 74:29-34 CE 61:29-34

गत्वा परममध्वानमुपर्युपरि सागरम् ।
हिमवन्तं नगश्रेष्ठं हनूमन्गन्तुमर्हसि ॥ २९॥

ततः काञ्चनमत्युग्रमृषभं पर्वतोत्तमम् ।
कैलासशिखरं चापि द्रक्ष्यस्यरिनिषूदन ॥ ३०॥
तयोः शिखरयोर्मध्ये प्रदीप्तमतुलप्रभम् ।
सर्वौषधियुतं वीर द्रक्ष्यस्यौषधिपर्वतम् ॥ ३१॥

तस्य वानरशार्दूलचतसो मूर्ध्नि सम्भवाः ।
द्रक्ष्यस्योषधयो दीप्ता दीपयन्त्यो दिशो दश ॥ ३२॥
मृतसञ्जीवनीं चैव विशल्यकरणीम् अपि ।
सौवर्णकरणीं चैव सन्धानीं च महौषधीम् ॥ ३३॥

ताः सर्वा हनुमन्गृह्य क्षिप्रमागन्तुमर्हसि ।
आश्वासय हरीन्प्राणैर्याज्य गन्धवहात्मज ॥ ३४॥

256.

Yuddha GP 74:40 CE 61:40

स घूर्णितमहाद्वारा प्रभग्नगृहगोपुरा ।
लङ्का त्रासाकुला रात्रौ प्रनृत्तेवाभवत्तदा ॥ ४०॥

257.

Yuddha GP 74:69-70 CE 61:63-64

स भास्कराध्वानमनुप्रपन्नस्
तद्भास्कराभं शिखरं प्रगृह्य ।
बभौ तदा भास्करसंनिकाशो
रवेः समीपे प्रतिभास्कराभः ॥ ६३॥

स तेन शैलेन भृशं रराज
शैलोपमो गन्धवहात्मजस्तु ।
सहस्रधारेण सपावकेन
चक्रेण खे विष्णुरिवोद्धृतेन ॥ ६४॥

258.

Yuddha GP 74:74

सर्वे विशल्या विरुजाः क्षणेन ।
हरिप्रवीराश्च हता श्च ये स्युः ।
गन्धेन तासाम् प्रवरौषधीनां ।
सुप्ता निशान्तेष्विव संप्रबुद्धाः ॥ ६-७४-७४ ॥

259.

Yuddha GP 75:4 CE 62:4

ततोऽस्तं गत आदित्ये रौद्रे तस्मिन्निशामुखे ।
लङ्कामभिमुखाः सोल्का जग्मुस्ते प्लवगर्षभाः ॥ ४॥

260.

Yuddha GP 75:26 CE 62:19

हर्म्यार्थैर्दह्यमानैश्च ज्वालाप्रज्वलितैरपि ।
रात्रौ सा दृश्यते लङ्का पुष्पितैरिव किंशुकैः ॥ १९॥

261.

Yuddha GP 75:41 CE 62:32

तेषां संनह्यमानानां सिंहनादं च कुर्वताम् ।
शर्वरी राक्षसेन्द्राणां रौद्रीव समपद्यत ॥ ३२॥

262.

Yuddha GP 75:51-52

तत्र चाग्निप्रदीप्तानां गृहाणाम् सागरः पुनः ।
भाभिः संसक्तसलिलश्चलोर्मिः शुशुभेऽधिकम् ॥ ६-७५-५४

चन्द्राभा भूषणाभा च ग्रहाणाम् ज्वलिता च भा ।
हरिराक्षससैन्यानि भाजयामास सर्वतः ॥ ६-७५-५३

263.

Yuddha GP 81:1, CE 68:1

विज्ञाय तु मनस्तस्य राघवस्य महात्मनः ।
संनिवृत्याहवात्तस्मात्प्रविवेश पुरं ततः ॥ १॥

264.

Yuddha GP 82:24-25 CE 69:23

ततः प्रेक्ष्य हनुमन्तं व्रजन्तं यत्र राघवः ॥ ६-८२-२४
स होतुकामो दुष्टात्मा गतश्चैतं निकुम्भिलाम् ।
निकुम्भिलामधिष्ठाय पावकं जुहुवे न्द्रजित् ॥ ६-८२-२५

स तु प्रेक्ष्य हनुमन्तं व्रजन्तं यत्र राघवः ।
निकुम्भिलामधिष्ठाय पावकं जुहुवे न्द्रजित् ॥ २३॥

265.

Yuddha GP 82:27 CE 69:25

सोऽर्चिः पिनद्धो ददृशे होमशोणिततर्पितः ।
सन्ध्यागत इवादित्यः स तीव्राग्निः समुत्थितः ॥ २५॥

266.

Yuddha GP 85:36 CE 72:33

विविधममलशस्त्रभास्वरं तद्
ध्वजगहनं विपुलं महारथैश्च ।
प्रतिभयतममप्रमेयवेगं
तिमिरमिव द्विषतां बलं विवेश ॥ ३३॥

267.

Yuddha GP 86:15 CE 73:14

वृक्षान्धकारान्निष्क्रम्य जातक्रोधः स रावणिः ।
आरुरोह रथं सज्जं पूर्वयुक्तं स राक्षसः ॥ १४॥

268.

Yuddha GP 88:5

हनुमत्पृष्ठमारूढमुदयस्थरविप्रभम् ।
उवाचैनं सुसंरब्धः सौमित्रिं सविभीषणम् ॥ ८८-६-५
तांश्च वानरशार्दूलान् पश्यध्वं मे पराक्रमम् ।

269.

Yuddha GP 88:31

सुपत्रवाजिता बाणा ज्वलिता इव पन्नगाः ॥ ८८-६-३१
नैरृतोरस्यभासन्त सवितू रश्मयो यथा ।

270.

Yuddha GP 88:55 CE 76:20

विधूतवर्मा नाराचैर्बभूव स कृतव्रणः ।
इन्द्रजित्समरे वीरः प्रत्यूषे भानुमानिव ॥ ८८-६-५७

विधूतवर्मा नाराचैर्बभूव स कृतव्रणः ।
इन्द्रजित्समरे शूरः प्ररूढ इव सानुमान् ॥ २०॥

271.

Yuddha GP 89:31, CE 77:26-27

न मुष्टिप्रतिसन्धानं न लक्ष्यप्रतिपादनम् ।
अदृश्यत तयोस्तत्र युध्यतोः पाणिलाघवात् ॥ २६॥

चापवेगप्रमुक्तैश्च बाणजालैः समन्ततः ।
अन्तरिक्षेऽभिसञ्छन्ने न रूपाणि चकाशिरे ।
तमसा पिहितं सर्वमासीद्धीमतरं महत् ॥ २७॥

272.
Yuddha GP 89:34-35

निरन्तरमिवाकाशं बभूव तमसा वृतम
तैः पतद्भिश्च बहुभिस्तयो शरशतैः शितैः
दिशश्च प्रदिशश्चैव बभूवुः शरसंकुलाः
तमसा विहितं सर्वमासीत प्रतिभयं महत

273.
Yuddha GP 89:36

अस्तं गते सहस्त्रांशौ संवृते तमसा च वै
रुधिरौघा महानद्यः प्रावर्तन्त सहस्त्रशः

274.
GP 90:5 CE

तमसा बहुलेनेमा संसक्ताः सर्वतो दिशः
नेह विज्ञायते स्वो वा परो वा राक्षसोत्तमाः

275.
Yuddha GP 90:81 CE 78:43

यथास्तं गत आदित्ये नावतिष्ठन्ति रश्मयः ।
तथा तस्मिन्निपतिते राक्षसास्ते गता दिशः ॥ ४३॥

276.
Yuddha GP 90:82 CE 78:44

शान्तरश्मिरिवादित्यो निर्वाण इव पावकः ।
स बभूव महातेजा व्यपास्त गतजीवितः ॥ ४४॥

277.
Yuddha GP 91:16

अहोरात्रैस्त्रिभिर्वीरः कथंचिद विनिपातितः
निरमित्रः कृतोऽस्म्यद्य निर्यास्यति हि रावणः

278.
Yuddha GP 92:66 CE 80:55

अभ्युत्थानं त्वमद्यैव कृष्णपक्षचतुर्दशीम् ।
कृत्वा निर्याह्यमावास्यां विजयाय बलैर्वृतः ॥ ५५॥

279.
Yuddha GP 101:29-32 CE 89:13-16

एवमुक्त्वा तु वाक्यज्ञः सुपर्णे राघवं वचः ।
समीप्स्थमृग्वावेदं हनूमन्तमभित्वरन् ॥ १३॥

सौम्य शीघ्रमितो गत्वा शैलमौषधिपर्वतम् ।
पूर्वं हि कथितो योऽसौ वीर जाम्बवता शुभः ॥ १४॥

दक्षिणे शिखरे तस्य जातामोषधिमानय ।
विशल्यकरणीं नाम विशल्यकरणीं शुभाम् ॥ १५॥

सौवर्णकरणीं चापि तथा सञ्जीवनीम् अपि ।
सन्धानकरणीं चापि गत्वा शीघ्रमिहानय ।
सञ्जीवनार्थं वीरस्य लक्ष्मणस्य महात्मनः ॥ १६॥

280.
Yuddha GP 101:55 CE 89:34

अहं तु वधमिच्छामि शीघ्रमस्य दुरात्मनः ।
यावदस्तं न यात्येष कृतकर्मा दिवाकरः ॥ ३४॥

281.
Yuddha GP 102:8-12 CE 90:5-7

ततः काञ्चनचित्राङ्गः किङ्किणीशतभूषितः ।
तरुणादित्यसङ्काशो वैदूर्यमयकूबरः ॥ ५॥

सदश्वैः काञ्चनापीडैर्युक्तः श्वेतप्रकीर्णकैः ।
हरिभिः सूर्यसङ्काशैर्हेमजालविभूषितैः ॥ ६॥

रुक्मवेणुध्वजः श्रीमान्देवराजरथो वरः ।
अभ्यवर्तत काकुत्स्थमवतीर्य त्रिविष्टपात् ॥ ७॥

282.
Yuddha GP 102:32-33 CE 90:26-27

व्यथिता वानरेन्द्राश्च बभूवुः सविभीषणाः ।
रामचन्द्रमसं दृष्ट्वा ग्रस्तं रावणराहुणा ॥ २६॥

प्राजापत्यं च नक्षत्रं रोहिणी शशिनः प्रियाम् ।
समाक्रम्य बुधस्तस्थौ प्रजानामशुभावहः ॥ २७॥

283.
Yuddha GP 102:34-36 CE 90:30

कोसलानां च नक्षत्रं व्यक्तमिन्द्राग्निदैवतम् ।
आक्रम्याङ्गारकस्तस्थौ विशाखामपि चाम्बरे ॥ ३०॥

284.
Yuddha GP 107:65-66 CE 96:30-31

देवदानवयक्षाणां पिशाचोरगरक्षसाम् ।
पश्यतां तन्महद्युद्धं सर्वरात्रमवर्तत ॥ ३०॥

नैव रात्रिं न दिवसं न मुहूर्तं न चक्षणम् ।
रामरावणयोर्युद्धं विराममुपगच्छति ॥ ३१॥

285.
Yuddha GP 108:4 CE 97:4

यमस्मै प्रथमं प्रादादगस्त्यो भगवानृषिः ।
ब्रह्मदत्तं महद्बाणममोघं युधि वीर्यवान् ॥ ४॥

286.
Yuddha GP 121:1 CE 109:1

तां रात्रिमुषितं रामं सुखोत्थितमरिन्दमम् ।
अब्रवीत्प्राञ्जलिर्वाक्यं जयं पृष्ट्वा विभीषणः ॥ १॥

287.
Yuddha GP 121:7 CE 109:7

इत एव पथा क्षिप्रं प्रतिगच्छाम तां पुरीम् ।
अयोध्यामायतो ह्येष पन्थाः परमदुर्गमः ॥ ७॥

288.

Yuddha GP 121:8-11 CE 109:8-10

एवमुक्तस्तु काकुत्स्थं प्रत्युवाच विभीषणः ।
अह्ना त्वां प्रापयिष्यामि तां पुरीं पार्थिवात्मज ॥ ८॥

पुष्पकं नाम भद्रं ते विमानं सूर्यसंनिभम् ।
मम भातुः कुबेरस्य रावणेनाहृतं बलात् ॥ ९॥

तदिदं मेघसङ्काशं विमानमिह तिष्ठति ।
तेन यास्यसि यानेन त्वमयोध्यां गजव्रजः ॥ १०॥

289.

Yuddha GP 121:30

तत्पुष्पकं कामगमं विमानमुपस्थितं भूभरसंनिकाशम् ।
दृष्ट्वा तदा विस्मयमाजगाम रामः ससौमित्रिस्तारसन्नः ॥ ३० ॥

290.

Yuddha GP 122:25-27 CE 110:22-23

तेष्वारूढेषु सर्वेषु कौबेरं परमासनम् ।
राघवेणाभ्यनुज्ञातमुत्पपात विहायसम् ॥ २२॥

ययौ तेन विमानेन हंसयुक्तेन भास्वता ।
प्रहृष्टश्च प्रतीतश्च बभौ रामः कुबेरवत् ॥ २३॥

291.

Yuddha GP 123:1 CE 111:1

अनुज्ञातं तु रामेण तद्विमानमनुत्तमम् ।
उत्पपात महामेघः श्वसनेनोद्धतो यथा ॥ १॥

292.

Yuddha GP 124:17 CE 112:15

अहमप्यत्र ते दद्मि वरं शस्त्रभृतां वर ।
अर्घ्यं प्रतिगृहाणेदमयोध्यां श्वो गमिष्यसि ॥ १५॥

293.

Yuddha GP 127:9 CE 115:7

समुच्छ्रितपताकास्तु रथ्याः पुरवरोत्तमे ।
शोभयन्तु च वेश्मानि सूर्यस्योदयनं प्रति ॥ ७॥

294.

Yuddha GP 127:32

तरुणादित्य संकाशं विमानं रामवाहनं
धनदस्य प्रसादेन दिव्यमेतन्मनोजवं

295.

Yuddha GP 128:9 CE 116:9

जगद्द्याभिषिक्तं त्वामनुपश्यतु सर्वतः ।
प्रतपन्तमिवादित्यं मध्याह्ने दीप्ततेजसं ॥ ९॥

296.

Uttara GP 39:26-27, CE 38:14-15

पप्रुष्चैव सुगन्धीनि मधूनि विविधानि च ।
मांसानि च सुमृष्टानि फलान्यास्वादयन्ति च ॥ १४॥

एवं तेषां निवसतां मासः साग्रो गतस्तदा ।
मुहूर्तमिव तत्सर्वं रामभक्त्या समर्थयन् ॥ १५॥

297.

Uttara GP 39:28-30, CE 38:16-17

रेमे रामः स तैः सार्धं वानरैः कामरूपिभिः ।
राजभिश्च महावीर्यैं राक्षसैश्च महाबलैः ॥ १६॥

एवं तेषां ययौ मासो द्वितीयः शैशिरः सुखम् ।
वानराणां प्रहृष्टानां राक्षसानां च सर्वशः ॥ १७॥

298.

Uttara GP 40:2, CE 39:2

गम्यतां सौम्य किष्किन्धां दुराधर्ष सुरासुरैः ।
पालयस्व सहामात्यै राज्यं निहतकण्टकम् ॥ २॥

299.

Uttara GP 42:26, CE 41:17

अत्यक्रामच्छुभः कालः शैशिरो भेगद: सदा । [ईश्वर्षसहस्राणि गतानि सुमहात्मनोः ॥]
शास्त्रयोर्विचित्रभोगानलीत: शिशिरगमः । ॥ २६ ॥

तथा तु रममाणस्य तस्यैवं शिशिरः शुभः ।
अत्यक्रामन्नरेन्द्रस्य राघवस्य महात्मनः ॥ १७॥

300.

Uttara GP 42:1-15, 41:1-10

स विसृज्य ततो रामः पुष्पकं हेमभूषितम् ।
प्रविवेश महाबाहुरशोकवनिकां तदा ॥ १॥

चन्दनागरु चूतैश्च तुङ्ग कालेयकैरपि ।
देवदारुवनैश्चापि समन्तादुपशोभिताम् ॥ २॥

प्रियङ्गुभिः कदम्बैश्च तथा कुरबकैरपि ।
जम्बूभिः पाटलीभिश्च कोविदारैश्च संवृताम् ॥ ३॥

सर्वदा कुसुमै रम्यैः फलवद्भिर्मनोरमैः ।
चारुपल्लववपुष्पाढ्यैर्मत्तभ्रमरसङ्कुलैः ॥ ४॥

कोकिलैर्भृङ्गराजैश्च नानावर्णैश्च पक्षिभिः ।
शोभितां शतशश्चित्रैश्चूतवृक्षावतंसकैः ॥ ५॥

शातकुम्भनिभाः के चित्के चिदग्निशिखोपमाः ।
नीलाञ्जननिभाश्चान्ये भान्ति तत्र स्म पादपाः ॥ ६॥

दीर्घिका विविधाकाराः पूर्णाः परमवारिणा ।
महाईमणिसोपानस्फटिकान्तरकुट्टिमाः ॥ ७॥

फुल्लपद्मोत्पलवनाश्चक्रवाकोपशोभिताः ।
प्राकारैर्विविधाकारैः शोभिताश्च शिलातलैः ॥ ८॥

तत्र तत्र वनोद्देशे वैदूर्यमणिसंनिभैः ।
शाद्वलैः परमोपेताः पुष्पितद्रुमसयुताः ॥ ९॥

नन्दनं हि यथेन्द्रस्य ब्राह्मं चैत्ररथं यथा ।
तथारूपं हि रामस्य काननं तन्निवेशितम् ॥ १०॥

301.

Uttara GP 42:30-31, CE 41:21-22

दृष्ट्वा तु राघवः पत्नीं कल्याणेन समन्विताम् ।
प्रहर्षमतुलं लेभे साधु साध्विति चाब्रवीत् ॥ २१॥

अपत्यलाभो वैदेहि ममायं समुपस्थितः ।
किमिच्छसि हि तद्ब्रूहि कः कामः क्रियतां तव ॥ २२॥

302.

Uttara GP 64:10, CE 56:10

स ग्रीष्मे व्यपयाते तु वर्षरात्रे उपस्थिते ।
हन्यास्त्वं लवणं सौम्य स हि कालोऽस्य दुर्मते ॥ १०॥

303.

Uttara GP 64:18

निर्याय सेनाभय सोऽग्रतस्तदा गजेन्द्रवाजिभवरौघसंकुलाम् ।
उपास्यमानः स नरेन्द्रपार्थवैः भैन्त्रिमयातो रघुवंशवर्धनः ।

304.

Uttara GP 65:1-5, CE 57:1-5

प्रस्थाप्य तद्बलं सर्वं मासमात्रोषितः पथि ।
एक एवाशु शत्रुघ्नो जगाम त्वरितस्तदा ॥ १॥

द्विरात्रमन्तरे शूर उष्य राघवनन्दनः ।
वाल्मीकेराश्रमं पुण्यमगच्छद्वासमुत्तमम् ॥ २॥

सोऽभिवाद्य महात्मानं वाल्मीकिं मुनिसत्तमम् ।
कृताञ्जलिरथो भूत्वा वाक्यमेतदुवाच ह ॥ ३॥

भगवन्नद्य तुमिच्छामि गुरोः कृत्यादिहागतः ।
श्वः प्रभाते गमिष्यामि प्रतीचीं वारुणीं दिशम् ॥ ४॥

शत्रुघ्नस्य वचः श्रुत्वा प्रहस्य मुनिपुङ्गवः ।
प्रत्युवाच महात्मानं स्वागतं ते महायशः ॥ ५॥

305.

Uttara GP 66:1-12, CE 58:1-10

यामेव रात्रिं शत्रुघ्न पर्णशालां समाविशत् ।
तामेव रात्रिं सीतापि प्रसूता दारकद्वयम् ॥ १॥

ततोऽर्धरात्रसमये बालका मुनिदारकाः ।
वाल्मीकेः प्रियमाचख्युः सीतायाः प्रसवं शुभम् ।
तस्य रक्षां महातेजः कुरु भूतविनाशिनीम् ॥ २॥

तेषां तद्वचनं श्रुत्वा मुनिर्हर्षमुपागमत् ।
भूतघ्नीं चाकरोत्ताभ्यां रक्षां रक्षोविनाशिनीम् ॥ ३॥

कुशमुष्टिमुपादाय लवं चैव तु स द्विजः ।
वाल्मीकिः प्रददौ ताभ्यां रक्षां भूतविनाशिनीम् ॥ ४॥

यस्तयोः पूर्वजो जातः स कुशैर्मन्त्रसंस्कृतैः ।
निर्माजनीयस्तु भवेत्कुश इत्यस्य नामतः ॥ ५॥

यश्चापरो भवेत्ताभ्यां लवेन सुसमाहितः ।
निर्माजनीयो वृद्धाभिर्लवश्चेति स नामतः ॥ ६॥

एवं कुशलवौ नाम्ना तावुभौ यमजातकौ ।
मत्कृताभ्यां च नमाभ्यां ख्यातियुक्तौ भविष्यतः ॥ ७॥

ते रक्षा जगृहुस्ता च मुनिहस्तात्समाहिता ।
अकुर्वंश्च ततो रक्षां तयोर्विगतकल्मषाः ॥ ८॥

तथा तां क्रियमाणां तु रक्षां गोत्रं च नाम च ।
सङ्कीर्तनं च रामस्य सीतायाः प्रसवौ शुभौ ॥ ९॥

अर्धरात्रे तु शत्रुघ्नः शुश्राव सुमहत्प्रियम् ।
पर्णशालां गतो रात्रौ दिष्ट्या दिष्ट्येति चाब्रवीत् ॥ १०॥

306.

Uttara GP 66:13, CE 58:11

तथ तस्य प्रहृष्टस्य शत्रुघ्नस्य महात्मनः ।
व्यतीता वार्षिकी रात्रिः श्रावणी लघुविक्रमा ॥ ११॥

307.

Uttara GP 70:8-9, CE 62:8-9

सा सेन शीघ्रमागच्छच्छ्रुत्वा शत्रुघ्नशासनम् ।
निवेशनं च शत्रुघ्नः शासनेन समारभत् ॥ ८॥

सा पुरी दिव्यसङ्काशा वर्षे द्वादशमे शुभा ।
निविष्टा शूरसेनानां विषयश्चाकुतोभयः ॥ ९॥

308.

Uttara GP 70:16, CE 62:14

तस्य बुद्धिः समुत्पन्ना निवेश्य मधुरां पुरीम् ।
रामपादौ निरीक्षेयं वर्षे द्वादशमे शुभे ॥ १४॥

309.

Uttara GP 71:1-5, CE 63:1-5

ततो द्वादशमे वर्षे शत्रुघ्नो रामपालिताम् ।
अयोध्यां चक्रमे गन्तुमल्पभृत्यबलानुगः ॥ १॥

मन्त्रिणो बलमुख्यांश्च निवर्त्य च पुरोधसं ।
जगाम रथमुख्येन हययुक्तेन आस्तवता ॥ २॥

स गत्वा गणितान्वासान्सप्ताष्टौ रघुनन्दनः ।
अयोध्यामगमत्तूर्णं राघवोत्सुकदर्शनः ॥ ३॥

स प्रविश्य पुरीं रम्यां श्रीमानिक्ष्वाकुनन्दनः ।
प्रविवेश महाबाहुर्यत्र रामो महाद्युतिः ॥ ४॥

सोऽभिवाद्य महात्मानं ज्वलन्तमिव तेजसा ।
उवाच प्राञ्जलिर्भूत्वा रामं सत्यपराक्रमम् ॥ ५॥

310.

Uttara GP 71:14-17

स ह्रुकराक्षरश्रेष्ठो गीत्ज्ञार्थमृदुघ्नचमम् । शुश्राव रामचरितं तस्मिन्काले यथा क्रमम् ॥ १४ ॥
तन्त्रीलयसमायुक्तं विस्थानकरणान्वितम् । संस्कृतं लक्षणोपेतं समतालसमन्वितम् ॥ १५ ॥
शुश्राव रामचरितं तस्मिन्काले पुरा कृतम् । वान्यसराणि सत्वानि व्याहृतानि पूर्वश्च ॥ १६ ॥
श्रुत्वा पुरुषव्यादेशो विस्मितो बाष्णलोचनः । स ह्रुष्टेश्वरिज्ञो विनिःश्वस्य हृद्वहृढेः ॥ १७ ॥

311.

Gorresio Text Ayodhya 17:35

ग्रत्नैव महणां मे प्रस्तु को बार्षी तीविविनि मे ।
ग्रय ज्ञानस्य वर्षाणि दश चार्धी च तेऽनघ ॥ ३५ ॥

312.

Gorresio Text Aranya 4:20

पतिसंयोगसुलभं वयो दृष्ट्वा च मे पिता ।

चिन्तामभ्यगमद्दीनो विननाशादिवाधनः ॥ २० ॥

GP Ayodhya 118:34

पति सम्योग सुलभम् वयो दृष्ट्वा तु मे पिता ।
चिन्ताम् अभ्यगमद् दीनो वित्त नाशाद् इव अधनः ॥ २-११८-३४

CE Ayodhya 110:33

पतिसंयोगसुलभं वयो दृष्ट्वा तु मे पिता ।
चिन्तामभ्यगमद्दीनो वित्तनाशादिवाधनः ॥ ३३॥

313.

Gorresio Text Aranya 53:3-4

मंत्रसरं चाध्युषिता राघवस्य निवेशने ।
भुंजाना मानुषान् भोगान् मर्त्यकाममसृद्धिनी ॥ ३ ॥
ततः मंत्रसारार्द्धं ममन्यत मे पतिं ।
अभिषेचयितुं राता मंगल्यं माचित्रैः महः ॥ ४ ॥

314.

Aranya GP 47:3-4

उषित्वा दवा दश समाः इक्ष्वाकुणाम् निवेशने ।
भुंजाना मानुषान् भोगान् सर्वे काम समृद्धिनी ॥ ३-४७-४
तत्र त्रयो दशे वर्षे राज अमंत्र्यत प्रभुः ।
अभिषेचयितुम् रामम् समेतो राज मन्त्रिभिः ॥ ३-४७-५

315.

Aranya CE 45:4-5

संवत्सरं चाध्युषिता राघवस्य निवेशने ।
भुञ्जाना मानुषान्भोगान्सर्वकामसमृद्धिनी ॥ ४॥

ततः संवत्सरादूर्ध्वं सममन्यत मे पतिम् ।
अभिषेचयितुं रामं समेतो राजमन्त्रिभिः ॥ ५॥

316.

Sundara GP 33:17-18

समा द्वादश तत्र अहम् राघवस्य निवेशने ॥ ५-३३-१७
भुन्जाना मानुषान् भोगान् सर्वे काम समृद्धिनी ।
ततः त्रयोदशे वर्षे राज्येन इक्ष्वाकु नन्दनम् ॥ ५-३३-१८
अभिषेचयितुम् राजा स उपाध्यायः प्रचक्रमे ।

317.

Sundara CE 31:13-14

समा द्वादश तत्राह राघवस्य निवेशने ।
भुञ्जाना मानुषान्भोगान्सर्वकामसमृद्धिनी ॥ १३॥

ततस्त्रयोदशे वर्षे राज्येनेक्ष्वाकुनन्दनम् ।
अभिषेचयितुं राजा सोपाध्यायः प्रचक्रमे ॥ १४॥

318.

Aranya GP 47:10-11,

मम भर्ता महातेजा वयसा पंच विंशकः ॥ ३-४७-१०
अष्टा दश हि वर्षाणि मम जन्मनि गण्यते ।

319.

Aranya CE 45:10

मम भर्ता महातेजा वयसा पञ्चविंशकः ।
रामेति प्रथितो लोके गुणवान्सत्यवाक्शुचिः ।
विशालाक्षो महाबाहुः सर्वभूतहिते रतः ॥ १०॥

320.

Kishkindha GP 26:14, CE 25:12

पूर्वोऽयं वार्षिको मासः श्रावणः सलिलागमः ।
प्रवृत्ताः सौम्य चत्वारो मासा वार्षिकसंज्ञिताः ॥ १२

321.

Kishkindha GP 26:17, CE 25:15

कार्तिके समनुप्राप्ते त्वं रावणवधे यत ।
एष नः समयः सौम्य प्रविश त्वं स्वमालयम् ।
अभिषिञ्चस्व राज्ये च सुहृदः सम्प्रहर्षय ॥ १५

322.

Kishkindha GP 28:54, CE 27:34

नासि पौष्टपदे ब्रह्म ब्राह्मणानां विषक्षताम् ।
अयमध्यायसमयः सामगानानुपस्थितः ॥ ३४

323.

Kishkindha GP 28:55, CE 27:35

नियृत्तकर्मीयतनो नूतं सञ्चितसञ्चयः ।
आषाढीमभ्युपगतो भरतः कोषकाधिपः ॥ ३५

324.

Kishkindha GP 30:64, CE 29:32

चत्वारो वार्षिका मासा गता वर्षशतोपमाः ।
मम शोकाभितप्तस्य सौम्य सीताम्पश्यतः ॥ ३२

325.

Kishkindha GP GP 30:78, CE 29:45

वर्षासमयकालं तु प्रतिज्ञाय हरीश्वरः ।
व्यतीतांश्चतुरो मासान्पिहरन्नावबुध्यते ॥ ४५

326.

Aranya GP 56:23-25, CE 54:21-22

सीताया वचनं श्रुत्वा परुषं रोमहर्षणम् ।
प्रत्युवाच ततः सीता भयदर्शन वचः ॥ २१

शृणु मैथिलि मद्वाक्यं मासान्द्वादश भामिनि ।
कालेनानेन नाभ्येषि यदि मां वशवर्तिनि ।
ततस्त्वा प्रातराशार्थे सूदाश्छेत्स्यन्ति लेशशः ॥ २२

327.

Aranya GP 56:31, CE 56:28

तर्जैना तर्जनाघोरैः पुनः सान्त्वैश्च मैथिलीम् ।
आनयध्वं वशं सर्वा वन्यां गजवधूम् इव ॥ २८॥

328.

Sundara GP 22:8-9, CE 20:8-9

द्वौ मासौ रक्षितव्यौ मे योऽवधिस्ते मया कृतः ।
ततः शयनमारोह मम त्वं वरवर्णिनि ॥ ८

द्वाउयाम्पूर्वं तु मासाभ्यां भर्तार मामनिच्छतीम् ।
मम त्वां प्रातराशार्थमारभन्ते महानसे ॥ ९

329.

Bala GP 77:14, CE

अभिवाद्याभिवाद्यांश्च सर्वी राजसुतास्तदा ।
रेमिरे मुदिताः सर्वा भर्तृभिः सहिता रहः ॥ ११॥

330.

Aranya GP 38:5-6

इति एवम् उक्तो धर्मात्मा राजा दशरथः तदा ॥ ३-३८-५
प्रत्युवाच महाभागम् विश्वामित्रम् महामुनिम् ।
ऊन द्वादश वर्षं अयम् अकृत अङ्गः च राघवः ॥ ३-३८-६
कामम् तु मास यत् सैन्यम् मया सह गमिष्यति ।

331.

Aranya CE 36:5-6

इत्येवमुक्ती धर्मात्मा राजा दशरथस्तदा ।
प्रत्युवाच महाभागं विश्वामित्रं महामुनिम् ॥ ५॥

ऊन पीड़श तर्पाऽयमकृतात्प्रश्च राघवः ।
कामं तु मम यत्सैन्यं मया सह गमिष्यति ।
वधिष्यामि मुनिश्रेष्ठ शत्रुं तव यथेप्सितम् ॥ ६॥

332.

Ayodhya GP 26:9, CE 23:8

अद्य बाहस्पतः श्रीमान्युक्तः पुष्यो न राघव ।
प्रोच्यते ब्राह्मणैः प्राज्ञैः केन त्वमसि दुर्मनाः ॥ ८॥

333.

Bala GP 18:34-36, CE 17:21

ते यदा ज्ञानसम्पन्नाः सर्वे समुदिता गुणैः ।
ह्रीमन्तः कीर्तिमन्तश्च सर्वज्ञा दीर्घदर्शिनः ॥ २१॥

334.

Bala GP 18:37-38, CE 17:22

अथ राजा दशरथस्तेषां दारक्रियां प्रति ।
चिन्तयामास धर्मात्मा सोपाध्यायः सबान्धवः ॥ २२॥

335.

Bala GP 18:38-39, CE 17:23

तस्य चिन्तयमानस्य मन्त्रिमध्ये महात्मनः ।
अभ्यागच्छन्महातेजो विश्वामित्रो महामुनिः ॥ २३॥

336.

Bala GP 26:15

उद् धुन्वाना रजो घोरम् ताटका राघवौ उभौ ।
रजो मेघेन महता मुहूर्तम् सा व्यमोहयत् ॥ १-२६-१५

337.

Bala GP 24:13-16, CE 23:12-14

अहो वनमिदं दुर्गं झिल्लिकागणनादितम् ।
भैरतैः श्वापदैः कीर्णं शकुन्तैर्दारुणारवैः ॥ १२॥

नानाप्रकारैः शकुनैर्नाद्यश्चभैरवस्वनैः ।
सिंहव्याघ्रवराहैश्च वारणैश्चापि शोभितम् ॥ १३॥

धवाश्वकर्णककुभैर्बिल्वतिन्दुकपाटलैः ।
सङ्कीर्णं बदरीभिश्च किं न्विदं दारुणं वनम् ॥ १४॥

338.

Bala GP 12:1, CE 11:1

ततः काले बहुतिथे कस्मिंश्च चित्सुमनोहरे ।
वसन्ते समनुप्राप्ते राजो यष्टुं मनोऽभवत् ॥ १॥

339.

Ayodhya GP 41:8-15, CE 36:8-12

स तमन्तःपुरे घोरमार्तशब्दं महीपतिः ।
पुत्रशोकमिसन्तप्तः श्रुत्वा चासीत्सुदुःखितः ॥ ८॥

नाग्निहोत्राण्यहूयन्त सूर्यश्चान्तरधीयत ।
व्यसृजन्कवलान्नागा गावो वत्सान् पाययन् ॥ ९॥

त्रिशङ्कुलर्लोहिताङ्गश्च बृहस्पतिबुधावपि ।
दारुणाः सोममभ्येत्य यहाः सर्वे व्यवस्थिताः ॥ १०॥

नक्षत्राणि गतार्चींषि ग्रहाश्च गततेजसः ।
विशाखाश्च सधूमाश्च नभसि प्रचकाशिरे ॥ ११॥

अकस्मान्नागरः सर्वो जनो दैन्यमुपागमत् ।
आहारे वा विहारे वा न कश्चिदकरोन्मनः ॥ १२॥

340.

MBH Adi Parva GP 71:34, CE 65:34

चक्रवान्यं च लोकं वै क्रुद्धो नक्षत्रसम्पदा ।
प्रतिष्ठन्नापूर्वाणि नक्षत्राणि चकार यः ।
गुरुशापहतस्यापि भिराब्धो शरणं ददौ ॥३४॥

अति नक्षत्रवंशांश्च क्रुद्धो नक्षत्रसम्पदा
प्रति श्रवणपूर्वाणि नक्षत्राणि ससर्ज यः ३४

341.

MBH Ashwamedha Parva GP 44:2

अहः पूर्वं ततो रात्रिर्मासाः शुक्लादयः स्मृताः ।
धवषाश्वीनि ऋतुक्षणि ऋतवः शिशिरादयः ॥ २ ॥

342.

Mbh Ashwamedha Parva CE 44:2

अहः पूर्वं ततो रात्रिर्मासाः शुक्लादयः स्मृताः
श्रविष्ठादीनि ऋृक्षाणि ऋतवः शिशिरादयः २

343.

Aranya GP 13:22-27, CE 10:21-25

प्रविश्य सह वैदेह्या लक्ष्मणेन च राघवः ।
तदा तस्मिन्स काकुत्स्थः श्रीमत्याश्रममण्डले ॥ २१॥

उषित्वा सुसुखं तत्र पूज्यमानो महर्षिभिः ।
जगाम चाश्रमांस्तेषां पर्यायेण तपस्विनाम् ॥ २२॥

येषामुषितवान्पूर्वं सकाशे स महास्त्रवित् ।
क्व चित्परिदशान्मासानेकं संवत्सरं क्व चित् ॥ २३॥

क्व चिच्च चतुरो मासान्पञ्चषट्चापरान्क्व चित् ।
अपराण्यधिकान्मासानध्यर्धमधिकं क्व चित् ॥ २४॥

त्रीन्मासानष्टमासांश्च राघवो न्यवसत्सुखम् ।
तथा संवत्सतस्तस्य मुनीनामाश्रमेषु वै ।
रमतश्चानुकूल्येन ययुः संवत्सरा दश ॥ २५॥

344.

Sundara GP 4:27-28

रथैः यातैः विमानैः च तथा गज हयैः शुभैः ।
वारणैः च चतुः दन्तैः श्वेत अभ्र निचय उपमैः ॥ ५-४-२७

345.

Sundara GP 9:5, CE 7:4

चतुर्विषाणैर्द्विरदैस्त्रिविषाणैस्तथैव च ।
परिक्षिप्तमसम्बाधं रक्ष्यमाणमुदायुधैः ॥ ५॥

346.

GP 71:1-6, CE 65:1-4

स ज्ञान् मुखी राजा गृहात् अभिनिश्चय वीर्यवान् ।
ततः सुदामानं द्युतिमान् सम्तीववैश्य ताम् नदीम् ॥ २-७१-१
हलदिनीम् दुर पारामं च प्रत्यक्षु सोतं तरङ्गिणीम् ।
शतद्रूम अतरत् श्रीमान् नदीमं इक्ष्वाकु नन्दनः ॥ २-७१-२
एनं धाने नदीम् तीर्त्वा प्राप्य च अपर पर्षटान् ।
शिवामं आकुवतीम् तीर्त्वाग्नेयम् शल्य कर्तनम् ॥ २-७१-३
सत्यं सघः शुद्धिः श्रीमान् पेक्षमाणः शिला वहाम् ।
अत्यायत् स महा शीलान् वनम् चैव रथम् प्रति ॥ २-७१-४
सरस्वतीम् च गङ्गाम् च उग्मेन पतिपद्य च ।
उत्तरम् वीरमत्स्यानाम् भारण्डम् प्राविशद्वनम् ॥ २-७१-५
वेणीनीम् च कुलिन्ग आख्याम् हादिनीम् पर्वत आवृताम् ।
यमुनाम् प्राप्य सम्तीर्णां बलम् आश्वासयत् तदा ॥ २-७१-६

स प्राङ्मुखो राजगृहादभिनिर्याय वीर्यवान् ।
ह्लादिनीं दूरपारां च प्रत्यक्स्रोतस्तरङ्गिणीम् ।
शतद्रूमतरच्छ्रीमान्नदीमिक्ष्वाकुनन्दनः ॥ १॥

एलधाने नदीं तीर्त्वा प्राप्य चापरपर्पटान् ।
शिलामाकुर्वतीं तीर्त्वा आग्नेयं शल्यकर्तनम् ॥ २॥

सत्यसन्धः शुचिः श्रीमान्प्रेक्षमाणः शिलावहाम् ।
अत्ययात्स महाशैलान्वनं चैत्ररथं प्रति ॥ ३॥

तेगिनीं च कुलिङ्गाख्यां ह्लादिनीं पर्वतावृताम् ।
यमुनां प्राप्य सन्तीर्णो बलमाश्वासयत्तदा ॥ ४॥

347.

Ayodhya GP 15:5, CE 13:5

गङ्गायमुनयोः पुण्यात्सङ्गमादाहृतं जलम् ।
याश्चान्याः सरितः पुण्या ह्रदाः कूपाः सरांसि च ॥ ५॥

348.

Bala GP 6:22-25, CE 6:20-23

कांभोज विषये जातैः बाह्लिकैः च हय उत्तमैः ।
वनायुजैः नदीजैः च पूर्णा हरिहय उत्तमैः ॥ १-६-२२
विन्ध्य पर्वतजैः मत्तैः पूर्णा हैमवतैः अपि ।
मदान्वितैः अतिबलैः मातङ्गैः पर्वतौपमैः ॥ १-६-२३

इरावत कुलीनैः च महापद्म कुलैः तथा ।
अंजनादपि निष्क्रान्तैः वामनादपि च द्विपैः ॥ १-६-२४
भद्रैः मन्द्रैः मृगैः च एव भद्र मन्द्र मृगैः थथा ।
भद्र मन्द्रैः भद्र मृगैः मृग मन्द्रैः च सा पुरी ॥ १-६-२५
नित्य मत्तैः सदा पूर्णा नागैः अचल सन्निभैः ।
काम्बोजविषये जातैर्बाह्लीकैश्च हयोत्तमैः ।
वनायुजैर्नदीजैश्च पूर्णाहरिहयोपमैः ॥ २०॥

विन्ध्यपर्वपजैर्मतैः पूर्णा हैमवतैरपि ।
मदान्वितैरतिबलैर्मातङ्गैः पर्वतोपमैः ॥ २१॥

अञ्जनादपि निष्क्रान्तैर्वामनादपि च द्विपैः ।
भद्रमन्द्रैर्भद्रमृगैर्मृगमन्द्रैश्च सा पुरी ॥ २२॥

नित्यमत्तैः सदा पूर्णा नागैरचलसंनिभैः ।
सा योजने च द्वे भूयः सत्यनामा प्रकाशते ॥ २३॥

281

ABOUT THE AUTHOR

Nilesh Nilkanth Oak, is the author of ***When did the Mahabharata War Happen? The Mystery of Arundhati***, where he freshly evaluated astronomy observations of Mahabharata text. His work led to validation of 5561 BCE as the year of Mahabharata War while falsifying more than 120 alternate claims.

The book was nominated for ***the Lakatos award***; the award is given annually by London School of Economics for a contribution to the philosophy of science.

Nilesh researches in astronomy, archeology, anthropology, quantum mechanics, economics, ancient narratives and philosophy.

Nilesh's writes on 'Ancient Indian History' blog at: http://nileshoak.wordpress.com/

Book pages on Facebook can be accessed at:

https://www.facebook.com/TheHistoricRama

https://www.facebook.com/pages/When-did-the-Mahabharata-War-happen-The-Mystery-of-Arundhati/171011776255177

Printed in Great Britain
by Amazon

42393746R00159